Informatik-Fachberichte 276

Herausgeber: W. Brauer
im Auftrag der Gesellschaft für Informatik (GI)

H. Maurer (Hrsg.)

Hypertext / Hypermedia '91

Tagung der GI, SI und OCG
Graz, 27. / 28. Mai 1991

Proceedings

 **Springer-Verlag**

Berlin Heidelberg New York London Paris
Tokyo Hong Kong Barcelona Budapest

Herausgeber

Hermann Maurer
Technische Universität Graz
Institut für Grundlagen der Informationsverarbeitung
und Computergestützte neue Medien
Schießstattgasse 4a, A-8010 Graz

CR Subject Classification (1991): E.2, H.1.2, H.3.3, H.4

ISBN-13: 978-3-540-54145-5   e-ISBN-13: 978-3-642-76698-5
DOI: 10.1007/978-3-642-76698-5

2133/3140-543210 – Gedruckt auf säurefreiem Papier

Vorwort

Die Tagung Hypertext/Hypermedia'91 in Graz/Österreich setzt zwei erfolgreiche Workshops 1990 in Basel und Darmstadt (siehe IFB 249) fort. Hypertext/Hypermedia'91 ist die erste Tagung auf diesem Gebiet, die gemeinsam von den großen Informatikorganisationen Deutschlands (GI), der Schweiz (SI) und Österreichs (OCG) veranstaltet wird. Um auch in Zukunft weitere ähnlich gelagerte Tagungen für den deutschsprachigen Bereich zu koordinieren – als Ergänzung zu der alle zwei Jahre stattfindenden europäischen Tagung über Hypermediasysteme (ECHT) und zeitlich von ihr abgesetzt –, wurde ein informeller Beirat, bestehend aus A. Aders (Universität Zürich), H. Maurer (TU Graz und IMMIS Graz), H. Raffler (Siemens München) und N.A. Streitz (GMD/IPSI, Darmstadt) konstituiert.

Der vorliegende Band enthält 27 Beiträge, die vom Programmkomitee aus den zahlreichen eingereichten Arbeiten ausgewählt wurden, und wird ergänzt durch ein eingeladenes Referat von N. Magnenat-Thalmann zum aktuellen Thema "Multimedia, Virtual Reality and Computer Animation".

Das Programmkomitee bestand aus den Herren A. Aders (Universität Zürich), R. Albrecht (Universität Innsbruck), R. Cordes (Telenorma Frankfurt), P. Gloor (Hypermedia AG, Zürich), H. Maurer (TU Graz und IMMIS Graz) (Vorsitzender), W. Janko (WU Wien), R. Kuhlen (Universität Konstanz), G. Müller (Universität Freiburg), J. Nievergelt (ETH Zürich), W. Rauch (Universität Graz) und N.A. Streitz (GMD/IPSI, Darmstadt), die bei der Auswahl durch eine Reihe von zusätzlichen Gutachtern unterstützt wurden; nämlich G. Holweg, F. Kappe, H. Mülner, H. Peyn, P. Sammer, W. Schinnerl, R. Stubenrauch, A. Taudes, Th. Töpperwien und Th. Weidenfeller. Ihnen allen gebührt Dank und Anerkennung für die umfangreich investierte Arbeit.

Besonderer Dank gilt auch dem Springer-Verlag für die ausgezeichnete Zusammenarbeit bei der Drucklegung des Bandes.

H. Maurer
Graz, März 1991

Inhaltsverzeichnis

MULTIMEDIA , VIRTUAL REALITY AND COMPUTER ANIMATION

Nadia Magnenat-Thalmann
MIRALab, CUI
University of Geneva
Switzerland

1. Introduction

Most events and actions in the today world are typically dynamic. They evolve over time. Three-dimensional real-time computer animation is the most appropriate media to simulate these events and actions. It is the key media; but, accompagnied by other media such as synthesized sound, speech and music, it will bring in the near future a new dimension to the multimedia. Moreover, interactive techniques are now essential to this multimedia approach. In particular, the advent of powerful 3D interactive devices brought a new approach to the virtual reality. The animator may now enter in the synthetic world that he/she has created, admire it, modify it and truly perceive it. Finally, computer-generated human beings should be present and active in the synthetic world. They should be the synthetic actors (Magnenat-Thalmann and Thalmann 1990) playing their unique role in the theater representing the scene to be simulated.

This paper presents the main techniques of Computer Animation and the impact of virtual reality on these techniques. In Section 2, we describe the main concepts of computer animation. Section 3 explains the problematics of human animation. Section 4 presents an overview of main 3D interactive devices for virtual reality. Then the last section presents four examples of using a virtual reality approach to problems of animation.

2. Concepts and Problems of Computer Animation

2.1 Introduction

Designing an animation sequence (Magnenat-Thalmann and Thalmann 1990b) consists of creating a scene, characterized by a description, called a script. Each scene contains static objects grouped into a decor and animated objects that change over time according to motion laws. Moreover, in a 3D space, scenes are viewed using virtual cameras and they may be lit by synthetic light sources. These cameras and lights may evolve over time as though manipulated by cameramen. In order to create all the entities and motions, coordinate and synchronize them, known collectively as choreography, it is necessary to know the appearance of the scene at this time and then Computer Graphics techniques allow us to build and display the scene according to viewing and lighting parameters. The problems to solve are how to express time dependence in the scene, and how to make it evolve over time.

2.2 Motion control

A computer animated sequence is obtained by a series of images produced by the computer according to the animator's directives. We may distinguish three general methodologies:

1. All frames are given to the computer by the animator. A typical example is the **rotoscopy**, consisting of recording the motion by a specific device for each frame and using this information to generate the image by computer.

2. The second and most used method is called **keyframe animation**. It consists mainly of giving to the computer a certain number of frames, called **keyframes**, and the computer derives the other frames using interpolation procedures like interpolating splines (Kochanek and Bartels 1984).

3. In the third approach, called **procedural animation**, motion is algorithmically described. With such an approach, any kind of law may be applied to the parameters. For example, the variation of a joint angle may be controlled by kinematic laws as well as dynamic laws.

2.3 Decors and actors

As in a theater, a decor is a collection of static objects. For example, a room may be a decor for a scene. Even in the absence of actors, an animated scene may be produced by moving a camera or changing a light parameter over time.

Actors are not necessarily human; a film may involve animals or any object which changes over time. For example, a clock is a non-human actor. Its animation consists of moving the clock pendulum using the corresponding physical law. More generally, we shall define an animated object that changes over time according to a list of transformations.

2.4 Camera animation

A scene is only meaningful when it is viewed. But there are many ways a scene may be viewed. It depends on the position of the viewer, where the view is directed, and the viewing angle. Such characteristics, and others, are generally grouped into an entity called a **virtual camera**. Specifying virtual camera motion is an important problem in a number of different computer graphics areas. Animation, scientific visualization, CAD and virtual environments all make considerable use of virtual camera motion in a three-dimensional environment (Brooks et al 1986; Baum et al 1990; Magnenat-Thalmann and Thalmann 1986; Shinagawa et al 1990). A basic virtual camera is characterized by at least two parameters: the eye and the interest point. The eye is a point and it represents the location of the camera; the interest point is the point towards which the camera is directed. A viewing angle may also be defined for controlling how wide the observer view is.

One of the most impressive effects in computer-generated films is the possibility of rotating around a three-dimensional object or entering inside any complex solid. Although classical camera motions are often used, there are many situations where it may be more attractive to design a nonlinear trajectory for the camera. We call such a trajectory a **camera path**. One of the most common is the design of control points to generated a spline.

2.5 Animation of Lights

A scene should also receive light to be realistic. Synthetic lights should be created; their characteristics may also vary over time. In particular, intensities and positions of source lights may change according to evolution laws (Fig.1).

Fig.1 Animating lights

3. Creation and Animation of Synthetic Actors

In three-dimensional character animation, the complexity of motion may be arbitrarily divided into three parts: body animation, hand animation, facial animation.

3.1 Anatomy and geometry of a synthetic actor

The human body has a complex and irregular surface that is difficult to model. Traditional methods based on real persons or reduced models (plaster models) are the following ones:

- **Three-dimensional reconstruction from two-dimensional photographs**

  Two or three projections (photos) are entered and the computer is used to derive the 3D coordinates. Synthetic Marilyn and Bogey in the film *Rendez-vous in Montreal* (Magnenat Thalmann and Thalmann 1987) were created using this approach.

- **Reconstruction from cross sections**

  This popular method consists of reconstructing an object from a set of serial cross sections, like tracing the contours from a topographic map. This method (Magnenat Thalmann and Thalmann 1990) has been used to create *Eglantine*, a computerized mannequin, who never existed before.

- **Three-dimensional digitizing**

  The technique is simply to enter the 3D coordinates using a 3D digitizer. We used for example, the Polhemus 3D-digitizer (based on magnetic fields) to create various objects. The method is less time-consuming than the two other methods, because no photos are needed. However, there are limitations in the shapes, which can be digitized; cavities and small parts cannot be entered.

3.2 Skeleton and body animation

Basically a synthetic actor is structured as an articulated body defined by a skeleton. When the animator specifies the animation sequence, he/she defines the motion using a skeleton. A skeleton is a connected set of segments, corresponding to limbs, and joints. A joint is the intersection of two segments, which means it is a skeleton point where the limb which is linked to the point may move. The angle between the two segments is called the joint angle. A joint may have at most three kinds of position angles: flexion, pivot and twisting.

The mapping of surfaces onto the skeleton may be based on various techniques. Chadwick et al. (1989) propose an approach where the control points of geometric modeling deformations are constrained by an underlying articulated robotics skeleton. Komatsu (1988) describes the synthesis and the transformation of a new human skin model using the Bézier surfaces. Magnenat-Thalmann and Thalmann (1987) introduced the concept of Joint-dependent Local Deformation (JLD) operators, which are specific local deformation operators depending on the nature of the joints. These JLD operators control the evolution of surfaces and may be considered as operators on these surfaces. Fig.2 shows examples of actors based on JLD operators.

Fig.2 Family photo

Skeleton animation consists in animating joint angles. According to section 2.2, there are two main ways to do that: parametric keyframe animation and procedural animation based on mechanical laws. For example, to bend an arm with parametric keyframe animation, it is necessary to enter into the computer the elbow angle at different selected times. Then the software is able to find any angle at any time using for example interpolating splines. In the second approach, angles are calculated by applying forces and torques to the limbs in order to vary the angles. This latter approach has been recently introduced by several authors (Armstrong and Green 1985; Wilhelms and Barsky 1985; Isaacs and Cohen 1987; Arnaldi et al. 1989).

A high-level approach consists in specifying the animation in terms of tasks. With task level control, the animator can only specify the broad outlines of a particular movement and the animation system fills in the details. In task-level animation, the animator specifies what the synthetic actor has to do, for instance, "jump from here to there". Task-level animation requires high-level models of human actions.

3.4 Facial animation

One of the ultimate objectives is to model exactly the human facial anatomy and movements which satisfy both structural and functional aspects of simulation. This however, involves many problems to be solved simultaneously. Some of these are: the geometric representation must be very close to the actual facial structure and shape, modeling of interior facial details such as muscles, bones, tissues, and incorporating the dynamics and movements involved in making expressions etc. Each one of these is, in itself, a potential area of research.

This complexity leads to what is commonly called facial expressions. The properties of these facial expressions have been studied for 25 years by Psychologist Ekman, who proposed a parameterization of muscles with their relationships to emotions: the Facial Action Coding System (FACS) (Ekman and Friesen, 1978). FACS describes the set of all possible basic actions performable on a human face. Various facial animation approaches have been proposed: parameterized models (Parke 1982), muscle model for facial expressions (Platt and Badler 1981; Waters 1987), abstract muscle action procedures, interactive simulation system for human expressions (Guenter 1989).

Fig.3 A facial expression

Kalra et al. (1991) describe a methodology for specifying facial animation based on a multi-layered approach. Each successive layer defines entities from a more abstract point of view, starting with phonemes, and working up through words, sentences, expressions, and emotions. Finally, the high level layer allows the manipulation of these entities, ensuring synchronization of the eye motion with emotions and word flow of a sentence. A language for synchronizing speech, emotions and eye motions is developed to provide a way to naturally specify animation sequences.

The basic level is based on the concept of abstract muscle action (AMA) procedures (Magnenat-Thalmann et al. 1988). An AMA procedure is a specialized procedure which simulates specific action of a face muscle. These procedures work on certain regions of the human face which must be defined when the face is constructed. Each AMA procedure is responsible for a facial parameter corresponding approximately to a muscle., for example, vertical jaw, close upper lip, close lower lip, lip raiser etc. Fig.3 shows an example.

3.3 Impact of the environment

Synthetic actors are moving in an environment comprising models of physical objects. Their animation is dependent on this environment and the environment may be modified by these actors. Moreover several synthetic actors may interact with each other. Several very complex problems must be solved in order to render three-dimensional animation involving actors in their environment. For example, Gourret et al (1989) introduced a finite element method to model the deformations of human flesh due to flexion of members and/or contact with objects. The method is able to deal with penetrating impacts and true contacts. Simulation of impact with penetration can be used to model the grasping of ductile objects, and requires decomposition of objects into small geometrically simple objects. All the advantages of physical modeling of objects can also be transferred to human flesh. For example, the hand grasp of an object is expected to lead to realistic flesh deformation as well as an exchange of information between the object and the hand which will not only be geometrical.

3.4 Cloth modelling and animation

In our film "Rendez-vous à Montréal" featuring Humphrey Bogart and Marilyn Monroe, clothes were simulated as a part of the body with no autonomous motion. For modeling more realistic clothes, two separated problems have to be solved: the motion of the cloth without collision detection and the collision detection of the cloth with the body and with itself. A flexible or deformable object is different from a rigid object because it cannot be considered as a whole and its movement cannot be computed from a small set of its points. The flexible object must be divided into small parts and each point is submitted to a set of local and global constraints. These constraints create forces which prevent the violation of these constraints. Solving the dynamic system requires finding an equilibrium between all these forces. Recent research deals with dynamic models for flexible or deformable objects. In every case, the system is perturbed by external and internal constraints and the solution consists of finding an equilibrium between these forces.

Collision detection adds extra constraints and requires a specific algorithm. For very flexible objects like clothes, it is necessary to introduce a self-detection. In our method (Lafleur et al. 1991), collision avoidance consists of creating a very thin force field around the obstacle surface to avoid collisions. This force field acts like a shield rejecting the points. This volume is divided into small contiguous non-overlapped cells which completely surround the surface. As soon as a point enters into a cell, a force is applied. The direction and the magnitude of this force are dependent on the velocities, the normals and the distance between the point and the surface. Fig.4 shows aframe of the film Flashback with cloth animation.

Fig. 4 A frame of the film *Flashback*

3.5 Hair modeling and rendering

For synthesized images containing humans beings, realistic hair has long been an unresolved problem and therefore has always been absent from these images. The great number of geometrical primitives involved and the potential diversity of the curvature of each strand of hair makes it a formidable task to manage. Typically, there can be from 50 000 to 200 000 individual hairs on a human scalp and their width may vary from approximately 0.05 mm to 0.1 mm. It is however not the characteristics of width and number that are the main contributing factors for covering the skin of the scalp, but rather the length of the hair. A new and efficient method for rendering realistic human hair is introduced by Leblanc et al. (1991b). Based on alpha-blending concepts, the generated images are completely free of aliasing artifacts and are calculated faster than with previous methods used for rendering fur. A simple but effective anisotropic illumination model is formulated to simulate diffuse backlighting and strong reflected highlights present around each hair. A method is also shown to incorporate the hair among objects generated by other conventional rendering algorithms.

4. 3D interactive devices for virtual reality

4.1 Introduction to virtual reality

Visual feedback, in a typical computer graphics application that requires items to be positioned or moved in 3-D space, usually consists of a few orthogonal and perspective projection views of the same object in a multiple window format. This layout may be welcomed in a CAD system where, in particular, an engineer might want to create fairly smooth and regular shapes and then acquire some quantitative information about his design. But in 3-D applications where highly irregular shapes are created and altered in a purely visual and esthetic fashion, like in sculpting or keyframe positioning, this window layout creates a virtually unsolvable puzzle for the brain and makes it very difficult (if not impossible) for the user of such interfaces to fully understand his work and to decide where further alterations should be made.

Until recently, the greatest obstacles in the elaboration of intuitive human-machine interaction methods for 3-D graphical applications came from basically insufficient computing power, slow frame rates and the lack of adequate multi-dimensional input devices. Highly interactive applications that require uninterrupted interaction in 3-D space rely on fast display rates in order to assure that the user may view the result of his actions without any perceived time delays. To keep up with these fast refresh rates when making changes to the state of the environment, good computing power is also an important asset. Completing this list of hardware requirements is the need for multi-dimensional input devices that can relate user information to the computer in an intuitive fashion. Indeed, advances in all these areas have provided us with a wide set tools for building interaction methods that are more intuitive for 3-D applications.

In the next sections, we present three popular 3D devices for virtual reality: the exephone, the dataglove and the Spaceball. More details may be found in (Balaguer and Mangili 1991).

4.2 The eyephone (Fig.5)

This is a head-mounted display system which presents the rich 3D cues of head-motion parallax and stereopsis. It is designed to take advantage of human binocular vision capabilities and presents the general following characteristics:

- headgear with two small display devices (generally LCD color screens), each optically channeled to one eye, for binocular vision.
- special optics in front of the screens, for wide field of view
- a tracking system for precise location of the user's head in real time; it is the Polhemus 3Space Isotrack composed of a source generating a low frequency magnetic field detected by a sensor.

Fig. 5. eyephone

4.3 DataGlove

Hand measurement devices must sense both the flexion angles of the fingers and the position and orientation of the wrist in real-time. Currently, the most common hand measurement device is the DataGlove (see Fig. 6) from VPL Research. The DataGlove consists of a lightweight nylon glove with optical sensors mounted along the fingers. In its basic configuration, the sensors measure the bending angles of the joints of the thumb and the lower and middle knuckles of the others fingers, and the DataGlove can be extended to measure abduction angles between the fingers. Each sensor is a short length of fiberoptic cable, with a light-emitting diode (LED) at one end and a phototransistor at the other end. When the cable is flexed, some of the LED's light is lost, so less light is received by the phototransistor. Attached to the back is a 3Space Isotrack system (see previous section for description) to measure orientation and position of the gloved hand. This information, along with the ten flex angles for the knuckles is transmitted through a serial communication line to the host computer. Knuckle data can be sampled at up to 60 Hz.

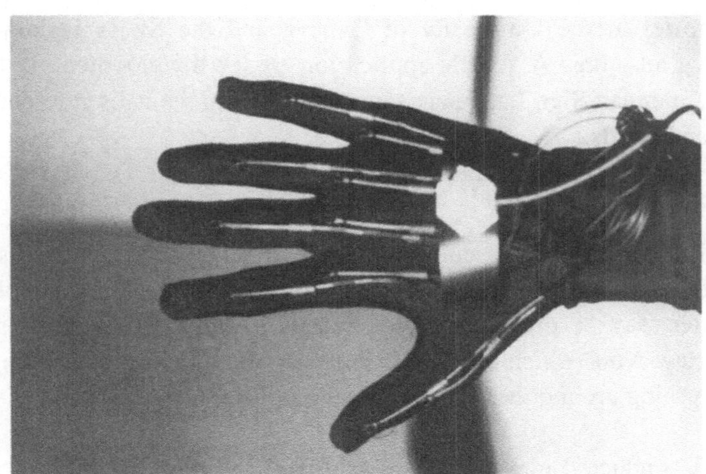

Fig.6: VPL DataGlove

4.4 Spaceball

Some people have tried to extend the concept of the mouse to 3D. In order to address this problem, Spatial Systems designed a 6 DOF interactive input device called the Spaceball. This is essentially a "force" sensitive device that relates the forces and torques applied to the ball mounted on top of the device. These force and torque vectors are sent to the computer in real time where they are interpreted and may be composited into homogeneous transformation matrices that can be applied to objects. Buttons mounted on a small panel facing the user control the sensitivity of the Spaceball and may be adjusted according to the scale or distance of the object currently being manipulated. Other buttons are used to filter the incoming forces to restrict or stop translations or rotations of the object.

4. Virtual reality approach to animation problems

4.1 Introduction

Now, with the existence of graphics workstations able to display complex scenes containing several thousands of polygons at interactive speed, and with the advent of such new interactive devices as the Spaceball, Eyephone, and DataGlove, it is possible to create applications based on a full 3D interaction metaphor in which the specifications of deformations or motion are given in real-time. We describe three applications developed in our laboratories at the University of Geneva and the Swiss Federal Institute of technology in Lausanne. A fourth application under development is an automatic generation of American Sign Language sequences. Dataglove is used to enter hand signs for sentences and words.

4.2 Sculpting using a spaceball and a mouse

Our first application consists of sculpting highly irregular polygon mesh surfaces, such as character faces or any other surfaces of arbitrary shape. For example, a realistic human character may be produced (Paouri et al. 1991) with a method similar to the modelling of clay, work which essentially consists of adding or eliminating parts of the material, and turning around the object when the principal form has been set up.

The operations conducted in a traditional sculpture can be performed by computer for computer generated objects. A sculpting software (LeBlanc et al. 1991) which is based on the Spaceball. This allows the user to create a polygon mesh surface. When used in conjunction with a common 2-D mouse such that the Spaceball is held in one hand and the mouse in the other, full three-dimensional user interaction is achieved.

The Spaceball device is used to move around the object being sculpted in order to examine it from various points of view, while the mouse carries out the picking and deformation work onto a magnifying image in order to see every small detail in real time (e.g. vertex creation, primitive selection and local surface deformations). In this way, the user not only sees the object from every angle but he can also apply and correct deformations from every angle interactively.

This input device is designed to use a person's spatial intuitions to move and orient objects in space with greater dexterity. When object movements can be produced with this device and displayed in real-time, depth perception on traditional 2-D displays may be considerably enhanced by exploiting a psychological phenomena called *motion parallax* (Cahen 1990, Forrest 1986). In essence, this consists of the human brain's ability to render a three-dimensional mental picture of an object simply from the way it moves in relation to the eye. In a perspective projection, depth perception is further accentuated by the speed in which features flow in the field of view æ points located closer to the eyes move faster than the ones situated in back. In order to improve our approach using stereo display, we also use "Stereoview".

With our ball and mouse approach, the operations performed while sculpting an object closely resemble traditional sculpting. The major operations performed using this software include:

Creation of primitives: Typically, the sculpting process may be initiated in two ways: by loading and altering an existing shape or by simply starting one from scratch. Then polygons may be added or removed according to the details needed.

Selection: To select parts of the objects, the mouse is used in conjunction with the Spaceball to quickly mark out the desired primitives in and around the object. This amounts to pressing the mouse button and sweeping the mouse cursor on the screen while moving the object with the Spaceball.

Local deformations: It is possible to produce local elevations or depressions on the surface and to even out unwanted bumps once the work is nearing completion. Local deformations are applied while the Spaceball device is used to move the object and examine the progression of the deformation from different angles, mouse movements on the screen are used to produce vertex movements in 3D space from the current viewpoint. The technique is intended to be a metaphor analogous to pinching, lifting and moving of a stretchable fabric material. Pushing the apex vertex inwards renders a believable effect of pressing a mould into clay.

4.3 Designing human animation using spaceball and mouse

A facial animation is under development based on the sculpting software; it also uses the ball and mouse metaphor. Generation of facial expressions are based on the free form deformations on a volume inside a control box. Free form deformations are defined in terms of a tensor product trivariate Bernstein polynomials. Any expression is considerd as the composition of many muscle actions. The free form deformation is applied to a specific region for generating a particular muscle action (similar to an AMA procedure). A muscle action can easily be mapped into the deformation of the control box i.e. how a muscle would provide a force to the region of interest can be seen as the displacement of the control box vertices. There are several types of deformations included which can be applied to the control box as a whole. In addition, individual plan eor vertex of the control box can also be deformed. The deformations are scale, translate, shear, shift, rotate, taper, and bend.

4.4 Physically-Based Interactive Camera Motion Control Using 3D Input Devices

In this application (Turner et al. 1991), naturalistic interaction and realistic-looking motion is achieved by using a physically-based model of the virtual camera's behavior. The approach consists to create an abstract physical model of the camera, using the laws of classical mechanics, which is used to simulate the virtual camera motion in real time in response to force data from the various 3D input devices (e.g. the Spaceball or DataGlove). The behavior of the model is determined by several physical parameters such as mass, moment of inertia, and various friction coefficients which can all be varied interactively, and by constraints on the camera's degrees of freedom which can be simulated by setting certain friction parameters to very high values. This allows us to explore a continuous range of physically-based metaphors for controlling the camera motion. A physically-based camera control model provides a powerful, general-purpose metaphor for controlling virtual cameras in interactive 3D environments. Because it is based on a real camera model, it is natural for the user to control. Its parameters are physically-based and, therefore, easy to understand and intuitive for the user to manipulate. Its generality and control parameters make it configurable to emulate a continuum of camera behaviors ranging from pure position control to pure acceleration control. As it is fully described by its physical parameters, it is possible to construct more sophisticated virtual camera control metaphors by varying the parameters as a function of space, time, application data or other user input. Also, when used with force-calibrated input devices, the camera metaphor can be reproduced exactly on different hardware and software platforms, providing a predictable standard interactive "feel". Obviously, pressure-sensitive input devices are usually more appropriate because they provide a passive form of "force-feedback". In our case, the device that gave the best results is the Spaceball.

For example, in a virtual environment application the camera becomes the virtual "eyeball" with which the user inspects the virtual reality; in architectural CAD applications, the user has the ability to walk through virtual buildings and inspect them from any angle; in computer animation systems, the animator can specify the camera motion for a scene interactively in real time; for scientific visualization, large multi-dimensional data sets can be inspected by walking through 3D projections.

The relationship between device input and virtual camera motion is not as straightforward as one might think. Usually, some sort of mathematical function or "filter" has to be placed between the raw 3D input device data and the virtual camera viewing parameters. Several recent papers have proposed and compared different metaphors for virtual camera motion control in virtual environments using input devices with six degrees of freedom (Ware and Osborne 1990, Mackinlay et al 1990). These metaphors are usually based on a kinematic model of control, where the virtual camera position, orientation, or velocity is set as a direct function of an input device coordinate.

The interactive camera control metaphor is based on physical modeling of the virtual camera, using forward dynamics for motion specification. The important mechanical properties of this model which affect its motion are its mass, its moments of inertia, and the coefficients of friction and elastic forces imposed by the camera mount. The general motion of a rigid body such as a camera can be decomposed into a linear motion of its center of mass under the control of an external net force and a rotational motion about the center of mass under the control of an external net torque.

Conclusion

We have shown how a virtual reality approach may considerably improve the animator-computer interface. Future computer animation systems will certainly take advantage of 3D input devices like the dataglove or the Spaceball. The advent of force-feedback devices and image processing programs to analyze images coming from video cameras will bring a new dimensions to such systems.

Acknowledgements

The project has been partly sponsored by le Fonds National Suisse pour la Recherche Scientifique. The author is grateful to Arghyro Paouri for the design of most pictures of this paper.

References

Armstrong WW and Green MW (1985) Dynamics for Animation of Characters with Deformable Surfaces in: N.Magnenat-Thalmann and D.Thalmann (Eds) Computer-generated Images, Springer, pp.209-229.

Arnaldi B., Dumont G., Hégron G., Magnenat-Thalmann N., Thalmann D. (1989) Animation Control with Dynamics in: State-of-the-Art in Computer Animation, Springer, Tokyo, pp.113-124

Balaguer F, Mangili A (1991) Virtual Environments in: N.Magnenat-Thalmann and D.Thalmann (Eds) New Trends in Animation and Visualization, John Wiley and Sons

Baum R., Wingel J.W (1990) Real Time Radiosity Through Parallel Processing and Hardware Acceleration Proceedings 1990 Workshop on Interactive 3D Graphics ACM: 67-75

Brooks F.P. Jr (1986) Walkthrough - A Dynamic Graphics System for Simulating Virtual Buildings Proceedings 1986 Workshop on Interactive 3D Graphics ACM : 9-22

Cahen O (1990), L'image en relief, de la photographie stéréoscopique à la vidéo 3D, 1990, MASSON.

Chadwick J, Haumann DR, Parent RE (1989) Layered Construction for Deformable Animated Characters, Proc. SIGGRAPH '89, Computer Graphics, Vol. 23, No3, pp.234-243

Ekman P and Friesen W (1978) Facial Action Coding System, Consulting Psychologists Press, Palo Alto.

Fisher S.S., McGreevy M., Humphries J., Robinett W.,(1986), "Virtual Environment Display System", Proceeding 1986 Workshop on Interactive 3D Graphics, ACM, pp 77-87

Forrest AR (1986), User Interfaces for Three-Dimensional Geometric Modelling, Proceedings 1986 Workshop on Interactive 3D Graphics, ACM Press, pp. 237-249.

Gourret JP, Magnenat-Thalmann N, Thalmann D (1989) Simulation of Object and Human Skin Deformations in a Grasping Task, Proc. SIGGRAPH '89, Computer Graphics, Vol.23, Vol.4, pp.21-30.

Guenter B (1989) A System for Simulating Human Facial Expression, in: Magnenat-Thalmann N, Thalmann D (Eds) State-of-the-Art in Computer Animation, Springer, Tokyo, pp. 191-202

Isaacs PM and Cohen MF (1987) Controlling Dynamic Simulation with Kinematic Constraints, Bahavior Functions and Inverse Dynamics, Proc. SIGGRAPH'87, Computer Graphics, Vol.21, No4, pp.215-224

Kalra P, Mangili A, Magnenat-Thalmann N, Thalmann D (1991), "SMILE: a Multilayered Facial Animation System", Proc. IFIP Conf. on Graphics Modeling, Tokyo, Japan

Kochanek D and Bartels R (1984) Interpolating Splines with Local Tension, Continuity and Bias Tension, Proc. SIGGRAPH '84, Computer Graphics, Vol.18, No3, pp.33-41.

Komatsu K (1988) Human Skin Model Capable of Natural Shape Variation, The Visual Computer, Vol.3, No5, pp.265-271

Lafleur B, Magnenat-Thalmann N, Thalmann D (1991), "Cloth Animation with Self-Collision Detection", Proc. IFIP Conf. on Graphics Modeling, Tokyo, Japan (to appear in April '91)

LeBlanc A, Kalra P, Magnenat-Thalmann N, Thalmann D (1991) Sculpting With the "Ball & Mouse" Metaphor - Proc. Graphics Interface '91, Calgary, Canada

LeBlanc A, Turner R, Thalmann D (1991b) Rendering Naturalistic Hair using Pixel-Blending and Shadow-Buffers, Journal of Visualization and Computer Animation, Vol.2, No3

Mackinlay J.D., Card S.K, Robertson G. (1990) Rapid Controlled Movement Through a Virtual 3D Workspace, Computer Graphics 24(4) : 171-176

Magnenat Thalmann N, Thalmann D (1990), Synthetic Actors in Computer-Generated 3D Films, Springer-verlag, Tokyo

Magnenat-Thalmann N, Primeau E, Thalmann D (1988) Abstract Muscle Action Procedures for Human Face Animation, The Visual Computer, Vol.3, No5

Magnenat-Thalmann N, Thalmann D (1990b) Computer Animation: Theory and Practice, Springer, Tokyo, 2nd edition

Magnenat-Thalmann N, Thalmann D (1987) The direction of synthetic actors in the film Rendez-vous à Montréal, IEEE Computer Graphics and Applications, Vol.7, No12, pp.9-19

Magnenat-Thalmann N., Thalmann D. (1986) Special Cinematographic Effects Using Multiple Virtual Movie Cameras, IEEE Computer Graphics & Applications 6(4): 43-50

Paouri A, Magnenat Thalmann N, Thalmann D (1991) Creating Realistic Three-Dimensional Human Shape Characters for Computer-Generated Films, Proc. Computer Animation '91, Geneva, Springer-Verlag, Tokyo

Parke FI (1982) Parameterized Models for Facial Animation, IEEE Computer Graphics and Applications, Vol.2, No 9, pp.61-68

Platt S, Badler N (1981) Animating Facial Expressions, Proc. SIGGRAPH '81, Computer Graphics, Vol.15, No3, pp.245-252.

Shinogawa Y., Kunii T.L., Nomura Y., Okuno T., Young Y. (1990) Automating View Function Generation for Walkthrough Animation Using a Reeb Graph, Proceedings Computer Animation 90 Springer, Tokyo: 227-238

Turner R, Balaguer F, Gobbetti E, Thalmann D (1991), Physically-Based Interactive Camera Motion Control Using 3D Input Devices, Proc. Computer Graphics International '91, Springer, Tokyo

Ware C, Osborne S, "Exploration and Virtual Camera Control in Virtual Three Dimensional Environments", Computer Graphics, 24 (2), pp. 175-183.

Waters K (1987) A Muscle Model for Animating Three-Dimensional Facial Expression, Proc. SIGGRAPH '87, Computer Graphics, Vol.21, No4, pp.17-24.

Wilhelms J and Barsky B (1985) Using Dynamic Analysis to Animate Articulated Bodies such as Humans and Robots, in: N.Magnenat-Thalmann and D.Thalmann (Eds) Computer-generated Images, Springer, pp.209-229.

MULTI-MEDIA ALS BENUTZERSCHNITTSTELLE ZU WISSENSBASIERTEN ANWENDUNGEN

Rainer Angstmann
IBM Deutschland GMBH
Pascalstraße 100, D-7000 Stuttgart 80

Unter dem Schlagwort "Multi-Media" verbergen sich neue Wege der Informationsvermittlung durch Einbindung von Bildern und Ton in computergestützte Anwendungen. Hierbei werden Video-Standbilder, Graphik, Sprache und Musik digital gespeichert und unter einer gemeinsamen Steuerung präsentiert. Je nach Hardwareaufwand können auch bewegte Bilder digitalisiert sein bzw. bewegte Bildsequenzen auf einer Bildplatte angesteuert werden. Durch die Gestaltungsvielfalt, die die bisherigen Möglichkeiten weit übertrifft, eignen sich Multimedia-Systeme als benutzergerechte Frontends zu operationalen wissensbasierten Systemen. Einsatzgebiete sind beispielsweise Diagnosesysteme, bei denen Prüfanleitungen, Meßpunkte oder Einstellparameter im Video-Standbild gezeigt und über Sprache erläutert werden, Konfiguratoren mit Bildern der Einzelteile und des Ergebnisses, Beratungssysteme mit Präsentation der auszuwählenden Objekte.

Multi-Media und Hyper-Media

Multi-Media und Hypermedia Systeme weisen bei prinzipiell unterschiedlichen Anwendungsschwerpunkten eine Vielzahl gemeinsamer Mechanismen und Eigenschaften auf. In Grenzfällen gehen sie ineinander über.

Multi-Media Systeme werden überwiegend zur Präsentation von Sachverhalten und Dokumenten eingesetzt. Die Dokumentenstücke, nämlich Bilder und Graphiken in der Größe einer Bildschirmseite beziehungsweise Teilbilder, Texte und Ton stehen in einem engen logischen Zusammenhang. Die definierten Strukturen sind weniger vernetzt als die in Hypermedia Systemen. Sieht man Informationen in Graphiken bzw. Bildern und Tondaten als Knoten in einem Netz an, so werden einem Benutzer die einzelnen Knoten in einer stückweisen sequentiellen Standardanordnung vorgegeben. Durch interaktive Eingriffe werden Teilfolgen angewählt und durch Verzweigen zu anderen Präsentationsteilen wird die sequentielle Ordnung durchbrochen. Hier vereinigen sich Eigenschaften von Multi-Media Systemen und Hypermedia Systemen. Dem Entwickler einer Präsentation steht ein Satz von Werkzeugen zu Verfügung wie Text-, Graphik- und Bildeditoren, Konvertierungswerkzeuge, Tonaufnahme- und Scannerunterstützung, Strukturierungsysteme. Im Gegensatz zu typischen Hypermedia Systemen wird jedoch einem Benutzer keine spezielle Unterstützung zum "Browsen" durch die Information geboten, sondern die Navigation über interaktive Verweise zu anderen Präsentationsteilen wird anwendungsspezifisch explizit programmiert.

Bei Hypermedia Systemen steht der Zugriff und die Verwaltung von nur lose gekoppelten Informationen im Vordergrund. Die verhältnismäßig kleinen Informationsstücke sind zu Informationsnetzen verbunden. Die Struktur der Beziehungen der Informationen steht nicht eindeutig fest. Ein Benutzer navigiert in diesen Netzen. Er stellt sich die von ihm gewünschten Informationen entsprechend seiner individuellen Sicht zusammen, indem er den Verweisen folgt. Hypermedia Systeme unterstützen diese Arbeitsweise durch Hilfmittel zur Strukturierung , spezielle Browser, Editoren, Suchhilfen und als "History" die Anzeige bereits besuchter Knoten.

Wird eine wissensbasierte Anwendung mit einer Multimedia- oder Hypermediaanwendung gekoppelt, ändert sich die Art der Navigation. Das Expertensystem bestimmt im Verlauf des Schlußfolgerns den Zugriff auf die Informationsfragmente und wandelt die zunächst nicht-lineare Struktur dynamisch in eine auf die jeweilige Expertise abgestimmte quasi-lineare Ausgabestruktur um. Dabei können einzelne Strukturteile durchaus die ursprüngliche lose Kopplung beibehalten und dem Anwender Verzweigungen zu "außerplanmäßigen" Knoten erlauben, die jedoch regelmäßig zu ihrem Ausgangspunkt zurückkehren. Solche außerplanmäßigen Verzweigungen können, wie in Abb. 1 angedeutet, z.B. nähere Erläuterungen, graphische oder bildhafte Details, Einblendungen von bewegten Bildsequenzen oder Tonfolgen sein.

Multi-Media und Expertensysteme am Beispiel einer Anwendung

In Zusammenarbeit mit einem Unternehmen der Maschinenbaubranche wird für Rotorspinnmaschinen eine Diagnoseanwendung entwickelt, die die Eigenschaften von Multi-Media und Expertensystemen zusammenführt. Als Werkzeuge werden das Multi-Media System IBM Audio Vido Connection (AVC) und das Expertensystementwicklungswerkzeug IBM AD/Cycle The Integrated Reasoning Shell (TIRS) eingesetzt. Hierbei treten unter anderem die folgenden Teilaufgaben auf: die Aufbereitung von Bild-Informationen aus vielfältigen Quellen, die Erweiterung eines bestehenden Diagnosesystems in TIRS und die Kommunikation zwischen einer TIRS-Anwendung und einer AVC-Anwendung unter OS/2. Über das genannte Projekt hinaus sind die Ergebnisse auf andere Anwendungen ohne Einschränkungen übertragbar.

Das Expertensystem optimiert die Garnproduktion. Beim Anspinnvorgang werden Produktionsstörungen an einer "Spinnstelle", die z.B. durch Schwankungen in der Qualität des Rohmaterials oder durch Verunreinigungen auftreten können, automatisch durch den Einsatz eines Roboterwagens, des "Anspinnwagens", beseitigt. Die richtige Einstellung des Anspinnwagens bestimmt Erfolg oder Mißerfolg des Anspinn-

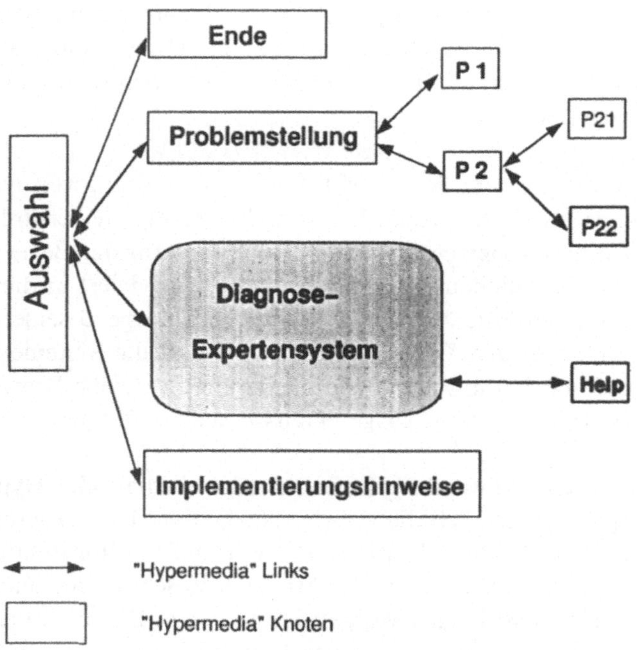

Abbildung 1. Diagnoseanwendung mit Multimedia- und Hypertexteigenschaften

vorgangs und beeinflußt maßgeblich die Güte der produzierten Garne und die Wirt-schaftlichkeit der Produktion.

Audio Video Connection

Audio Video Connection (AVC) ist ein Multimediasystem, mit dem Präsentationen mit nur geringen zusätzlichen Aufwand an Hardware und Software auf IBM Personal Computern erstellt, verwaltet und wiedergegeben werden können. Digital gespeicherte Video-Standbilder, Zeichen- und Textgraphiken und Audio-Elemente, also Musik, Sprache, Geräusche, werden mit Hilfe der Multi-Media-Technik kontrolliert zusammengeführt. Weiter ist die Ansteuerung einer Bildplatte möglich. Als Ergebnis liefert AVC interaktive Anwendungen mit umfassenden Datenverarbeitungs-möglichkeiten unter Verwendung der genannten Elemente. Das AVC System besteht aus zwei Einsteckkarten und dem AVC Autorensystem, welches die gesamte Steue-rung des AVC auf dem PS/2 übernimmt.

Der AVC Audio Adapter ermöglicht die Eingabe von Tönen wie z.B. von Mikrophonaufnahmen, Schallplatten, CD Player oder Tonband. Mit Hilfe des Audio Adapters werden die analogen Signale in digitale Form konvertiert und auf der Fest-platte komprimiert als Datei abgespeichert. Die Tonausgabe über Kopfhörer, Laut-sprecher oder Verstärker erfolgt wiederum über den Audio-Adapter.

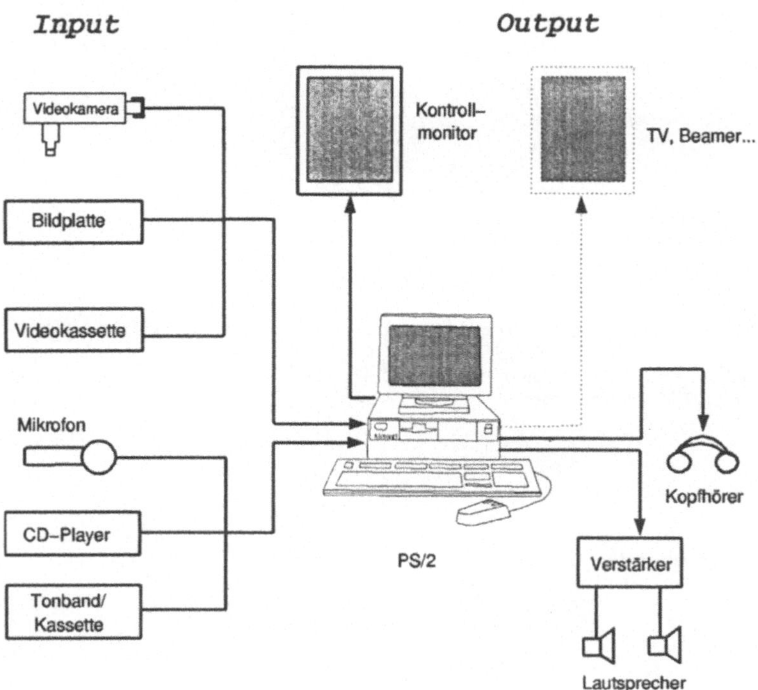

Abbildung 2. AVC-Konfiguration mit PS/2

Video-Standbilder lassen sich mit einer handelsüblichen Video-Kamera, über Video-Standbild Kameras oder über Video-Recorder in den AVC Video Adapter einspielen, digitalisieren und ähnlich wie Audio-Dateien in stark komprimierter Form abspeichern. Für die Wiedergabe auf dem Bildschirm wird der Video-Adapter nicht mehr benötigt. Die Ausgabe erfolgt im VGA-Standard mit bis zu 256 Farben.

Die AVC-Autorensprache AVA ist eine vollständige prozedurale Programmiersprache, erweitert um Sprachelemente zur Behandlung von Bild und Ton, z.B. SHOW, PASTE, PLAY. AVA-Programme integrieren Bild und Ton und steuert die Reihenfolge einer Präsentation. Dabei können über Benutzereingriffe mit Menü- und Tastatureingaben Daten eingegeben und der Ablauf der Präsentation beeinflußt werden. Abb. 3 zeigt einen Auszug aus der Realisierung der "Anspinnen" Anwendung mit verschiedenen Sprachelementen.

Verzweigungen zu anderen Informationselementen werden mit einer Kombination aus Trigger-Feldern und einem Stück Code in AVA-Sprache realisiert. Auf einem Bildelement können mit dem Graphikeditor statische Trigger-Felder definiert werden. Ein Trigger-Feld ist ein markierter rechtwinkliger Bereich beliebiger Größe mit einem Namen. Klickt ein Benutzer den Bereich an, z.B. mit der Maus, so wird der Namen einer speziellen AVA-Variablen zugewiesen. Programmatisch wird der Inhalt dieser Variablen ausgewertet und aufgrund des Namens eine Verzweigung z.B. zu einer anderen Story oder Anzeige eines entsprechenden Bildes durchgeführt. Ein

```
/* main story
main:

   ...
   STORIES.auswertungsart = 'AUSWRTA'

   ...
   @M_DRIVER @M_XPS                         /* start XPS system

   ...
   /* Interpreter main loop
   do forever

    ...
    call PREAD                             /* read action from pipe

    ...
    parse var COMDATA_IN ':' instruction varname arguments

       ...
       when instruction = 'STORY' then do  /* test and call story
            call var STORIES.varname arguments
       end /*STORY*/
       ...
   end /*do*/
   /* End interpreter main loop

   ...

/* AUSWRTA procedure Auswertungsart
auswrta:
   show qauswrta                   /* display image with trigger fields
   COMDATA_OUT = @TF               /* assign trigger variable to variable
   ...
   call PWRITE                     /* write result to pipe
   ...
   return
```

Abbildung 3. AVA-Sprache: Auszug aus der Story "Anspinnen"

Bildelement kann beliebig viele solcher Trigger-Felder enthalten Eine Story kann
dann entweder weiter verzweigen oder zum Ausgangspunkt zurückkehren. Für Exper-
tensysteme bietet sich besonders der Einsatz von "Triggern" dadurch an, durch die
mit einfachem Maus-Klicken auf ausgezeichneten Bildelementen komplexe Dateicn-
gaben ausgelöst werden können. Abb. 4 gibt schematisch einen solchen Dialogbild-
schirms wieder.

Eine Präsentation wird in Applikationen gegliedert. Eine Applikation besteht aus
einem Komponentenverzeichnis, einer oder mehreren Stories, d.h. in AVA-Sprache
geschriebenen Programmen, den Bilddateien und den Tondateien. Die Stückliste kann
auch Referenzen auf andere Applikationen, Bild- und Tondateien enthalten. Der
Entwickler wird bei der Strukturierung von der Editierumgebung unterstützt. Ein
Benutzer sieht nur die ganze Präsentation, die Struktur bleibt ihm verborgen.

Die Autorensprache ermöglicht weiter den Aufruf von in einer beliebigen Program-
miersprachen geschriebenen externen Programmen. Über diese Schnittstelle kann auch
eine Verbindung zu anderen Anwendungen hergestellt werden, unter anderem auch zu
solchen, die mit The Integrated Reasoning Shell (TIRS) erstellt sind.

Abbildung 4. Schema eines Dialogs mit Triggerfeldern

The Integrated Reasoning Shell

 AD/Cycle The Integrated Reasoning Shell ist ein Werkzeug mit umfangreichen regel-
und frame-basierten KI-Funktionen zur Erstellung wissensbasierter Systeme. Für den
hier entwickelten Prototyp kommen als Eigenschaften besonders zum tragen:

- lauffähing unter OS/2
- hohe Performance
- externe "C"-Routinen aufrufbar
- kann leicht in andere Anwendungen integriert werden
- Procedure Sources, externe Routinen und einfache Änderungen der standardmäßig
  vorgesehenen Ein-Ausgaberoutinen ermöglichen die Verknüpfung mit beliebigen
  Nicht-TIRS-Anwendungen, also auch mit AVC.

Die Entwicklung des Prototyps

Die Realisierung trennt in den wissensverarbeitenden Teil, implementiert als in TIRS
und "C" geschriebene Anwendung, und den Präsentationsteil. Dieser ist eine
AVC-Anwendung, oder "Story", erstellt in der AVA (Audio Visual Authoring)
Sprache mit unterstützendem Bild-, Graphik- und Tonmaterial.

Die Eingabe wird zunächst auf das Einlesen von Zeichenketten und Zahlen
zurückgeführt und als TIRS "Question Source" realisiert. Als Ausgabe tritt nur die
Ausgabe von Zeichenketten entsprechend dem TIRS "SHOW" Befehl auf. Nach dem
Austesten der Wissensbasis mit dem TIRS Standard-Entwicklerdialog werden die
Standard- Ein- und Ausgaberoutinen durch äquivalente Aufrufe von Systemroutinen
ersetzt, die den Datenfluß mit der AVC-Anwendung sicherstellen.

Die AVC- und die TIRS-Anwendung kommunizieren im Server-Client Konzept über
einen Kommunikationsmechanismus, der "named pipe" genannt wird. Die AVC-
Anwendung ist hierbei Server. Sie ist Eigentümer und erzeugt die named pipe.

Die TIRS-Wissensbasis treibt die AVC-Anwendung. Nach der Initialisierungsphase
tritt sie in eine Interpretierschleife ein, die von der TIRS-Anwendung eine Zeichen-
kette einliest, ausgewertet und in der Regel in ein entsprechendes AVA- Unterprogramm verzweigt. Das Unterprogramm führt die anwendungsspezifische Aktionen
durch, zum Beispiel Anzeigen von bestimmten Bildern und Zurücksenden einer
Antwort als Ergebnis eines "Trigger-"Feldes.

Bilder werden bei der Gestaltung des Dialogs herangezogen zur Darstellung der
Bedeutung von Trigger-Feldern und zur Verdeutlichung von Handlungsvorschlägen,
denn "ein Bild sagt mehr als tausend Worte". Als besonders vorteilhaft für die Erstellung des Bildmaterials erweist sich, daß gegebenenfalls bereits vorhandene Schulungs-
und Marketing- Videobänder verwendet werden können, ergänzt um weitere Auf-
nahmen mit einer Video-Standbild Kamera oder Video-Film Kamera. Die Festlegung
einer bildabhängigen Farbpalette bei der Digitalisierung gewährleistet eine hohe
Bildqualität der Wiedergabe.

Zusammenfassung

Mit Expertensystemen und Multimedia/ Hypermedia Techniken lassen sich wissensbasierte Anwendungen verwirklichen,die besonders aussagekräftige Benutzeroberflächen
aufweisen. Der Prototyp eines Diagnosesystems zeigt, wie hierfür die unterschiedlichen Systemkomponenten integriert werden können. Die dabei entwickelten Techniken sind auf andere wissensbasierte Systeme übertragbar.

Literatur

1. Carlson, D. A., Suda Ram: HyperIntelligence: The Next Frontier. Commun.ACM 33,3
   (March 1990), 311-321
2. Hofmann, M., Cordes, R., Langendörfer, H.:Hypertext/Hypermedia. Informatik Spektrum
   12,4 (August 1989), 218-220
3. IBM Corporation: Audio Visual Connection Authoring Language Reference. Part No.
   90X8367 (1990)
4. IBM Corporation: Audio Visual Connection User' Guide. Part No. 33F9455 (1990)
5. IBM Corporation: The Integrated Reasoning Shell Reference Manual. Order No.
   SH21-1007 (1990)
6. IBM Corporation: The Integrated Reasoning Shell Development/2 Application Design and
   Development Guide. Order No. SH21-1006 (1990)
7. Halasz, F. G.: Reflections on Notecards: Seven Issues for the Next Generation of
   Hypermedia Systems. Commun.ACM 31,7 (July 1988), 836-852
8. Nielsen, J.: The Art of Navigating through Hypertext. Commun.ACM 33,3 (March 1990),
   296-310
9. W. Schlafhorst & Co.: AUTOCORO ® [1] ASW_Heft Anspinner II
10. Van Dam, A.: Hypertext'87 Keynote Address. Commun.ACM 31,7 (July 1988), 887-895

---

[1] AUTOCORO ® ist ein Warenzeichen der W. Schlafhorst &Co. Mönchengladbach

Ein typ- und regelgesteuertes Autorensystem

Friedrich Augenstein, Thomas Ottmann, Jürgen Schöning
Institut für Informatik, Universität Freiburg
Rheinstraße 10-12, D-7800 Freiburg

Zusammenfassung

Aufbauend auf Erfahrungen, die im Rahmen eines großen Projekts zum Aufbau einer Bibliothek von Unterrichtslektionen für den Informatikunterricht an der Hochschule gesammelt wurden, untersuchen wir die Frage, ob überhaupt und ggfs. wie man das Wissen erfahrener Entwickler von Lehrsoftware in rechnergestützte Werkzeuge für Autoren integrieren kann. Wir berichten über die Konzeption des Kerns eines typ- und regelgesteuerten Autorensystems, das die mediengerechte Aufbereitung von Lehrinhalten besser unterstützen soll als herkömmliche Systeme.

1 Kontext

Seit Mitte der 50er Jahre wurde versucht, Rechner für Unterrichtszwecke nutzbar zu machen. Man kann heute drei Hauptentwicklungslinien beobachten, zwischen denen es allerdings fließende Übergänge gibt: *Traditionelle Systeme* mit dem an der University of Illinois Mitte der 70er Jahre entwickelten PLATO-System als prägenden Repräsentanten, *Hypertext- und Hypermediasysteme* mit Hypercard für Macintosh-Rechner als bekanntesten Vertreter und *Intelligente Tutorielle Systeme*, für die es einige interessante Prototypen, z.B. den LISP-Tutor von Anderson gibt. Mit System ist dabei jeweils das ganze Bündel von Unterrichtssoftware, Ablauf- und Lernumgebungen und Werkzeugen für Autoren gemeint.

Besonders für die ersten beiden Typen spielt die mediengerechte Aufbereitung von Lehrinhalten eine zentrale Rolle. Die den Autoren dazu zur Verfügung gestellten Werkzeuge erlauben die Erstellung von Informationseinheiten bestehend aus Text, Graphik, Animationen (Trickfilme), und die Einbindung von Audio- und Videosequenzen. Diese Informationseinheiten (Frames bei traditionellen Systemen und Karten oder Knoten bei Hypertextsystemen) werden miteinander vernetzt. Der Benutzer kann sich in dieser Informationswelt mehr oder weniger frei bewegen.

Bei Hypertextsystemen ist eine nichthierarchische, sehr freie Vernetzung durch markierte Links möglich. Dieses assoziative Speichermodell erlaubt einerseits ein an der menschlichen Informationsverarbeitung orientiertes "entdeckendes Lernen", führt aber andererseits auch zu dem bekannten "getting lost" Problem [Hal].

Der Funktionsumfang heutiger Systeme ist gegenüber noch vor wenigen Jahren verfügbaren "traditionellen" Systemen so erweitert worden, daß man sie als mächtige Instrumente zur Aufbereitung von Inhalten für die computergestützte Lehre ansehen kann. Allerdings bieten Autorensysteme ihre Funktionen in der Regel auf sehr niedriger, objektnaher Ebene an ohne ausreichende Systemunterstützung für gelegentliche Autoren. Denn insbesondere im Hochschulbereich sind Autoren von Lehrsoftware zwar Fachleute für ein Sachgebiet aber keine Designexperten, Didaktiker oder Kognitionswissenschaftler. Daher wird häufig sowohl für traditionelle Lehrsoftware als auch für mit Hypertextsystemen erstellte Information über die mangelnde Qualität ("Coloritis", "Fontitis", "Linkitis") [vD] geklagt.

Diese Beobachtung wird auch durch umfangreiche eigene Erfahrungen im abgeschlossenen COSTOC - Projekt bestätigt [OW][MMO]. Im Rahmen dieses Projekts wurden Teile des Informatikwissens als Bibliothek von ca. 350 Unterrichtslektionen aufbereitet. Die Autoren haben einen integrierten, teilweise direkt manipulierenden Editor für Text, Graphik, Animation, Struktur und Dialog (Antwortanalyse) verwendet. Die Qualitätskontrolle geschah durch schriftliche Richtlinien [KM] sowie Fehlersuche und Korrektur durch Benutzer und Herausgeber — ein oft wenig erfolgreiches und mühsames Verfahren.

Wesentlich und im Vergleich zu vielen anderen Versuchen positiv war jedoch, daß eine eingeschränkte Hardwareunabhängigkeit durch Offenlegen des Objektcodes erzielt werden konnte. Dadurch wurde die erstellte Kursbibliothek auf einer größeren Zahl unterschiedlicher Rechner ablauffähig. Ein großer Nachteil ist allerdings, daß der Objektcode zu "flach" und ohne erkennbare Struktur direkt auf der Ebene der Text- und Graphikprimitive angesiedelt ist. Das hat nicht nur einen enormen Entwicklungsaufwand für Autoren zur Folge sondern macht auch verschiedene Sichten und Interpretationen derselben Informationsmenge unmöglich.

Trotz stark erweiterter Funktionalität moderner Autorensysteme, wie etwa Course of Action, einer sehr komfortablen Benutzeroberfläche und gewisser Ansätze in Richtung "Typisierung" ist das verwendete Datenmodell und das unterliegende Grundprinzip vom prägenden Vorbild PLATO nicht wesentlich verschieden. Der Objekt-Code ist nicht öffentlich; eine darüber liegende logische Ebene scheint nicht zu existieren oder ist zumindest nicht zugänglich.

2 Vorbilder

Aufgrund der genannten Erfahrungen zeigen wir konstruktive Wege auf, wie das Wissen erfahrener Entwickler von Lehrsoftware in rechnergestützte Werkzeuge für Autoren integriert werden kann.

In Anlehnung an Erfahrungen, die mit Text- und Satzsystemen gemacht wurden [Bru], besteht ein möglicher Weg in der konsequenten Trennung der logischen (inhaltlichen) Struktur der Unterrichtssoftware von der formalen Struktur. Dies läuft auf eine Abkehr von den heute vorherrschenden, direkt manipulierenden Systemen für die Erstellung von Multimedia-Dokumenten und eine klare Trennung der Funktion und Verantwortlichkeit von (professionellen) Designern, Didaktikern und für den Inhalt verantwortlichen Fachleuten hinaus. Wesentliche Schritte hierzu sind:

- Eine Änderung des für Hypertextsysteme vorherrschenden Datenmodells in die von F. Tompa [Tom] vorgeschlagene Richtung, sodaß verschiedene Sichten auf dieselbe Informationsmenge möglich werden.

- Eine Anhebung der Sprachebene über die Ebene von Text- und Graphikprimitiven hinaus unter Beibehaltung der Maschinenunabhängigkeit.

- Die Möglichkeit zur Steuerung des Editiervorgangs durch von Designspezialisten bzw. Didaktikern vordefinierte Typen (Typsteuerung).

- Die regelgesteuerte Überwachung des Entwurfsprozesses durch Messung und Auswertung von das Entwurfsergebnis beeinflussenden Parametern (Regelsteuerung).

3 Typsteuerung

Wir unterscheiden *Bildschirmtypen* zur Festlegung der logischen Struktur von Seiten (wobei eine Seite die kleinste Informationseinheit im Datenmodell von Tompa ist), *Strukturtypen* zur Festlegung der Verbindungs- / Ablaufstruktur und *Interaktionstypen* zur Festlegung von Interaktionsmustern. Typen können entweder (implizit) vordefiniert oder selbstdefiniert sein. Als Sprache zur Spezifikation von Bildschirmtypen und zur Charakterisierung von Objekten eines bestimmten Typs verwenden wir eine an SGML [Bry] angelehnte Notation.

Die Typspezifikation, d.h. die Definition einer generischen Struktur einer Bildschirmklasse, ebenso wie die zur Erzeugung des Objekt-Codes in einem geräteunabhängigen Format erforderlichen Layout-Direktiven, werden von einem Designexperten erstellt. Der Autor erzeugt durch einen weitgehend typgesteuerten Editiervorgang auf möglichst hoher Ebene logisch ausgezeichnete, individuelle Seiten mit spezifischer Struktur. Abbildung 1 zeigt eine schematische Übersicht über diesen Systemteil. Abbildung 2 zeigt ein Beispiel für eine Definition der generischen Struktur einer Bildschirmklasse, Abbildung 3 eine dieser Struktur entsprechende individuelle Seite und Abbildung 4 eine nach bestimmten Layout-Direktiven gesetzte Bildschirmseite.

Zur Spezifikation von Strukturtypen müssen Klassen von (mindestens zweistufigen) Hypergraphen festgelegt werden. Das kann mit verschieden formalen Hilfsmitteln (Graphgrammatiken, verbotene Wege) geschehen. Über die Spezifikation von Interaktionstypen ist noch nicht entschieden.

4 Regelsteuerung

Die Regelsteuerung wird in drei Stufen gegliedert: Die erste Stufe, wie sie bereits bei [Hub] andiskutiert wird, ist die Überprüfung des Kursentwurfs nach jedem Kursentwurfsschritt. Als Kursentwurfsschritt kann eine "task" eines Autorensystems angesehen werden, wie sie in [MB] definiert werden. Diese tasks werden in create-, modify- oder delete-Operationen in Form von Skripten den einzelnen Kurstypen zugeordnet. Skripte beinhalten prozedurale Bestandteile von Hypermedia-Dokumenten und werden z.B. in [Glo][Zel] beschrieben. Diese Skripte werden an die konkreten Instanzen eines Typs beim Editiervorgang weitergegeben und ausgeführt. Die zweite Stufe ist die Überprüfung nach Beendigung des gesamten Kursentwurfs, also eine Gesamtkursanalyse. Die dritte Stufe ist die Auswertung von Daten, die bei Benutzung des Kurses durch Schüler gesammelt wurden. Die jeweils anwendbaren Regeln zur Qualitätsüberwachung werden kurstypabhängig gewählt. So gelten für einen Kurstyp "Drillkurs" andere Maßstäbe als für einen Kurstyp "Simulation".

Zur Kursentwurfsschritt-Analyse wird nach Abschluß jeder Operation ein Kurszustand gemessen, der von der Menge aller instantiierten Struktur-, Interaktions- und Bildschirmobjekte abhängt. Dazu müssen Typen und Objekte als Instanzen dieser Typen mit prozeduralen Elementen verknüpft werden. Das geschieht mit Hilfe der oben genannten Skripte, die operationsgebunden sind: Die Bearbeitung eines Objekts eines bestimmten Typs löst die Ausführung der an die Operation gebundenen Skripte aus. Die Skripte messen bestimmte Parameter. Abhängig von diesen Parametern werden dann über mit den Parametern verbundene Regeln bestimmte Feedbacks an den Autor ausgelöst.

Die Gesamtkursanalyse kann als Anwendung der Kursentwurfsschritt-Analyse auf das Objekt vom Typ "Gesamtkurs" angesehen werden. Hier finden allerdings sehr komplexe Überprüfungen statt wie beispielsweise die Überprüfung des Kurses auf "Sackgassen", auf Teile, die nicht durchlaufen werden können oder auf konsistente Verwendung bestimmter Auszeichnungsmerkmale.

Die Schülerdaten-Analyse hat die Aufgabe, die Interaktion von Schülern mit dem zu analysierenden Kurs aufzuzeichnen und auszuwerten. Dazu gehört u.a. die Messung des Grads der Abweichung von dem vom Autor vorgesehenen, "empfohlenen" Pfad durch den Kurs, und der Abweichung von Schülerantworten von den richtigen. So wird eine Generalisierung über mehrere Schülersitzungen hinweg erreicht, also eine Durchschnittsermittlung und daraus abgeleitete Schlußfolgerungen, die zu Verbesserungsvorschlägen für den Autor führen.

Ein Entwicklungsziel ist die Erstellung von kurstypabhängigen Regeldateien. Sie enthalten die zu überwachenden Regeln und müssen von einem Regeldesigner gewartet werden. Dabei treten ähnliche Probleme wie bei der Entwicklung von Expertensystemen auf, z.B. die Frage der Konsistenzsicherung von Regeldateien.

5 Stand der Implementierung

Es wurde begonnen, zunächst den Kern eines Autorensystems, bestehend aus einem Text- und Grafikeditor, einem Animationseditor und einem Struktureditor, zu implementieren. Grundlage für den Text- und Grafikeditor ist ein im Quellcode (Object Pascal) vorliegender, direkt manipulierender Editor, der die Erstellung farbiger Text- und Grafikobjekte zuläßt. Er erzeugt zunächst nur unstrukturierte Listen von Bildschirmobjekten. Diese interne Datendarstellung wird schrittweise angehoben. Der Editor erzeugt dann ein File wie in Abbildung 3. Dieses wird nach jedem Entwurfsschritt gemäß den Layout-Direktiven interpretiert und auf dem Bildschirm dargestellt.

Abbildungen

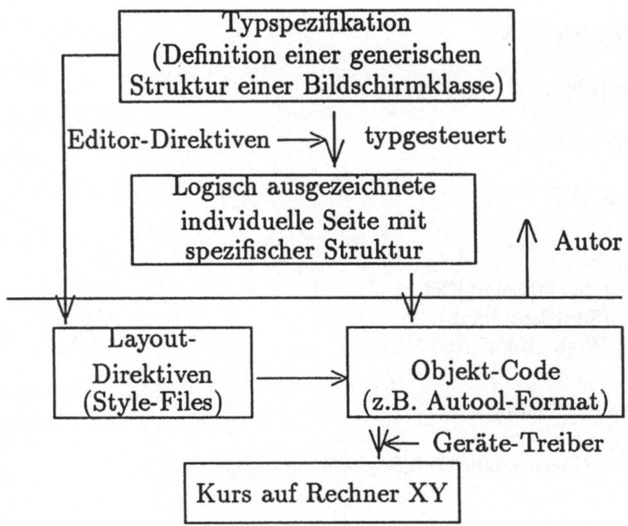

Abbildung 1: Bildschirmtypen

```
<!ELEMENT NFrame (Explain, Example?) >

<!ELEMENT (Explain|Example) (Title?,((Graphic,Text?)|Text)+)>

<!ATTLIST (Explain| Example)
Position                (gltr|grtl|gotu|guto|g|t)                              'gltr'>

<!ELEMENT Title #PCDATA >

<!ELEMENT Text (p)+ >

<!ELEMENT p (phrase)+ >

<!ELEMENT phrase #PCDATA >

<!ATTLIST phrase
Color           (Color1|Color2|Color3|Color4)           'Color1'
Position        (Sup|Center|Sub)                         'Center'
High            (High1|High2|High3|High4)                'High1' >

<!ELEMENT Graphic (Shape)+ >

<!ELEMENT Shape (Picture|Line|Oval|Region|Rectangle|Word) >

<!ATTLIST Shape
Color           (Color1|Color2|Color3|Color4|defCol|gbc)        'Color1'
FStyle          (full|empty|FStyle1|FStyle2|FStyle3)            'empty'
LWidth          (LWidth1|LWidth2|LWidth3|LWidth4)               'LWidth1'
ColVal          NUTOKENS                                        '0,0,0' >

<!ELEMENT Picture (#PCDATA,X,Y,X,Y) >

<!ELEMENT Line (X,Y,X,Y) >

<!ELEMENT Oval (X,Y,X,Y) >

<!ELEMENT Region (X,Y,X,Y,(X,Y)+) >

<!ELEMENT Rectangle (X,Y,X,Y) >

<!ELEMENT Word (X,Y,#PCDATA) >

<!ELEMENT (X|Y) #PCDATA >
```

Abbildung 2: Beispiel für eine Definition der generischen Struktur einer Bildschirmklasse

```
<NFrame>
  <Explain>
    <Title>
          Zusammenfassung
    </Title>
    <Graphic>
          <Shape Color='defCol' ColVal='21567,34897,1098'>
                <Rectangle>
                      <x>03000000</x>
                      <y>15999999</y>
                      <x>15000000</x>
                      <y>22000000</y>
                </Rectangle>
          </Shape>
          <Shape FStyle='full' Color='defCol' LWidth='LWidth2' ColVal='32367,2897,31098'>
                <Circle>
                      <x>39999999</x>
                      <y>15999999</y>
                      <x>60000000</x>
                      <y>25000000</y>
                </Circle>
          </Shape>
    </Graphic>
    <Text>
          <p>
                <phrase>Dies ist normaler Text.
                Es folgt</phrase>
                <phrase High='High2'>hervorgehobener Text</phrase>
                <phrase High='High1'>und</phrase>
                <phrase High='High3'>besonders hervorgehobener Text</phrase>
          </p>
    </Text>
  </Explain>
</NFrame>
```

Abbildung 3: Beispiel für eine logisch ausgezeichnete individuelle Seite

Zusammenfassung

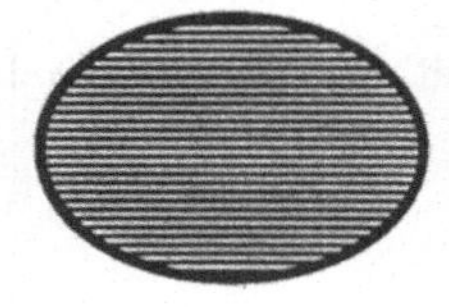

Dies ist normaler Text in einem Textfenster.
Es folgt hervorgehobener Text und besonders hervorgehobener Text.
Text im Textfenster erklärt die im nebenstehenden Grafikfenster gezeigten Grafiken.

Abbildung 4: nach Layoutdirektiven gesetzte Bildschirmseite

Literatur

[Bru] A. Brüggemann-Klein. *Einführung in die Dokumentenverarbeitung. Leitfäden der angew. Informatik*, Teubner, 1989.

[Bry] M. Bryan. *SGML: an author's guide to the Standard Generalized Markup Language*. Addison-Wesley Publishing Company, 1988.

[Glo] P.A. Gloor. *Hypermedia-Anwendungsentwicklung. Leitfäden der angew. Informatik*, Teubner, 1990.

[Hal] F.G. Halasz. Reflections on notecards: seven issuses for the next generation of hypermedia systems. *Comm. ACM*, 31(7):836 ff., 1988.

[Hub] F. Huber. A proposal for an authoring system avoiding common errors in tutorial lessons. In H. Maurer, editor, *Computer Assisted Learning, Proceedings of ICCAL 89*, Springer-Verlag, Dallas, TX, 1989.

[KM] D. Kaiser and H. Maurer. *How to write a COSTOC course*. Report 229, IIG Graz, 1987.

[MB] C. MacKnight and S. Balagopalan. An evaluation tool for measuring authoring system performance. *Comm. ACM*, 32:1231ff, 1989.

[MMO] F. Makedon, H. Maurer, and Th. Ottmann. Computer learning: a step beyond the book. In B. Krause and A. Schreiner, editors, *HECTOR VOL I: New Ways in Education and Research*, Springer Verlag, Berlin, 1988.

[OW] Th. Ottmann and P. Widmayer. Erstellung und Nutzung von Präsentations-graphiklektionen für die Informatik. In *CIP Status-Seminar 1987*, Schriftenreihe Studien zu Bildung und Wissenschaft, 1987.

[Tom] F. Tompa. A data model for flexible hypertext database systems. *ACM Transactions on Information Systems*, 7(1):85–100, 1989.

[vD] A. van Dam. Hypertext 87. *Comm. ACM*, 31(7):17–41, 1988.

[Zel] P. Zellweger. Active paths through multimedia documents. In J.C. van Vliet, editor, *Document Manipulation and Typography*, page 19ff, Cambridge University Press, 1988.

Relational Back-Ends in the management of large Hypertexts

Gilberto Barbieri, Luigi Colazzo, Andrea Molinari

Istituto di Informatica, Università di Trento
Via Inama 13, 38100 Trento (TN), Italy

Abstract [*]

In this paper we present an overview of the back-end layer of current hypertext systems, expecially with regard of the use of a relational data base management system. This kind of storage mechanism allows generalized management of links, which solves a series of problems related to the traditional network data model of hypertext systems. We present some examples derived from a prototype in Toolbook under development at our Institute. Finally we discuss the adoption of post-relational models of back-ends, in particular those based on Nested Algebra, where we can manage complex objects and re-define the concept of "type of link" from a structural point of view.

Introduction

A hypertext [Bush45], [Nels74], [Nels81], [Conk87] is made up of a collection of documents which can be read by following a number of alternative paths. A hypertext system (**HTS**) is a software tool that represents and manages the links between the nodes which form the information space. The *browsing* mechanism allows the collection of documents to be read in different ways. It is based on the technique of making parts of a document sensitive to the mouse (or to the contact of a finger on a screen in the case of "touch screen" technology) and to associate to each sensitive area a *"link"* to another portion of the same or other documents. Once the connection has been constructed, the activation of the sensitive area activates the underlying link, transforming the action of the user into a *"go to"*.

In large hypertexts the browsing mechanism on its own, often proves itself to be insufficient [Hala87]. Having to follow a long path to reach the desired information, often brings about an information

[*] Partially financed by CNR - "Progetto finalizzato Informatica e Calcolo Parallelo" contract n. 89.00022.69; IBM Study Contract n. 0401 1990 0058 2039; Informatica Trentina S.p.A.

overload and, as a consequence, confusion and disorientation due to the change in context. It is therefore necessary to supply the user with generalized query mechanisms on the information space, using Information Retrieval [Agos88], [Crof89], [Fris89], [Cola89], or Data Base techniques.

The aim of this work is to present some advantages that the adoption of Data Base techniques introduce into the HTS.

With regards to what we have said up to now, from a *conceptual* point of view it is possible to identify a hypertext using the metaphor of network. A large number of current systems maintain this metaphor also from a *physical* point of view. In this way a storage structure organized as a multi-list is implemented [Pryw63], [Wied77], in which nodes contain the documents and arcs represent the links (relations) between parts of documents. Often this structure is an integral part of the system. This way performance is improved but generality is limited. In other words, the system components employed in storage, management and search of nodes and links (*back-end*) are rarely separated from the components which take care of interaction with the user (*front-end*). In addition, in literature and in commercial systems we can note sophisticated structures at the front-end level and storage mechanisms that remain mostly at file system level. In this way the hypertext data structure is not very clear or layered, causing a series of problems: interaction complexity, notable maintenance difficulty and above all lack of generalized functions which act on an extended set of documents.

It is possible to start from the consideration that a link is simply the connection between two points in a space made up of object addresses (the sensitive areas). It therefore becomes possible to pass from a network model of link management (metaphor of the net) to a more efficient relational model (metaphor of the table). All this implies a clear distinction between the management of the link data base and the management of the front-end aspects. As will be demonstrated by the examples contained in the following pages, the RDBMS solution allows many of the problems present in hypertexts to be avoided, especially for those hypertexts which undergo frequent changes and on which different authors work (HTS used in argumentation or cooperative work support systems).

The work is organized in five sections.

Section one discusses the terminology used in the description of hypertext conceptual models, in relation to that used in this paper.

Section two describes the different applications of *front-end* and *back-end* concepts in current hypertext systems.

Section three is an overall view of the back-end layer architecture.

Section four presents in detail the approach that uses the technology of relational data bases for the management of the back-end layer.

In conclusion section five presents a data abstraction approach based on Nested algebra.

1. Terminology

The macro components of our argumentation are collections of *documents* in an electronic form, the contents of which are divided into a collection of *nodes*. A *hypertext link* connects between them two *hypertext anchors* contained in the same or in two different nodes. A *button* is a visible indicator (audible, ...) of the presence of an anchor and can be in a textual form (then one talks of a *sticky button* or a *hotword*) or in a graphic form (*icon*) [Irle90].

As at the moment hypertext terminology is poorly defined, we briefly consider the terms **node, link** and **anchor.**

A **node** is an object container. This is basically a "fuzzy" concept: a node can in fact be a card (Hypercard), a page (Toolbook), a frame (KMS) or a scrolling window (Guide). From a storage point of view, each node can be a file (a KMS frame). However we can have more than one node in a file (a Hypercard stack or the KMS frames), or more than one file in a node (the table top cards of NoteCards). As contents, it is possible to have text, vector graphics, bitmaps, tables, video, animations, photos, spreadsheets, voices, audio, music etc. *Hypermedia* is talked about when the system is able to manage text and other types of "media".

A **link** is the hypertext system component in which the connection (or relation) between two anchors is codified. The connection can be stored in a permanent manner (*extensional* or stored links) or it can depend on the result of a program (*intensional* or calculated links) [DeRo89]. Type of links (explanations, bibliographic notes, references etc.) are also talked about in [Trig83]. Finally we can find labelled links, in the case where keywords are used to indicate to the user the meaning of a link (for example giving a name to the arc that joins the graphical representation of two nodes in the graphical network browsers).

An **anchor** is an area of the node (or the node itself) which can be selected and identified in a permanent way, and from which links leave or arrive [Meyr89a]. One talks of "node to node" (gIBIS), "point-to-node" (NoteCards) or "span-to-span" (Intermedia) systems. For our aims it is necessary that the anchor has a name, a source identifier and/or a link destination, and a series of attributes defined by the system (the node and/or the document to which it belongs, creation date, author, etc.) or by the user (keywords, contexts, etc). The storage of this information in data base tables allows, through SQL query, to carry out operations such as the use environment setting (for example the desired authors or contexts) or the listing of the nodes connected to the current one.

Therefore, what is generically called a link, in reality contains several objects: the anchor and the program which executes the link (forming part of the back-end of the system) and the button, icon, or hotword (forming part of the front-end).

2. Towards a stratification in the architecture of hypertext systems

The necessity of separating the components of a hypertext system is not a new aspect in literature [Camp87], [Hala89]. The advantages of this approach are a clearer project, greater modularity and versatility. When one speaks of a network system with multi-user functionality, this characteristic becomes indispensable. However, few systems have followed this direction, from both a conceptual and physical point of view.

The first item to deal with is the user interface. The link activation mechanism is not the principal characteristic of a hypertext, but it is part of a functional element which Myers [Myer88] calls a *Windows Manager*. A windows manager is an advanced graphical interface, the main function of which is to divide a physical terminal into a number of logical terminals (ie windows).

Therefore, the problem of designing a hypertext system does not lie in the implementation of display mechanisms (already provided at the graphical interface level) but in the management (user dependent) of the actions produced by a display mechanism applied to a universe of words and graphical signs.

There are many possible alternatives concerning this, the simplest of which consists of associating every sensitive area with a program which carries out an action. In such a case every click on a mark starts the program off. One of the main paradigms of hypertexts is the construction of a generalized program which carries out a "go to" another node. In this way the display of a mark in the starting node (document, document fragment or image) allows the jump to the destination node associated to the mark chosen by the user.

In many hypertext systems the data necessary for the "go to" program (or others similar), are physically stored in the application data structure and this causes something similar to an application programming environment when the definition of a file schema is contained in the application program using it. In the case of a schema definition this limits the system functionality. As it is well known, the schema modification brings about a program modification, and a change in the program could bring about a re-structuring of the file. In a similar way, when the "link" data are maintained together with the document data or in other data structures defined at application level and not accessible to the user, the re-organization of a hypertext becomes laborious because the links cannot be treated in a generalized way.

In commercial hypertexts this problem has different solutions. The discussion about five different approaches will be illustrated by the presentation of five systems: OWL Guide, Asymetrix Toolbook, IRIS Intermedia Sun Link Service and GMD SEPIA.

OWL Guide [Brow87], [Brow89], [Guid90]. An hypertext shell based on the Ms-Dos operating system and the graphical interface Ms-Windows. Text, graphics, anchors and the programs which execute the links are stored together in the GUI files. The programs are constructed using a pull-down menu and cannot be accessed directly. The *"command buttons"* are the exception to this rule: using the "Windows Definitions" it is possible to edit programs in LOGiiX.
Also in KMS information about links are stored together with the nodes [Aksc87].

Asymetrix Toolbook [Tool90]. A hypertext shell based on the Ms-Dos operating system and the graphical interface Ms-Windows. The main difference between Toolbook and Guide is that in the former is possible to associate a script (in the **OpenScript** language) to each object, which is always accessible to the author.

The other "script-oriented" programs (HyperCard [Appl88], [Good88], Supercard [Supe90], Plus [Plus90], HyperPAD [Hype90] etc.) behave in the same way.

With Toolbook we can separate the back-end and front-end using a DLL, supplied with the product, which manages the DBIII files. In this case Toolbook supplies the front-end and the DLL manages the back-end using the files in DBIII format. A similar interaction mechanism is also present between HyperCard and Oracle in a Macintosh environment.

IRIS Intermedia [Yank88], [Meyr86], [Walt89]. An hypertext environment made up of a series of "client" application modules which manage different types of media (InterWord, InterDraw, InterPix, InterVal timeline editor, InterVideo, InterPlay) and by a relational data base which acts as a "server". Intermedia version 3.0 is based on A/UX, the UNIX version for the Macintosh, which retains all the standard characteristics of the Mac interface.

One of the key concepts of Intermedia is that the hypertext links are maintained in a data base separate from the documents. This allows:

- multi-user access;
- the grouping together all the links which form part of a context in what is called *web*;
- the construction and modification of the links on read-only supports (CD-ROM etc).

In particular the web structure provides visual assistance for navigation in extended documentary bases, by displaying only the links belonging to a specific context. Before creating or following a link, it is necessary to create or open a web, so that each link, from any application created, belongs to at least one web. Two users can have different webs open in the same document. Each web can be graphically displayed as a *map*.

Sun Link Service [Pear89]. An "*open*" system from Sun Corp. which allows permanent connections to be constructed between documents created by generic applications in a UNIX environment. In contrast to "*monolithic*" systems, the creation of the connections is made without having to import the documents produced by various editors (text, graphics, etc.) into the hypertext shell (as in Guide) and without the requirement of constructing "ad hoc" editors for the system (as in the case of Intermedia). The usual user applications and the Sun Link Service control panel form the front end, while the separate and divided back-end deals with the majority of link related functionality. The back-end is for now quite primitive, as to reach the destination anchor (which in Sun Link is associated to a line of text) the system carries out a "find" in the destination document to the first occurrence of the text string which acts as a button. The adoption of OpenLook by Unix applications will also allow the use of a common graphic interface.

The designers of Intermedia are also moving in this direction [Meyr89b].

SEPIA [Stre89], [Schü90]. An "authoring" and "idea-processing" instrument designed by GMD (Gesellschaft für Mathematik und Datenverarbeitung Mbh) to support the creation and modification of documents in a hypertext environment. The system is made up of a series of modules, among which an expert system which provides active feedback and control support on the consistency of the hypertext. From our point of view this system is important as it separates two components at the back-end level: the hypertext engine (HyperBase) which deals with the management of the hypertext objects and an RDBMS (Sybase) which deals with storage, data sharing and distribution on LAN.

A generic software architecture for a hypertext environment could be that shown in figure 1.

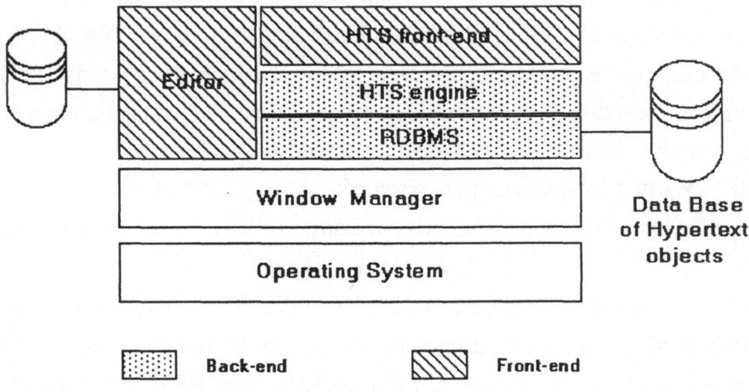

Figure 1

3. Types of Back-ends

We dwell a little on the aspects connected to the component that manages and stores the hypertext objects. The back-end of hypertext systems can be grouped, at the moment, in four types:

a) File system

In this case the back-end coincides with the operating system. Therefore inside the system no distinction exists between back-end and front-end. As already mentioned, most of existing systems follow this approach.

An interesting example is **PlaneText** [Gull86], a hypertext system made up on the Unix file system which uses SunView as a window manager. With PlaneText the storage of the nodes is separated from that of the links. The nodes are in fact normal Unix files, while the links are implemented as pointers, and stored in separate files. In this way the files are not modified when connections are installed between them.

b) Relational DBMS

Actually there are a certain number of systems which use an RDBMS as a back-end. The data base stores the hypertext objects with their attributes. This allows them to be filtered using relational queries. These "*filters*" can be of two types [Meyr89a]:
- *collection filters* which return a list of documents that matches a query on certain attributes;
- *exposure filters* which allow the visualization only of objects that match one specific choice
    criteria.

The hypertext system examples we take into consideration are: gIBIS, WE, Idex, Virtual Notebook and Intermedia.

In **gIBIS** [Conk87b], an argumentation system developed by MCC, the hypertext construction and browsing actions are based on a relational data base which acts as a server. The gIBIS query system is based on a "query by example" approach: the user searches in the data base by constructing a proto-node, the structure of which reflects that of the node being sought. The system stores a node table, a link table and a layout table. When an "issue group" is loaded the three tables are merged.

WE [Smit87a] (Writing Environment), a system for writing support, uses an RDBMS to maintain the nodes and network connections. One of the five windows of WE is used to search for information in the data base.

Idex [Cook89] is a system for the display of large text data bases in a hypertext format. It has been designed on the basis of the most important international standards: Windows and Presentation Manager for the user interface, SGLM (Standard General Mark-up Language) [ISO86] for the layout, Ethernet for the LAN and SQL for the interaction with the data base. This latter aspect provides a standard access method, irrespective of the type of DBMS used.
The data base stores a series of attributes of each document (the status and the type of document, the context, the author and the creation date etc). The attributes can be accessed using the "Catalog Cards" and allow the user to filter the documentary base (collection filters).

Virtual Notebook [Ship89] is a distributed hypertext system for cooperative work implemented on the Sybase relational data base. The system uses X Window on the basis of the client/server mechanism. The elements of the hypertext (information objects, links, pages, notebooks and users) are stored in the data base with a series of system or user constructed attributes. For example, for the object "page" the system can store the composition (that is characteristics, layout and dimensions of each object present in the page), the author, the title and the creation date. When the user moves the mouse over an anchor, a pop-up menu appears containing this information together with that on the links. In this way a **HyperTIES** [Shne87] type of preview is created. Navigation takes place by dynamically constructing the nodes: when the user requests a certain page the hypertext system loads the links and the appropriate objects containing the information from the data base using an SQL query and displays them inside a window.

The server of **Intermedia** is based on a relational data base (CTree) in which the links are objects with associated properties: the starting and destination anchors with the originating document, the name of the link with the keywords which describe it, the author and the creation date. On the basis of these attributes it is therefore possible, (but not yet implemented), to carry out link search and sort operations. From our point of view the web mechanism could be considered as an exposure filter on contexts.

c) Object Oriented DBMS

Sometimes it can be difficult to represent complex networks of objects in a series of relations expressed by means of a table. Some researchers [Smit87b] are studying the possibility of replacing the relational data base with an object oriented data base that is able to deal with more complex data structures (object hierarchies, etc.) in a more appropriate way. To our knowledge, the only system that operate using an object-oriented data base are an Intermedia prototype developed at IRIS and a prototype of SEPIA under development at GMD of Darmstadt (West Germany).

d) Hypertext data base

Up to now we have dealt with back-end types which use technology developed outside of the hypertext environment. In literature it is possible to find back-end models which have been developed "ad hoc" for hypertext systems.

The most important example of hypertext storage system is the **Hypertext Abstract Machine (HAM)** **[Camp87]**, a general-purpose, transaction-based server designed to handle multiple users in a networked environment. The storage model of HAM consists of five objects organized hierarchically:

Graphs, which contain general hypertext information;

Contexts, i.e. logical partitions inside the graph that contain zero or several nodes and links;

Nodes;

Links;

Attributes, which can be associated to contexts, nodes or links.

The pair attribute/value gives the HAM objects a semantic. Using the pair attribute/value it is possible to define the filter mechanism for the entire graph. A filter operation needs a predicate, an execution date and a list of attributes.

HAM provides for the version management and a group of primitives which acts on the objects: create, delete, destroy, change, get, etc.

HAM works directly on the Unix file system. However in **[Bige88]** the author talks about the possibility of using an RDBMS when the number of hypertext objects is too high.

Hypertext Abstract Machine is the hypertext engine of **DynamicDesign** **[Bige87]**, a CASE environment for C programming language developed by **Tektronix.**

As it has already been mentioned, the hypertext engine of SEPIA is **HyperBase** **[Schü90]**. This is a system which supports the creation, management and storage of nodes, links, complex objects and user defined attributes, maintaining a "history list" for each object. In contrast to HAM, this module does not work directly on the file system but uses the storage and multi-user capabilities of an RDBMS.

One of the main aims of the designers of HyperBase is to make the hypertext engine independent from the front-end, that is from the various editors used.

The data base is composed of objects (*HB_Objects*) which possess an arbitrary number of attributes. HB_Objects are divided into three sub-classes:

- *HB_Nodes*, which are objects that have a content and a history;

- *HB_Links*, that are objects which connect two existing HB_Objects;

- *HB_Complex-Objects*, a collection of references to existing HB_Objects which are defined by the user and which are dealt with a single body (for example they can be sorted in some manner). These objects can be: the result of a query on the data base, a selection of several objects, a "guided tour", etc.

HB_Attributes exist only if they are connected to an HB_Object. System or user defined attributes exist.

The AT&T Bell Laboratories developed **Eggs** [**Putt90**], the storage system interface of a *hypermedia toolkit* that manages the integration of new and existing tools in a software development environment. Eggs, which is a simplified version of the HAM, makes the application's interface independent of the storage system. The data model components are *Graphs*, *Contexts*, *Nodes*, *Links*, *Attributes* and *Symbols*.

Along with HAM, HyperBase and Eggs, there exist some hypertext engine models which are at the theoretical stage. The work of P.K. Garg [**Garg87**], F.WM Tompa [**Tomp89**] and Dexter Hypertext Group [**Hala90**] is moving in this direction.

In [**Garg87**] the possibility of implementing abstraction mechanisms based on a distinction between primitive objects (<document texts>) and informative objects (<document models>) is discussed. In this case a hypertext **H** is a collection of objects composed of:

a) a series of primitive objects **P0** and an series of informative objects **I0** under the condition that I0 intersects P0 = {_};

b) a series of predicates **Q**;

c) a series of attributes or properties **A** which collectively define the I0 schema.

"Keyword" is a particular user definable attribute which can be used to place filters on the objects and their abstraction.

F.WM. Tompa in [**Tomp89**] also maintains the necessity of a clear cut separation between the hypertext structure and its contents in order to create and manage several superstructures on the same documentary base. The author proposes the use of a "directed and labelled **hypergraph**" to represent the state of the document base. This model also allows the definition of personalized "views", the execution of queries and the management of updates, while maintaining track of previous versions. The nodes and links are "labelled", but it is not possible to associate attributes to them.

In [**Hala90**] the Dexter Hypertext Group defined a proposal for hypertext system architecture on three levels:

- Runtime Layer (interface);
- Within Component Layer (hypertext engine);
- Storage Layer (storage module).

In conclusion it is possible to note that there does exist a sufficiently delineated and homogeneous direction regarding hypertext architecture of the future.

4. Opportunities offered by an RDBMS type of back-end.

In this paragraph we present some examples that can be carried out with systems that use an RDBMS as back-end. Works in this direction are a paper by L. Gallagher, R. Furuta and P. D. Stotts [**Gall90**] and a paper by our group which appeared in the proceedings of AICA'90 [**Cola90**]. The prototypes proposed were constructed in environments which have similar characteristics: HyperCard and Oracle in the first case, Toolbook and DBIII in the second.

In [Gall90] an RDBMS was used for two purposes:

- supporting the work of the authors of the hypertext;
- supporting the work of the men who maintain the hypertext.

The physical properties of the HyperCard objects are translated into five relations of a data base: *Button, Card, Field, Background, Stack*. As well as the physical properties the user can also define the logical properties (keywords associated to the objects, etc.). The function of "message passing" and interconnections between the cards are represented by the tables *Handle* and *Link*.

The prototype under development at our Institute [Cola90] has a ToolBook hypertext shell as a front-end and a DLL which operates on the DBIII files as a back-end. Toolbook has a larger number of physical objects than HyperCard and for this reason the schema of our data base provides the following relations:

Hotword   *<HW_id, HW_name, PG_id, BOOK_id, author_id, HW_date, context_id, HW_properties, ...>*

Field   *<FL_id, FL_name, PG_id, BOOK_id, author_id, FL_date, context_id, FL_properties, ...>*

Button   *<BT_id, BT_name, PG_id, BOOK_id, author_id, BT_date, context_id, BT_properties, ...>*

Graphic object   *<GP_id, GP_name, PG_id, BOOK_id, author_id, GP_date, context_id, GP_properties, ...>*

Group   *<GR_id, GR_name, PG_id, BOOK_id, author_id, GR_date, context_id, GR_properties, ...>*

Page   *<PG_id, PG_name, BOOK_id, BK_id, author_id, HW_date, context_id, PG_properties, ...>*

Record Field   *<RFL_id, RFL_name, BK_id, PG_id, BOOK_id, author_id, RFL_date, context_id, RFL_properties, ...>*

Background   *<BK_id, BOOK_id, author_id, BK_date, context_id, BK_properties, ...>*

Book   *<BOOK_id, author_id, BOOK_date, context_id, BOOK_properties, ...>*

The function of "message passing" and interconnections between the pages are also represented in our case by two tables with the following schema:

Handle   *<handle_name, PG_id, BOOK_id, contain_obj_id, ...>*

Link   *<LK_id, source_PG, target_PG, target_BOOK, source_BOOK, source_obj_id, type_obj, handle_name, author_id, LK_date, context_id, LK_type, LK_label, LK_properties....>*

In our prototype the relational representation of hypertext objects has a double function:

a) supporting the authoring and maintenance of the hypertext as in [Gall90];
b) allowing the usual mechanisms of navigation to be varied.

For this reason, in the schema appear not only the attributes that can be directly referred to the physical properties of ToolBook objects, but also other attributes the function of which is to support navigation in the hypertext environment. The schema is completed by other two tables:

Context   <*id_context, context_name, id_author, context_date, context_properties, ...*>
Author   <*id_author, author_name, author_surname, author_properties, ...*>

In the examples that follow different queries are shown which can be used to assist the navigation and management of a hypertext. The queries are expressed in SQL, even though in our prototype they are effectively implemented by means of DBIII programs.

Example 1: Find all the links associated to an anchor

SELECT *target_PG, target_BOOK, context_id, LK_label, LK_properties*
FROM *Link*.
WHERE *source_obj_id* = current_obj_id

Example 2: Find all the links which exit from a page

SELECT *target_PG, target_BOOK, context_id, LK_label, LK_properties*
FROM *Link*.
WHERE *source_PG* = current_PG

Example 3: Change all the properties of all the buttons of a Book

UPDATE Button
WHERE *BOOK_id* = current_Book
SET *HighLight* = True, *FontSize* = 12, *FontStyle* = "italic", *FontFace* = "Tms Rmn"

Example 4: Find all the links associated to the current anchor and defined by the context of indentifier XYZ

SELECT *target_PG, target_BOOK, context_id, LK_label, LK_properties*
FROM *Link*.
WHERE *source_obj_id* = current_obj_id
    and *context_id* = "XYZ"

From the navigation viewpoint, the most interesting operations are the "setting" of the contexts or of the authors, combining their functional characteristics. In this way it is possible to navigate in the hypertext only seeing those objects (for example the buttons or hotwords) created by authors X and Y for context Z. These opportunities are very useful in a didactic hypertext.

5. Abstract operations on the hypertext objects Data Base

In this section we discuss the possibility of defining *abstract objects* on the relations of the hypertext objects data base. In this way it becomes possible to interrogate and manage some macro-object defined in the hypertext and increase the potential of the system.

The proposed approach is discussed through the presentation of an example in which a collection of geographic maps of different scales is used as the access and navigation mechanism of a hypertext. The example is the result of our ideas and experience of the construction of a hypertext-like geographical interface for a collection of information on members of a philanthropic international association (*).

The prototype under construction uses Toolbook to access text files and a data base in DBIII containing general information and the legal documents of each institution that has relations with the main office in Vatican City. The maps which represent the countries in which a Caritas member works are departure anchors for Toolbook pages on which the prototype show predefined selection on the values of DBIII files and the opportune text files. Due to the relatively small size of the hypertext, we have not, up to now, used the link storage mechanisms described in the preceding paragraph.

Currently, if a system user is interested in aggregated information on a number of countries - eg for drafting a report - he must interrogate the data base using DBIII and its language. Obviously this operation would be difficult for inexpert users. It is therefore necessary to provide sophisticated access functionality to data, while maintaining, however, the same hypertext style of interaction.

The approach we are studying is based on the use of a Nested-algebra [Maki77], [Sche82], [Abit84], [Roth84], [Thom86] for the creation and manipulation of the abstract objects stored in the data base.

A Nested Algebra allows us to apply to unnormalized relations a series of operators which transform "flat" relations into nested hierarchical ones or viceversa. The operators that principally interest our model are:

- the *NEST* operator, which acts on a series of defined objects in order to aggregate them in a new object of a superior hierarchical level;

- the *UNNEST* operator, which divides an object into its basic components.

As we will see in what follows, the adoption of abstraction mechanisms on the data base of hypertext objects allows us to solve a series of problems similar to those mentioned earlier. It also brings us to extend the concept of link and to take another look at the definition of *"type of link"* presented in [Trig83]. In fact from the point of view of the data structure, the normal notion of type of link coincides with the concept of *"label of link"*. An effective type of link requires the definition of the abstract objects of a higher logic level.

We will clarify what we have said up to now using figures 2, 3 and 4. Figure 2 shows an example of the current functioning of the prototype. The maps of Norway, Sweden and Finland (A1, A2, A3) are the departure anchors to nodes N1, N2 and N3 which contain information on the respective Caritas member. The three links (L1, L2, L3) are normal links of the "go to" type.

(*) Caritas Internationalis.

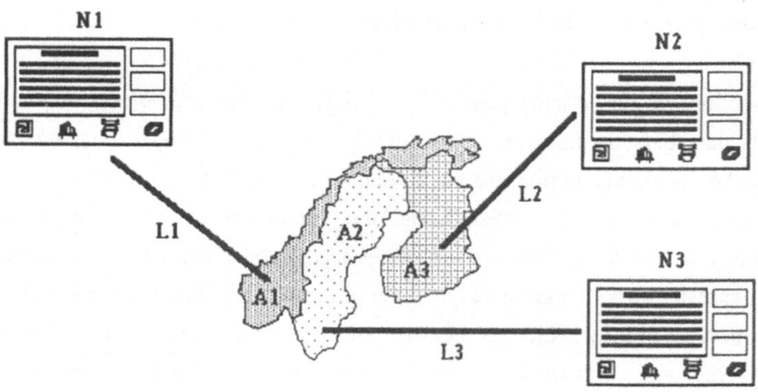

Figure 2

Adopting the notation used in [Güti87], the data base structure for the proposed example can be represented as follows:

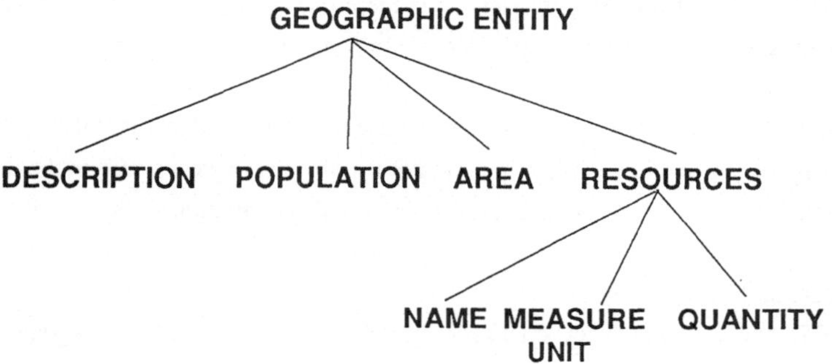

Figure 3

In this data base, the occurrences of the "geographic entity" schema assume the following values:

```
< (FINLAND,  337.032,  4.758.000,  < (BARLEY, TONS, 1.800.000) >
                                    < (FISHING, TONS, 146.000) >
                                    < (OAT, TONS, 1.400.000) >
                                    < (POTATO, TONS, 800.000) >
                                    < (TIMBER, M³, 39.000.000) > ) >
< (NORWAY,  323.895,  4.079.500,  < (BARLEY, TONS, 700.000) >
                                    < (FISHING, TONS, 2.500.000) >
                                    < (OAT, TONS, 400.000) >
                                    < (POTATO, TONS, 600.000) >
                                    < (TIMBER, M³, 8.000.000) > ) >
```

```
< (SWEDEN,  411.613,  8.318.000,   < (BARLEY, TONS, 2.000.000) >
                                   < (FISHING, TONS, 250.000) >
                                   < (OAT, TONS, 1.300.000) >
                                   < (POTATO, TONS, 1.000.000) >
                                   < (TIMBER, M³, 53.000.000) > ) >
```

An interesting feature of the system could be the creation of new areas derived from the aggregation of previous defined entities. However, when in the example the user defines the new zone "Scandinavian Region", (labelled as A4 in fig. 4), what is the meaning of the link L4 and of the node N4?

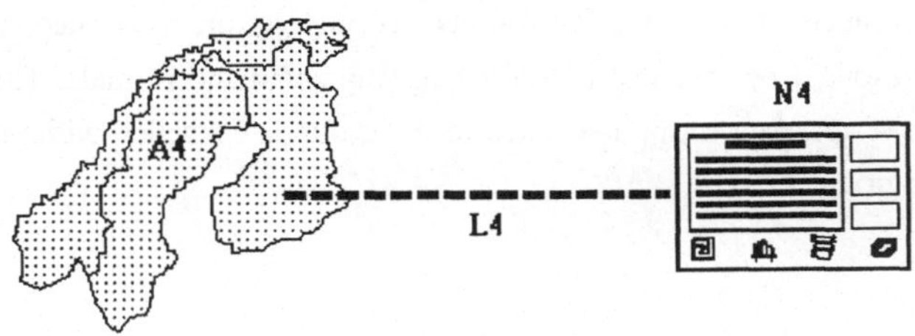

Figure 4

It is possible to think that once the new area has been defined ("*Nest*" operation) the user can choose between a predefined series of type of links which determine the rules and the composition of the destination nodes. In other words one realizes something similar to "composite nodes" and "virtual structures", two of "Halasz' seven issues" presented at Hypertext '87 [Hala87].

For example, applying the NEST operator to the occurrences of the relations defined previously, we obtain:

```
< (SCANDINAVIAN REGION,  337.032,  4.758.000, < (BARLEY, TONS, 4.500.000) >
                                              < (FISHING, TONS, 2.896.000) >
                                              < (OAT, TONS, 3.100.000) >
                                              < (POTATO, TONS, 2.400.000) >
                                              < (TIMBER, M³, 100.000.000) > ) >
```

In this case the composition rule of the type of link L4 is "connect the alpha-numeric fields and add up the numeric fields of the destination nodes". The node N4 contains the aggregate information created by the NEST operator on the data base.

Other composition rules that determine the type of link could, for example, be the following:
- "connect the associative links (hotword) and execute the union of the navigation links" (button or graphic object);
- "execute the intersection of the keywords associated to the destination nodes".

Opposite operations could occur when the user carries out an "Unnest", that is dividing an area into its base components.

A concept similar to that just mentioned - even if it is much more primitive - is present in the commands "*Group*" and "*Ungroup*" of some object orientated hypertext systems such as Toolbook and SuperCard.

If a Group of objects, to which script has been previously associated, is made using **Toolbook**, each of them maintains and is able to execute its own script. This also occurs when a script is associated to the Group just created. The decomposition rule in the case of an Ungroup operation is the following: if different objects have associated scripts, each conserves its own; if the Group possesses a name or a script the system advises the user that execution of the operation will destroy them.

If a Group of objects is created using **SuperCard** any scripts associated to them will remain stored, but they can no longer be executed until the Ungroup command is made. This also occurs if the group does not have a script. Any script associated to the group is cancelled without warning when the user carries out the Ungroup.

Conclusions

From a realizational point of view, greater map granularity (the base object becomes the region instead of the state) would give the system considerable generality and potential. However, the environment used does not allow a similar level of efficiency.

Abstraction mechanisms similar to those exposed can be thought also for other hypertext macro-objects: guided tours, history lists, table tops, tables of contents, query results, and so on.

The adoption of abstraction mechanisms on the hypertext object data base entails a different concept of "*type of link*" with regard to those defined in current systems. In fact a set of links are not different because of the shape of the cursor or the label of the "go to" program, but because of the structural properties that define what their characteristics are and how they behave in different situations. True link type can provide an higher level of flexibility as well as an increase in representational power.

Acknowledgments

We would like to thank the Caritas Internationalis for suggestions in the construction of the prototype. We also thank W. J. Irler and M. Margoni of the Istituto di Informatica of the University of Trento for the collaboration during the discussion and implementation of the interface aspects.

References

[AAVV] Hypertext '87 (1987), Hypertext '87 Workshop, UNC, Chapel Hill, NC, Nov. 1987, ACM: New York.

[AAVV] Hypertext '89 (1989), Hypertext '89 Workshop, Pittsburgh, PA, Nov.5-8 1989. ACM: New York.

[Abit84] Abiteboul S, Bidoi N (1984), Non-First-Normal-Form-Relations to represent hierarchically organized data. In Proc. 3rd ACM PODS, 1984, and also in Journal of Computer and System Sciences.

[Agos88] Agosti M (1988), Is hypertext a new model of information retrieval? In: (Online'88), Vol.I, 57-62.

[Aksc87] Akscyn R, McCracken D, Yoder E (1988), KMS: A distributed hypermedia system for managing knowledge in organizations. Comm. ACM, Vol. 31, 7, pp. 820-835. also in: (Hypertext '87), pp. 1-20.

[Appl88] Apple (1988), HyperCard Stack Design Guidelines. Addison-Wesley Apple Technical Library: Menlo Park, CA.

[Bige87] Bigelow J, Riley V (1987), Manipulating source code in dynamic design. In: (Hypertext '87), 397-408.

[Bige88] Bigelow J (1988), Hypertext and CASE. IEEE Software, Mar.1988, 23-27.

[Brow87] Brown P J (1987), Turning ideas into products: The Guide System. In: (Hypertext '87), pp. 33-40.

[Brow89] Brown P J (1989), A hypertext system for Unix [Guide]. Comput.Syst. (USA), Vol.2, n.2, Wint.1989, 37-53.

[Bush45] Bush V (1945), As we may think. Atl.Month., 176, 101-108; reprinted in: (Nelson , 1987), (Lambert & Ropiequet, 1986).

[Camp87] Campbell B, Goodman J M (1987), HAM: A general-purpose hypertext abstract machine. C ACM, Jul.1988, Vol.31, n.7, 856-861; also in: (Hypertext '87), pp. 21-32.

[Cola89] Colazzo L, Irler W J (1989), Interpretare ovvero produrre conoscenza. (Interpreting or producing knowledge). In: (AICA'89), Vol. I, 493-509.

[Cola90] Colazzo L, Barbieri G, Irler W J (1990), Tecnologie delle basi di dati analitiche & tecnologie ipertestuali. La prospettiva della comunicazione. In Proc. AICA'90 Bari, Sept. 1990.

[Conk87a] Conklin E J (1987), Hypertext: An introduction and survey. IEEE Computer 20, 9 (Sept.87), 17-41; Ital.trad. in Informatica Oggi, No.43 (1988), 20-62.

[Conk87b] Conklin J Begeman M L (1987), gIBIS: A hypertext tool for team design deliberation. In: (Hypertext '87), pp. 247-251; also: ACM Trans.Off.Inf.Syst., Oct.1988, Vol.6, n.4, 303-331.

[Cook89] Cook P, Williams I (1989), Design issues in large hypertext systems for technical documentation. In: (McAleese, 1989), 93-104.

[Crof89] Croft W B, Turtle H (1989), A retrieval model incorporating hypertext links. In: (Hypertext '89).

[DeRo89] DeRose S (1989), Expanding the notion of links. In: (Hypertext '89), 249-258.

[**Fris89**] Frisse M E, Cousins S (1989), Information retrieval from hypertext: update on the Dynamic Medical Handbook Project. In: (Hypertext '89), 199-212.

[**Gall90**] L. Gallagher, R Furuta, P.D. Stotts (1990), Increasing the power of hypertext search with relational queries. Hypermedia, Vol. 2, n.1, 1-14.

[**Garg87**] Garg P K (1987), Abstraction mechanisms in hypertext. In: (Hypertext'87), 375-395; also: (1988), C ACM, Jul.1988, Vol.31, n.7, 862-870.

[**Good88**] Goodman D (1988,2.ed.), The Complete HyperCard Handbook. Bantam Books: New York.

[**Guid90**] Guide 3.0, OWL International Inc., 14218 Northeast 21st. St., Bellevue, WA 98007.

[**Gull86**] Gullichsen E, D'Souza D, Lincoln P, Casey T (1986), The PlaneText Book. MCC TR n. STP-333-86(P).

[**Güti87**] Güting R H, Zicari, R Choy D M (1987), An algebra for structured office documents. Research report, IBM Research Division, Yorktown Heights, New York.

[**Hala87**] Halasz F (1987), Reflections on NoteCards: seven issues for the next generation of hypermedia systems. In: (Hypertext '87), pp. 345-366; C ACM, Jul.1988, Vol.31, n.7, 836-861.

[**Hala89**] Halasz F, Conklin J (1989), Issues in the design and application of hypermedia systems. SIGCHI '89 Tutorial.

[**Hala90**] Halasz F, Schwartz (1990), The Dexter Hypertext Reference Model. In Proc. of NIST Hypertext Standardization Workshop, Gaithersburg, MD, Jan 90.

[**Hype90**] HyperPAD 2.0, Brightbill-Roberts &Co. Ltd., 120 E. Washington St., Suite 421, Syracuse, NY 13202.

[**Irle90**] Irler W J, Barbieri G (1990), Non-intrusive hypertext anchors and individual colour markings. In Proc. ECTH'90, Versailles, 27-30 Nov. 1990, pp. 261-273.

[**ISO86**] ISO 8879.(1986) Standard Generalised Markup Language (SGLM). Genevra.

[**Maki77**] Makinouchi A (1977), A consideration on Normal Form of Not-Necesserely-Normalized-Relation in the Relational Data Model. In Proc. VLDB, Tokio, 1977.

[**Meyr86**] Meyrowitz N (1986), Intermedia: The architecture and construction of an Object-oriented hypermedia system and application framework. In: (OOPSLA '86).

[**Meyr89a**] Meyrowitz N (1989), I sistemi ipermediali e l'interfaccia "a scrivania" di domani. In Navigare con gli ipertesti, Ed. Spec. Zero Uno, Dec 1989, 85-106

[**Meyr89b**] Meyrowitz N (1989), The missing link: why we're all doing hypertext wrong. TR 89-1, Brown University, 1989.

[**Myer88**] Myers B A (1988), A taxonomy of window manager user interface. IEEE Computer Graphics 5-8 Nov. 1989.

[**Nels74**] Nelson T H (1974), Computer Lib / Dream Machines (2nd ed., 1987). Microsoft Press: Redmond WA.

[**Nels81**] Nelson T H (1981), Literary machines,Ed.87.1. (1987). The Distributors: South Bend IN.

[**Pear89**] Pearl A (1989), Sun's link sevice: a protocol for open linking. In: (Hypertext '89).

[**Plus90**] Plus, Spinnaker Software, 1 Kendall Square, Cambridge, MA 02139.

[**Pryw63**] Prywes N, Gray H J (1963), The organization of a multi-list type associative memory. IEEE Trans. on Comp. and Elec, Sept 1963, 488-492.

[**Putt90**] Puttres J J, Guimaraes N M (1990), The Toolkit approach to hypermedia. In Proc. ECTH'90, Versailles, 27-30 Nov. 1990, pp. 25-37.

[**Roth84**] Roth M A, Korth H K, Silberschartz A (1984), Theory of Non-First-Normal-Form-Relation Databases. Univ. of Texas, Austin, TR 84-36, 1984.

[**Sche82**] Schek H J, Pistor P (1982), Data structures for an Integrated Database Management and Information Retrieval System. In Proc. VLDB, Mexico City, 1982.

[**Schü90**] Schütt H, Streitz N A (1990), HyperBase: a hypermedia engine based on a relational database management system. In Proc. ECTH'90, Versailles, 27-30 Nov. 1990, pp. 95-108.

[**Ship89**] Shipman F, Chaney R, Gory G (1989), The virtual notebook system: distributed hypertext for collaborative research. In: (Hypertext '89), pp 129-136.

[**Shne87**] Shneiderman B (1987), User interface design for the Hyperties electronic encyclopedia. In: (Hypertext '87), pp. 189-194.

[**Smit87a**] Smith J B, Weiss S F, Ferguson G J (1987), A hypertext Writing Environment and its cognitive basis. In: (Hypertext '87), pp 195-214.

[**Smit87b**] Smith K E, Zdonik S B (1987), Intermedia: a case study of the differences between relational and object-oriented datebase systems. In: (OOPSLA'87).

[**Stre89**] Streiz N A, Hannemann J, Thüring M (1989), From ideas and arguments to hyperdocuments: travelling through activity spaces. In: (Hypertext '89), 195-214.

[**Supe90**] SuperCard 1.5, Aldus Corp., 411 First Ave. S., Seattle, WA 98104.

[**Thom86**] Thomas S J, Fischer P C (1986), Nested Relational Structures. In Advances in Computing Research, (Kannelakis ed.), JAI Press, 1986.

[**Tomp89**] Tompa F WM (1989), A data model for flexible hypertext database systems. ACM Trans. Information Systems, Vol.7, n.1, Jan.1989, 85-100.

[**Tool90**] Toolbook 1.0, Asymetrix Corp., 110 110th Ave., Suite 717, Bellevue, WA 98004.

[**Trig83**] Trigg R (1983), A network-based approach to text handling for the online scientific community. Ph.D Thesis, dept. of Computer Science, Univ. of Maryland 1983.

[**Walt89**] Walter M (1989), IRIS Intermedia: pushing the boundaries of hypertext. Seybold Rep.Publ.Syst. (USA), Vol.18, n.21, Aug.1989, 21-32.

[**Wied77**] Wiederhold G (1977), Database Design. McGraw Hill Book Company, NY 1977.

[**Yank88**] Yankelovich N, Haan BJ, Meyrowitz N Drucker S M (1988), Intermedia: the concept and the construction of a seamless information environment. IEEE Computer, Jan. 1988, 81-96.

Vom Prototyp zum Produkt

Empirische Untersuchung zum Akzeptanzverhalten einer Hypertextapplikation

Eva Bertha und Erich J. Schwarz
Institut für Informationswissenschaft, Karl-Franzens-Universität Graz
Strassoldogasse 10, A-8010 Graz

Zusammenfassung

Ein am Institut für Informationswissenschaft erstellter Bibliotheksführer auf Hypertext-Basis wurde von den potentiellen Nutzern, hauptsächlich Studenten und Mitarbeitern der Technischen Universität Graz, in einem Feldversuch getestet, wobei folgende Punkte besonders untersucht wurden:

- Benutzerklassen
- Hardware und Systembedienung
- Benutzeroberfläche
- Inhalt des Systems
- Navigieren im System
- Medium Hypertext

Die inhaltliche Aufarbeitung der Problemstellung sowie die graphische Umsetzung und die Bedienung mit der Maus fanden bei den Testpersonen große Zustimmung. Auch Hypertext als neues Medium wurde von den Benutzern positiv aufgenommen. Als Schwachstelle dieser Applikation erwies sich die Navigation durch das System. Eine Einbindung bereits bestehender Systeme bzw. die Vernetzung mit dem Online Public Access Catalog (OPAC) wurde häufig von den Testpersonen gefordert.

Die wichtigste Erkenntnis aus diesem Feldversuch ist, daß bei derartigen Applikationen vorwiegend die einfachen und traditionellen Navigationshilfen genutzt werden. Typische Hypertext-Werkzeuge wie die Volltextsuche werden nicht entsprechend angenommen. Die Testpersonen hatten auch erhebliche Probleme, die Mehrdimensionalität dieser Hypertextapplikation zu erfassen, was sich darin äußerte, daß sie das Gefühl hatten, im System verloren zu sein. Die zum Teil zu abstrakten Symbole beim Dimensionsselektor dürften dieses Gefühl der Desorientierung verstärkt haben.

Plant man also, ein derartiges System für gelegentliche Benutzer zu entwickeln, müssen die verwendeten Symbole und die vorgegebenen Suchstrategien besonders sorgfältig gestaltet werden. Nicht komplizierte Benutzeroberflächen sollen das Ziel der Entwicklung sein. Es muß versucht werden, durch Einfachheit der Benutzerschnittstellen und Klarheit der Strukturen die Bedienung des Systems zu erleichtern.

1. Einleitung

Am Institut für Informationswissenschaft der Karl-Franzens-Universität wurde für die Universitätsbibliothek der Technischen Universität Graz im vergangenen Jahr ein elektronischer Bibliotheksführer "UBTUG Scout" erstellt (Fasching 1991). Dieses elektronische Auskunftssystem enthält Informationen zu den Öffnungszeiten, Katalogen und Entlehnmodalitäten der Bibliothek sowie zur Lehrbuchsammlung, zum Personal und zu den Institutsbibliotheken. Da dieses Produkt allen Benützern der Bibliothek zur Verfügung gestellt werden sollte, war die leichte Bedienbarkeit das entscheidende Kriterium für die Auswahl der eingesetzten Software. Aus diesem Grund wurde diese Applikation auf einem Macintosh mit HyperCard entwickelt.

Dem Benutzer werden mehrere Navigationsmöglichkeiten angeboten, um die gesuchte Information in der netzwerkartig aufgebauten Applikation zu finden. So steht neben Tasten zum Vor- und Rückwärtsblättern (Kontrollpaneel) auch ein Dimensionsselektor zur Verfügung, der an der jeweiligen Stelle der Applikation Auskunft über Person, Inhalt, Art der Informationsvermittlung, Ort und Zeit gibt. Versucht man etwa zusätzliche Informationen über den Entlehnvorgang zu erhalten, so bekommt man durch Anklicken der "Wann"-Taste im Dimensionsselektor die Öffnungszeiten der Entlehnstelle angezeigt. Weiters sollen integrierte Volltextsuche, Hilfefunktion und Suche mittels Index dem Benutzer die Inhaltserschließung erleichtern. Aufgrund der Konzeption von HyperCard ist es möglich, ohne Verwendung der Tastatur nur mit Hilfe der Maus die gewünschten Informationen abzurufen.

Um die Akzeptanz der Applikation zu untersuchen, wurde der Prototyp des Bibliotheksführers von potentiellen Nutzern in einem Feldversuch getestet. Der vorliegende Beitrag berichtet über die Ergebnisse dieses Feldversuches und über die daraus entstehenden Konsequenzen sowohl für die getestete Applikation als auch für das Design neuer Hypertextsysteme. Obwohl bereits unzählige Hypertextapplikationen erstellt wurden, gibt es in der Literatur kaum Untersuchungen über ihre Akzeptanz. Aus diesem Grund können die Ergebnisse dieses Beitrages bei Neuerstellungen von derartigen Systemen Hilfestellung leisten.

2. Erstellung des Fragebogens und Testanordnung

Beim Feldversuch wurden standardisierte Interviews und Fragebögen als Erhebungsmethoden eingesetzt (Schwarz 1989, Dillman 1978). Besonderes Augenmerk galt der Erstellung des Fragebogens. Mehrere Personen mit und ohne Computererfahrung wurden eingeladen, das System zu testen, wobei ihre Interaktionen mit dem System beobachtet und aufgezeichnet wurden. Die dabei auftretenden Fragen und Probleme bildeten die Grundlage für den Rohentwurf des Fragebogens. Um sprachliche und inhaltliche Fehler in der endgültigen Version des Fragebogens zu vermeiden, wurde zusätzlich ein dreitägiger Vortest unter gleichen Bedingungen wie beim späteren Haupttest durchgeführt. Die Ergebnisse dieses Vortests wurden analysiert und der Fragebogen in einigen Punkten noch ergänzt bzw. korrigiert. Um für den Haupttest auch genug Testpersonen zur Verfügung zu haben, wurde fünf Tage vor der Testperiode begonnen, für die Applikation zu werben. In allen wichtigen Bereichen der Bibliothek wurden Plakate mit Informationen über das neue System angebracht. Der Haupttest fand dann im Dezember 1990 im Entlehnbereich der Bibliothek statt (Kappel, Bagary 1991).

Aufgrund der geringen Anzahl an freiwilligen Testpersonen während des Vortests (acht Personen/Testtag) und der fehlenden Information über die Merkmale der Grundgesamtheit (Summe aller Bibliotheksbenutzer) wurde von einer Auswahl der Testpersonen im Stichprobenverfahren abgesehen und eine Vollerhebung durchgeführt. Da diese Erhebung mitten im Semester und über einen längeren Zeitraum anberaumt war, kann davon ausgegangen werden, daß diese Versuchspersonen eine repräsentative Auswahl darstellen. Selbst der hohe Prozentsatz an computererfahrenen Testpersonen schränkt diese Annahme nicht ein, weil mit hoher Wahrscheinlichkeit davon ausgegangen werden kann, daß die Bibliotheksbenutzer einer technischen Universität häufig mit Computern konfrontiert sind. Die einzige Restriktion bezüglich der Testpersonen bestand darin, daß für die Befragung grundsätzlich nur jene Personen herangezogen wurden, die ohne Aufforderung mindestens drei Minuten das System benutzt hatten, wie Abbildung 1 zu entnehmen ist. Die große Zahl der "Kurztester" (Testdauer weniger als drei Minuten) wurde nicht in die Statistik aufgenommen. Insgesamt wurden beim Haupttest 85 Personen befragt.

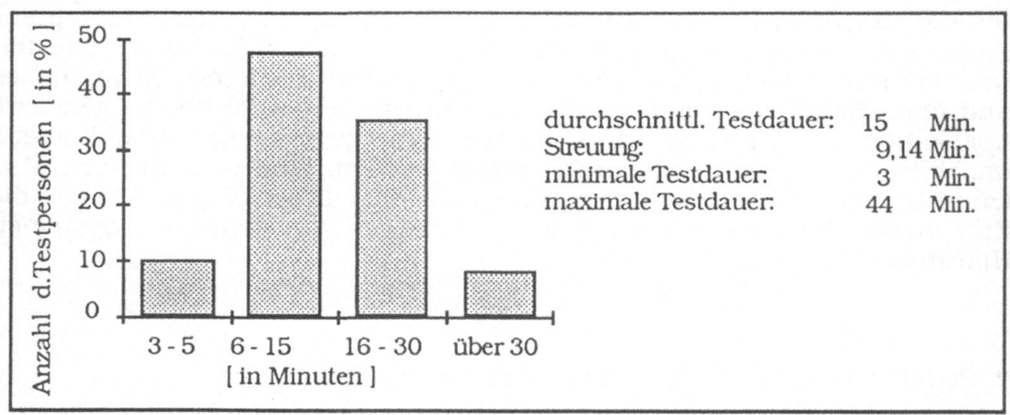

Abb. 1: Testdauer

Die Befragung der Testpersonen erfolgte unmittelbar nach den praktischen Tests in drei Abschnitten. Die 13 zum Teil offen gestellten Fragen des I. Abschnittes wurden vom Interviewer vorgelesen und mußten mündlich beantwortet werden. Diese Fragen bezogen sich auf den Gesamteindruck der Applikation sowie auf die Verständlichkeit einiger vom System angebotener

Navigationshilfen wie Volltextsuche oder Bedienung eines Indexfensters. Um etwaigen sprachlichen Mißverständnissen vorzubeugen, wurden den Befragten die Navigationshilfen in Form von Graphiken gezeigt.

Abschnitt II beinhaltete Fragen zur Bedienung des Systems, zur formalen Suche von Information sowie Fragen zur Informationsaufbereitung und -nutzung. Alle 15 "Fragen" des II. Abschnittes wurden als Statements formuliert und mußten schriftlich beantwortet werden. Um die statistische Auswertung dieser Aussagen zu erleichtern, wurde eine einheitliche Skalierung bei den Antwortmöglichkeiten gewählt.

Den Abschluß jedes Interviews bildete Abschnitt III des Fragebogens, der aufgrund einiger offener Fragen wiederum vorgelesen wurde und daher von den Testpersonen mündlich beantwortet werden mußte. Mit Hilfe des III. Abschnittes sollten vor allem Fragen die allgemeine Bedienung, die Präsentation und die Aufstellung des Systems betreffend sowie allgemeine Fragen zu den Testpersonen (Geschlecht, Computererfahrung etc..) und zum Computertyp untersucht werden.

3. Ergebnisse und Auswertung der Tests

Von den 85 Fragebögen konnten einige wegen widersprüchlicher Angaben bzw. wegen Beeinflussung durch Dritte (etwa durch positive Mundpropaganda) nicht zur Analyse herangezogen werden, sodaß letztlich 78 Fragebögen statistisch ausgewertet wurden.

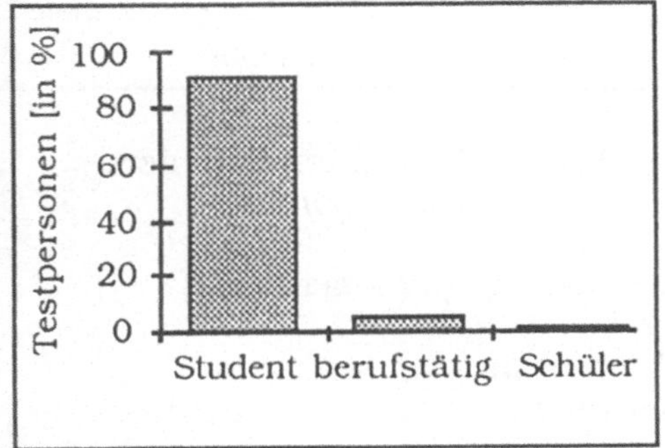

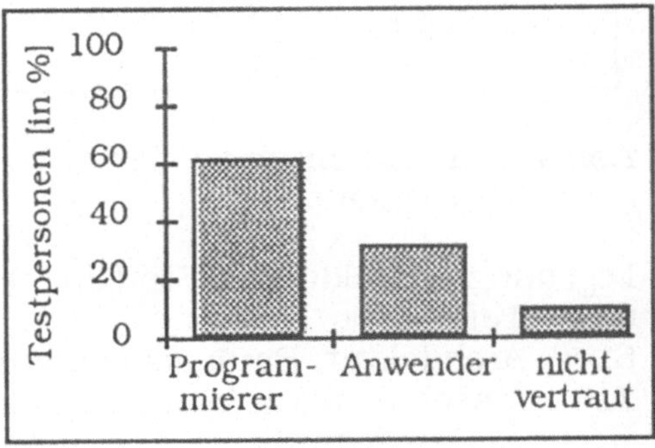

Abb. 2: Tätigkeit der Testpersonen

Abb.3: Computererfahrung der Testpersonen

Wie bereits erwähnt, hatte der Großteil der Testpersonen bereits persönliche Erfahrung mit Computern. So gaben etwa 60% an, selbst zu programmieren, 30% Anwendungsprogramme zu verwenden und 10% nicht mit Computern vertraut zu sein. Ein interessanter Aspekt dabei war, daß lediglich zwei Tester bisher mit Apple PCs Kontakt hatten. Aufgrund mangelnder Erfahrung der Testpersonen sowohl mit dem Medium Hypertext als auch mit der graphischen Benutzeroberfläche des MacIntosh ergab sich für die meisten Testpersonen eine ähnliche Ausgangssituation, wodurch die Vergleichbarkeit der Ergebnisse erleichtert wurde.

Bei der statistischen Auswertung der Fragebögen ergaben sich keine signifikanten Unterschiede in den Beurteilungen durch unerfahrene Benutzer, Anwender und Programmierer. Dieses Ergebnis ist insofern interessant, da es sich sich vom Resultat einer ähnlichen Studie unterscheidet, die von der schottischen Universität Strathclyde durchgeführt wurde (Baird 1990). Bei der schottischen Untersuchung zeigte sich, daß Testpersonen mit geringerer Computererfahrung die Möglichkeiten eines Informationssystems auf Hypertext weit höher bewerteten bzw. wesentlich stärker von dieser Hyper-Card-Applikation beeindruckt waren, als die Gruppe mit der größeren EDV-Erfahrung.

Bei der Auswertung der Fragebögen konnten auch bezüglich der Studienrichtung bzw. der Studiendauer keine signifikanten Unterschiede in den Ergebnissen festgestellt werden.

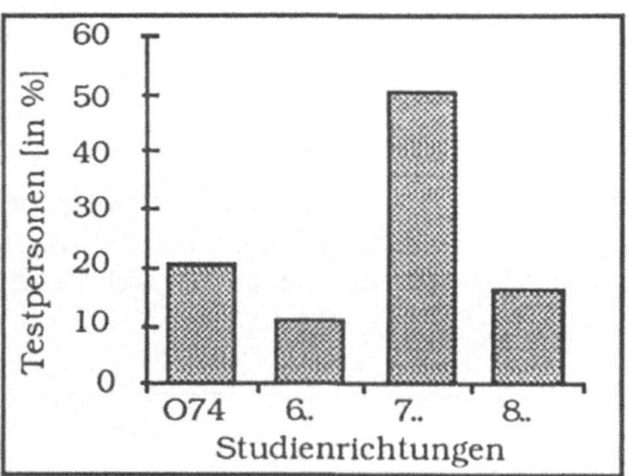

Abb.4: Studienrichtungen der
Testpersonen

Abb. 5: Semesteranzahl der
Testpersonen

Legende zu Abbildung 4 (Studienrichtungen der Testpersonen):
074   Telematik
6..   Architektur, Bauingenieurwesen, Vermessungswesen
7..   Maschinenbau, Wirtschaftsingenieurwesen, Verfahrenstechnik, Elektrotechnik
8..   Chemie, Physik, Mathematik

Die Ergebnisse des schriftlich zu beantwortenden Teiles des Fragebogens sind Abbildung 6 zu entnehmen. Bereits bei Erstellung des Fragebogens wurde festgelegt, daß alle Punkte der Applikation mit einer schlechteren Durchschnittsbenotung als 2,5 (auf einer fünfteiligen Skala von 1 = "sehr gut" bis 5 = "nicht genügend") bei einer weiteren Systemversion korrigiert werden müssen. Bei allen anderen Punkten sollte der notwendige Änderungsaufwand im Verhältnis zum erwarteten Nutzen betrachtet werden.

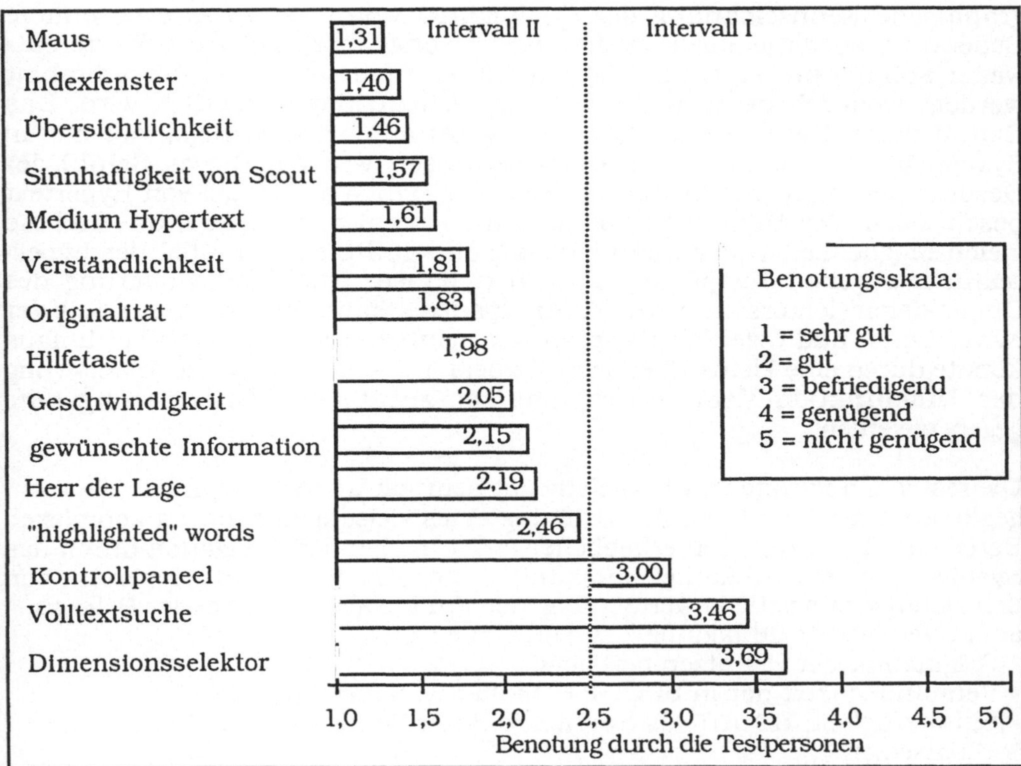

Abb. 6: Systembenotung durch die Testpersonen

Zur Diskussion wurden die erhaltenen Werte in zwei Intervalle zusammengefaßt:
Intervall 1: Werte > 2,5
Intervall 2: Werte ≤ 2,5

Wie aus Abbildung 6 ersichtlich, fallen der Dimensionsselektor, die Volltextsuche und das Kontrollpaneel in Intervall I und müssen daher verbessert werden. Die schlechte Beurteilung dieser Navigationshilfen ist sicherlich nicht nur auf mangelhafte Erklärung in der Hilfefunktion oder zum Teil stark abstrakte Symbolik beim Dimensionsselektor zurückzuführen, sondern zeigten, daß die Testpersonen durch die vielen Möglichkeiten der Informationsgewinnung in diesem Hypertextsystem überfordert wurden (Rauch 1990). Die Änderungsvorschläge bzw. die Konsequenzen aus diesen Ergebnisse werden in Abschnitt 4 dieser Arbeit diskutiert.

Aus dem Intervall II wurden die letzten beiden Punkte einer genauen Analyse unterzogen. Es sind dies das Statement, daß man sich als Benutzer im "Großen und Ganzen als Herr der Lage " fühlt und die sogenannten "highlighted words" - d.h. all jene Worte, die einmal kurz am Bildschirm aufleuchten und die direkte Verbindung zu einer weiteren Karte - mit zusätzlicher Information zum jeweiligen Begriff - anzeigen. Durch eine bessere graphische Kennzeichnung der "highlighted words" kann ihre besondere Bedeutung hervorgehoben werden. Es ist vorstellbar, daß diese Worte entweder ständig mit einem auffälligen Hintergrund unterlegt oder umrahmt werden, wodurch deren besondere Eigenschaft klar ersichtlich wird. Das Gefühl nicht "Herr der Lage" zu sein, weist auf Orientierungsprobleme im System hin und kann direkt kaum verbessert werden. Dieses Gefühl der Desorientierung wurde bereits von Conklin 1987 als Nachteil von Hypertext beschrieben. Die Mehrdimensionalität dieser Hypertextapplikation und die vielen Möglichkeiten der Informationssuche dürfte den Großteil der hypertextunerfahrenen Testpersonen verwirrt haben. Durch die Änderung des Dimensionsselektors und des Kontrollpaneels kann sicherlich ein Teil der Navigations- und Orientierungsprobleme gemindert werden. Darüber hinaus könnte durch eine kleine Übersicht - "stackmap" - oder durch die Erweiterung der Hilfefunktion dem Systembenutzer zusätzliche Orientierungshilfe gegeben werden.

Die restlichen Punkte wurden relativ gut beurteilt und widerspiegeln die recht geglückte Umsetzung und Aufbereitung eines vielschichtigen und komplexen Bereiches. Trotz zum Teil erheblicher Probleme bei der Navigation durch das System, wird ein Bibliotheksauskunftssystem basierend auf Hypertext von den Benutzern positiv bewertet. Folgende Punkte schnitten bei der Befragung am besten ab, wie Abbildung 7 zu entnehmen ist:
- Originalität der Benutzeroberfläche
- Verständlichkeit der in SCOUT enthaltenen Informationen
- Sinnhaftigkeit, SCOUT als Informationsmedium für die TU-Bibliothek einzusetzen
- Verwendung eines Bibliotheksführers mit Hypertext
- Übersichtlichkeit der Bildschirme
- Bedienung der Indexfenster
- Mausbedienung.

Die durchgeführte Stärken-Schwächen Analyse basierte auf folgenden drei offenen Fragen:
Frage 1: Was gefällt an Scout besonders gut?
Frage 2: Was stört an Scout besonders?
Frage 3: Was sollte an Scout geändert werden?

Pro Frage durften bis zu drei Nennungen abgegeben werden. Bei der ersten Frage wurden insgesamt 121 , bei der zweiten 97 und bei der dritten Frage 72 Nennungen abgegeben. Die Ergebnisse der Auswertung sind in Abbildung 7 dargestellt. Die meisten abgegebenen Nennungen waren entweder positiv oder negativ belegt worden. Lediglich bei den Punkten, Benutzerführung, Systemgeschwindigkeit und dargebotener Inhalt, gab es sowohl pro als auch contra Meinungen, wobei nur beim Punkt Geschwindigkeit die negativen Wertungen leicht überwogen. Besonders gut gefiel den Versuchspersonen die Bedienung des Systems mit der Maus, sowie die inhaltliche und graphische Aufbereitung der Information. Auch das neue Medium Hypertext wurde von den Benutzern positiv aufgenommen. Wie bereits durch andere Fragestellungen erhoben, waren die Symbole zur Navigation nicht klar genug und wurden auch bei der offenen Befragung am häufigsten kritisiert. Dieses Ergebnis untermauert eindrucksvoll die Resultate des geschlossenen Fragebogens (siehe dazu Abb. 6).

Im unmittelbaren Zusammenhang mit der unklaren Symbolik steht das Problem der zu langen Einarbeitungszeit, die durch die bereits angekündigten Verbesserungen bei den Piktogrammen reduziert werden kann. Auch die beim Drücken der START-Taste ablaufende Bildschirmsequenz wurde als störend empfunden, weil sie nicht umgangen werden kann.

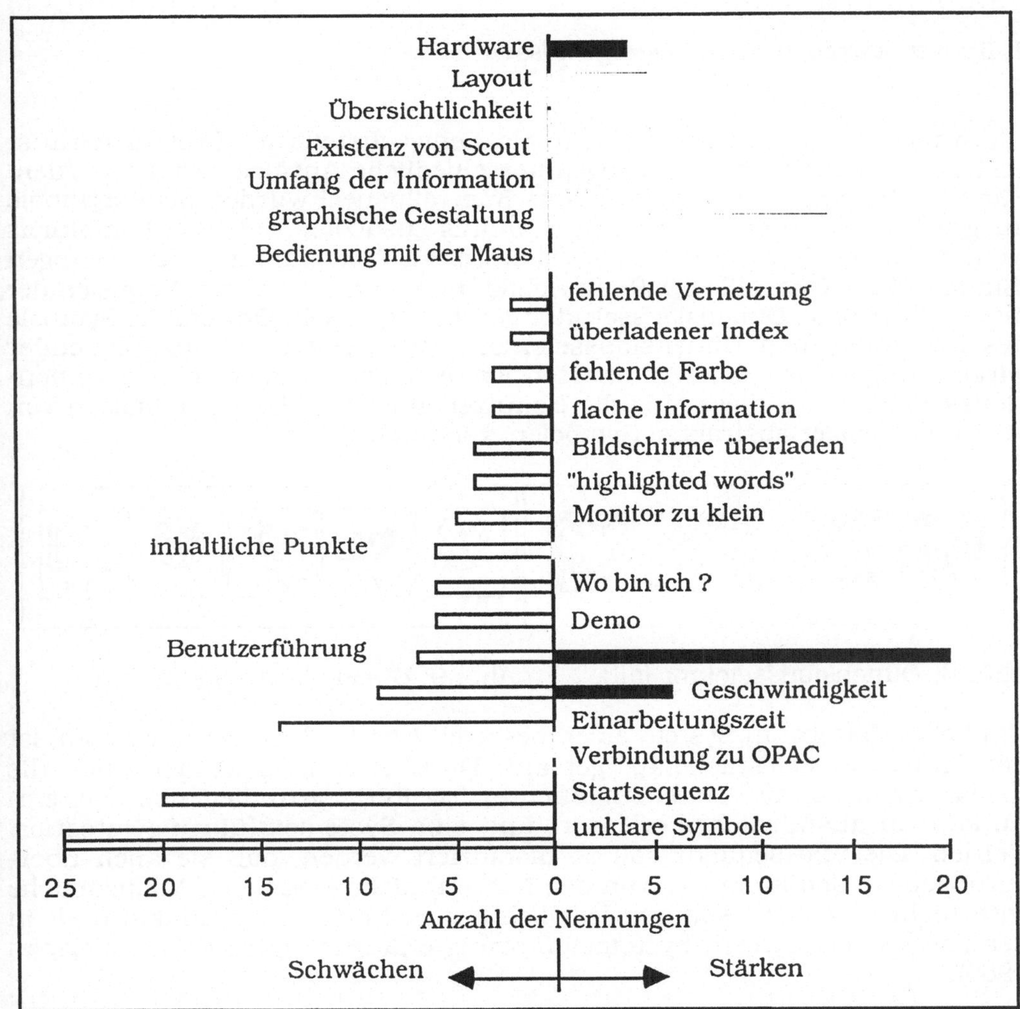

Abb. 7: Stärken-Schwächen Analyse

Mit SCOUT wurde ein Auskunftssystem entwickelt, das auf generelle Fragen in der Bibliotheksbenutzung Antwort geben soll. Es enthält daher nicht den an der Universitätsbibliothek der TU Graz ebenfalls angeboten Online Katalog (OPAC). Aufgrund der zahlreichen Wünsche der Testpersonen, diesen

Online Katalog auch von SCOUT aufrufen zu können, wird überlegt, eine geeignete Schnittstelle zu schaffen. Weiters wurde der Bildschirm als zu klein empfunden und die fehlende Farbe beanstandet. Diese Applikation wurde zu einem Zeitpunkt konzipiert, als HyperCard nur in der Version 1.2 (ohne Farbe) zur Verfügung stand. Die Überarbeitung von SCOUT wird bereits mit der neuen Softwareversion 2.0 durchgeführt. Grund für die Verwendung des kleinen Bildschirmes waren die kaum vorhandenen finanziellen Mittel.

4. Konsequenzen aus den Testergebnissen

Die Navigation hat sich sehr klar als Schwachstelle im System herausgestellt, wobei zur Verbesserung unterschiedliche Ansätze verfolgt werden. Für den Dimensionsselektor und das Kontrollpaneel wurden neue Symbole ausgewählt, die zum besseren Verständnis zusätzlich mit Text kombiniert werden. Dabei wurde einschlägige Literatur zu Piktogrammen herangezogen (Staufer 1987, Guastello 1989). In Abbildung 8 und 9 sind zum Vergleich der alte und der neue Dimensionsselektor gegenübergestellt. Obwohl die Symbole des ursprünglichen Dimensionsselektors vom Design her ansprechender wirken, zeigen die bisher gemachten Erfahrungen mit dem neuen Dimensionsselektor, daß dieser für die Benutzer aufgrund der Kombination von Text und weniger abstrakten Symbolen verständlicher ist.

Abb. 8: Dimensionsselektor (alt)   Abb. 9: Dimensionsselektor (neu)

Um beim Blättern im System einen besseren Überblick zu gewährleisten, ist der Einbau einer "stackmap" geplant. Darüber hinaus werden auch die Erklärungen in der Hilfekomponente erweitert, grundlegende Systemfunktionen ausführlicher erläutert und eine Systemeinführung integriert werden. Die Startsequenz soll so modifiziert werden, daß sie auch übersprungen werden kann. Die von den Nutzern nicht akzeptierte Volltextsuche wird nicht verändert, sondern lediglich besser in der Hilfefunktion und in der neu zu schaffenden Systemeinführung erläutert werden (Shneiderman 1989).

Um die Akzeptanz bei den Benutzern zu erhöhen, können folgende Erweiterungen ins Auge gefaßt werden:
- Vernetzung und Integration mit anderen Systemen und
- Aufstellung an mehreren Standorten innerhalb des Universitätsgeländes.

Wie bereits erwähnt, wird die Verbindung zwischen dem Online Katalog der Bibliothek und dem Benutzerführer "SCOUT" häufig von den Testpersonen gefordert. Aber nicht nur diese Vernetzung wäre erstrebenswert, sondern auch die Integration von weiteren universitären Informationsquellen wie etwa Ankündigungen zu Vorlesungen und Prüfungen, Sprechstunden, u.a.m. Ein einheitlicher Zugriff auf all diese Informationen von zahlreichen Standorten innerhalb der Universität könnte die Transparenz erhöhen. An der Lösung und Durchführung der oben genannten Möglichkeiten wird bereits im Rahmen von weiteren Studien gearbeitet. Es sind auch Untersuchungen geplant, die den Echteinsatz des Systems in Hinblick auf Wartung und Aktualisierung der Daten prüft.

Das Resümee dieses Feldversuches ist, daß Applikationen, die lediglich für gelegentliche Benutzer erstellt werden, so einfach wie möglich gebaut sein müssen. Es ist in diesem Zusammenhang auf einen für den Benutzer verständlichen Aufbau des Systems, auf klare und eindeutige Symbolik und und einfache Suchstrategien zu achten. Dieses Ergebnis wirft die Frage auf, ob Systeme die für gelegentliche Benutzer konzipiert werden, auch den Anforderungen professioneller Benutzer genügen.

Anerkennung

Die Autoren bedanken sich bei Univ. Prof. Dr. Wolf Rauch, Dipl. Ing. Mag. Christian Schlögl und HR Dr. Karl. F. Stock für die Unterstützungen und Anregungen, die zur Abfassung dieses Beitrages geführt haben. Unser Dank gilt auch den zahlreichen Studenten des Instituts für Informationswissenschaft die zur Zeit Diplomarbeiten zum Thema Hypermedien verfassen, insbesondere Herbert Fasching, Herbert Kappel und Gudrun Bagary.

Literatur

Baird, Patricia; Percival, Marc: Glasgow Online. Database Development using Apple´s HyperCard. In: Hypertext theory into practice. Ed. by R. MacAleese. Oxford: Blackwell 1989, 75-92

Bagary, Gudrun E.: Von der Laborversion zum fertigen Produkt. Weiterentwicklung einer HyperCard Applikation. 1991. Diplomarb. am Inst. f. Informationswissenschaft, Universität Graz. In Vorbereitung

Conklin, Jeff: Hypertext. An Introduction and Survey. IEEE Computer 20 (1987) 9, 17-41

Dillman, D. A.: Mail and Telephone Surveys. The Total Design Method. Wiley: New York 1978

Fasching, Herbert: Erstellung eines Benutzerführers für die Bibliothek der Technischen Universität Graz mit HyperCard. 1991. Diplomarb. am Inst. f. Informationswissenschaft, Universität Graz

Guastello, Stephen J.; Traut, Mary; Korienek, Gene: Verbal versus pictorial representations of objects in a human-computer interface. Int. J. Man Machine Studies, 31 (1989) 1, 99-120

Kappel, Herbert J.: Test eines HyperCard-Informationssystems. 1991. Diplomarb. am Inst. f. Informationswissenschaft, Universität Graz. In Vorbereitung

Rauch, Wolf: Spekulationen über die Informationsgesellschaft. In: Schwimmende Vorträge. Ein Nachtrag zum 1. Internationalen Symposium für Informationswissenschaft, ISI´90 in Konstanz. Bericht 2/90. Universität Konstanz 1990, 25-39

Schwarz, Erich J.; Kanet, John J.; Leigh, H. David: Quality Control Practices. Am. Ceram. Soc. Bul. 68 (1989) 3, 530-544

Shneiderman, Ben; Kearsley, Greg: Hypertext Hands-On! Reading, MA: Addison-Wesley 1989. ISBN 0-201-13546-9

Staufer, Michael J. : Piktogramme für Computer. Kognitive Verarbeitung, Methoden zur Produktion und Evaluation. Berlin: de Gruyter 1987. ISBN 3-11-010917-4

Der S*P*A*R*K-Teacher - eine Hypertext Applikation

Ronald Bogaschewsky
Abteilung für Unternehmensplanung, Universität Göttingen
Platz der Göttinger Sieben 3, D-3400 Göttingen

Zusammenfassung

Der Teacher ist ein Modul in dem System S*P*A*R*K, das weiterhin eine wissensbasierte Komponente und eine multimediale Beispieledatenbank umfaßt. S*P*A*R*K soll bei der Suche nach strategischen, wettbewerbsbezogenen Einsatzmöglichkeiten von Informationen und Informationstechnologie unterstützen. Schwerpunkt bei der inhaltlichen Konzeption des Teachers war das Vorhaben, dem Benutzer des Systems die in der wissensbasierten Komponente von S*P*A*R*K enthaltenen Methoden, Techniken und Vorgehensweisen zur inhaltlichen Problemlösung auf Anforderung zu erläutern. Weiterhin sollte mit dem Teacher das inhaltliche Konzept von S*P*A*R*K verdeutlicht werden.

Der Teacher könnte somit in die Klasse "Informationssysteme" [1] mit dem Schwerpunkt "Erklärung" und "Schulung" innerhalb möglicher Hypertext-Anwendungen eingeordnet werden.

Für die Realisierung des Teachers wurde die Audio Visual Connection (AVC) von IBM eingesetzt. Diese Software ist grundsätzlich als Präsentations-Management-System, auch für multimediale Anwendungen, anzusehen. Durch entsprechende Programmierung mit der Audio Visual Authoring Language (AVA), wurde eine typische Hypertext-Struktur geschaffen, wobei der Benutzer die Kontrolle über den Präsentationsablauf übernimmt.

Der Beitrag zeigt zunächst auf, welche Zielsetzungen und Problemcharakteristika zur Entscheidung führten, den Teacher als Hypertext zu realisieren. Anschließend wird die Struktur des Teachers und die Benutzungsoberfläche dargestellt. Die geschilderten Implementierungsaspekte nehmen Bezug auf die Rolle der Erstellung des Teachers innerhalb der Entwicklung des Gesamtsystems S*P*A*R*K. Abschließend werden Verbesserungsvorschläge für die Ausgestaltung der Benutzungsoberfläche sowie Ansätze zum Einsatz des Hypertext-Konzepts bei der Realisierung der Beispieledatenbank und deren Zugriffskomponente innerhalb des Systems S*P*A*R*K aufgezeigt.

1 Das Teacher-Modul im System S*P*A*R*K

Der Teacher wurde vom Autor für das System S*P*A*R*K konzipiert und realisiert. S*P*A*R*K wurde als prototypisches System am Los Angeles Scientific Center (LASC) der IBM im Rahmen der Forschungsarbeiten zum "Strategic Information Management Support"[1] entwickelt [3,4]. Die Zielsetzung war, mit diesem Prototypen Managern von Unternehmen beliebiger Branche und Größe ein Hilfsmittel an die Hand zu geben, das sie bei der Suche nach strategischen Einsatzmöglichkeiten von Informationen und Informationstechnologie (IIT) unterstützt. Betriebswirtschaftlicher Hintergrund ist dabei die Erlangung von Wettbewerbsvorteilen, die nicht nur kurzfristig Bestand haben sollten.

Die Komponenten des Systems S*P*A*R*K lassen sich auf die folgende Weise darstellen:

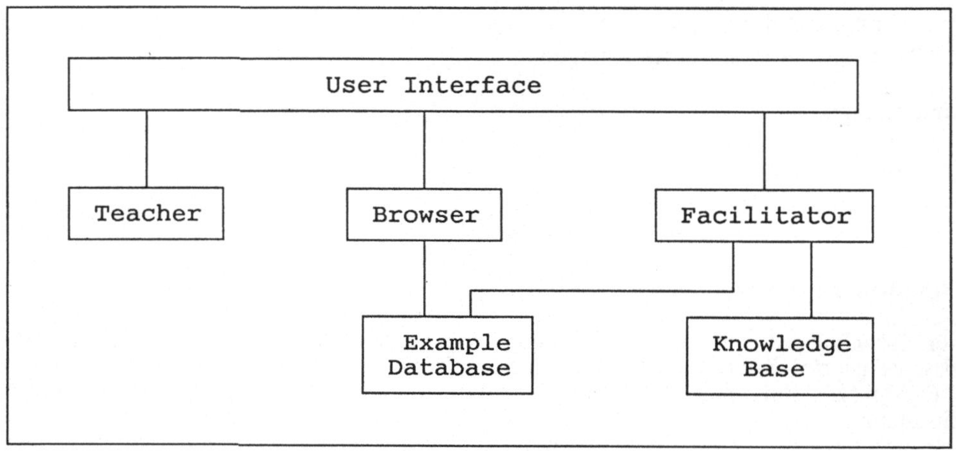

*Abb.1: S*P*A*R*K Systemüberblick*

Der Benutzer tritt mit dem System über die einheitliche Benutzerschnittstelle, die mittels des Presentation Managers unter OS/2 [7] verwirklicht wurde, in Kontakt. Dort besteht die Möglichkeit unter den Modulen Teacher, Browser und Facilitator zu wählen.

Der *Facilitator* stellt die wissensbasierte Komponente[2] von S*P*A*R*K dar. Hier wurde Expertenwissen in Form von Analysetechniken aus der Literatur extrahiert. Im Facilitator versuchen mehrere "Experten" parallel, den Benutzer bei seiner Suche nach strategischen Einsatzmöglichkeiten von IIT zu unterstützen. Jeder "Experte" legt dabei andere Schwerpunkte bei der wettbewerbsbezogenen Analyse des betroffenen Unternehmens. Es werden mögliche Strategien vom System vorgeschlagen und passende Beispiele aus der Datenbank zur Ansicht empfohlen.

---

[1] Der Autor gehörte dieser Forschungsgruppe im Rahmen eines Post-Doctoral Fellowship Program von August 1989 bis August 1990 an.

[2] Auf den Inhalt der Wissensbasis von S*P*A*R*K sowie verwendete Wissensakquisitions- und -repräsentationstechniken soll in diesem Beitrag nicht eingegangen werden. Vgl. hierzu [2].

Der *Browser* bietet ein einfach zu bedienendes Zugriffssystem zur Beispieledatenbank an. Die Beispiele (ca. 100 von etwa 300 gesammelten Praxisbeispielen wurden bisher in die Datenbank aufgenommen) zeigen reale Anwendungen auf, in denen IIT zur Erlangung von Wettbewerbsvorteilen eingesetzt wurde, sowie Gründe für den Erfolg oder das Scheitern dieser Projekte. Durch die Kombination von Attributen, die den jeweiligen Beispielen zugeordnet sind, können entsprechend dieser Kriterien Teilmengen aus der Datenbank extrahiert werden. Alternativ besteht die Möglichkeit, direkt auf Beispiele über ihren zugeordneten Namen zuzugreifen. Die Beispiele sind In Form von schriftlichen Darstellungen, statischen und dynamischen Grafiken sowie gesprochenen Texten realisiert.

Jede der genannten Systemkomponenten kann wiederholt und in beliebiger Reihenfolge vom Benutzer angesprochen werden. Ein "elektronischer Notizblock", der als Window auf dem Bildschirm realisiert ist, steht für Notizen, Bemerkungen und als Gedächtnishilfe zur Verfügung.

2 Der S*P*A*R*K-Teacher

2.1 Zielsetzung bei der Entwicklung

Einsatzschwerpunkt für den Teacher ist, dem Benutzer den *inhaltlichen* Zugang zu den eingesetzten Analysetechniken und damit zum S*P*A*R*K-System selbst zu vereinfachen. Dabei werden keine bedienungstechnischen Fragen angesprochen; es handelt sich nicht um eine Hilfe-Funktion.

Im Teacher wird das Konzept von S*P*A*R*K vorgestellt und eine Einführung in die in der Wissensbasis repräsentierten Methoden und Techniken sowie deren wissenschaftliche Grundlagen gegeben. Auf diese Weise soll der Erstbenutzer für die Problematik des strategischen Einsatzes von IIT sensibilisiert und auf diesem Gebiet weitergebildet werden. Weiterhin werden die Sichtweisen der in der Wissensbasis verfügbaren "Experten" verdeutlicht. Damit wird eine problemunabhängige Zugangsmöglichkeit zu den Methoden und Techniken bereitgestellt, wodurch die Erklärungskomponente des Facilitators sinnvoll ergänzt wird. Auf diese Weise erhält der Benutzer die Möglichkeit, sich theoretisch mit dem Problemgebiet zu beschäftigen und so die Arbeitsweise des Systems besser verstehen und nachvollziehen sowie die Empfehlungen des Systems besser bewerten zu können.

Eine technische Anforderung an den Teacher war eine Bedienbarkeit, die keinerlei EDV-technische Vorkenntnisse erfordern sollte. Es mußte davon ausgegangen werden, daß der Benutzer so stark mit inhaltlichen Problemen beschäftigt ist, daß jede erforderliche Konzentration auf bedienungstechnische Aspekte als außerordentlich störend empfunden werden würde und das System dann vom Benutzer abgelehnt werden könnte.

2.2 Gründe für einen Hypertext-Ansatz

Bereits in der Konzeptionsphase boten sich mehrere Alternativen zur Realisierung des Teachers an. Die Implementierung auf einem Rechner und nicht als papiergebundenes Dokument war dabei quasi vorgegeben, da auf Dokumentationsmaterial in Papierform aus Gründen der Einfachheit und Flexibilität im gesamten Projekt weitgehend verzichtet werden sollte.

Eine Analyse des abzubildenden Problemgebiets und die benutzerseitigen Anforderungen führten zu den folgenden Feststellungen:

- Zwischen den in die Wissensbasis einzubringenden Methoden und Techniken existieren zahlreiche Verbindungen.

- Für viele verwendete Fachtermini sollten im Bedarfsfall schnell und einfach zugreifbare Erklärungen verfügbar sein.

- Benutzer sollten jederzeit auf die sie interessierenden Themenbereiche zugreifen können.

- Benutzer sollten auf Verbindungen zu anderen Informationen aufmerksam gemacht werden.

- Es sollten nur minimale bedienungstechnische Anforderungen gestellt werden, damit sich der Benutzer voll auf das Problem konzentrieren kann.

Die genannten Anforderungen können bevorzugt durch ein auf dem Hypertext-Konzept basierenden System erfüllt werden. Lineare Darstellungen von Informationen, wie sie z.B. in typischen schriftlichen Darstellungen vorherrschen, konnten damit ausgeschlossen werden. Des weiteren wurde die Kombination des Teachers und der Beispieledatenbank auf einem Video, wie in einer früheren Version von S*P*A*R*K realisiert [8], aus den oben angeführten Gründen als ungeeignet betrachtet.

Eine Verwendung der Medien Bild und Ton mit ihrem unbestreitbar hohen Wert als Informationsträger, wurde zunächst nicht als zwingend erforderlich angesehen. Mit AVC wurde eine Implementierungssoftware verwendet, die multimediale Darstellungen optional ermöglicht.

2.3 Die Informationsstruktur

Bei der Gestaltung der Struktur eines Hypertextes als Informationssystem können durchaus Freiheitsgrade bestehen, die in erster Linie durch die Komplexität des behandelten Problemgebiets, die Zielgruppe und die Intention des Autors bedingt sind [1].

Das *behandelte Problemgebiet* kann im vorliegenden Fall grundsätzlich auf mehrere parallel darstellbare Gebiete festgelegt werden (siehe Abbildung 2). Diese Gebiete weisen jedoch zahlreiche Verknüpfungspunkte auf und stehen in definierter Weise zueinander in Beziehung. So ist das "Allgemeine Konzept der Wettbewerbsstrategien" und die "Strategische Bedeutung von IIT" zumindest teilweise Voraussetzung für das Verständnis der "Methoden und Techniken". Letztere weisen wiederum untereinander zahlreiche

Überschneidungen und Ähnlichkeiten auf. Neben der Darstellung dieser Verknüpfungspunkte zwischen Themenbereichen, die sich durch Links realisieren lassen, müssen auch direkte Zugangsmöglichkeiten zu den Informationseinheiten geschaffen werden, um dem Benutzer die Möglichkeit zu geben, sich zielgerichtet über bestimmte Fragestellungen zu informieren. Gleichzeitig müssen übergeordnete Informationen für die Einordnung des Problemgebiets z.B. in die Strategische Planung und in das Zielsystem der Unternehmung sowie für eine Orientierung innerhalb der betrachteten Domäne verfügbar sein.

Als *Zielgruppe* kamen grundsätzlich "Informations-Manager" in Betracht, jedoch auch Fachleute für Strategische Planung, Marketingpersonal von Hard- und Software-Herstellern sowie Nachwuchskräfte, die das System als Schulungsinstrument nutzen wollen. Je nach Erfahrungsstand in Hinsicht auf das angesprochene Problemfeld konnte daher ein sehr unterschiedlicher Wissensstand erwartet werden. Damit mußten detaillierte Informationen und Erläuterungen verfügbar sein, sollten jedoch nur auf Anfrage zur Verfügung gestellt werden.

Die *Intention des Autors* lag daher darin, den Hypertext so zu gestalten, daß die Informationsbedürfnisse aller potentiellen Nutzertypen in der Zielgruppe adäquat befriedigt werden können. Dies sollte u.a. durch die Konzeption einer klaren und übersichtlichen Informationsstruktur und die Konzentration auf für die Problemstellung wesentliche Aspekte erreicht werden. Daneben war der zu erwartende Erstellungsaufwand für den Hypertext im Rahmen eines Prototyps zu berücksichtigen.

Auf der Basis dieser Analyse entstand ein Konzept, das die gesamten darzustellenden Informationen in eine Baumstruktur gliedert, wobei Querverbindungen zwischen den einzelnen Knoten des Baumes auftreten können. Auf diese Weise ergibt sich eine Netzstruktur, die sich im Kern an einer Baumstruktur orientiert. Die Abbildung 2 verzichtet auf die Darstellung der Querverbindungen, um den inhaltlichen Überblick zu erleichtern.

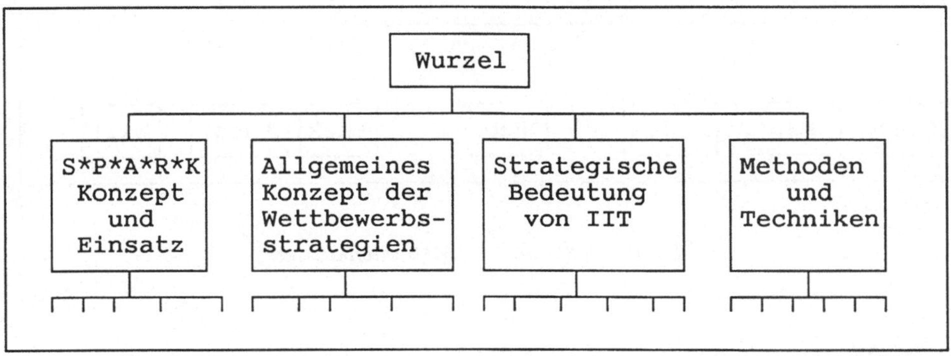

Abb. 2: Obere Ebene der Baumstruktur des Teachers

Als Beispiel für eine strukturierte Zugangsmöglichkeit zu den einzelnen Methoden und Techniken (rechter Kasten in Abbildung 2), sind diese Vorgehensweisen in Klassen eingeteilt worden. Auf diese Weise erhält der Benutzer eine zielgerichtete Anleitung bei der Auswahl einer Methode. Die Klassifizierung berücksichtigt die unterschiedlichen Ausrichtungen der Techniken:

- Konzentration auf ein Zielobjekt (Target): Kunden, Lieferanten, Konkurrenten, neue Marktteilnehmer, Substitutionsprodukte.

- Geschäftsstrategie (Focus): Differenzierung des Produkts oder des Service, Kostenführerschaft, Konzentration auf Schwerpunkte.

- Allgemeiner Einsatz von Informationen und Informationstechnologie (IIT Use).

Dabei sind Überschneidungen zwischen diesen Klassen möglich (FT, FI, TI, FTI). Die Abbildung 3 zeigt den das Klassifizierungsschema abbildenden Knoten des Hypertextes und damit die Auswahlmöglichkeiten des Benutzers:[3]

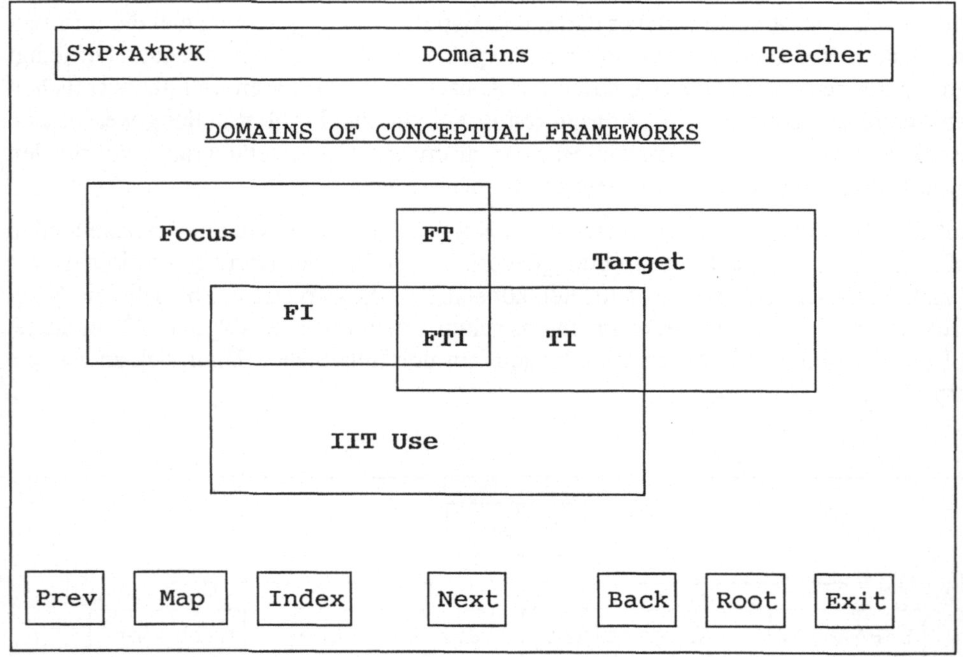

Abb.3: Darstellung der Methodenklassen

2.4 Realisierte Zugriffsformen und Benutzungsoberfläche

Die Hypertexte im Gegensatz zu linearen Texten grundsätzlich auszeichnende Möglichkeit, "verstreute" Informationseinheiten physisch direkt untereinander zu verknüpfen,

---

[3] Aus technischen Gründen können in diesem Beitrag die qualitativ höherwertigen und farbigen Grafiken, wie sie im Teacher realisiert sind, nicht abgedruckt werden.

bringt noch nicht zwangsläufig ein benutzerfreundliches System mit sich. Prinzipiell ist eher Vorsicht walten zu lassen, da die erweiterten Möglichkeiten und die höhere Flexibilität eines Hypertextes gegenüber linearen Darstellungsweisen auch zu unübersichtlichen Darstellungen führen können. Daher sind zahlreiche benutzerseitige Anforderungen bei der Konzeption und Implementierung eines Hypertextes zu berücksichtigen. Im folgenden wird dargestellt, welche Anforderungen auf welche Weise beim Teacher berücksichtigt wurden.

Da bei der Konzeption des Teachers eine möglichst einfache Bedienbarkeit gefordert war, wurde eine *mausgesteuerte Eingabe*, ohne jegliche Benutzung der Tastatur präferiert. Über die Definition optisch hervorgehobener Bildschirmbereiche bzw. Felder (highlighted fields), die zumeist Textstellen entsprechen, werden Ausgangspunkte für Verbindungen (Links) zu anderen Informationseinheiten verdeutlicht. Eine Informationseinheit entspricht einem Bildschirminhalt oder, wenn es sich um nur in Zusammenhang mit einer anderen Informationseinheit sinngebenden Information handelt, einem Window-Inhalt. Von der Definition unterschiedlicher Link-Typen wurde abgesehen, da die Problemdomäne eine solche Differenzierung nicht unbedingt notwendig erscheinen ließ.

Zur weiteren Systemsteuerung wurden *"Buttons"* ("Bedienungsknöpfe") auf dem Bildschirm definiert. Diese erscheinen auf einer definierten Zeile am unteren Rand des Bildschirms (siehe Abbildung 3). Jeder Button hat eine festgelegte Position und Farbe und trägt zur Verdeutlichung eine Kurzbezeichnung. Momentan nicht aktivierbare Buttons werden dabei ausgeblendet, um die Übersichtlichkeit zu erhöhen. Die Windows benutzen die gleichen Buttons am unteren Rand des entsprechenden Bildschirmfensters. Dabei sind die Window-Buttons zur Abgrenzung von den Bildschirmseiten-Buttons nicht mit der entsprechenden Button-Farbe ausgefüllt, sondern nur gerändert. Im einzelnen stehen die folgenden Buttons zur Verfügung:

- **Buttons zum sequentiellen Blättern**

Für das sequentielle Blättern von einer Bildschirmseite zur nächsten bzw. zur vorherigen Seite dienen die Buttons "Next" (Nächste Seite) und "Previous" (Vorige Seite). Diese Zugriffsmöglichkeit ist beim Vorliegen quasi-linearer Strukturen innerhalb des Informationsnetzes sinnvoll. Als quasi-linear werden hier sequentielle Abfolgen mehrerer Seiten zusammenhängenden Inhalts bezeichnet, die jedoch jeweils auch Links zu anderen Informationseinheiten aufweisen können. Die gleichen Buttons können zur Führung des Benutzers auf vordefinierten Informationswegen (guided tours) dienen.

- **Buttons für den Direktzugriff**

Nach dem Traversieren eines Teils des Hypertextes, besteht beim Benutzer unter Umständen der Wunsch, zu einem bestimmten Ausgangspunkt zurückzukehren. Zur Abkürzung dieses Rückwegs, der auch durch wiederholtes Betätigen des "Previous"-Buttons "begehbar" wäre, wurden der "Root"-Button (Start) und der "Back"-Button (Zurück) definiert.

Der "Back"-Button führt den Benutzer zum Anfang der momentan im Zugriff befindlichen quasi-linearen Struktur. Ob sich der Benutzer momentan innerhalb einer solchen

Struktur befindet, wird duch eine Seitennumerierung (Page x of y) angezeigt. Liegt eine solche Struktur im Augenblick nicht vor, wirkt diese Funktion wie die "Previous"-Funktion.

Bei Aktivierung der "Root"-Funktion erfolgt ein direkter Sprung zum Wurzelknoten des Informationsbaumes, also der Informationseinheit, die immer als erste nach Aufruf des Systems angesprochen wird.

- Verlassen des Systems und Schließen eines Windows

Das System kann jederzeit durch Aktivierung des "Exit"-(Ende) Buttons verlassen werden. In den Windows hat der Button an dieser relativen Position die Bezeichnung "Quit" und bewirkt das Schließen des jeweiligen Fensters.

- Direktzugriff über den Index

Eine wichtige Anforderung zur Vereinfachung der Arbeit mit Hypertexten ist die Bereitstellung eines Indexes, mit dessen Hilfe Stichworte und Themenbereiche ausgewählt und direkt in Zugriff genommen werden können. Dabei sind Themenbereiche repräsentierende Indexeinträge (Schlagworte) häufig als Oberbegriff angelegt, die sich jeweils in mehrere Unterbegriffe aufgliedern und so gezielte Zugriffe erlauben.

Eine solche Indexfunktion ist ein unverzichtbares Hilfsmittel für den direkten Zugang zu ausgewählten Sachverhalten und dient auch als Überblickshilfe. Aufgrund des hohen Detailliertheitsgrades des Indexes wurde auf die Implementierung einer Suchfunktion verzichtet.

- Grafischer Browser

Die Darstellung der Informationsstruktur eines Hypertextes unter Anzeige der momentanen Position des Benutzers im Informationsnetz, stellt eine wertvolle Hilfestellung dar. Auf diese Weise kann dem leicht auftretenden Phänomen des "Verlaufens" in Hypertexten ("lost in hyperspace") entgegengewirkt werden. Eine deutliche Erhöhung der Benutzerfreundlichkeit wird erreicht, indem der Direktzugriff auf die im Grafischen Browser dargestellten Informationseinheiten ermöglicht wird.

Die Abbildung 4 zeigt einen Ausschnitt aus dem implementierten Hypertext. Auf die mit durchgehenden Rändern versehenen Kästen, die jeweils eine Informationseinheit darstellen, kann direkt zugegriffen werden. Die gestrichelt geränderten Kästen sind nicht direkt ansprechbar, da deren inhaltliche Aussage nur in Zusammenhang mit der hierarchisch höherliegenden Informationseinheit interpretiert werden soll. Durch Anwählen des Knotens mit der Markierung "C" (Continue), werden die Knoten des angrenzenden Bereichs des Hypertext-Dokuments angezeigt.

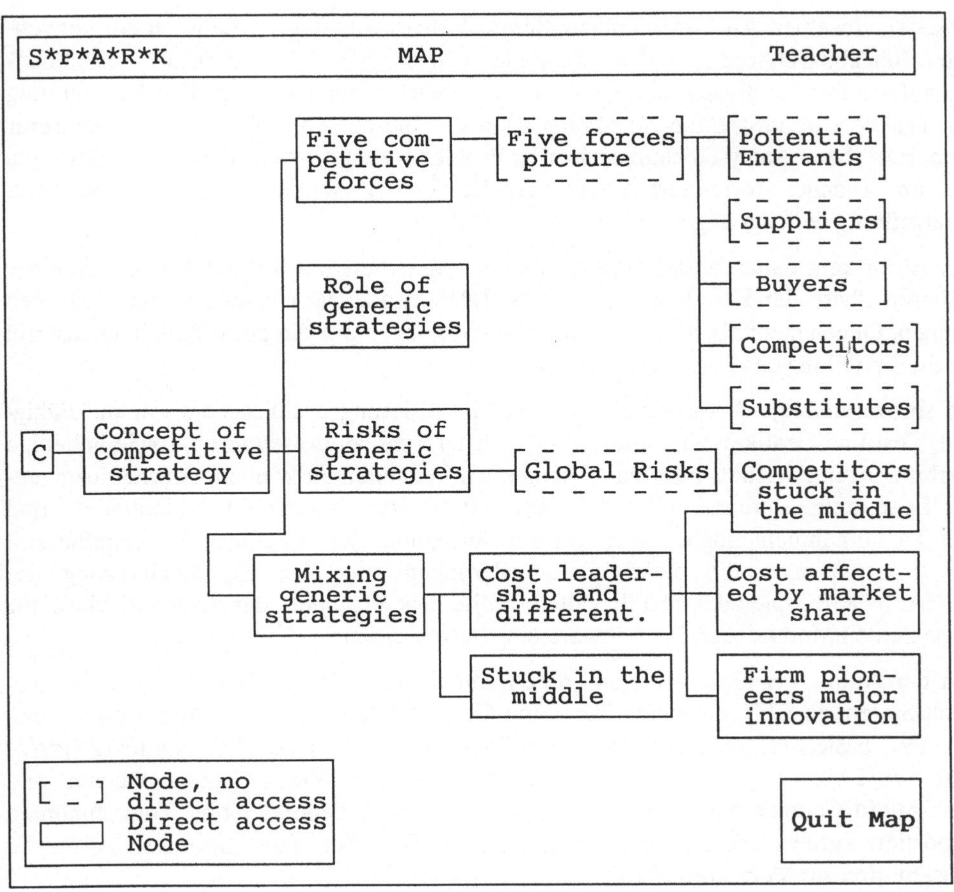

Abb.4: Grafischer Browser

2.5 Implementierungsaspekte

Die Erstellung von Hypertexten zu Informationszwecken erfordert häufig einen gegen-über linearen Darstellungsformen erhöhten Aufwand. Dies ist u.a. mit dem Aufwand für die Definition und Einrichtung der Informationsverknüpfungen auf Grundlage einer wohldefinierten Gesamtstruktur zu erklären. Das zu berücksichtigende Problemgebiet ließ sich auf der Basis des inhaltlichen Konzepts der wissensbasierten Komponente von S*P*A*R*K relativ gut eingrenzen (siehe auch Kapitel 2.3).

Die eingehende Analyse des Problemgebiets mit seinen wissenschaftlichen Grundlagen sowie den spezifischen Analysetechniken erwies sich als außerordentlich förderlich für das tiefgehende Verständnis der Gesamtproblematik und existierender Zusammen-hänge zwischen Einzelfragen. Auf diese Weise trug die Erstellung des Teachers als Hy-pertext entscheidend zur Wissensakquisition für den Facilitator bei. Insbesondere zeigten sich bereits vor der eigentlichen Formulierung des Wissens in der eigens hierfür entwickelten Knowledge Representation Language (KRL) [2] Interdependenzen zwischen einzelnen Analysetechniken, deren Berücksichtigung im Rahmen der verwendeten Blackboard-Architektur[4] von besonderer Wichtigkeit war. Auf diese Weise konnten aufwendige Neuformulierungen des Wissens vermieden werden. Die Realisierung des Teachers bestätigte die Forderung nach der "parallelen"[5] Einbeziehung mehrerer "Experten" bzw. Analysetechniken in den Problemlösungsprozeß. Des weiteren trugen die im Teacher formulierten Sachverhalte und Zusammenhänge zur positiven Überprüfung der Eignung der verwendeten KRL bei.

Der Autor kam daher zu dem Schluß, daß die Erstellung des Teachers bereits in einer früheren Phase der Erstellung von S*P*A*R*K zusätzliche Nutzeffekte hätte bringen können. Gegebenenfalls hätte dies auch Auswirkungen auf die getroffene Toolauswahl für die Erstellung des Facilitators gehabt.

Als softwaremäßige Anforderungen bei der Realisierung des Teachers war die Fähigkeit, Text und Grafiken zu editieren, zu speichern und zu präsentieren, sowie beliebige Verbindungen zwischen Informationseinheiten herstellen zu können, von herausragender Bedeutung. Optional sollte die Verarbeitung von importierten Videobildern und von Tonaufnahmen möglich sein. Da mit Ausnahme der beliebigen Verknüpfbarkeit von Informationen die gleichen Anforderungen auch für die Realisierung der S*P*A*R*K-Beispieledatenbank galten, sollte aus Gründen der Einheitlichkeit für diese beiden Module dieselbe Software eingesetzt werden.

Mit der Audio Visual Connection (AVC) von IBM wurde ein Präsentations-Management-System gewählt, das einen Text- und Grafikeditor sowie einen Audio-Editor bietet. AVC basiert teilweise auf Storyboard Plus und ist auf Personal Computer/2 (PS/2) unter OS/2 ablauffähig. Durch Einsatz eines zusätzlichen "Video Capture Adapter" und des "Audio Capture and Playback Adapter" können Videobilder und Tonaufnahmen importiert werden. Diese stehen anschließend als Datei für eine Editierung und für die Präsentation zur Verfügung [5,6].

Für jeden Bildschirminhalt können "maus-sensitive" Bereiche (trigger fields) definiert werden, die dem Benutzer als Ausgangspunkt für das Verfolgen von Verknüpfungen zwischen Informationseinheiten dienen. Unter Einsatz der auf der Steuersprache REXX basierenden Audio Visual Authoring Language (AVA) können Ablaufstrukturen für die Präsentation von Bildschirminhalten programmiert werden. Dabei kann dem Benutzer die Kontrolle über den Ablauf der Präsentation übergeben werden. Somit wurde keine spezifische Hypertext-Software eingesetzt, das heißt, daß z.B. die Links zwischen Informationseinheiten nicht durch einfache Systembefehle hergestellt werden konnten, sondern im einzelnen programmiert werden mußten. Entsprechend wurde die Erstellung des Indexes und des grafischen Browsers nicht vom System unterstützt.

Ein Vorteil der Nutzung von AVC war u.a. das Vorhandensein eines kombinierten Text- und Grafikeditors, mit dessen Hilfe qualitativ hochwertige Grafiken auf relativ einfache Weise erstellt werden konnten. Mittels der Programmiersprache AVA konnten die er-

---

[4] Das Blackboard-Konzept sieht vereinfachend formuliert die gleichzeitige Aktivierungsfähigkeit unabhängiger Wissensquellen (Knowledge Sources) vor, die alle auf ein sog. Blackboard zugreifen und dieses durch Einbringung von Daten, Fakten und (Zwischen-)Ergebnissen verändern können. Vgl. hierzu [9,2].

[5] Der Ausdruck "parallel" ist hier konzeptuell zu sehen. Solange das System auf Rechnern mit sequentieller Prozessor-Architektur realisiert wird, ist eine echte Parallelverarbeitung natürlich nicht möglich.

stellten Text- und Grafikeinheiten auf beliebige Weise, auch in Teilen, für Präsentationen kombiniert werden. Dabei sind dynamische Darstellungen durch Bewegungen von Grafiken und Texten auf dem Bildschirm möglich. Weiterhin konnte auf diese Weise eine anwendungsspezifische Benutzungsoberfläche ohne maßgebliche Einschränkungen seitens der verwendeten Software konstruiert werden. Die Möglichkeiten der Verarbeitung von Videobildern und Tonaufnahmen bieten die oben genannten Vorteile gegenüber reinen Hypertext-Systemen.

Der erhöhte Erstellungsaufwand von Hypertexten oder Hypermedia-Anwendungen mit Präsentations-Management-Systemen ist allerdings nur zu vertreten, wenn diese besonderen Möglichkeiten als unverzichtbar angesehen werden.

2.6 Mögliche Weiterentwicklungen

Zur Verbesserung der Bedienungsfreundlichkeit lassen sich prinzipiell weitere Funktionen zur Verfügung stellen, die im Teacher bislang nicht realisiert wurden. Allerdings erschienen diese, im folgenden aufgeführten Funktionen unter Berücksichtigung der realisierten Funktionen und der oben aufgezeigten Anforderungen nicht zwangsläufig erforderlich zu sein.

Suchfunktionen, die das direkte Auffinden von Stichworten ermöglichen, können eine wertvolle Hilfe sein. Dies gilt insbesondere, falls der Index nicht alle wichtigen Stichworte abdecken kann. Beim Teacher wurde versucht, eine weitgehende Abdeckung der wichtigen Stichworte über den Index zu erreichen.

Die *gleichzeitige Darstellung mehrerer Informationseinheiten* in mehreren Windows kann bei Hypertext-Anwendungen sinnvoll sein. Dies erfolgt beim Teacher nur begrenzt und in vordefinierter Form, d.h. der Benutzer selbst kann nicht beliebige Windows auf dem Bildschirm anordnen. Sinnvoll wäre eine solche Möglichkeit z.B. auch für das wahlweise permanente Anzeigen des grafischen Browsers, um auf diese Weise immer einen Überblick der momentanen "Umgebung" im Informationsnetz vor Augen zu haben.

Die vorgenommene Einschränkung auf *seitenweises Blättern* erfordert teilweise eine künstliche Modularisierung von Informationseinheiten. Das heißt, die physischen Ausmaße eines Bildschirms bzw. eines definierten Windows beschränken die Anzahl an Zeichen und Grafiken sowie deren Größe in einer Informationseinheit. Wäre ein stufenloses Blättern möglich, könnte diese Restriktion aufgehoben werden, wobei eventuell Probleme bei der Übersichtlichkeit eines Informationsknotens für den Benutzer auftreten können. Beim Teacher wurde durch die Einführung der problemlosen und schnellen Steuerung durch Buttons innerhalb einer sequentiellen Abfolge von Knoten eine akzeptable Lösung geschaffen.

Als Alternativentwicklung zum jetzigen Konzept von S*P*A*R*K könnte der verstärkte Einsatz des Hypertext-Ansatzes auch in den anderen Modulen des Systems sinnvoll sein. Insbesondere könnte die Beispieledatenbank und ihre Zugriffskomponente (Browser) als Hypertext realisiert werden. Da ohnehin für den Teacher und die Beispieledatenbank mit AVC die gleiche Software verwendet wurde, dürften sich hierbei keine technischen Schwierigkeiten ergeben. Zusätzlich zum jetzigen Konzept wären dann jedoch Verknüpfungen zwischen einzelnen Beispielen möglich, z.B. zwischen ähnlichen Fällen, bei denen jedoch einige scheiterten, während die anderen erfolgreich waren. Verknüpfungen zwischen den Beispielen und den wissenschaftlichen Grundlagen der spezifischen Anwendung könnten ebenfalls vorteilhaft sein.

Weiterhin könnte geprüft werden, inwieweit die Erklärungskomponente des Facilitators sinnvoll durch ein Hypertext-Modul verbessert werden könnte.

Anmerkungen

Der Autor dankt den weiteren Mitgliedern des S*P*A*R*K-Teams am Los Angeles Scientific Center (LASC) der IBM, mit denen er von August 1989 bis August 1990 zusammenarbeiten konnte, für die konstruktiven Beiträge bei der Erstellung des Teachers. Besonderer Dank gilt den geistigen Eltern des S*P*A*R*K-Projektes, Patricia Gongla und Gene Sakamoto, mit denen die Zusammenarbeit eine besondere Freude und wertvolle Erfahrung war. Rita Summers, Projektmanagerin am LASC, und der IBM Deutschland sei für die Ermöglichung meines Aufenthalts am LASC gedankt.

Literatur

[1] **Bogaschewsky, R.** (1991), Hypertext/Hypermedia - Ein Überblick, in: Informatik-Spektrum (zur Veröffentlichung angenommen).

[2] **Bogaschewsky, R.** (1991), S*P*A*R*K: Ein Wissensbasiertes System zur Identifizierung strategischer Einsatzmöglichkeiten von Informationen und Informationstechnologie, in: Biethahn, J., Bloech, J., Bogaschewsky, R., Hoppe, U. (Hrsg.): Wissensbasierte Systeme in der Betriebswirtschaft, 2. Symposium des Göttinger Arbeitskreises für Wissensbasierte Systeme (GAWS), Göttingen 11.1.91, Wiesbaden.

[3] **Gongla, P. et al.** (1989), S*P*A*R*K: A knowledge-based system for identifying competitive uses of information and information technology, IBM Systems Journal, Vol.28, No.4, S.628-645.

[4] **Gongla, P. et al.** (1988), Strategic Information Management Support (SIMS). Project Overview, Los Angeles Scientific Center Report No. 1988-2829.

[5] **IBM Corp.** (1989), Audio Visual Connection. User's Guide, IBM-No. 01F0344.

[6] **IBM Corp.** (1989), Audio Visual Authoring Language Reference, IBM-No. 01F0383.

[7] **IBM Corp.** (1989), Operating System/2. Programming Tools and Information, IBM-No. 64F0273.

[8] **Ives, B., Sakamoto, G., Gongla, P.** (1986), A Facilitative System for Identifying Competitive Applications of Information Technology, IBM Los Angeles Scientific Center Report No. G320-2789.

[9] **Nii, P.** (1986), Blackboard Systems: The Blackboard Model of Problem Solving and the Evolution of Blackboard Architectures, in: The AI Magazine, Summer 1986, S.38-53.

Browsing in unstrukturierten Hyperdokumenten

Dittrich G., Tochtermann K.
Universität Dortmund
Fachbereich Informatik
Postfach 50 05 00
D-4600 Dortmund 50

Schlüsselwörter

Browsing in unstrukturierten Hyperdokumenten, Benutzerführung, Fish-Eye-View

Zusammenfassung

In diesem Beitrag werden Ergebnisse des theoretischen Teils einer Diplomarbeit über Browser in unstrukturierten Hyperdokumenten vorgestellt. Die dabei gewonnenen Erkenntnisse lassen sich entweder direkt oder indirekt auf strukturierte Hyperdokumente übertragen, so daß ihre Anwendung auch in solchen Umgebungen ermöglicht wird. Um auf einer formalen Grundlage aufbauen zu können, wird eine auf der Graphentheorie basierende Vorgehensweise verwendet.

Dieser Beitrag behandelt zunächst Konzepte für Browser in unstrukturierten Hyperdokumenten. Daraus werden anschließend entsprechende Anforderungen für solche Browser abgeleitet. Diese Anforderungen konzentrieren sich im wesentlichen darauf, wie der Benutzer im Falle eines Orientierungsverlustes unterstützt werden kann. Um einem solchen Orientierungsverlust auf seiten des Benutzers auch vorbeugen zu können, wird im nächsten Abschnitt auf eine bislang vernachlässigte Komponente von Browsern eingegangen: die Benutzerführung. Die hierzu eingeführten Definitionen liefern insbesondere die Voraussetzung für einen Fish-Eye-View in unstrukturierten Hyperdokumenten, der zum Abschluß dieses Beitrags vorgestellt wird.

1. Einleitung

Unter einem *Hyperdokument* wird hier ein Text verstanden, dessen logische Einheiten, die *Knoten*, in nichtlinearer Weise über sogenannte *Verweise* miteinander verbunden sind. Bei dem Begriff Hyperdokument kann zwischen *strukturiertem* und *unstrukturiertem Hyperdokument* unterschieden werden. In einem unstrukturierten Hyperdokument besteht die Menge der Knoten nur aus Knoten, die Informationen wie etwa Text, Graphik oder Ton beinhalten. Demgegenüber enthält die Menge der Knoten eines strukturierten Hyperdokumentes zudem noch ausgezeichnete Knoten, die dazu dienen, die Knoten eines Hyperdokumentes zu organisieren und zu kategorisieren. Somit können in strukturierten Hyperdokumenten themengleiche Knoten etwa zu einem Kapitel zusammengefaßt werden.

Aufgrund der Vielzahl von Knoten und Verweisen in einem Hyperdokument kann ein Benutzer bei der Navigation durch das Dokument leicht die Orientierung verlieren. Um den Benutzer in einem solchen Fall zu unterstützen, werden sogenannte *Browser* eingesetzt.

Mit diesem Beitrag werden theoretische Ergebnisse einer Arbeit [9] über Browser in unstrukturierten Hyperdokumenten vorgestellt. Aufbauend auf diesen Ergebnissen wurde ein Browser für unstrukturierte Hyperdokumente implementiert. Damit kann gezeigt werden, daß die entwickelten Theorien zum einen realisierbar sind und zum anderen einen weiterführenden Beitrag zum Thema Browsing leisten.

Um formal exakt und möglichst allgemein formulieren zu können, wurde ein in der Graphentheorie eingebettetes Begriffsgerüst aufgebaut.

2. Konzepte für Browser in unstrukturierten Hyperdokumenten

Um graphentheoretische Formalisierungen zu ermöglichen, wird folgende Definition für ein Hyperdokument eingeführt:

Definition 2.1 (Hyperdokument)

Ein Hyperdokument H wird durch einen gerichteten Graphen G = (K,V) repräsentiert, wobei K die Menge der Knoten und V die Menge der Verweise ist (Schreibweise: H = (K,V)) [4].

Hat ein Benutzer bei der Navigation durch ein Hyperdokument die Orientierung verloren, so ist die Darstellung des Kontextes des aktuellen Knotens bei der Orientierungsfindung sehr hilfreich. Als aktueller Knoten wird dabei der Knoten bezeichnet, der im augenblicklichen Interesse des Benutzers steht.

In strukturierten Hyperdokumenten kann der Kontext eines Knotens in eine globale und eine lokale Komponente differenziert werden [5]. In unstrukturierten Hyperdokumenten ist eine solche Unterscheidung zunächst nicht mehr möglich, da keine Strukturierungsmöglichkeiten zur Verfügung stehen und somit ein wie in [5] beschriebener globaler Kontext nicht mehr existiert.

Vor diesem Hintergrund wird daher eine Beschreibung für den Kontext eines Knotens aus einem unstrukturierten Hyperdokument vorgestellt. Insbesondere ist die im folgenden formulierte Beschreibung auch auf strukturierte Hyperdokumente übertragbar.

Der Kontext eines Knotens in einem unstrukturierten Hyperdokument enthält Knoten, die über eine beliebige Anzahl von Verweisen von dem aktuellen Knoten aus erreichbar sind bzw. über die der aktuelle Knoten mit einer beliebigen Anzahl von Verweisen erreicht werden kann. Der Kontext eines Knotens läßt sich für die folgenden Betrachtungen in zwei duale Komponenten, eine zukunfts- und eine vergangenheitsorientierte, zerlegen. Wegen ihrer größeren Bedeutung soll an dieser Stelle nur die zukunftsorientierte Komponente vorgestellt werden.

Definition 2.2 (zukunftsorientierter Kontext)

Sei $H = (K,V)$ ein Hyperdokument. Sei $TV(V)$ die transitive Verweishülle von V (vgl. [4]). Für $k \in K$ seien

$U_z(k) := \{l \mid l \in K \wedge (k,l) \in TV(V)\} \cup \{k\}$,

$V_z(k) := \{(l,m) \mid l,m \in U_z(k) \wedge (l,m) \in V\}$.

Dann heißt $KON_z(k) := (U_z(k), V_z(k))$ der zukunftsorientierte Kontext von k.

Der zukunftsorientierte Kontext eines Knotens beinhaltet also alle Knoten, die von dem aktuellen Knoten k aus erreichbar sind, und die Verweise dieser Knoten untereinander. Eine Darstellung des zukunftsorientierten Kontextes ermöglicht dem Benutzer einen Blick auf die von dem aktuellen Knoten aus erreichbaren Knoten. Anhand der Knotennamen können von dem aktuellen Knoten aus erreichbare Themengebiete identifiziert werden. Um nun eine solche Darstellung nicht zu unübersichtlich werden zu lassen, soll dem Benutzer die Möglichkeit eingeräumt werden, den Grad n des zukunftsorientierten Kontextes festzulegen

Definition 2.3 (zukunftsorientierter Kontext vom Grad n)

Sei $H = (K,V)$ ein Hyperdokument. Sei $TV(V)$ die transitive Verweishülle von V (vgl. [4]). Für $k \in K$ und $n \in \mathbb{N}$ seien

$U_{z,n}(k) := \{l \mid l \in K \wedge \exists j \in \mathbb{N} \backslash \{0\} \wedge j \leq n \wedge \exists y_0, \ldots, y_j \in K$ mit $(y_i, y_{i+1}) \in V$, für $i = 0, \ldots, j\text{-}1$
　　　　　derart, daß $y_0 = k$ und $y_j = l\} \cup \{k\}$,

$V_{z,n}(k) := \{(l,m) \mid l,m \in U_{z,n}(k) \wedge (l,m) \in V\}$.

Dann heißt $KON_{z,n}(k) := (U_{z,n}(k), V_{z,n}(k))$ der zukunftsorientierte Kontext vom Grad n von k.

Ein Knoten l muß also über mindestens einen Weg der Länge kleiner oder gleich n von dem aktuellen Knoten k aus erreichbar sein, um in dessen zukunftsorientierten Kontext vom Grad n zu liegen.

Für die Knoten, über die der Benutzer zu dem aktuellen Knoten gelangt ist, soll ebenfalls der zukunftsorientierte Kontext mit Grad n dargestellt werden können. Mit dieser Darstellung erhält der Benutzer einen Einblick in den Kontext, aus dem er zu dem aktuellen Knoten gelangt ist. Dieser Einblick ist insbesondere dann wichtig, wenn der Benutzer zu einem der bereits besuchten Knoten zurückkehren möchte. Durch die Darstellung dieser zukunftsorientierten Kontexte kann der Benutzer abschätzen, welcher der besuchten Knoten der geeignetste ist, um beispielsweise ein bestimmtes Themengebiet weiterzubearbeiten.

Für die Verfahren zur Erzeugung eines zukunftsorientierten Kontextes vom Grad n können die Grundprinzipien von Algorithmen aus dem Bereich der systematischen Erforschung von Graphen übernommen werden (vgl. [4]). Für diese Verfahren kann ferner gezeigt werden, daß sie ein lineares Zeitverhalten besitzen. Dieser Aspekt ist insofern sehr hoch zu bewerten, als daß ein Browser schnell auf von einem Benutzer gestellte Anforderungen reagieren muß.

Um Darstellungen des zukunftsorientierten Kontextes aufgrund von einer hohen Anzahl von Knoten und Verweisen nicht zu unübersichtlich werden zu lassen, wurde ein geeigneter Filtermechanismus für

Verweise entwickelt. Mit Hilfe dieses Mechanismus kann der Benutzer die Zahl der darzustellenden Verweise beeinflussen.

3. Benutzerführung in unstrukturierten Hyperdokumenten

Alle in der Literatur (etwa [1], [3], [5], [6], [10]) vorgestellten Browser vernachlässigen eine nicht zu unterschätzende Komponente eines Browsers: die Benutzerführung. Lediglich in [8] wird ein Schwerpunkt auf die Benutzerführung gelegt, wobei die dort zugrunde gelegte Struktur eines Hyperdokumentes nicht ohne weiteres auf beliebige Hyperdokumente übertragbar ist.

Vor diesem Hintergrund wurden Strategien entwickelt, die eine Benutzerführung durch einen Browser ermöglicht. Die zugrundeliegende Idee besteht darin, Wissen der Autoren über semantische Zusammenhänge der Knoten eines Hyperdokumentes auch späteren Benutzern zugänglich zu machen. Dabei soll den Autoren die Möglichkeit eingeräumt werden, die semantische Beziehung zwischen Knoten über eine Gewichtung der sie verbindenden Verweise auszudrücken. Die Frage, wie eine solche Gewichtung in der Praxis zu bestimmen ist, steht hier zunächst im Hintergrund. Vielmehr wird untersucht, welche neuen Möglichkeiten sich mit einer solchen Vorgehensweise eröffnen. Es wird vorgeschlagen, diese Gewichtung über eine Gewichtung von Sourcen vorzunehmen, die als der spezifische Ursprung eines Verweises zu verstehen sind.

Definition 3.1 (Gewichtung einer Source)
Seien $H = (K,V)$ ein Hyperdokument, $k \in K$. Die durch $w_{max} \in \mathbb{N} \setminus \{0\}$ beschränkte Gewichtung einer Source in einem Knoten $k \in K$ ist eine Abbildung $G: \{s \mid s$ ist Source in $k \in K\} \rightarrow \{1,\ldots,w_{max}\}$.

Daraus läßt sich wie folgt die semantische Relevanz zwischen zwei Knoten ableiten:

Definition 3.2 (semantische Relevanz)
Seien $H = (K,V)$ ein Hyperdokument. Für $k,l \in K$ ist die semantische Relevanz eines Verweises $(k,l) \in V$ eine Abbildung $R_{sem}: V \rightarrow \mathbb{N} \setminus \{0\}$ derart, daß gilt:

$$R_{sem}(k,l) := \max.\{G(s) \mid s \text{ ist Source des Verweises } (k,l) \in V\}.$$

Die semantische Relevanz des Knotens l für den Knoten k wird also durch das Gewicht der am höchsten gewichteten Source eines Verweises (k,l) repräsentiert.

Für die Benutzerführung werden zwei Strategien vorgeschlagen:

Die erste Strategie beruht darauf, daß der Browser die Navigation des Benutzers durch das Hyperdokument mitverfolgt und immer den zukunftsorientierten Kontext vom Grad n für den gerade aktuellen Knoten darstellt. Wird einem Verweis von einem Knoten k zu einem Knoten l gefolgt, so registriert der Browser diese Veränderung und paßt seine Darstellung dem neuen zukunftsorientierten Kontext des Knotens l an. Bei dieser Strategie ist der Benutzer jederzeit über die möglichen erreichbaren Knoten und die damit verbundenen Themengebiete informiert. Somit ist der Benutzer mental vorbereitet, wenn einer dieser Knoten durch das Folgen eines Verweises geöffnet wird.

Die zweite Strategie dient dazu, sich aus dem zukunftsorientierten Kontext des aktuellen Knotens heraus den „wichtigsten" Weg zu einem Endknoten des Kontextes anzeigen zu lassen. Mit seiner Hilfe soll dem Leser ein „roter Faden" für den gerade dargestellten Kontext angeboten werden. Eine optisch hervorgehobene Darstellung eines solchen Weges ist insbesondere dann wertvoll, wenn der Benutzer mit dem Hyperdokument oder Teilen desselben noch nicht vertraut ist.

Auf die Problematik, daß ein zukunftsorientierter Kontext zyklische Wege enthalten kann, oder daß aufgrund vorkommender Zyklen keine Endknoten existieren, wird in [9] ausführlich eingegangen.

Aufgrund der Verweisgewichte wird in drei Filtrationsphasen der „wichtigste" Weg ermittelt. Es sei bemerkt, daß auch durchaus mehrere „wichtigste" Wege existieren können.

Die erste Phase filtert Wege heraus, deren semantische Relevanz relativ zu den anderen Wegen gering ist. Unter der semantischen Relevanz eines Weges versteht man eine Größe, die die durchschnittliche semantische Relevanz eines Verweises dieses Weges beschreibt. Um sie zu erhalten, werden die semantischen Relevanzen der Verweise des Weges addiert und anschließend mit der Länge des Weges in Beziehung gesetzt.

Zu Beginn der zweiten Phase liegen nur noch Wege mit einer hohen semantischen Relevanz vor. Nun kann es jedoch sein, daß ein Weg in der ersten Phase nicht herausgefiltert wurde, weil einige wenige Verweise in diesem Weg eine sehr hohe semantische Relevanz besitzen, während die übrigen Verweise relativ niedrig gewichtet sind. Die zweite Phase überprüft daher alle verbliebenen Wege bezüglich ihrer semantischen Homogenität. Unter der semantischen Homogenität eines Weges werden dabei die Unterschiede der semantischen Relevanzen der Verweise dieses Weges verstanden: Je geringer diese Unterschiede sind, desto homogener ist die semantische Relevanz des zugehörigen Weges. Mit ihrer Hilfe kann festgestellt werden, wie sehr die semantischen Relevanzen der Verweise innerhalb eines Weges differieren. Die semantische Homogenität eine Weges $(k,l) \in TV(V)$ wird wie folgt formal beschrieben.

Definition 3.3 (semantische Homogenität eines Weges)

Sei $H = (K,V)$ ein Hyperdokument. Seien $k,l \in K$ und $(k,l) \in TV(V)$ ein Weg von k nach l. Dann existieren für diesen Weg $y_0, \ldots, y_n \in K$ mit $y_0 = k$ und $y_n = l$, wobei $(y_i, y_{i+1}) \in V$, für $i = 0, \ldots, n-1$ für ein $n \in \mathbb{N} \setminus \{0\}$.

Die semantische Homogenität $H_{(k,l)}$ des Weges $(k,l) \in TV(V)$ ist definiert als:

$$H_{(k,l)} := \frac{\displaystyle\sum_{i=0}^{n-2} \sum_{j=i+1}^{n-1} |\, R_{sem}(y_i, y_{i+1}) - R_{sem}(y_j, y_{j+1}) \,|}{\displaystyle\sum_{i=1}^{n-1} i}$$

Je näher die semantische Homogenität eines Weges bei dem Wert 0 liegt, desto weniger unterscheiden sich die einzelnen semantischen Relevanzen der Verweise dieses Weges voneinander. Die Untersuchung der semantischen Homogenität erfolgt erst in der zweiten Phase, da ein Weg eine hohe semantische Homogenität aufweisen kann, obwohl seine semantische Relevanz gering ist.

Nachdem diese beiden Schritte durchgeführt wurden, verbleiben nur noch Wege, die zum einen eine hohe semantische Relevanz aufweisen und zum anderen relativ homogen sind. In der dritten Phase werden daher die Verweisgewichte innerhalb der verbliebenen Wege miteinander verglichen. Dabei werden zunächst die semantischen Relevanzen der Verweise betrachtet, die von dem aktuellen Knoten ausgehen. Anschließend werden die semantischen Relevanzen der nächsten Verweise innerhalb der verbliebenen Wege miteinander verglichen. Dieses Prinzip setzt sich solange fort, bis die Endknoten eines Weges erreicht werden. Um diese Vergleiche zeiteffizient gestalten zu können, wird die Gewichtung eines Weges eingeführt. Zu diesem Zweck werden Verfahren aus der Codierungstheorie verwendet (vgl. [11]): Zunächst wird die maximale Länge eines Weges in dem gegebenen zukunftsorientierten Kontext ermittelt. Die semantischen Relevanzen der Verweise eines jeden Weges können nun bezüglich der oberen Schranke einer beschränkten Gewichtung G von Sourcen gewichtet werden. Diese Gewichtungen der sematischen Relevanzen werden aufsummiert und repräsentieren eine eindeutige Gewichtung des zugehörigen Weges. Diese Vorgehensweise führt zu folgender Formalisierung:

Definition 3.4 (Gewichtung eines Weges)

Sei H = (K,V) ein Hyperdokument. Seien k,l $\in$ K und (k,l) $\in$ TV(V) ein Weg von k nach l.

Es gelte :

(i) w_{max} ist die obere Schranke einer beschränkten Gewichtung G von Sourcen

(ii) Für den Weg von k nach l existieren $y_0, \ldots, y_n \in$ K mit $y_0 = k$ und $y_n = l$, wobei $(y_i, y_{i+1}) \in$ V, für i = 0,...,n-1 für ein n $\in \mathbb{N} \setminus \{0\}$.

(iii) r := max. {length(s,t) | s,t $\in$ K $\wedge$ (s,t) $\in$ TV(V)}, wobei mit length(s,t) die Länge des Weges (s,t) bezeichnet wird.

Die Gewichtung $C_{(k,l)}$ für den Weg (k,l) $\in$ TV(V) ist definiert als:

$$C_{(k,l)} := \sum_{i=0}^{n-1} R_{sem}(y_i, y_{i+1}) * (w_{max}+1)^{r-i}$$

Beispiel

Im praktischen Teil dieser Arbeit [9] wurde ein Hypertextsystem entwickelt, das einen graphischen Browser mit der beschriebenen Funktionalität anbietet. Die folgende Abbildung 3.1 zeigt einen Ausschnitt eines mit diesem System erstellten Hyperdokumentes, das die fünf neuen Bundesländer Deutschlands vorstellt. Für den Knoten „Sachsen" wurde der zukunftsorientierte Kontext vom Grad 3 bestimmt. Als maximale Gewichtung von Sourcen sei $w_{max} = 5$ angenommen. In Abbildung 3.1 sind die semantischen Relevanzen der einzelnen Verweise durch die entsprechende Beschriftung repräsentiert. Für diesen

Kontext wurde nun der „wichtigste" Weg zu einem der Endknoten des Kontextes ermittelt. Dieser Weg ist in der Darstellung optisch hervorgehoben.

Gemäß den obigen Erklärungen verfügt dieser Weg über eine hohe semantische Relevanz. Desweiteren beträgt die semantische Homogenität des selektierten Weges 1 und ist ebenfalls als relativ hoch einzustufen. Um diesen Weg gezielt verfolgen zu können, wird ein Mechanismus angeboten, der den Benutzer in der Navigation entlang dieses Weges unterstützt. Der augenblicklich aktuelle Knoten des „wichtigsten" Weges wird in seiner Darstellung invertiert. In Abbildung 3.1 ist dies der Knoten „Rotes Sachsen". Wird nun einem Verweis zu dem Knoten „Sachsen im Königreich" gefolgt, wechselt die invertierte Darstellung von dem Knoten „Rotes Sachsen" zu dem Knoten „Sachsen im Königreich".

Desweiteren besteht die Möglichkeit, sich in dem Knoten „Rotes Sachsen" die am höchsten gewichtete Source selektieren zu lassen, die Ursprung eines Verweises zu dem Knoten „Sachsen im Königreich" ist. Damit wird der Benutzer automatisch in den „wichtigsten" Kontext des Knotens „Rotes Sachsen" gebracht, von dem aus der Knoten „Sachsen im Königreich" erreicht werden kann.

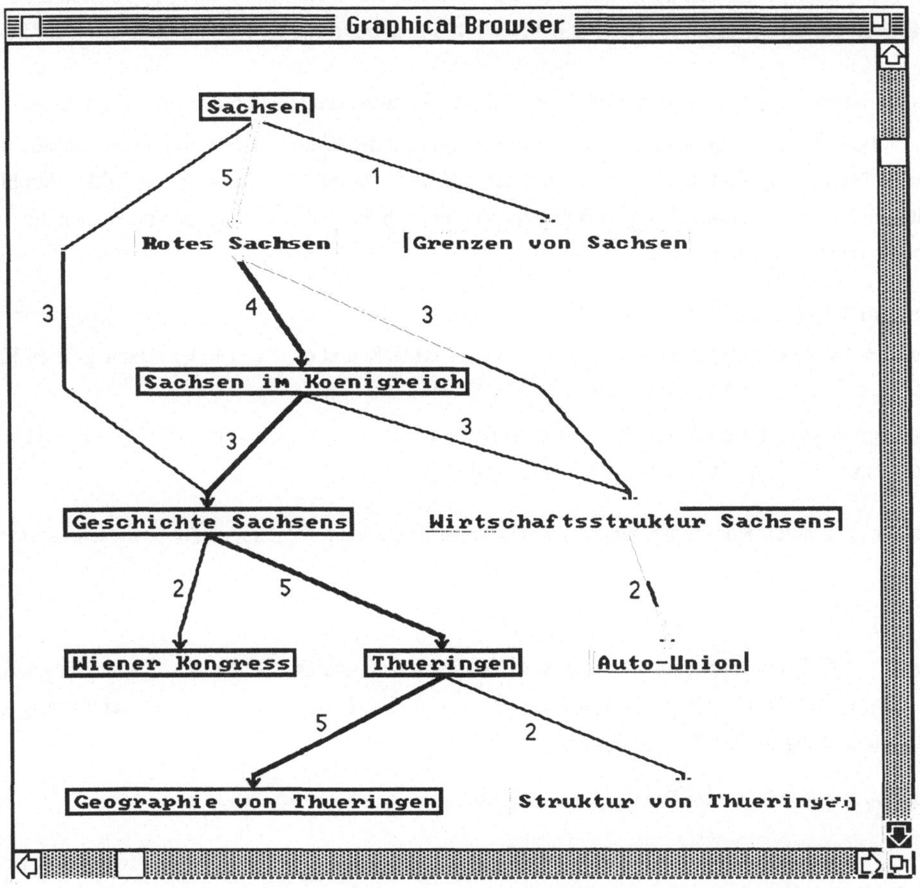

Abbildung 3.1: Darstellung des wichtigsten Weges

4. Fish-Eye-View in unstrukturierten Hyperdokumenten

Der in [2] vorgestellte und in [3] bzw. [7] am Beispiel illustrierte Fish-Eye-View kann angewendet werden, wenn die einem Hyperdokument zugrundegelegte Struktur hierarchisch ist. Diese Tatsache war Anlaß, einen Fish-Eye-View für unstrukturierte Hyperdokumente zu entwickeln.

Durch die obige Definition der semantischen Relevanz kann bislang nur die Beziehung zwischen zwei Knoten ausgedrückt werden, die nur einen Verweis auseinanderliegen. Um auch den semantischen Zusammenhang zwischen weiter entfernt liegenden Knoten ermitteln zu können, wird daher die a priori Wichtigkeit APW(k,l) für zwei Knoten k und l definiert. Diese a priori Wichtigkeit hängt dabei von den Verweisgewichten der Wege von k nach l ab. Da es in unstrukturierten Hyperdokumenten in der Regel mehrere Wege unterschiedlicher Länge von k nach l gibt, muß dabei berücksichtigt werden, daß nicht immer der kürzeste Weg zwischen beiden Knoten auch gleichzeitig der semantisch wichtigste ist. Des weiteren soll der Fish-Eye-View auch auf hierarchische Strukturen anwendbar sein. Diese Vorgabe kann eingehalten werden, wenn die in [2] gestellten Anforderungen erfüllt bleiben. Das heißt, bei der Anwendung der a priori Wichtigkeit auf solche Strukturen muß mit der Entfernung von k auch die a priori Wichtigkeit der erreichbaren Knoten l abnehmen. Da in unstrukturierten Hyperdokumenten der kürzeste Weg zwischen zwei Knoten nicht immer der semantisch wichtigste ist, gilt diese Anforderung in unstrukturierten Hyperdokument nur unter bestimmten Voraussetzungen, auf die später eingegangen wird.

Aufgrund eventuell vorkommender Zyklen kann die Anzahl der Wege von k nach l unendlich sein. Daher wird eine Markierungsfunktion eingeführt, mit deren Hilfe festgestellt werden kann, ob Zyklen durchlaufen werden. In diesem Zusammenhang kann gezeigt werden, daß durch das Vermeiden von Zyklen die a priori Wichtigkeit nicht beeinflußt wird.

Definition 4.1 (Knotenmarkierung in Wegen)

Seien $H = (K,V)$ ein Hyperdokument, $n \in \mathbb{N} \setminus \{0\}$, $k,l \in K$ und $(k,l) \in TV(V)$. Dann gibt es Knoten $y_0, \ldots, y_n \in K$ mit $y_0 = k$, $y_n = l$ und $(y_i, y_{i+1}) \in V$ für $i = 0, \ldots, n-1$.

Eine Knotenmarkierung für die Knoten $y_i \in K$ für $i = 0, \ldots, n$ eines Weges (k,l) ist eine Abbildung $\text{mark}_{(k,l)}$ mit $\text{mark}_{(k,l)} : \{y_i \mid y_i \in K \text{ für } i = 0, \ldots, n\} \to \mathbb{N} \cup \{-1\}$.

Mit einer geeigneten Konkretisierung der Funktion $\text{mark}_{(k,l)}$ kann folgender Satz bewiesen werden (vgl. [9]).

Satz 4.1

Seien $H = (K,V)$ ein Hyperdokument, $n \in \mathbb{N} \setminus \{0\}$, $k,l \in K$ und $(k,l) \in TV(V)$. Dann gibt es Knoten $y_0, \ldots, y_n \in K$ mit $y_0 = k$, $y_n = l$ und $(y_i, y_{i+1}) \in V$ für $i = 0, \ldots, n-1$. Ist ferner $\text{mark}_{(k,l)}$ eine Knotenmarkierung für den Weg (k,l), dann gilt:

$$\sum_{i=0}^{n} \text{mark}_{(k,l)}(y_i) = 0 \Leftrightarrow \text{der Weg } (k,l) \text{ ist azyklisch.}$$

Die a priori Wichtigkeit kann nun wie folgt definiert werden:

Definition 4.2 (a priori Wichtigkeit)

Seien $H = (K,V)$ Hyperdokument, $k,l \in K$ und $(k,l) \in TV(V)$. Es gelte :

(i) w_{max} ist die obere Schranke einer beschränkten Gewichtung G von Sourcen.

(ii) Es existieren $y_{0,j}, \ldots, y_{n_j,j} \in K$ mit $(y_{i,j}, y_{i+1,j}) \in V$ für $i = 0, \ldots, n_j - 1$ und $n_j \in \mathbb{N} \setminus \{0\}$, wobei $y_{0,j} = k$ und $y_{n_j,j} = l$ ist. Dabei ist $j \in \{1, \ldots, m\}$ für ein festes $m \in \mathbb{N} \setminus \{0\}$, falls es endlich viele Wege von k nach l gibt, andernfalls ist $j \in \mathbb{N}$.

(iii) Es sei $\mathrm{apw}_j(y_{0,j}, y_{n_j,j}) := \displaystyle\prod_{i=0}^{n_j-1} \frac{R_{sem}(y_{i,j}, y_{i+1,j})}{w_{max}}$.

Falls es unendlich viele Wege von k nach l gibt, berechne $\mathrm{apw}_j(y_{0,j}, y_{n_j,j})$ nur für die Wege $(y_{0,j}, y_{n_j,j}) \in TV(V)$, für die $\displaystyle\sum_{i=0}^{n_j} \mathrm{mark}_{(k,l)}(y_{i,j}) = 0$ ist. Andernfalls ist für jeden Weg von k nach l $\mathrm{apw}_j(y_{0,j}, y_{n_j,j})$ zu berechnen.

Die a priori Wichtigkeit von l für k ist definiert als :

$$APW(k,l) := \mathrm{maximum} \ \{\mathrm{apw}_j(y_{0,j}, y_{n_j,j}) \mid j \in M \wedge M \subset \mathbb{N} \wedge M \text{ endlich} \wedge n_j \in \mathbb{N} \setminus \{0\} \wedge \text{ für}$$
$$y_{0,j} = k \text{ und } y_{n_j,j} = l \text{ ist } (y_{0,j}, y_{n_j,j}) \in TV(V) \text{ ein Weg von } k \text{ nach } l\}.$$

Bemerkung

Da es aufgrund eventuell vorkommender Zyklen unendlich viele Wege zwischen zwei Knoten $k,l \in K$ geben kann, wird in (iii) $\mathrm{apw}_j(y_{0,j}, y_{n_j,j})$ nur für azyklische und damit endlich viele Wege berechnet. Die a priori Wichtigkeit von l für k wird dadurch nicht beeinflußt.

Um die oben formulierten Anforderungen erfüllen zu können, wurde das Verhalten der APW-Funktion studiert. Als ein Ergebnis dieser Untersuchung läßt sich folgender Satz formulieren:

Satz 4.2

Sei $H = (K,V)$ ein Hyperdokument. Seien $k,s,t \in K$, $(k,t) \in TV(V)$, $(k,s) \in TV(V)$ und $(s,t) \in TV(V)$. Unter der Voraussetzung, daß alle Wege von k nach t über den Knoten s führen, folgt :

$APW(k,t) \le APW(k,s)$.

Bemerkung

Wie folgendes Gegenbeispiel zeigt, kann obiger Satz nur mit der genannten Voraussetzung bewiesen werden (vgl. [9]) und gilt daher nicht in aller Allgemeinheit. Es sei angenommen, es gebe zwei Wege $w_1 = (k,m)$, (m,t) und $w_2 = (k,s)$, (s,t) von k nach t. Ferner sei s nur über den Verweis (k,s) von k aus erreichbar. Dann ist es möglich, daß für $w_{max} = 4$, $R_{sem}(k,m) = R_{sem}(m,t) = 4$ und $R_{sem}(k,s) = R_{sem}(s,t) = 2$ ist. Damit wäre aber $APW(k,t) = 1 > 0,5 = APW(k,s)$, obwohl t weiter von k entfernt ist als s.

Dennoch zeigt dieser Satz, daß obige Definition der a priori Wichtigkeit auch auf hierarchische Strukturen anwendbar ist. In den in [2] zugrundeliegenden baumartigen Strukturen gibt es immer nur genau einen Weg von einem aktuellen Knoten k zu einem beliebigen Knoten l. Damit ist die Voraussetzung in obigem Satz stets erfüllt und die a priori Wichtigkeit genügt der Anforderung, daß sie mit der Entfernung von dem aktuellen Knoten abnimmt.

Die a priori Wichtigkeit kann in obiger Form direkt auf Knoten strukturierter Hyperdokumente angewendet werden. Möchte man die a priori Wichtigkeit ähnlich wie in [3] auf ausgezeichnete Knoten eines strukturierten Hyperdokumentes anwenden, ist die Definition der semantischen Relevanz entsprechend zu erweitern.

Folgende Anwendung der a priori Wichtigkeit im Sinne des Fish-Eye-Views wurde im Rahmen dieser Arbeit implementiert: Der Benutzer gibt für einen zukunftsorientierten Kontext mit Grad n an, daß von den zugehörigen Knoten nur die Knoten dargestellt werden, die mindestens eine vorgegebene a priori Wichtigkeit für den aktuellen Knoten besitzen. Dies soll am Beispiel demonstriert werden.

Beispiel

Die Abbildung 4.1 auf der folgenden Seite stellt den zukunftsorientierten Kontext vom Grad 5 für den Knoten „Industrie in Thüringen" dar. Das heißt, daß es für jeden Knoten in der Darstellung einen Weg der Länge kleiner oder gleich fünf gibt, über den er von dem aktuellen Knoten „Industrie in Thüringen" erreicht werden kann. Als maximale Gewichtung von Sourcen sei $w_{max} = 5$ angenommen. Die semantischen Relevanzen der einzelnen Verweise werden durch die entsprechende Verweisbeschriftung repräsentiert.

In diesem Kontext wurde nun der Fish-Eye-View bezüglich einer a priori Wichtigkeit von 0,5 berechnet. Die Knoten, die diese a priori Wichtigkeit nicht besitzen, sind grau dargestellt, ebenso die Verweise, die zu diesen Knoten führen.

In der Abbildung erkennt man, daß erwartungsgemäß die a priori Wichtigkeit eines Knotens mit seiner Entfernung zu dem aktuellen Knoten abnimmt. So fallen vorwiegend die Knoten aus der Darstellung, die relativ weit von dem aktuellen Knoten entfernt liegen. Desweiteren wird die Gültigkeit des oben formulierten Satzes illustriert: Der Knoten „Sachsen-Anhalt" - unten links in der Darstellung - ist nur über den Knoten „Selbstbewußtsein der Thüringer" zu erreichen. Da der Knoten „Selbstbewußtsein der Thüringer" nicht im Fish-Eye-View liegt, kann auch der Knoten „Sachsen-Anhalt" nicht die erforderliche a priori Wichtigkeit erfüllen.

5. Ausblick

Wie die Vielfalt der hier vorgestellten Unterstützungsmechanismen für die Navigation durch ein Hyperdokument zeigt, scheint die Gewichtung von Sourcen und die daraus resultierende Verweisgewichtung eine sinnvolle Erweiterung des Hypertextkonzeptes zu sein. Mit der formal durchgeführten Vorgehensweise dürfte eine gute Grundlage geschaffen sein, um die verschiedenen

Komponenten des vorgestellten Browsers in bereits existierende oder noch zu entwickelnde Hypertextsysteme zu integrieren. Des weiteren werden verschiedene Möglichkeiten gesehen, die Gewichtung der Verweise für die Erzeugung von Touren in einem Hyperdokument einzusetzen.

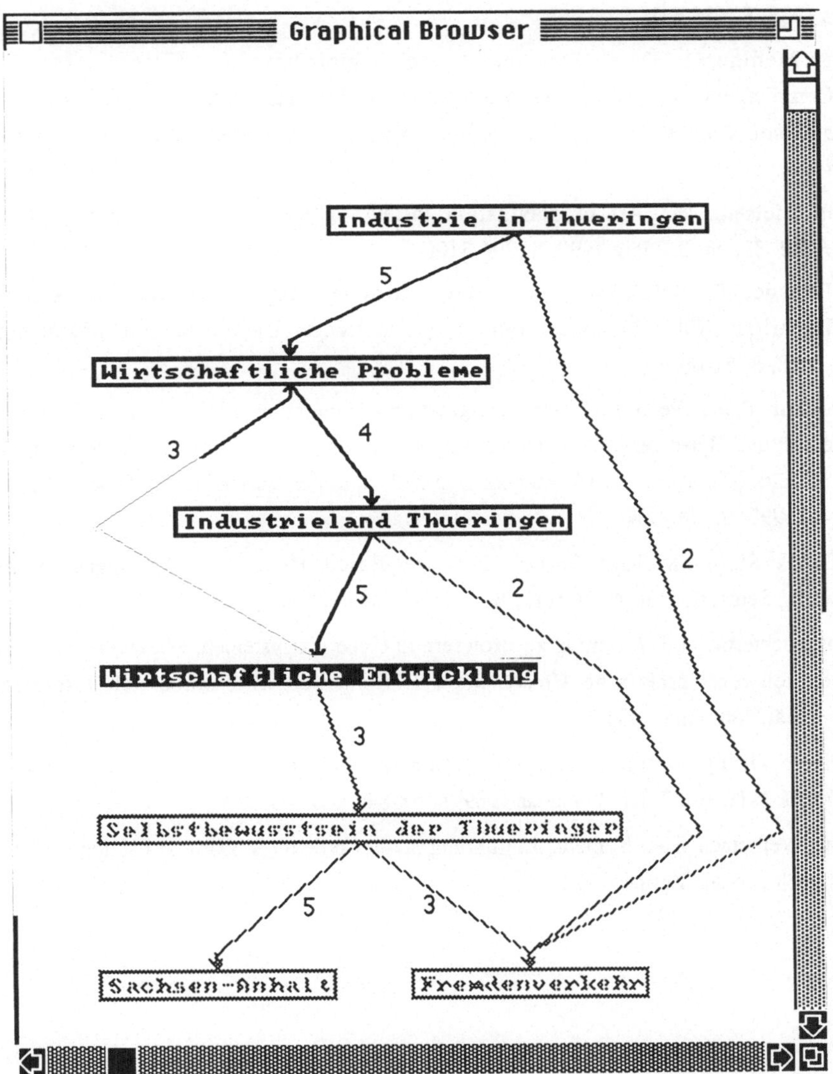

Abbildung 4.1: Ein Fish-Eye-View

Literaturverzeichnis

[1] Carolyn Foss; Effective Browsing in Hypertext Systems; in: *Proceedings RIAO´88, M.I.T. Cambridge (MA)*, März 1988, S. 82-98.

[2] George Furnas; Generalized Fisheye Views; in: *Proceedings of CHI´86, Human Factors in Computing Systems; Boston*, April 1986, S. 16-23.

[3] Henrik J. Komorowski, Robert A. Greenes et al.; Browsing and Authoring Tools for a Unified Medical Language System; in: *Proceedings RIAO´88,* M.I.T. Cambridge (MA), März 1988, S. 624-641.

[4] Kurt Mehlhorn; Data Structures and Algorithms 2: Graph Algorithms and NP-Completness; W. Brauer, G. Rozenberg, A. Salomaa (Eds.); *EACTS Monographs on Theoretical Computer Science*; Springer Verlag Berlin, Heidelberg, New York, Tokyo, 1984.

[5] Jakob Nielsen; The Art of Navigation through Hypertext; in: *Communications of the ACM*, Bd. 33, Nr. 3, März 1990, S. 296-310.

[6] X. Pintado, D. Tsichritis; An Affinity Browser; in: *Active Object Environments*, D. Tsichritzis (Ed.); Technical Report of the Centre Universitaire d´Informatique, Genf, Juni 1988, S. 51-60.

[7] Karl-Heinz Saxer, Peter A. Gloor; Navigation im Hyperraum: Fisheye Views in HyperCard; in: Hypertext und Hypermedia: Von theoretischen Konzepten zur praktischen Anwendung, P.A.Gloor, N.A. Streitz (Eds.); Informatik-Fachberichte 249, Springer Verlag Berlin, Heidelberg, New York, Tokyo, 1990, S. 190-204.

[8] P. Davis Stotts, Richard Furuta; Petri-Net-Based Hypertext: Document Structure with Browsing Semantics; in: *ACM ToIS*, Bd. 7, Nr. 1, Januar 1989, S. 3-29.

[9] Klaus Tochtermann; Ein Beitrag zu Browsern in Hypertextsystemen: Ein theoretischer Ansatz und dessen teilweise praktische Umsetzung . Diplomarbeit im Fachbereich Informatik an der Universität Dortmund, 1991.

[10] Kenneth Utting, Nicole Yankelovich; Context and Orientation in Hypermedia Networks; in: *ACM ToIS*, Bd. 7, Nr. 1, Januar 1989, S. 58-84.

[11] Klaus Weihrauch, Tiko Kameda; Einführung in die Codierungstheorie 1; Bibliographisches Institut Mannheim, Wien, Zürich, 1973.

Erweiterungen der ISO Normen ODA und DFR am Beispiel eines Hypertextservers

Heinz Fanderl
IBM - Deutschland GmbH
Europäisches Zentrum für Netzwerkforschung
Tiergartenstr. 8
6900 Heidelberg

Ernö Kovacs
Universität Kaiserlautern
AG Telematik

Kurzfassung

Die Dokumentenverarbeitung in offenen Systemen basiert auf internationalen Normen für Dokumentenarchitektur und Kommunikation. Ein Beispiel für eine normierte Dokumentenarchitektur ist die 'Open Document Architecture' (ODA). Inwieweit ODA die Anforderungen eines in einem heterogenen Umfeld verteilten Hypertext/Hypermedia Systems erfüllen kann, ist Inhalt dieses Beitrags. Dazu werden die Konzepte, die die heutige ODA Norm bietet und Bestrebungen der Standardisierungsgremien zur Architekturerweiterung untersucht. Dies resultiert in ein erweitertes Schema für Dokumententeile, welches in Form eines Prototyps auf seine Tauglichkeit hin überprüft wird.[1]

Einleitung

Der Austausch „elektronischer" Dokumente in heterogenen Umgebungen, welcher bei der Kommunikation über Unternehmensgrenzen hinweg, aber auch innerhalb von Unternehmen eine alltägliche Notwendigkeit ist, erfordert, daß sich die Kommunikationspartner auf eine einheitliche, normierte Dokumentenarchitektur und ebensolche Kommunikationsprotokolle einigen. Dazu haben die internationalen Standardisierungsgremien ISO und CCITT neben den Kommunikationsnormen im Rahmen des OSI Referenzmodells auch eine normierte Dokumentenarchitektur unter dem Namen 'Open Document Architecture' (ODA) [1] [2] verabschiedet. Gegenstand dieser Norm ist ein Architekturmodell und ein Austauschformat für integrierte Text/Grafik Dokumente, die sowohl zum Zweck des Weiterbearbeitens als auch zum Zweck der Wiedergabe in der vom Autor beabsichtigten Formatierung ausgetauscht werden.

ODA in seiner heutigen Form beschreibt zwar Prozesse, die das Bearbeiten und die Darstellung von Dokumenten betreffen, aber eine Unterstützung von Anwendungen, deren Inhalt das Navigieren in Dokumenten ist, wird in der Norm nicht vorgesehen. Insbesondere aber bei sehr großen Dokumentenbeständen wie Lexika oder Manualen

---

[1] Dieser Beitrag wurde teilweise durch das ESPRIT Projekt Nr. 2374 der Europäischen Gemeinschaft gefördert.

von technischen Großgeräten ist es jedoch unumgänglich, den Benutzer bei der Führung durch diese Hilfestellungen anzubieten. Sehr wünschenswert aus Gründen der Datenredundanz, aber auch wegen der Einsparung von Speicherungskapazitäten, ist die Speicherung solcher Dokumentenbestände an zentralen Stellen. Diese Dokumentenbestände zeichnen sich durch eine außerordentlich geringe Änderungsrate aus, was die Speicherung auf Massenspeichern wie CD-ROM nahelegt. Der Zugriff darauf erfolgt dann über Kommunikationsdienste in einer meist heterogenen Systemlandschaft, was die Verwendung von normierten Dokumentenarchitekturen und von normierten Speicherungs- und Zugriffsverfahren notwendig macht. Gerade aber beim entfernten Zugriff auf einen Dokumentenspeicher in einem Hypertextsystem ist ein Mangel in der ODA Norm deutlich sichtbar: ODA definiert Dokumente als Gesamtheit, der Zugriff auf Teile von Dokumenten, wie sie in diesem Szenario notwendig ist, um vor allem in Weitverkehrsnetzen die Übertragungszeiten in akzeptablen Grenzen zu halten, ist nicht Bestandteil der heutigen Norm.

In diesem Beitrag sollen die Möglichkeiten von ODA im Hinblick auf das dargestellte Szenario untersucht werden. Dazu wird zuerst die Integration der Hyperstrukturen in die Dokumentenarchitektur mit einer geschichteten Architektur, wie sie auch im Dexter Modell[2] [3] vorgeschlagen wird, verglichen, wobei der geschichteten Architektur der Vorzug gegeben wird. Diese benötigt jedoch die Definition von Dokumententeilen, wozu die Anwendbarkeit einer darauf hinzielenden Erweiterung der Norm, welche zur Zeit in den Standardisierungsgremien diskutiert wird, näher betrachtet wird. Daraus ergeben sich eine Reihe von nicht erfüllten Anforderungen, was zu einem allgemeineren Konzept für Dokumententeile führt.

Zur Erprobung dieses Konzepts, aber auch für die Ermittlung von Kommunikationsanforderungen an ein solches System, werden zwei Prototypen im Rahmen eines Esprit Projekts von unserer Gruppe in Zusammenarbeit mit Bull entwickelt. Dabei wird von Bull eine Hypertextapplikation, die das Navigieren auf lokalen ODA Dokumenten ermöglicht, und von unserer Gruppe die Speicherungs- und Zugriffsverfahren auf Dokumente in offener Umgebung, basierend auf der ISO Norm 'Document Filing and Retrieval' (DFR) [4] eingebracht. Demzufolge ist das Hauptziel dieser Arbeit die von der Dokumentenarchitektur zu leistende Unterstützung für Hypertextsysteme im Hinblick auf Zugriff, Referenzierung und Speicherung der Dokumententeile. Dies entspricht im wesentlichen dem 'Within-Component Layer' des Dexter Modells. Es sind weder die Hyperstruktur selbst noch die Benutzungsschnittstelle Schwerpunkte dieses Beitrags.

Hyperstruktur und ODA

In diesem Kapitel sollen zwei mögliche Systemarchitekturen diskutiert werden, die beide den Zugriff auf ODA Dokumente in Hypertextanwendungen zum Inhalt haben.

---

[2] Ziel des Dexter Referenzmodells ist die Schaffung einer gemeinsamen Basis für die Entwicklung von Hypertextsystemen. Das Modell ist in drei Schichten aufgeteilt: der 'runtime layer' konzentriert sich auf die Benutzerinteraktion mit dem Hypermediasystem, der 'storage layer' definiert ein Netz von 'nodes' und 'links', in diesem Beitrag oft als Hyperstruktur bezeichnet, und der 'within-component layer' ist den Inhalten und Strukturen der 'nodes' gewidmet und damit nicht der eigentliche Schwerpunkt des Dexter Modells.

Zuerst wird eine Systemarchitektur vorgestellt, die auf einer Veränderung von ODA zur Definition der Hyperstruktur beruht, anschließend eine Architektur mit einer Hyperstruktur, die vom Dokument völlig getrennt und damit von ODA unabhängig ist (geschichtete Architektur).

Die direkte Unterstützung von Hypertextanwendungen durch Veränderung der ODA Dokumente ist nur mit entsprechenden Erweiterungen der Norm möglich. Eine solche Erweiterung wird in [5] beschrieben. Dort wird ein allgemeiner Referenzierungsmechanismus innerhalb von Dokumenten eingeführt, der nicht nur für Hypertextanwendungen brauchbar ist. Dazu kann jedes logische Objekt eines Dokuments mit einem zusätzlichen Attribut LINK versehen werden, welches das Ziel der Referenz enthält. Durch Klassifikation dieser Referenzen können sie als Hypertext-Links benutzt werden. Dies muß noch um Referenzen auf andere Dokumente ergänzt werden (siehe dazu Abbildung 1).

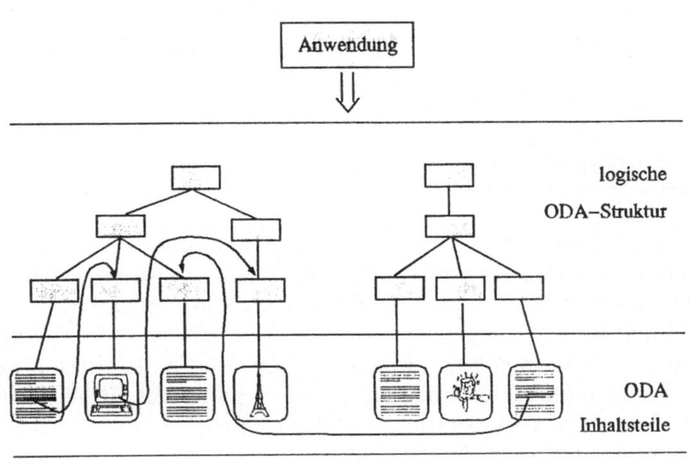

Abbildung 1. Integrierte Systemarchitektur

Die Vorteile dieses Ansatzes sind insbesondere die direkte Verwendbarkeit der, wenn auch erweiterten, ODA Norm für Hypertextanwendungen, eine weitgehende Konsistenz mit den heute existierenden ODA Strukturen und eine einfache Weiterentwicklung der aktuellen Austauschformate (ODIF und ODL).

Gegen diesen Ansatz sprechen im wesentlichen folgende Gründe: Die mit Hypertextinformation versehenen Inhaltsteile des Dokuments können nicht mit bereits existierenden ODA Produkten und Prototypen bearbeitet werden, was jedoch eine unverzichtbare Voraussetzung für die Akzeptanz einer Architekturerweiterung ist. Die Erweiterung ist, da spezifisch für ODA, lediglich auf ODA Dokumente anwendbar. Das bedeutet aber eine signifikante Einschränkung der Verwendbarkeit, denn die Integration in ein Hypertextsystem von Dokumenten oder von Dokumententeilen, die gemäß anderer Dokumentenarchitekturen dargestellt sind, ist mit diesem Ansatz nicht möglich.

Die geschichtete Architektur basiert auf unveränderten ODA Dokumenten und einer Hyperstruktur, die getrennt von diesen gespeichert wird (dazu Abbildung 2). Dies wird im übrigen auch von dem Dexter Referenz Modell vorgeschlagen.

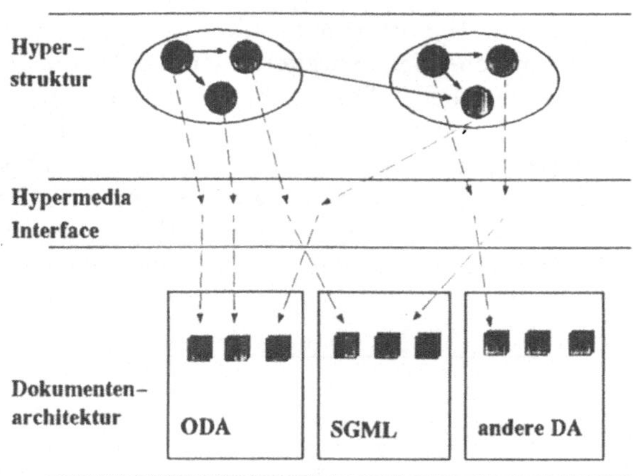

Abbildung 2. Geschichtete Systemarchitektur

Die Hyperstruktur definiert eine Menge von Objekten (nodes), die durch Referenzen (links) verbunden sind. Jedes Hypertextobjekt ist somit ein Anker einer Referenz oder der referenzierte Inhalt selbst. Aus der Sicht der Dokumentenarchitektur besteht zwischen diesen beiden Verwendungen eines Node kein Unterschied in der Definition, beide sind Teile von Dokumenten. Links können innerhalb eines Dokuments oder auch zwischen verschiedenen Dokumenten definiert sein. Wesentliche Eigenschaft dieses Ansatzes ist, daß die Hyperstruktur zwar Teile von Dokumenten und Beziehungen dazwischen beschreibt, daß aber diese keine Auswirkung auf die Dokumente selbst hat und deshalb auch nicht in der Dokumentenarchitektur definiert werden muß. Die Hyperstruktur ist getrennt von Dokument gespeichert, kann damit unabhängig vom Dokument bearbeitet werden und ist insbesondere auch individuell von Benutzern erzeugbar. Gerade dadurch ist dies für den heterogenen und individuellen Zugriff auf große zentrale Dokumentenspeicher (z.B. auf CD-ROM) besonders gut geeignet. Auch kann eine weitgehende Unabhängigkeit zwischen den zugrundeliegenden Dokumentenarchitekturen und der Hyperstruktur erreicht werden. Dies geschieht durch ein Hypermedia Interface, welches die abstrakt definierten Operationen der Hyperstruktur (z.B. Präsentation von Dokumententeilen, Hervorhebung von Ankern, Selektion und Verfolgung von Links) auf die entsprechenden Operationen der Werkzeuge (z.B. Editoren, Dokumentenspeicher) abbildet.

Der Nachteil dieses Ansatzes liegt in der notwendigen Definition der Hyperstruktur. Diese kann aber lokal zu einer spezifischen Anwendung gesehen werden und muß nicht notwendigerweise in einer offenen Umgebung übertragen werden. Dennoch sind Ansätze, die für die Hyperstruktur einen internationalen Standard festschreiben, sehr wünschenswert [6]. Da dies aber sehr applikationsspezifisch und architekturübergreifend ist, ist es nicht im Rahmen von ODA oder einer anderen Dokumentenarchitektur zu realisieren, sondern ist vielmehr als Aufgabe der Hypertext Standardisierung zu sehen.

Da sehr gewichtige Gründe für die geschichtete Architektur sprechen, soll im folgenden dieser Ansatz weiter verfolgt und in Prototypen erprobt werden. Eine Grundvoraussetzung dafür ist die Definition von Dokumententeilen. Inwieweit vorgeschlagene Erweiterungen der ODA Norm hier eine Hilfestellung geben können, wird im nächsten Abschnitt untersucht.

Partielle Dokumente

Dokumententeile stellen eine wichtige Anforderung für viele Applikationen, die auf der ODA Norm beruhen, dar. Sie werden nicht nur von Hypertextsystemen benötigt, sondern beispielsweise auch für die Vergabe von Zugriffsrechten auf Ausschnitte von Dokumenten und für die Realisierung von spezialisierten Servern. Deshalb werden in den Standardisierungsgremien Anstrengungen unternommen, um die Definition von Dokumententeilen in die existierende Norm zu integrieren. Eine Grundlage dazu ist ein Entwurf von Ute und Carsten Bormann [7], der im folgenden vorgestellt und auf seine Anwendbarkeit auf Hypertextanwendungen untersucht wird.

In diesem Vorschlag zur ODA Erweiterung wird die Möglichkeit geschaffen, Unterbäume der logischen Struktur oder der Layout Struktur eines Dokuments nicht mit zu übertragen, sondern diese aus referenzierten Dokumenten zu importieren. Notwendige Voraussetzung dazu ist, daß der Empfänger diese referenzierten Dokumente besitzt oder zumindest auf diese zugreifen kann und daß darin genau diese referenzierten Teile zur Verfügung gestellt werden. Bei der Auflösung einer Referenz (Resolution) wird diese durch die entsprechenden Teile des referenzierten Dokuments ersetzt, wobei stets ein gesamter Unterbaum dieses Dokuments zusammen mit allen angefügten Inhaltsteilen übernommen wird. Da möglicherweise auch in diesem Unterbaum weitere Referenzen vorkommen können, kann diese Auflösung von Referenzen als ein Prozeß angesehen werden, der möglicherweise erst nach mehreren Schritten zum Ziel führt.

Die Referenz im unvollständigen Dokument besteht aus einem eindeutigen Identifikator des externen Dokuments und aus einem Bezeichner für das betreffende Objekt, welches, mitsamt seines Unterbaums, anstatt der Referenz in das Dokument eingebaut werden soll. Im Gegensatz dazu findet sich im referenzierten Dokument eine Tabelle, die diese Bezeichner auf die realen ODA Identifikatioren abbildet und somit eine Liste der exportierten Dokumententeile darstellt.

Ein früherer Vorschlag, der im Rahmen des PODA-2 Projekts ausgearbeitet wurde, ist im wesentlichen eine Erweiterung des obigen Vorschlags um das Konzept der "region". Eine Region ist ein zusammenhängender Teil der logischen Struktur, welche nicht notwendigerweise mit einem vollständigen Unterbaum zusammenfällt und durch zwei Referenzpunkte begrenzt wird. Eine Region kann somit einige Buchstaben, Wörter, Sätze oder Kapitel aber auch ganze Dokumententeile umfassen. Im wesentlichen beschränkt sich dieses Konzept auf Textstellen, kann aber auf beliebige, in ODA erlaubte Inhaltsarchitekturen erweitert werden.

Für die Anwendung in einem Hypertextsystem ist die Definition eines Dokumententeils als Region Voraussetzung, da sowohl der Anker als auch die referenzierten Inhalte als Dokumententeile definiert sind und damit eine Einschränkung auf gesamte Unterbäume der logischen Struktur nicht akzeptabel ist. Zwei wesentliche Eigenschaften dieses Konzepts, die sich insbesondere bei der Speicherung von Dokumenten auf zentralen Dokumentenservern nachteilig auswirken, machen ein erweitertes Modell für Dokumententeile notwendig: In den vorgestellten Konzepten wird das explizite Exportieren der Dokumententeile erzwungen. Dies widerspricht der Anforderung im Hypertextsystem benutzerspezifische Nodes und Links zu definieren und zu verwenden, da in diesem Konzept lediglich vorgegebene Hyperstrukturen realisierbar sind. Die zweite Eigenschaft der beschriebenen Konzepte ist die nicht definierte Übertragung von Dokumententeilen. Partielle Dokumente in diesem Sinne wurden dazu geschaffen, um häufig benötigte, unveränderliche Dokumententeile von der Übertragung auszunehmen und diese aus bereits gespeicherten Dokumenten zu importieren. Dies ist aber in einer Hypertextanwendung nicht brauchbar, da hauptsächlich die Übertragung und Darstellung der Dokumententeile und nicht deren Unterdrückung im Vordergrund steht. Somit sind die diskutierten Konzepte wohl als erster Schritt zur Definition der Dokumententeile brauchbar, aber nicht für die formale Beschreibung, Darstellung und Übertragung von Dokumententeilen bei der Verwendung in Hypertextanwendungen. Hierzu muß ein erweitertes Konzept entwickelt werden.

Das erweiterte Konzept für partielle Dokumente soll für verschiedene Anwendungen eingesetzt werden. Neben der bereits erwähnten Hypertextanwendung können Systeme zum Remote oder Joint Editing die partiellen Dokumente gewinnbringend einsetzen. Auch als Spezifikationsformalismus für Dokumententeile, die dann einer weiteren Verarbeitung (z.B. Verschlüsseln) unterworfen werden, soll das Konzept geeignet sein. Diese vielfältigen Einsatzgebiete benötigen ein möglichst universell verwendbares Konzept. Dies wird es mit sich bringen, daß das Konzept für einige Anwendungen zu vielfältige Möglichkeiten bietet, während andere sich noch ganz spezielle Erweiterungen wünschen werden. Auf diese Problematik wird nach der Einführung des Konzeptes näher eingegangen.

Aus den skizzierten Anwendungen ergibt sich, daß neben der Darstellung und dem Austausch eines partiellen Dokuments auch eine Beschreibung eines Dokumententeiles möglich sein muß. Diese Beschreibung muß zwischen verschiedenen Systemen ausgetauscht werden, so daß hierfür ein Austauschformat in ASN.1 [8] definieren wird.

In der ODA-Norm werden sieben verschiedene Strukturen in einem ODA-Dokument unterschieden. Es sind dies das Profil, die generische logische und die generische Layout Struktur, die jeweiligen spezifischen Strukturen, die Layout und die Presentation Styles. Unser Beschreibungsformalismus bietet die Möglichkeit solche Strukturen als Ganzes zu referenzieren.

Die generischen Strukturen und die Styles sind Mengen von Objekten. Jedes dieser Objekte hat einen eindeutigen Identifikator, der aus einer Folge von Zahlen besteht, die durch Leerzeichen getrennt werden (z.B. "2 0 1 12"). Mit Hilfe dieses Identifikators kann ein einzelnes Objekt referenziert werden.

Auch die spezifischen Strukturen bestehen aus Objekten mit einer gleichartigen eindeutigen Kennzeichnung. Entsprechend können auch Objekte aus den spezifischen Strukturen einzeln referenziert werden. Im Gegensatz zu den generischen Strukturen bilden diese Objekte jedoch Bäume. Dies kann dazu benutzt werden, um abkürzende Schreibweisen einzuführen. Durch die Referenzierung seines Wurzelobjektes kann ein ganzer Unterbaum dieser Strukturen beschrieben werden. Daneben können auch speziellere Teilbäume selektiert werden, in dem außer dem Wurzelobjekt ausgewählte Söhne referenziert werden, die zu dem partiellen Dokument gehören. Da der ODA-Identifikator eines Sohnes sich aus dem ODA-Identifikator seines Vaters und einer eindeutigen weiteren Zahl zusammensetzt, genügt es, analog zur ODA-Norm, nur die zusätzliche Zahl zur Kennzeichnung des Sohnes anzugeben. Wendet man diesen Mechanismus rekursiv an, so kann man beliebige Teilbäume spezifizieren.

Ein allgemeines Konzept für Dokumententeile muß es zusätzlich ermöglichen, auch Teile eines Inhaltsstücks darzustellen. Dazu muß für jede Inhaltsarchitektur eine Darstellung zur Identifikation von Inhaltsteilen existieren. Diese Darstellung kann nun vielfältiger Art sein. Teile von Texten können mit Hilfe eines Offsets und einer Länge angegeben werden. Dabei werden nur darstellbare Zeichen gezählt, jedoch keine Kontrollzeichen. Andere Alternativen wären das Zählen von Worten oder Sätzen. Genauso reichen die Möglichkeiten bei Rastergrafiken von einem einfachen Rechteck über beliebige geometrische Formen bis hin zu einer Maske, die über das Bild gelegt wird und es so ermöglicht, jedes denkbare Teilstück darzustellen. Bei Vektorgrafiken kann man ebenfalls beliebige geometrische Formen benutzen, oder durch einen Abzählmechanismus direkt die ausgewählten Vektoren bestimmen. In unseren Prototypen haben wir uns für die jeweils einfachste Möglichkeit entschieden, d.h für die Offset / Länge Lösung bei Texten und für die Rechtecke bei den Grafiken. In einer Norm sollte man mehrere Möglichkeiten erlauben, so daß auch der allgemeine Fall abgedeckt werden kann.

Diese elementaren Beschreibungsmöglichkeiten werden nun zu einer Liste zusammengefaßt, mit welcher beliebige partielle Dokumente beschrieben werden.

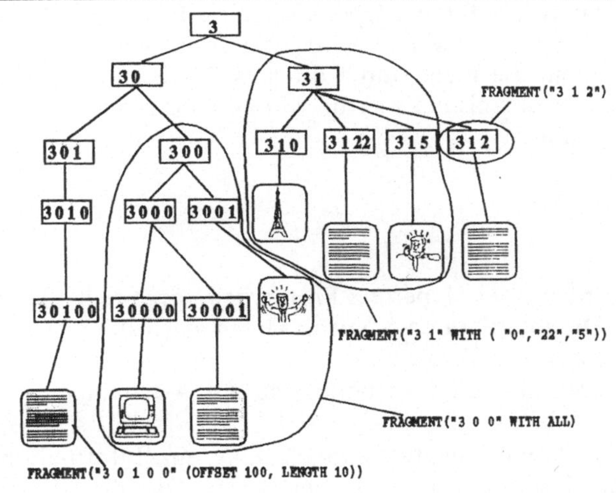

Abbildung 3. Beispiele für partielle Dokumente

Abbildung 3 zeigt einen Ausschnitt aus der speziellen logischen Struktur. Man erkennt, welche Teile der Struktur durch einen entsprechenden Ausdruck beschrieben werden - ein einzelnes Objekt mit Identifikator "3 1 2", ein ganzer Teilbaum mit der Wurzel "3

0 0", den speziellen Teilbaum mit der Wurzel "3 1" und ein Teil eines Textes, dessen zugehöriges logisches Objekt den Identifikator "3 0 1 0 0" trägt.

Zu diesen Beschreibungsmöglichkeiten wurde nun eine Darstellung in einer formalen Sprache und eine Spezifikation in ASN.1 erstellt. Dadurch ist es möglich, Beschreibungen von partiellen Dokumenten im heterogenen Systemverbund auszutauschen.

Das Austauschformat für die partiellen Dokumente ergibt sich aus dem normierten Austauschformat für ODA. Dort wird jedes Objekt einzeln kodiert und stellt dann eine 'Interchange Data Unit' dar. Die Strukturen des Dokuments werden mit Hilfe direkter Referenzen (ODA-Identifikatoren) in den 'Interchange Data Units' übertragen. Analog zu diesem Verfahren läßt sich auch ein partielles Dokument kodieren und übertragen. Dabei muß das Empfängersystem fehlende Referenzen erkennen und intern verwalten.

Werden Teile eines Inhaltsstückes kodiert, so muß zusätzliche Information übertragen werden, beispielsweise die Maske im Fall der Raster-Grafik oder die Rechteck-Koordinaten im Fall der Vektor-Grafik. Dafür werden zusätzliche Attribute zu den entsprechenden Inhaltsteilen hinzugefügt, die dann die genaue Selektion des Inhalts darstellen.

Es soll an dieser Stelle nicht unerwähnt bleiben, daß einige Anwendungen ein flexibleres Referenzierungsschema benötigen. So kann man sich vorstellen, daß zusätzlich zu einem beschriebenen Dokumententeil noch die aus diesem Teil referenzierten generischen Objekte und Styles benötigt werden. Dies kann momentan nicht beschrieben werden, ist aber auch in einem so starken Maße von der spezifischen Anwendung abhängig, daß wir entsprechende Mechanismen nicht in unser Modell für partielle Dokumente aufnehmen wollen. Sollten Anwendungen eine erweiterte Funktionalität benötigen, so schlagen wir vor, daß diese Operationen als Funktion beschrieben wird, die auf ein partielles Dokument angewandt wird. So kann das existierende Modell um zusätzliche Möglichkeiten, die nicht durch direktes Beschreiben erreicht werden können, erweitert werden. Ein Beispiel hierfür wird im Folgenden anhand unseres Hypertext-Prototyps vorgetellt.

Prototypen

In diesem Kapitel werden zwei Hypertext-Prototypen vorgestellt, die die dargestellten Konzepte umsetzen. Die internationale Norm 'Document Filing and Retrieval' (DFR) dient in beiden Ansätzen zur Verwaltung der von den eigentlichen Dokumenten getrennten Hyperstrukturen und zur Speicherung der ODA-Dokumente.

DFR spezifiziert ein Kommunikationsmodell und ein Informationsmodell. Das Kommunikationsmodell beruht auf den in der Norm 'Distributed Office Application Model' (DOAM) [9] festgelegten Richtlinien zur Definition eines Dienstes für eine verteilte Büroanwendung. Ein solcher Dienst besteht aus einem Client und einem Server beziehungsweise einem Serversystem. Zwischen diesen findet mit Hilfe der OSI-Schichten 1-6 und den 'Application Service Elements' ACSE, RTSE und ROSE [10] [11][12] ein Informationsaustausch statt, um den Dienst zu erbringen. In der aktuellen Version der DFR-Norm ist nur ein einzelner, zentraler Server vorgesehen. In Zukunft soll auch der Server auf verschiedene Knoten verteilt werden können. Es können unter anderem folgende Operationen auf den DFR-Objekten (z.B.: Dokumente, Gruppen von Dokumenten) erbracht werden: Create, Modify, Read, Copy, Move, Delete, Reserve, List, Search. Der DFR-Server kontrolliert die Zugriffsrechte, ermöglicht eine Versionsverwaltung und erlaubt mehreren Benutzern die Arbeit mit den Dokumenten. Die Abbildung 4 zeigt ein mögliches Anwendungsszenario.

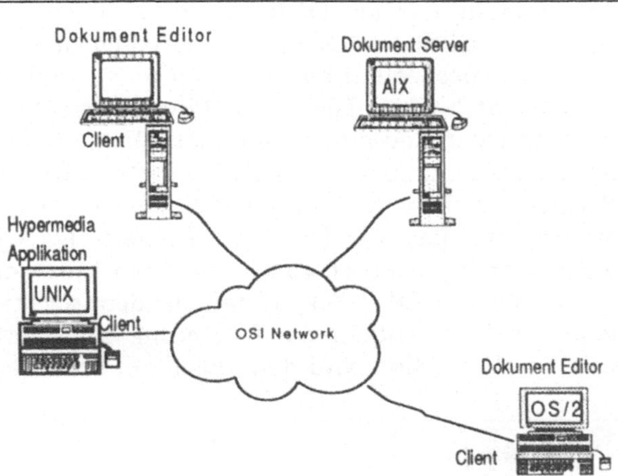

Abbildung 4.   Dokumentenbearbeitung im OSI-Netzwerk

Ein DFR-Server verwaltet Dokumente unabhängig von der zu Grunde liegenden Dokumentenarchitektur. Die Dokumente werden mit zusätzlichen Attributen versehen, die dann zum Wiederauffinden des Dokuments dienen. DFR definiert eine Menge von Attributen wie Titel, Autor, Schlüsselwörter etc., die standardmäßig zur Charakterisierung der Dokumente verwendet werden.

Unser erster Hypertext-Prototyp entstand in einer Zusammenarbeit zwischen Bull und unserer Gruppe. Bull erstellte die Hypertext-Applikation, während wir den DFR-Server und die Kommunikationsaspekte einbrachten. Das Hypertext System verwaltet Links, die zwei Nodes miteinander verbinden. Der Inhalt dieser Knoten ist ein Teil eines ODA-Dokuments, der durch zwei Referenzpunkte beschrieben wird. Ist ein Dokument in dem lokalen Hypertext System nicht vorhanden, so wird eine DFR-Operation angestoßen, die das fehlende Dokument beschafft. Die dazu nötigen Informationen - Name und Lokation des Dokuments - sind in der Hyperstruktur enthalten. Nach der Übertragung des gesamten ODA-Dokuments werden anschließend auf der lokalen Kopie die Hypertext-Operationen ausgeführt.

Der Vorteil dieses Systems ist darin zu sehen, daß die verwendeten Normen ODA und DFR nicht verändert werden mußten. Daraus ergibt sich aber auch der offensichtliche Nachteil dieser Lösung. Es werden immer vollständige Dokumente verwendet, was bei großen Dokumenten in offenen, langsamen Netzen zu langen Antwortzeiten führt. Auch muß der Client entsprechende Ressourcen zum Speichern des Dokuments haben.

Unser zweiter Ansatz beruht demzufolge darauf, nur den Teil des Dokuments vom Server zum Client zu übertragen, der auch wirklich angezeigt werden soll. Dazu muß die ODA-Norm um das oben beschriebene Konzept der partiellen Dokumente erweitert werden. Dies muß nun auch vom DFR-Server unterstützt werden, da das ODA-Dokument jetzt nicht mehr unverändert übertragen wird. Konzeptuell (d.h. gemäß DOAM) müßte dazu nun ein neuer Dienst eingeführt werden, der auf die DFR-Dokumente zugreifen und dann die Extraktionsoperation ausführen würde. Dazu ist insbesondere ein neues, nicht normiertes Protokoll zu definieren (vergl. Abbildung 5). Praktisch betrifft die Erweiterung nur die DFR-Operation 'Read'. Diese muß beim Aufruf die Beschreibung eines partiellen Dokuments erhalten und vor dem Zurücksenden des Dokuments die entsprechende Extract-Operation ausführen. Dies führt zu einer erweiterten DFR-Systemarchitektur (siehe Abbildung 5, rechter Teil). In dieser wird das Argument der Read-Operation um ein optionales Feld erweitert. Ohne dieses Feld entspricht das Argument genau dem normalen DFR-Read Argument. Für einen nicht erweiterten DFR-Client ist diese Änderung nicht sichtbar. Der erweiterte DFR-Server verhält sich konform zum Basisstandard, das erweiterte DFR-Protokoll ist bis auf die angesprochene Erweiterung identisch zum normierten Protokoll. Anhand dieses Feldes erkennt unser erweiterter DFR-Server, daß aus dem selektierten Dokument noch Teile zu extrahieren sind. Es enthält die Kodierung einer Beschreibung eines partiellen Dokuments. Diese Extraktion wird dann lokal am Server ausgeführt.

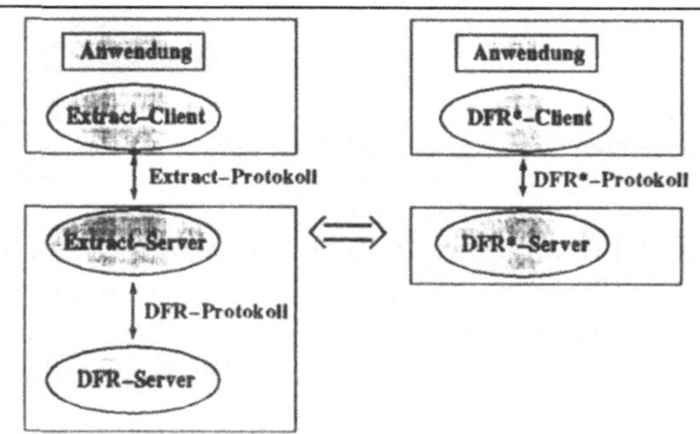

Abbildung 5.   Vergleich der Client-Server-Architekturen

Natürlich muß nun das Hypertextsystem partielle Dokumente präsentieren können. Beschränkt man sich auf bereits fertig formatierte Dokumente, so kann ein partielles Dokument unverändert zu dem entsprechenden Teil des Originaldokuments angezeigt werden. Wird das partielle Dokument in einem weiterverarbeitbaren Dokument definiert, so muß es vor der Präsentation noch formatiert werden. Dieser Formatierprozeß kann auf einem partiellen Dokument wegen fehlender Informationen nicht das gleiche Ergebnis erzielen wie auf dem ursprünglichen vollständigen Dokument. Man kann sich nun mit einem angenähertem Ergebnis zufrieden geben, oder zusätzlich zu den spezifizierten Teilen aus der logischen Struktur die dazu gehörenden Teile der Layout Struktur übertragen. Dazu benötigt man entweder ein Dokument, das beide Strukturen enthält (also in formatted-processable Form vorliegt), oder man formatiert das Dokument vor dem Extraktionsprozeß auf der Serverseite.

Zusammenfassend läßt sich sagen, daß durch Erweiterungen der Normen ODA und DFR sich der ursprüngliche Hypertext-Prototyp im Bereich der Übertragungszeiten wesentlich optimieren läßt. Die Erweiterungen sind in einer aufwärts-kompatiblen Art und Weise erfolgt, so daß sich vollständige ODA-Dokumente genauso weiterverwenden lassen wie der erweiterte DFR-Server. Es stellt sich nun die Frage, wie solche Erweiterungen in die Normierung eingebracht werden können, ohne daß sich die Normen ständig ändern müssen. Gerade im Bereich des DFR-Servers wäre es sehr wünschenswert, zusätzliche Funktionalität - beispielsweise zum Umgang mit speziellen Dokumentenarchitekturen - integrieren zu können, ohne die Normkonformität zu verlieren.

Zusammenfassung und Ausblick

Die in diesem Beitrag dargestellten Konzepte in der ODA Standardisierung sind nicht ausreichend um Hypertextanwendungen vollständig zu definieren. Dies ist aber auch nicht die Intention von ODA. Dennoch können durch den Basisstandard zusammen mit geeigneten Erweiterungen wertvolle Hilfestellungen zur Unterstützung solcher Anwendungen geleistet werden.

Bei den Erweiterungen sind im Wesentlichen die Bestrebungen zur Definition von Dokumententeilen, aber auch solche, die sich mit Datensicherheits- und Speicherungsanforderungen auseinandersetzen oder die zeitabhängige Medien wie Audio oder Bewegtbilder integrieren, als potentiell unterstützend für Hypertext/Hypermedia Anwendungen zu nennen.

Die Integration einer Vielzahl applikationsspezifischer Bestandteile in das ODA Architekturmodell, sei es aufgrund der Anforderungen aus den Bereichen Hypermedia, 'Computer Supported Cooperative Work' oder auch Dokumentenspeicherung, gefährdet allerdings den eigentlichen Zweck von ODA: eine Basis für den Dokumentenaustausch in offenen Netzen zu etablieren. Bei Weiterentwicklung der Norm in viele verschiedene Richtungen und damit verbundener zunehmender Komplexität wird keine Anwendung mehr in der Lage sein, den vollen Umfang der Norm zu unterstützen. Deshalb sind Konzepte notwendig, die aufbauend auf die existierende ODA Norm, Anwendungen unterstützen. Ein solches Konzept wurde in diesem Beitrag verfolgt.

Eine weitere Entwicklung von ODA, die Anwendungen aus unterschiedlichen Bereichen unterstützen wird, ist die Definition und die Realisierung eines 'Application Programmers Interface' (API) für ODA. Hiermit werden Möglichkeiten geschaffen, ODA Objekte in einer abstrakten Art und Weise zu bearbeiten und auf solche zuzugreifen. Inwieweit diese in der Diskussion befindlichen APIs den Anforderungen von Hypertextsystemen gerecht werden, ist allerdings erst nach Beendigung des Standardisierungsprozesses abzuschätzen. Auf alle Fälle wären solche APIs auch für andere Dokumentenarchitekturen, wie beispielsweise für SGML, denkbar. Damit wäre eine einheitliche Schnittstelle zwischen Hypermediaanwendungen und verschiedenen Dokumentenarchitekturen geschaffen.

Literatur

[1]   *CCITT Ninth Plenary Assembly: Recommendations T.411, T.412, T.414 - T.418. Open Document Architecture and Interchange Format*, CCITT Blue Book (1989), Volume VII.6, Melbourne, November 1988

[2]   *Information Processing - Text and Office Systems - Office Document Architecture (ODA) and Interchange Format*, ISO 8613 (part 1,2,4,5,6,7,8), 1989

[3]   F.Halasz, M.Schwartz, *The Dexter Hypertext Reference Model*, Proceedings of the Hypertext Standardization Workshop, NIST, 1990

[4]   *Information Technology - Document Filing and Retrieval (DFR)*, ISO/IEC DIS 10166, 1989

[5]   F.Cole, H.Brown, *ODA Modifications/Extensions*, ISO/IEC JTC1/SC 18/WG 3, 1989 1990

[6]   *MHEG - Multimedia and Hypermedia information coding Group: Coded representation of Multimedia and Hypermedia information*, Francis Kretz, SC2/WG12 MHEG Convenor, CCETT, France, Working Document for future MHEG standard, 1990

[7]   Carsten & Ute Bormann, TU Berlin, *Proposal for a First Working Draft on an Addendum to ISO 8613 on Partial Documents and External References between Documents*

[8]   *Information Processing Systems - Open Systems Interconnection - Specification of Abstract Syntax Notation One (ASN.1)*, ISO 8824, 1987

[9]   *Information Technology - Text and Office Systems - Distributed-Office-Application Model (DOAM)*, ISO/IEC 10031 (part 1 - 2), 1990

[10] *Information Processing Systems - Open System Interconnection - Service Definition for the Association Control Service Element*, ISO 8649

[11] *Information Processing Systems - Open System Interconnection - Protocol Specification for the Association Control Service Element*, ISO 8650

[12] *Information Processing Systems - Text Communication - Remote Operations*, ISO/IEC 9072 (part 1 - 2)

The Retrieval View, a Component of the Document Architecture

H.P. Frei, D. Stieger

Swiss Federal Institute of Technology (ETH) Zurich
Department of Computer Science
8092 Zurich, Switzerland

The problem addressed in this paper is the efficient retrieval of hypermedia documents in large document collections. In contrast to traditional information retrieval, both the indexing and the retrieval process have to be extended to non-textual information such as graphics, images, and speech. In addition to content related properties of the documents, structural properties are used for indexing and retrieval. Such structural properties are usually described in the logical and layout view of the document architecture and consist mainly of the logical structure, format information, and intra- and inter-document links. As structural information establishes the coherence of a document, it is an important part of a document's characterization and is, therefore, of high value when queries are evaluated. In order to facilitate access to the information necessary for the retrieval algorithms, we extended a traditional document architecture with a retrieval view. The content of this extended document architecture is created when multimedia collections are being put together, such as our test collection, consisting of patient data from an orthopedic clinic. Preliminary tests show that the quality of query results is significantly improved when information from the retrieval view is utilized by the retrieval algorithm.

1. Introduction

With the advent and increased use of hypermedia documents, it is to be expected that the number of such documents will grow. Eventually, there will be sizable hypermedia *document collections* covering specific fields. We identified such a field when putting together a test collection consisting of medical patient data: forms, written reports including graphical information, x-rays, slides, and even video tapes of operations performed. In the not too distant future, there will be many more such collections of hypermedia documents in the areas of education, advertisement, science, and the like.

The larger these collections grow, the more difficult it will be to find specific documents or parts thereof: *information retrieval (IR)* mechanisms will be necessary in order to support efficiently the retrieval of relevant information. The objective, therefore, is to develop an *information retrieval system* for hypermedia documents.

The backbone of a hypermedia document is an implementation of a directed graph or—most of the time—of several superimposed graphs. Every node of such a graph contains part of the content of the document: text, graphics, image, movie, sound, or even executable code. The arcs of the graph connect the nodes and are, therefore, responsible for the structure of the document. Typically, several arcs can originate or end in a single node. By activating the arcs, a user of a hypermedia system may move through the document and 'read' the content of the nodes he or she encounters.

In addition to the structural information, there is format and layout information pertinent to the definition of a hypermedia document. In practice, all this information is described by a so-called *document architecture*. It usually defines various kinds of *views* or models [Chr 86] under which a structured document can be seen. The document architecture also describes the *relationship* between these views or models. Examples of such views are

- the *logical view* describing the logical structure of the document, i.e. the way the different parts of the document (paragraphs, tables, figures etc.) are connected;
- the *layout view* describing the layout of the document, i.e. the way the document may be presented to the user; such a view partitions the document into pages, rectangular blocks, sound blocks etc.

Some of the classical document architectures employed at the present time, such as the *Office Document Architecture* ODA [ISO 87]—which handles structured, but linear documents—, distinguish between the logical and the layout view. The different views separate the intentions of the author (his message) from the result of the formatting process. This distinction is crucial, especially when multimedia documents are described.

Usually, information on the formatting process is encoded in the document formatter. With a *layout view* this information becomes an independent property of the document and adds considerable flexibility to its use. Furthermore, it can be used for other purposes such as to provide information for the retrieval process.

2. The Retrieval View

In order to conveniently provide pertinent information for the algorithms which search through hypermedia documents, we extended a document architecture consisting of a logical and a layout view by a third view, namely the *retrieval view*. The first two views—logical and layout—were essentially taken from ODA so that our architecture turns out to be an extension of ODA. In particular, the logical view was extended by the concept of *links* which allows the creation of hypermedia webs.

The retrieval view is composed of selected features taken from the logical and layout views as well as some additional features which are suited to describe the *content* of nodes. Special indexing methods are employed in order to determine these content-related features. As far as text is concerned, well-known indexing methods such as the use of stop lists and word stemming are used. It goes without saying, that there could be *several* distinct retrieval views for the same document collection each of which is suited to another retrieval purpose.

Figure 1 shows how the retrieval view was added to the two existing views and it gives an overview of the entire architecture of our test documents from an orthopedic clinic. Organizational links between different views within the same document are omitted for reasons of simplicity.

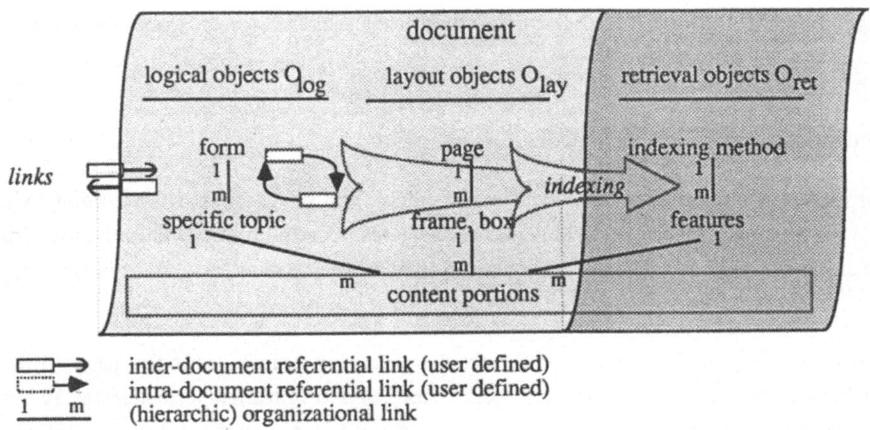

Figure 1: Extended Document Architecture

The retrieval view exclusively serves the retrieval algorithm; it can also support more effective browsing. It defines those logical and layout features vital to the retrieval algorithm in order to query and browse the collection for a specific purpose. In addition, the retrieval view contains the result of the semantically oriented indexing processes, i.e. values of selected fixed format attributes, (possibly weighted) text descriptors as well as indexing features extracted from graphical representations, images, speech and the like.

When documents are accepted by and stored in the hypermedia system, an indexing process is invoked automatically. This process runs simultaneously with the conversion of the documents into our document architecture [Sti 90]. Among other functions, it identifies formatted fields and puts them into the retrieval view. Unformatted (German) text is treated in a very simple fashion: We extract words or phrases according to a controlled vocabulary derived from the medical VESKA information structure [VES 88]. In case it becomes necessary to extend an existing information structure for a particular document this extension would become part of the retrieval view of this document. The extraction of content related features from images and audio data [Sch 90], in particular speech, is under development. For this reason the experiments presented in this paper are restricted to hypertext retrieval although the system is designed in a more general way.

The contribution of all these different features to the retrieval process is still under investigation. At the present time only those features which are obviously unsuited to information retrieval purposes are excluded from the retrieval view. These features include access privileges to certain nodes, document revision information, etc. Likewise, document properties which appear to be 'too hard' for retrieval purposes are weakened in order to make them fuzzier (exact absolute coordinates may be converted into less accurate relative coordinates in images).

In addition to the content- and structure-specific parts, the retrieval view also contains some administrative data, such as *when* and *by which algorithm* the indexing was performed. As a consequence, a retrieval algorithm may check whether a document adheres to its specifications before carrying out its task. Despite the fact that those retrieval view features taken from the other views are not stored twice, the additional data of the retrieval view needs some storage space. Our experience with MSWord® documents indicates that the storage requirement is substantial, but it hardly ever exceeds the storage space the document itself requires.

3. Extended Queries in a Hypermedia Environment

When conventional IR queries are executed, the query algorithms select documents according to indexing information consisting of formatted field values and features extracted from the unformatted parts of the documents. By means of the information contained in our retrieval view, new kinds of queries become possible:

- Elements describing the *logical structure* of the document can be included in the query. This feature means that searches can be performed in specific paragraphs or in paragraphs connected by referential links, in headers or footnotes only, in the references of a paper or in all the references of all the papers connected by inter-document links, etc.

- Elements describing the *layout* of the document can be included in the query. A human reader can often remember specific spatial references of parts of a document, i.e. how a document appeared on the screen or how it was printed on a piece of paper. Most of the time—especially with multimedia documents— the layout does not reflect the logical structure of the document. For this reason, it is important that users of a system may refer to what they perceived when they viewed the document.

These requirements constitute more than just a simple improvement of the usual retrieval activities. Novel kinds of query formulations are absolutely necessary as different 'readers' of the same hypermedia document may have seen this very document from completely different viewpoints. Therefore, they may have needs which do not arise in classical IR systems. In addition, it must be possible to include other kinds of information in the query formulation, such as graphics, image, or speech.

Classical descriptors d_i describe a text document d of a document collection D as follows:

$$d = (d_0, d_1, \dots , d_{n-1})^T.$$

In our context we deal with more general features $f_i{}^t \in F$ rather than descriptors where t stands for the media type. In this way, graphical features denote graphical primitives such as lines, arcs, circles, and the like; textual features denote classical text descriptors. In order to allow more elaborate retrieval, attributes are added to the features. Since every feature is attached to or derived from a certain (typed) object, it inherits the object's type and some of the object's attributes. Types of objects may be footnote, glossary entry, or operation report in the logical view. In the layout view pages or boxes may be object types. Examples of attributes to objects are the creation date or the name of the author in the case of logical objects, the display position or color in the case of layout objects. Since the number of such types and attributes may be very large (some of them are inherited along the object hierarchy) and the attributes may be fuzzy, this setup could be too complex for the user of the retrieval system to restrict and weight her or his subqueries. This complexity is why we attached some additional types and attributes $a \in A$ to the features, getting extended or typed features $f_{ext} \in F \times A$. This method allows the handling of types and attributes independently of each other but in a similar way to the methods by which regular features are usually handled. A weighting factor denotes the user's 'confidence' in a certain attribute; higher values signify stronger confidence. Furthermore, this method allows a second information structure to be used, operating on types and attributes.

Let us consider the following query

'Search for the medical history dated between 1985 and 1990 of all the patients with a <u>LCS knee prothesis</u> whose entrance examination was preferably performed by Dr. xyz. Only those medical histories are of interest which contain photographs of the actual operation.'

This example query clearly shows the power of typed features which—in this example—were originally derived from the logical view. The specified date (1985 to 1990) and the required photograph are unambiguous formatted fields. The name of the doctor performing the entrance examination has—though it is a formatted field—a confidence factor and becomes somewhat fuzzy. Therefore, the only text descriptor remaining might be '<u>LCS knee prothesis</u>.' An attribute 'patient number' may serve as an indirect reference to a photograph denoted by the same number. Only if this photograph exists is the query condition satisfied.

4. Retrieving Along Referential Links

As hypertext and multimedia documents became feasible only a few years ago, it is rather difficult to find real hypertext and/or multimedia collections. In order to create such material many researchers establish *'artificially' calculated links,* e.g. with the goal of breaking up a large encyclopedia into small portions which allows more efficient *browsing* facilities. Such links are a sort of *precalculated similarity* between a current node and its related nodes. However, this kind of link does not really provide additional information. Rather, such links serve as a browsing aid and can—in most cases—be established automatically.

A completely different type of link is one which is established *manually (intellectually)* in order to link related information together. In the most general case the two nodes involved do not contain visibly similar information portions which would be expressed by common features. Therefore, manually established links do indeed *add* information, usually provided by the author of the document or by attentive readers who chose to contribute to the document collection. References to further literature may be the starting point of such a link. The following paragraph shows an example:

'Our operation seems to be an adequate solution to the problems of the patient. Nevertheless, the author mentions a completely different | method without operation used in a clinic in the U.S.A. | which promises good results as well'

In most cases it would be rather difficult to retrieve the paper referenced by | method ... | by means of a classical IR system, especially when the alternative method has only few properties resulting in common features. In other words: a completely different query, consisting of features belonging to the documents to which the link points, would be necessary to pin down this alternative method. However, scientists reading a document are used to following promising references. This problem can be handled under the following conditions:

- a link from the text to the referenced document exists;
- the retrieval algorithms follow such links.

We distinguish four kinds of links which may be established in a hypermedia document, either by the author or a reader of the document. These different links can clearly be distinguished by the kind of information they transmit from the destination node to the source node:

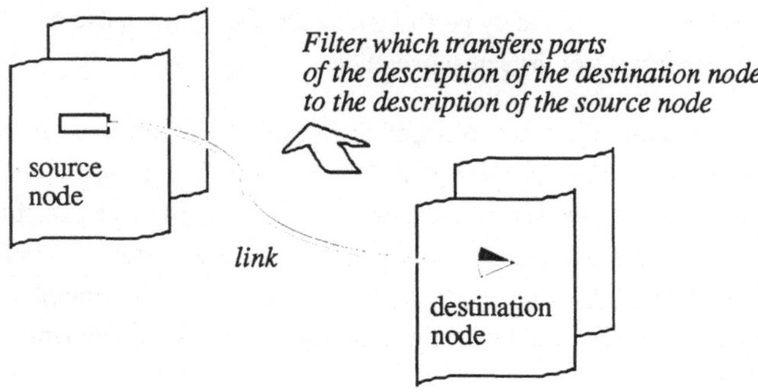

Figure 2: Link model

① *Pointing link:* no additional features are transferred to the source node.
② *Including link:* source node inherits all the features of the destination node.
③ *Related link:* source node inherits all the features of the destination node, a weighting factor determines the strength of the relation.
④ *Explaining link:* source node inherits selected features of the destination node, namely those associated with a certain subject.

A *pointing link* ① does not provide additional information for the retrieval process. The purpose of these links is to allow comfortable reading of the document (e.g. table of content, glossary, outlining etc.); we consider them of no value to the retrieval process. An *including link* ② subsumes the destination node under the source node, thus treating the destination node as if it were attached to the logical view of the source document. A *related link* ③ signifies that the node pointed to contains similar or more detailed information to the one of the source node. A weighting factor determines the strength of the relation between the two nodes. An *explaining link* ④ points to nodes which provide more information about a specific topic. This topic is defined (manually) by a few features attached to the link. These features are used to weight the link by evaluating the Retrieval Status Value (RSV) between them and the description of the destination node.

A user employing a hypermedia retrieval system may have two different needs:

- a wide *static search* in the entire collection;
- a *dynamic regional search* starting from a given document which is only possible by means of links.

The information necessary to meet these needs is contained in our retrieval view: intra-document link weights and a list of calculated inter-document link weights. In addition, the retrieval view keeps track of the browsing trail during a retrieval session, or during several logically connected physical sessions.

5. A Retrieval Experiment

When a new document is added to a hypermedia document base, links are established and maybe transferred into the retrieval view at the same time. As the medical document collection we are currently using as a test bed is still rather new and since there is no reasonable query set with its corresponding relevance assessments available, we decided to use a well known test collection for our first experiments.

The collection we employed was the Inspec test collection consisting of 2472 manually indexed documents and 65 sample natural language queries. However, the documents of the collection are written in a purely linear way and do not contain any links. For this reason we 'blew' the Inspec documents 'up' to hypertext documents by simply interpreting corresponding index terms (paragraph 'DE') as inter document links to all other documents with the same terms in this paragraph. It is to be noted that these manually assigned index terms were used exclusively to establish inter document links. In this way we got up to 158 links per document which seems both a satisfactory number of links and a reasonable way to link documents together.

Since the *pointing link* ① and the *including link* ② needs no verification we interpreted the automatically established links as *related* ③ or *explaining links* ④ . Usually, an author specifies whether a specific link is related or explaining. As such a classification is missing, we interpreted

a) all links as *related links;*
b) all links as *explaining links.*

With this assumption we carried out two experiments which we based on a reference evaluation without links.

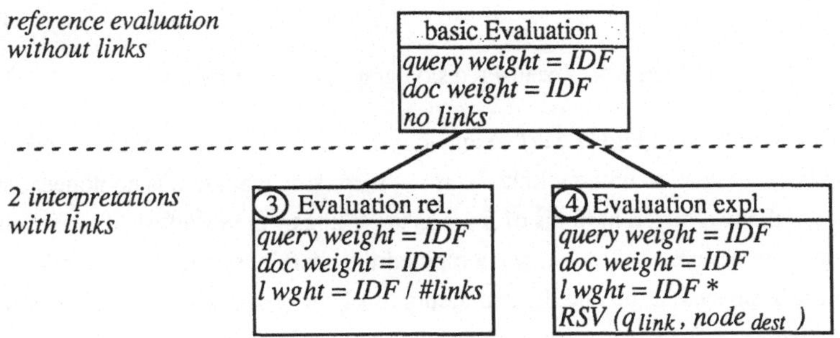

Figure 3: Experiments with INSPEC test collection

The above-mentioned *basic evaluation* serves as a reference for the two experiments. For the retrieval process both the Inspec documents and the Inspec queries were automatically indexed by applying a stop list and a modified version of Porter's stemming algorithm [Teu 89]. The term weights were set to the inverse document frequency (IDF) [Spa 72] multiplied by the number of term occurrences. As indicated in Figure 3, *evaluation rel* expands the description of a document by including all the terms from the linked documents. The weight of such a term is set to the IDF (already computed in the *basic evaluation*) divided by the number of outgoing links of this particular document. In this way we are simulating the *related links* ③ . With the *evaluation expl* the *explaining links* ④ are simulated. In this case the terms of paragraph 'DE' are interpreted as a description of the domain of discourse of the linked document. Accordingly, the weight of each link is the RSV between the above interpretation and the description of the linked document. For these experiments we chose the RSV to be the well-known cosine similarity multiplied by the IDF.

The two experiments carried out with linked documents basically follow the same lines. The description of the source document is expanded by terms which are 'pulled in' by the links. However, the weighting scheme differs for related and explaining links as pointed out above.

The results of the three experiments are plotted as Recall-Precision graphs in Figure 4.

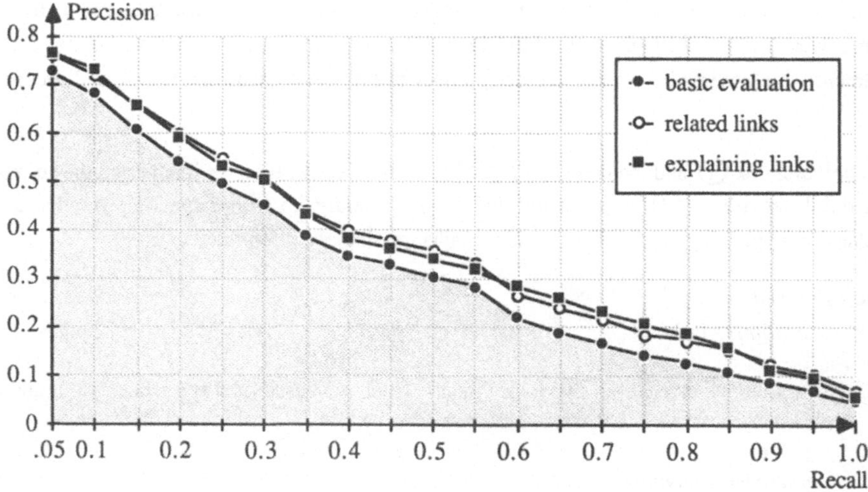

Figure 4: Recall-Precision graphs of experiments

These graphs clearly indicate a *higher performance* in the two cases where links are taken into account compared to the basic evaluation without links. It is not surprising that there is no noticeable performance difference between the two different kinds of links as these links were established by an automatic rather than an intellectual procedure. Likewise, we computed the usefulness [Fre 91] of both the related links compared with the basic evaluation and the explaining links compared with the basic evaluation. In both cases we found a *better performance* in cases of answer sets smaller than 100.

6 . Implementation and Future Work

The current test version of our IR system is implemented on a Sun® workstation and is written in Modula-2, using X-Windows. Many of the basic modules such as the associative arrays were taken from previous projects.

As stated above, our medical collection is being created at the present time. Since the conversion of the actual medical histories from paper into electronic form is rather expensive, time consuming, and requires much energy, we are still working with a rather limited document collection of roughly 2 MByte in size. It took up to four hours to scan a single patient history; we will therefore be able to convert only a small part of the 70,000 medical histories of the clinic. The data are indeed complex: in addition to the large text corpus, there are 32,000 literature references, 30,000 slides, and 200 partially commented video tapes.

Figure 6: A typical document

One of the open problems is the *immense feature set* which results when automatic indexing is performed. In such a case, relatively small document sets create rather high dimensional feature spaces. One of our objectives is to identify those features which are well suited to the retrieval algorithms.

Another problem is the *combination of retrieval results* emerging from the various kinds of information such as graphics, image, and speech. The problem which arises in this context is that these diverse kinds of information create inconsistent RSV values which have to be combined. It is rather natural that texts create many fewer features (mostly descriptors) than, for example, bit maps (in our case high resolution color images) which are rather difficult to analyze.

7 . Conclusions

In order to retrieve information from large collections of multimedia documents we introduced a *retrieval view* as a new component of the document architecture. This retrieval view contains the information necessary for the retrieval algorithms to perform their tasks.

However, it is not only the concentration of necessary data into a single view which gives us hope that the retrieval effectiveness will improve. It is the fact that information about the logical and layout structure is also included into the retrieval view which contributes to a higher performance. In particular, we showed that links can increase the retrieval effectiveness, even if the conditions are not optimal as in our experimental environment. It is to be assumed that in a real multimedia environment the increase in retrieval effectiveness will be even higher, provided the links are *manually* assigned by either the author or an authorized 'reader' of the multimedia material.

References

[Chr 86]   Christodoulakis, S. et al.: Multimedia Document Presentation, Information Extraction, and Document Formation in MINOS: A Model and a System. *ACM Trans. on Office Info Sys*, Vol. 4, No. 4, Oct 1986, pp. 345-383.

[Fre 91]   Frei, H.P., Schäuble, P.: Determining the Effectiveness of Retrieval Algorithms. *Information Processing & Management*, Vol. 27, No. 2, 1991.

[ISO 87]   ISO/DIS 8613: Information Processing - Text and Office Systems. *Office Document Architecture (ODA) and Interchange Format*, Parts 1-8, July 1987.

[Sch 90]   Schäuble, P., Glavitsch, U.: A Probabilistic Hypermedia Retrieval Model Based on Hidden Markov Models. *Proc. Workshop Intelligent Access to Information Systems*, Darmstadt, Nov. 1990.

[Spa 72]   Sparck Jones, J.: A statistical Interpretation of Term Specificity and Its Application in Retrieval. *Journal of Documentation*, Vol. 28, No. 1, March 1972, pp. 11-20.

[Sti 90]   Stieger, D.: Zur Integration von klassischen und hypermedialen Dokumenten und dem Retrieval in Datenbanken. *Hypertext und Hypermedia*, IFB 249, Springer Verlag, 1990, pp. 162-170.

[Teu 89]   Teufel, B.: *Informationsspuren zum numerischen und graphischen Vergleich von reduzierten natürlichsprachlichen Texten.* Informatik-Dissertationen ETH Zürich, Nr. 13, vdf, Zürich, 1989.

[VES 88]   *Diagnose-Schlüssel der Vereinigung Schweizerischer Krankenhäuser (VESKA).* Kommission für Statistik und Dokumentation, 3. Auflage, Aarau, 1988.

Presenting Hypermedia Concepts using Hypermedia Techniques

Peter A. Gloor
Lab for Computer Science, MIT
gloor@ptt.lcs.mit.edu

Abstract

The hypermedia technique is well suited as a basic presentation aid. In this paper the use of hypermedia for presentations is illustrated in an example of a lecture about hypermedia presented to computer science students. Advantages and disadvantages of the hypermedia presentation technique are discussed in comparison with more conventional presentation techniques. Conclusions about the strength and limitations of hypermedia for presentations are made from the practical experiences collected in the example lecture.

1   Introduction

Multimedia aids can greatly improve the quality of presentations. The combination of the computer with an adequate projection gives additional capabilities for presenting facts and algorithms that would be hard to explain with static aids such as the blackboard or slides. It was possible in the pre-computer-age to present animations and movies with film or video, but the use of the computer allows a level of interactivity that could not have been achieved with traditional means.

The hypertext concept is not only well suited for computer-aided instruction programs, on-line manuals and tutorials, technical documentations and sales presentations, but also for basic presentations in classroom teaching. Anybody who has ever tried to find a particular slide in a stack of unsorted slides in the middle of a presentation can appreciate the capability of direct access to any part of information at every point of the presentation.

For a one-semester course about hypermedia at the University of Zurich I decided to use hypermedia itself as the basic *technology* of presentation. I used the hypermedia lecture as a testbed for the use of hypermedia presentation techniques. For the hypermedia authoring system I chose Apple's HyperCard because

- Macintoshes are very popular at the university of Zurich. Every student could read the HyperCard stacks individually in parallel with the course.

- It is very easy to integrate simple animations directly into HyperCard[1] and the possibility always exists of launching other applications directly from within HyperCard.

- There are a lot of examples of hypermedia applications written in HyperCard, including computer aided instruction programs, on-line manuals and tutorials, technical documentations and sales presentations.

I had the students fill out a questionnaire about the use of hypermedia for presentations and improved my presentation system in the course of the lecture based on the students' reactions.

In the rest of the paper I will discuss briefly the advantages and disadvantages of using hypermedia techniques for presentations. I will then present my experiences with the hypermedia technology for classroom presentations. I will point out the original environment I used for the presentations and also mention the modifications I did on the original system as a reaction to the student's suggestions.

2 Use of Hypermedia for Classroom Presentations

In this paragraph a short comparison between hypermedia and traditional classroom presentation aids as slides, overhead transparencies and the blackboard will be given.

Advantages of hypermedia for presentations:

Multimedia aspects:

- *Integration of text, graphics and images:*
  Hypermedia allows for fast switching between different presentation media as text, graphics and images.

- *Integration of simulations and animations:*
  Hypermedia is well suited for the explanation of dynamic actions and processes. It is easy to integrate short animations and simulations directly into the normal presentation flow. It is not the aim of this paper to discuss, for example, algorithm animation for educational purposes (for an overview of this domain see e.g. [Bro88] and for the use of HyperCard for algorithm animation see [Glo89]).

- *Direct modification, adaptation and reuse:*
  In contrast to slides and overhead transparencies it is easy to modify a hypermedia based lecture:

---

[1] As well as in the algorithm and data structure lecture as in the operating system lecture at the university of Zurich, HyperCard animations of most of the basic algorithms have been successfully used [Glo89]. These animations were developed by students at the university of Zurich.

- in the middle of the presentation a screen can be modified by using the editing tools of the hypermedia authoring system.
- the whole presentation or parts of it can be reused easily for the construction of new presentations.

Hypertext aspects:

- *Clear structure of the whole lecture:*
  By using outlining techniques (as in MORE for the Macintosh) a clear and concise structure of the whole content of the lecture can be achieved. Ideally the whole lecture is organized hierarchically.

- *Direct access to every part of the lecture:*
  Every part of the whole lecture can be accessed directly. If the presentation is organized logically, and navigation in the hyperspace is supported by a clear structure of the document, every node of the hypertext document can be reached (in at most a few mouse clicks) by following the correct links.

- *Attractive medium:*
  The bare fact of using hypermedia as a presentation means makes the presentation more attractive for a technically interested audience.

Disadvantages of hypermedia for presentations:

- *Labor intensive preparation:*
  Contrary to a blackboard-based lecture a hypermedia presentation needs the same amount of preparation as a slide- or overhead transparency-based lecture.

- *Expensive and even immature hardware:*
  Hypermedia presentations need adequate hardware. This means that in addition to the computer some projection facilities, such as a video beamer or LCD display (to be put on an overhead projector) have to be available. Prices for LCD displays have declined considerably in the last few years, but overhead projectors for transparencies or a simple blackboard are much cheaper. Until today there are often technical problems concerning the projection quality:
  - Video beamers often whistle in operation and it is sometimes difficult to get an image which is free of flickering.
  - The refresh rate of LCD displays often is not fast enough for fast running animations. Only today the first LCD displays with color capabilites are appearing.

- *Difficulties to produce the hardcopy manuscript:*
  Hardcopy production is a general problem for hypermedia documents. The non-sequential structure can only partly be brought to a sequential medium like paper. (For my lecture I used the easiest approach by offering a printed manuscript as a sequence of screen copies and by not using scrolling fields for the presentation (about the use of scrolling fields vs. fixed pages see below).)

- *Presentation speed:*
  Hypermedia offers the same possibilities and dangers of information overload as

overhead transparencies, i.e., it is possible to present to the audience too much material in a short period of time. The elimination of this problem demands a lot of discipline and self restriction from the speaker.

3 Description of the Hypermedia Presentation System

For the purpose of the hypermedia lecture, I designed a simple authoring environment in HyperCard that is described below.

To ease the navigational task (problem of being lost in hyperspace) I used a strictly hierarchical structure (fig. 1) for the organization of the information contained in the lecture. The hierarchical structure has been directly transferred to the HyperCard implementation.

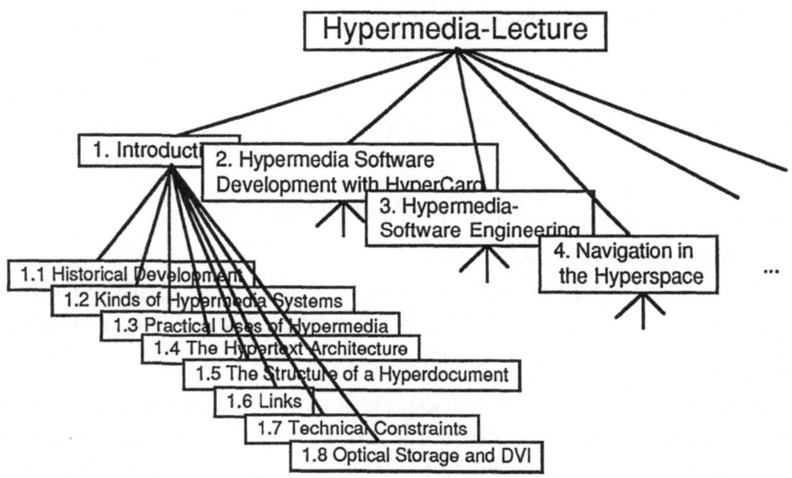

fig. 1 hierarchical structure of the hypermedia lecture

To keep the presentations as simple as possible and to avoid cluttering up the screen, I declined using unnecessary graphical elements on the screen. (This decision was criticized by the students and will be revised in the next version of the hypermedia presentation system.)

There is a node[2] at the top, from which every chapter can be reached. Each chapter is implemented as a HyperCard stack. For practical reasons, the node at the top is integrated in the HyperCard Home stack. Every text card has four navigational buttons (fig. 2).

---

[2] In HyperCard a node is called "card".

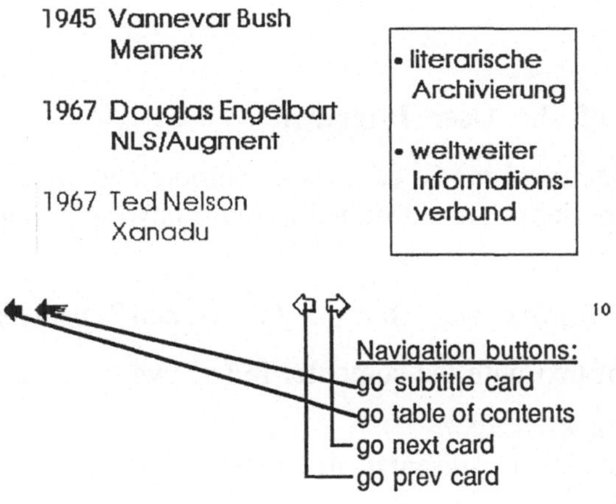

fig. 2 text card

The navigation buttons allow the direct jump to the topmost card in the home stack (table of contents), to the subtitle card of the particular chapter, to the previous card inside the chapter and to the next card inside the chapter (fig. 3)

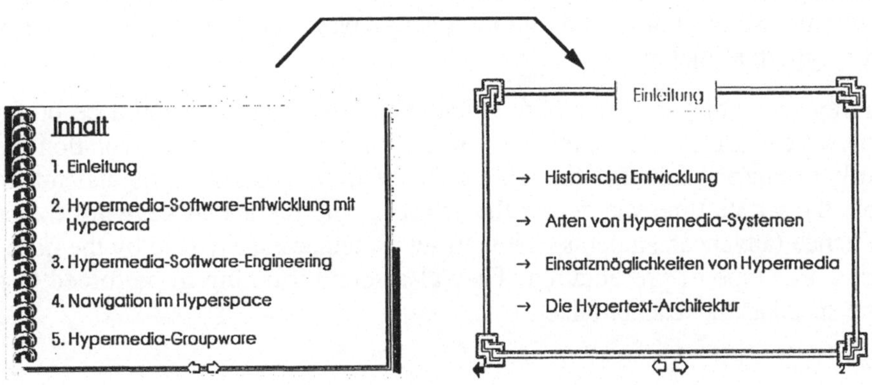

fig. 3 table of content card (left) and subtitle card (right)

If the user jumps back to the table of contents or to the subtitle card, the entry in the table of contents or the arrow in the subtitle card belonging to the original text card will be highlighted.

This mechanism works like an overview map [Tri88] and gives the reader the necessary information about where he is in the document at every location in the document.

4 Evaluation of the User Interface

In the course of the lecture I modified various components of the user interface. The focal points of my experience are subsumed in the following paragraphs:

"Typewriter" presentation vs. "screen for screen" presentation:

For the presentation of text with the computer I used two methods:

- *Typewriter like presentation*
  "Typewriter" text cards presented line after line of text with the same speed as the speaker talked. This method was appreciated because it offered a quick orientation to an easily distracted auditor.

- *Presentation card by card*
  For the most part ordinary text cards were used where all text contained in a card could be seen by the audience the whole time. This method offered a greater degree of freedom to the auditor to read ahead and to find contextual information. It was also easier for the auditor to get a global impression and to see logical connections. In addition the (small) card size forced the teacher to structure all the information into logically-connected chunks, thus fitting well to the hypertext metaphor.

In a survey the audience was asked which of the two methods would be preferred if only one were available. The audience voted clearly (9:6) for the presentation of whole text cards because it felt that the additional freedom to have contextual information available the whole time was worth the effort to find the actual keyword themselves. The audience (advanced students) felt themselves unnecessarily lead by the nose by the typewriter like type of presentation. They also found it boring to be forced to read at the same speed as the teacher talked.

Text size limited to cards vs. unlimited text in scrolling fields:

Sometimes the teacher finds it impossible to shrink or to divide logically coherent information. As a quick solution to this problem scrolling fields were used to present bigger chunks of text which could not be placed on one card. The use of scrolling fields offers the possibility of demonstrating the unity of text. But the audience soon voted against the presentation of text in scrolling fields (10:6). Text on scrolling fields proved to be hardly readable on the projection screen. In addition it was hard to maintain orientation in the scrolling text. It was found that by additional effort by the teacher, every one of those scrolling text fields could have been subdivided further in card sized text chunks, a process which would have added considerably to the readability and understandability of the content.

Non bordered text vs. bordered text:

As can be seen in (fig. 2) and (fig. 3) only the subtitle cards were bordered in the original presentation system, while for the sake of simplicity and so as not to distract the reader, the ordinary text card was not bordered. I made this decision thinking that the screen border would be frame enough. But in the survey the audience clearly opted (11:6) for borders around the text on the grounds that the frame aided in concentrating on the text and improved the structure of the card.

Black text on white background vs. white text on black background:

The audience clearly preferred (15:1) black text on white background. As [McK90] has noted, the human reading habits have been formed by printed books and newspapers which usually have the same arrangement. Knowing this I first wanted to present all text "black on white", but some people in the audience voted for a better readability of "white on black". With video beamer and LCD display it is very easy to switch between the two formats (all one has to do is to press the button "invert") so I tested both variants on the auditorium, which indeed voted clearly (as expected) for the "black on white" variant.

Use of visual effects for the navigation:

To ease the navigational task, buttons with different icons were used as principal navigational aids, the different shapes of the icons indicating the position of a text card in the chapter: E.g., the "go table of contents" button of the last card in a subchapter has a different shape than on the other text cards ("⬑"instead of "⬅"). In addition to different shaped buttons, visual effects were used as navigational aids

- to go back to the subtitle card ("visual effect checkerboard to black")
- to go to the first card of a subchapter ("visual effect iris close to grey")
- to go to the table of content ("visual effect iris open to black")
- to go from the previous card to the next card and inverse ("visual effect scroll right/left")
- to jump across chapters ("visual effect zoom open")

In the first version of the hypermedia presentation system every time a subchapter was finished and a new one started the screen flashed in order to elucidate the change.

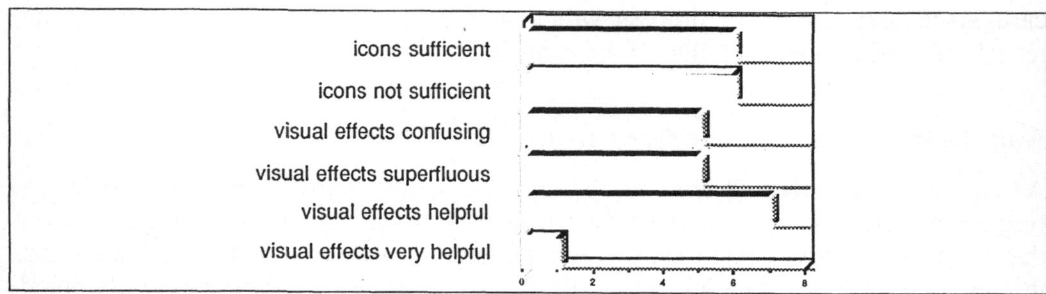

fig. 4 survey: use of visual effects for the navigation

As can be seen in (fig. 4) one half of the audience was satisfied by just using buttons for the navigation and were able to dispense with visual effects for the navigation. The bigger part of the audience found the visual effects more confusing than helpful, but the controversy mainly originated from the flash at the change between two subchapters. The other visual effects were found helpful and thus will be used also in future presentation systems.

5   The Improved Hypermedia Presentation System

After evaluating the student feedback and my own experiences I decided to integrate the following changes in a future version of my hypermedia instruction program. These changes are in a wide range consistent with the stack design guidelines for HyperCard stacks as suggested by Apple [App89][3].

Present text in card sized textual chunks
In the next version of the hypermedia lecture, text will be presented primarily on window sized cards. This presentation style forces the hypertextual organization into small chunks of information and results in a well structured organization of the whole text.

Use typewriter cards sparingly
This technique is only advantageous if a sequence of essential keywords has to be presented where the speaker whishes to emphasize every word. I will not dispense with typewriter cards totally, but I will use this technique even more sparingly.

Eliminate scrolling fields
Because of disorientation problems and reading difficulties, this presentation style will be eliminated.

---

[3]Apple applies the guidelines only to HyperCard stacks, but I claim that most of the findings mentioned in this paragraph are valid for any hypertext system used for presentation purposes.

Border screens with a simple border
The improved text card will include a plain border for better readability.

Use sounds sparingly
In the first version the typewriter cards used a typewriter sound, but this sound disturbed more than it helped in the orientation. Repeated use of the same piece of music in every introduction belongs to a radio or TV show, but not to a speaker-based presentation.

Use visual effects for navigation economically and carefully
Consistent use of visual effects for the transition to a predetermined part of the presentation seems to support the navigational task. It will be used more in the next version.

Add the capability to add hypertext notes to the hypermedia manuscript
The first version of the hyperdocument had no built in capability to add notes. Every student had to program this extension himself in HyperCard. The next version of the hypermedia manuscript will include this useful feature.

Extent of the presentation cards with annotation fields
A speaker often needs more information for his talk than just the keywords he presents to the audience. In the first version of the hypermedia lecture, notes written on paper were used; but there should be a capability to add notes to the hyperdocument that are invisible to the auditorium. On the Macintosh this means the use of an auxiliary screen that is not projected on the wall. On this auxiliary screen the notes for the speaker can appear. This is not a hardware problem (it is possible to connect several screens to a Macintosh), but this is impossible in bare HyperCard 1.2, because in HyperCard 1.2 the window size is restricted to one small sized rectangle. This extension can easily be implemented in the newer version of HyperCard (2.0) and other products (e.g., SuperCard) capable of using multiple freely sizable and locatable windows.

6   Conclusion

The primary disadvantage of hypermedia today is the immaturity of the technology. The multimedia presentation aids of today (LCD display and video projector) are usable, but improvable. Their reliability is good[4], but the projection quality is sometimes poor and does not achieve the quality of transparencies on an overhead projector.

Hypermedia offers good possibilities as a presentation aid in classroom presentations. For the presentation of plain text, slides or overhead transparencies are almost always sufficient. However, in special cases, in particular, if the presentation flow is dynamic and the sequence of the text cannot completely be prepared in advance, the use of hypermedia technologies offers clear advantages.

---

[4] I had an overhead transparencies backup of the whole lecture that I never used.

The real strength of hypermedia for presentation becomes apparent if graphics, sounds or animations need to be integrated in the presentation. It is natural that algorithm animations and simulations are used at first in lectures and presentations in the computer science domain[5], but there are numerous other application fields (e.g., geography, biology etc.) where the hypermedia technology would be extremely helpful in explaining ideas and concepts.

Acknowledgements

I would like to thank Professor Bauknecht and the other faculty members in the Computer Science Department of the University of Zurich for giving me the possibility to test my ideas in practice. I would also like to thank Chris Lindblad for the thoughtful proofreading of an earlier version of this paper.

Literature

[App89]   Apple; *"HyperCard Stack Design Guidelines"*; Addison-Wesley, Reading MA, (1989)

[Bro88]   Brown, M.H.; *"Algorithm Animation"*; MIT Press, Cambridge MA, (1988)

[Glo89]   Gloor, P.; "Algorithmen-Animation mit Hypercard"; *Proc. GI-Jahrestagung 89*, München, Informatik Fachberichte 222, Springer, Berlin, Heidelberg, New York (1989)

[Glo90]   Gloor, P. *"Hypermedia-Anwendungsentwicklung - Eine Einführung mit Hypercard Beispielen"*; Teubner, Stuttgart (1990)

[McK90]   McKnight, C.; Dillon. A.; Richardson, J.; "Problems in Hyperland? A Human Factors Perspective"; *Hypermedia*, Vol.1, No. 2; Autumn, (1990)

[Sax90]   Saxer, K.H.; Gloor, P.; "Navigation im Hyperraum: Fish Eye Views in HyperCard"; *Hypertext und Hypermedia*, Proceedings of the Hypertext/Hypermedia Fachtagung der SI/GI; Basel, 6. April 1990, Informatik Fachberichte 249, Springer, Berlin, Heidelberg, New York (1990)

[Tri88]   Trigg, R.H.; "Guided Tours and Tabletops: Tools for Communicating in a Hypertext Environment"; *ACM Trans. on Office Information Systems*, Vol. 6., No. 4.; October (1988)

---

[5]See footnote 1.

Ein Ansatz zur Organisation von Hyperdokumenten

Jörg M. Haake, Jörg Hannemann & Manfred Thüring
Institut für integrierte Publikations- und Informationssysteme (IPSI)
Gesellschaft für Mathematik und Datenverarbeitung (GMD)
Postfach 104326
6100 Darmstadt

e–mail: haake@darmstadt.gmd.dbp.de

Zusammenfassung

In diesem Beitrag wird ein Ansatz zur Strukturierung von Hyperdokumenten vorgestellt. Die Forschung zum Textverstehen hat gezeigt, daß sowohl die Orientierung in einem linearen Text als auch dessen Verständnis entscheidend durch Gestaltungsmittel beinflußt wird, die es Lesern erlauben, eine *kohärente* mentale Repräsentation des Textinhalts aufzubauen. Zu Beginn dieses Beitrags werden daher die Kohärenzmerkmale linearer Texte diskutiert und auf Hyperdokumente übertragen. Anschließend werden vor dem Hintergrund eines Designkonzeptes Strukturierungsmittel für die Produktion von Hypertexten beschrieben, die ein Autor einsetzen kann, um die Kohärenzbildung seiner Leser zu fördern. Dabei wird von drei funktionell verschiedenen Komponenten eines Hyperdokumentes ausgegangen, die wir als Inhalts–, Organisations– und Präsentationskomponente bezeichnen. Abschließend werden die vorgestellten Strukturierungskonzepte anhand eines Beispieldokuments illustriert.

1 Einleitung

Das Medium Hypertext stellt Autoren innovative Gestaltungsformen zur Realisierung von elektronischen Dokumenten zur Verfügung. Neben den traditionellen Maßnahmen der hierarchischen Gliederung, Reihung und Bezugnahme auf andere Dokumentteile (Fußnote, Verweis, Zitat) bieten sich neue Möglichkeiten der Textorganisation, die von linearen Strukturen prinzipiell verschieden sind und Autoren eine wesentlich größere Flexibilität als bisher erlauben. Darüberhinaus lassen sich Hyperdokumente einfacher und vielfältiger erweitern als konventionelle Dokumente, indem andere, bereits bestehende Texte, Graphiken oder Bilder in das Hypertextnetz eingebunden werden. Dies führt nicht nur zu faszinierenden, multimedialen Dokumenten, sondern erhöht auch wesentlich die Wiederverwendbarkeit und Mehrfachnutzungsmöglichkeit der in einem Hypertextnetz enthaltenen Elemente. Außerdem ist es möglich, alternative Sichten auf einen Hypertext zu definieren, so daß ein Autor ein und dasselbe Dokument verschiedenen Leserkreisen auf unterschiedliche Weise zugänglich machen und deren spezifischen Bedürfnissen und Fähigkeiten flexibel anpassen kann.

Die Erhöhung der Freiheitsgrade für Entwurf und Nutzung von Dokumenten ist allerdings nicht nur mit Vorteilen verbunden, sondern kann auch Probleme für die Verfasser und Leser von Hypertexten mit sich bringen. Auf Seiten der *Autoren* sind eine Reihe von Aufgaben zu bewältigen, die über den Rahmen konventionellen Schreibens hinausgehen. So müssen Verfasser von Hypertexten beispielsweise entscheiden, welche Informationen sie in *verschiedenen* Hypertextknoten ablegen und welche sie in *einem* Knoten zusammenfassen, welche Knoten sie durch Links zueinander in Beziehung setzen und wie sie die Knoten (und ggf. die Links) ihres

Netzes benennen. Besonders die mit der Namensgebung verbundenen Anforderungen werden als kognitive Mehrbelastung (*cognitive overhead*) empfunden [Conklin, 1987] und können dazu führen, daß die Funktionalität eines Hypertextsystems nur eingeschränkt genutzt wird [Trigg, Irish, 1987].

Beobachtungen dieser Art deuten darauf hin, daß Autoren im Umgang mit Hypertextsystemen häufig überfordert sind. Eine Hauptursache hierfür könnte das Fehlen von Richtlinien für die Gestaltung von Hyperdokumenten sein. Im Gegensatz zu Autoren konventioneller Texte können sich die Verfasser von Hypertexten kaum an bewährten Konventionen orientieren und sind bei der Gestaltung ihrer Dokumente weitgehend auf sich allein gestellt. Dies mag in entscheidendem Maße dazu beitragen, daß die Qualität bislang produzierter Hyperdokumente vielfach zu wünschen übrig läßt [Brown, 1990].

Mangelnde Qualität von Hyperdokumenten hat unmittelbare Konsequenzen für deren *Leser*. Diese müssen vor allem mit zwei Erschwernissen rechnen, denen sie in linearen Dokumenten kaum ausgesetzt sind. Zum einen kann es aufgrund der Komplexität und des Netzcharakters des Dokuments sehr schwierig werden sich zurechtzufinden; d.h. ein Leser weiß häufig nicht mehr, wo er sich im Netz befindet, wohin er sich sinnvollerweise bewegen soll, oder wie er ein bestimmtes Ziel erreichen kann [Edwards, Hardman, 1989]. Diese Formen der *Desorientierung* konstituieren das sog. Navigationsproblem, das [Conklin, 1987] als *getting lost in hyperspace* charakterisiert. Zum anderen fällt es Lesern häufig schwer, ein Hyperdokument als eine zusammenhängende Einheit, als einen kohärenten Text, zu begreifen. Hierfür scheinen in erster Linie zwei Ursachen verantwortlich zu sein:

- Je unspezifischer die Bezeichnungen von Knoten in einem Hypertextnetz sind, und je weniger Links in diesem Netz ihrer inhaltlichen Bedeutung entsprechend benannt werden, desto geringer ist die Wahrscheinlichkeit, daß Leser in der Lage sind, die vom Autor intendierten *semantischen Relationen* zwischen den einzelnen Knoten zu rekonstruieren. In diesen Fällen ist zu erwarten, daß Leser Mühe haben, über "Knotengrenzen" hinweg Zusammenhänge zwischen den Inhalten verbundener Knoten herzustellen.

- Je ausgedehnter ein Hypertextnetz ist, und je spezifischer und heterogener die Inhalte seiner Knoten sind, desto geringer ist die Wahrscheinlichkeit, daß Leser einen *Gesamtzusammenhang* zwischen diesen Knoten erkennen und sie einem gemeinsamen inhaltlichen Thema unterordnen können[1]. Darüberhinaus fehlen in Hypertextnetzen zumeist erkennbare, benannte *Untereinheiten*, die – analog zu einer Gliederung linearer Texte – verdeutlichen, welche inhaltlichen Schwerpunkte bestehen und wie diese strukturell zusammenhängen. Unter derartigen Bedingungen fällt es nicht nur schwer, das übergreifende Thema eines Hypertextes zu identifizieren, sondern auch die Struktur nachzuvollziehen, die der inhaltlichen Auseinandersetzung mit diesem Thema zugrunde liegt.

Die bislang diskutierten Probleme für Autoren und Leser machen deutlich, daß sowohl der Entwurf von Hyperdokumenten strukturierter unterstützt als auch deren Qualität entscheidend verbessert werden muß. Von zentraler Bedeutung hierfür sind Gestaltungsmöglichkeiten, die: (a) auf Seiten der Autoren die Flexibilität des Dokumententwurfs möglichst erhalten sowie den kognitiven Mehraufwand durch geeignete Strukturierungs– und Organisationsformen weitgehend reduzieren und (b) auf Seiten der Leser die Navigation und ge-

---

1. Vergleiche hierzu auch die von [Marshall, Irish, 1989] diskutierten Probleme der Fragmentarisierung und Dekontextualisierung in Hypertexten.

zielte Suche nach Informationen erleichtern sowie das Verstehen und das Erfassen "knotenübergreifender" Zusammenhängen nachhaltig unterstützen.

2 Kohärenz: Eine Grundlage für Verstehen, Navigieren und Gestalten

Welche Ursachen den Schwierigkeiten zugrunde liegen könnten, denen sich Leser und Autoren von Hypertexten ausgesetzt sehen, wird deutlich, wenn man das Verstehen und Verfassen *linearer* Texte etwas genauer betrachtet.

Das Erfassen der Bedeutung eines Textes wird in neueren kognitionspsychologischen Ansätzen als die Konstruktion einer kohärenten (zusammenhängenden) mentalen Repräsentation des Textinhalts charakterisiert, die sich auf der Basis des Vorwissens des Rezipienten vollzieht [vgl. z.B. Schnotz, 1988]. Zwei Arten der Kohärenzstiftung spielen hierbei eine Rolle [van Dijk, Kintsch, 1983]. Auf der Ebene der **lokalen Kohärenz** werden Verbindungen zwischen einzelnen Sätzen oder Teilsätzen hergestellt; d.h. zwischen den Satzinhalten werden kausale, temporale, modale oder andere semantische Relationen etabliert. Die so entstehende mentale Repräsentation bezeichnet man als **Mikrostruktur** [Kintsch, van Dijk, 1979]. Auf der Ebene der **globalen Kohärenz** werden ausgehend vom erkannten Thema des Textes lokal kohärente Einheiten zu allgemeineren Aussagen, sog. Makropropositionen, zusammengefaßt. Verschiedene Makropropositionen haben wiederum inhaltliche Gemeinsamkeiten, die sie auf einer übergeordneten Ebene miteinander verbinden. Auf diese Weise bildet sich eine hierarchische **Makrostruktur** [Kintsch, van Dijk, 1979], auf deren oberster Ebene schließlich das Thema des Textes angesiedelt ist – d.h. alle Aussagen haben mit dem Thema zu tun und sind dadurch global miteinander verbunden. Aus dieser Perspektive erscheint Textverstehen als ein aktiver, fortschreitender Konstruktionsprozeß, der zum Erkennen lokaler und globaler Zusammenhänge beim Lesen führt und in einer hierarchischen Repräsentation des Textes mündet.

Der Aufbau einer kohärenten mentalen Repräsentation ist nicht nur von entscheidender Bedeutung für den Verstehensprozeß, sondern auch für die Navigation innerhalb eines linearen Textes. Da ein solcher Text hierarchisch organisiert ist, erschließt sich seine Struktur einem Rezipienten sukzessiv. Mit fortschreitendem Lesen erkennt er nicht nur, *welche* Inhalte der Text enthält und wie diese zusammenhängen, sondern er erfährt auch, *wo* sich diese Inhalte im Text befinden. Parallel zur semantischen Repräsentation kann ein Leser somit eine räumliche Struktur des Textes aufbauen, indem er rezipierte Textinhalte mit lokalisierbaren Textstellen verknüpft. Solch eine "kognitive Karte" scheint in erster Linie allgemeineren Makropropositionen topologische Informationen zuzuordnen und ist deshalb häufig nicht sehr detailliert. Aus dieser Perspektive kann sie als eine räumliche Repräsentation angesehen werden, die beschreibt, auf welche Weise die Makrostruktur linearisiert ist, und die die Basis für die Navigation in einem linearen Text darstellt. Leser benutzen derartige topologische Informationen vor allem, wenn sie gezielt nach Informationen suchen – sei es, wenn sie beim Lesen zurückblättern, um bereits Gelesenes nochmals anzuschauen, oder sei es, wenn sie in einem früher gelesenen Buch Informationen zu einem bestimmten Thema nachschlagen.

Da die Kohärenz eines Textes eine unabdingbare Voraussetzung für den Aufbau einer angemessenen mentalen Repräsentation darstellt, bestimmt sie in entscheidendem Maße, inwieweit ein Leser den Text versteht und sich in ihm zurechtfindet. Autoren setzen deshalb eine Vielzahl sprachlicher Mittel ein, um ihren Lesern bestimmte Zusammenhänge zu verdeutlichen. Auf der Ebene der *lokalen Kohärenz* spielen hierbei sog. **Kohärenzrelationen** eine entscheidende Rolle [Halliday, Hasan, 1976], zu denen neben den verschiedenen Formen von Referenz, Substitution und Ellipsis vor allem die Konjunktionen einer Sprache zählen. Sie dienen dazu, semantische Beziehungen zwischen Sätzen oder Teilsätzen zu spezifizieren und Lesern die Wahrnehmung jener lokalen Zusammenhänge zu ermöglichen, die ein Autor intendiert. Das Erkennen *globale Kohärenz* kann mit Hilfe von **Strukturierungsmaßnahmen**, wie z.B. dem Aufteilen in Kapitel und Unterkapitel, erleichtert werden. Hierzu fassen Autoren (lokal kohärente) Sätze in Abschnitte zusammen, ordnen sie einem Kapitel unter und benennen das Kapitel so, daß die thematische Gemeinsamkeit der in ihm enthaltenen Information möglichst gut charakterisiert wird. Hierdurch geben sie ihren Lesern wertvolle Hinweise auf höhere, übergeordnete Einheiten, an denen sich der Aufbau einer Makrostruktur orientieren kann. Lokale und globale Mittel der Kohärenzstiftung wirken somit zusammen, um Rezipienten Verständnis und Orientierung in einer Weise zu ermöglichen, die der jeweilige Verfasser für angemessen hält.

Wie verhält es sich nun mit der Kohärenz von *Hyperdokumenten*? Zum einen sind *in ihren Knoten* lineare Texte enthalten, für die die bereits genannten Kohärenzkriterien gelten und die deshalb im folgenden nicht weiter diskutiert werden. Zum anderen bestehen auf der Ebene der Knoten und Links (der **Netzebene**) Zusammenhänge, für die in Anlehnung an die Kohärenz linearer Texte ebenfalls lokale und globale Kohärenzmerkmale unterschieden werden können: *Lokale Kohärenz* liegt vor, wenn zwischen den Inhalten jeweils zweier Knoten eine semantische Beziehung besteht. *Globale Kohärenz* liegt vor, wenn sich die Inhalte verschiedener Knoten – analog zu verschiedenen Absätzen im Kapitel eines linearen Textes – auf ein gemeinsames Thema beziehen.

Wollen die Autoren von Hyperdokumenten ihren Lesern in vergleichbarem Maße beim Rezipieren und Navigieren helfen wie die Verfasser linearer Texte, so sehen sie sich mit einem neuartigen Problem konfrontiert: Während sie bei der Gestaltung der *Knoteninhalte* ihres Hypertextes auf vertraute Konventionen zurückgreifen können, stehen ihnen weder bewährte Richtlinien zur Vermittlung von Zusammenhängen auf der *Netzebene* zur Verfügung, noch bieten ihnen hier existierende Hypertextsysteme eine ausreichende Unterstützung: Lokale Kohärenz zwischen Knoten kann zwar durch das Einfügen eines Links *angezeigt* werden, doch genügt dies nicht, um einem Leser mitzuteilen, *welcher Art* der durch den Link etablierte Zusammenhang ist. Hierzu bedarf es getypter Links, die entsprechend ihrer Funktion benannt sind. Die Schaffung globaler Kohärenz zwischen Knoten wird derzeit noch weniger unterstützt. Um auf der Netzebene thematische Gemeinsamkeiten sowie deren Über– und Unterordnungsbeziehungen anzuzeigen, sind Strukturierungsmittel erforderlich, die beliebige Knoten zu Teilnetzen zusammenfassen und es erlauben, flache Hypertextnetze hierarchisch zu strukturieren.

Für die Entwicklung geeigneter Autorensysteme ist ein Ansatz zur Organisation von Hyperdokumenten notwendig, der Möglichkeiten zur Erstellung kohärenter Hyperdokumente bereitstellt, wie sie durch das Hypertextautorensystem SEPIA unterstützt werden soll [Streitz, Hannemann, Thüring, 1989] [Haake, Schütt, 1990] [Streitz, 1990]. In den nun folgenden Kapiteln werden Vorschläge zur Gestaltung von Hyperdokumenten entwickelt, die darauf abzielen, die Schaffung lokaler und globaler Kohärenz auf der Netzebene zu ermöglichen. *Dokumente*, in denen diese Vorschläge umgesetzt sind, sollten Lesern das Verstehen und Navigieren erleichtern, und *Systeme*, die entsprechende Gestaltungsmittel bieten, sollten die kognitive Mehrbelastung vermindern, der Autoren bei der Entwicklung von Hypertextnetzen ausgesetzt sind.

3 *Ein Vorschlag zur Organisation von Hyperdokumenten*

Ein Hyperdokument besteht aus einer Menge von Hypertextobjekten: Knoten und Links. Knoten präsentieren Informationseinheiten, während Links dem Transfer des aktuellen Standort im Hyperdokument zu einem Zielpunkt dienen. Wir unterscheiden atomare Knoten, die nicht weiter unterteilt sind, und zusammengesetzte Knoten (*composite nodes*, vgl. [Halasz, 1988]), die eine Menge anderer Knoten und Links referenzieren und damit zusammenfassen. Links können entweder vollständige Knoten verbinden oder vom Teil eines Knotens auf den Teil eines anderen Knotens zeigen (*embedded links*). Knoten und Links lassen sich nach ihren Eigenschaften weiter differenzieren, so daß eine Menge von Knoten- und Linktypen entsteht und ein Hyperdokument als ein Graph aus Knoten und Links verschiedener Typen aufgefaßt werden kann.

Ein Leser rezipiert ein Hyperdokument, indem er ausgehend von einem Einstiegsknoten durch Traversieren eines von dort ausgehenden Links dessen Zielknoten erreicht. Um die hierbei auftretenden Orientierungsschwierigkeiten zu vermindern, wurden in der Vergangenheit bereits einige Lösungsansätze entwickelt: [Conklin, 1987] unterscheidet organisatorische Links, die durch hierarchische Strukturen die Navigation unterstützen sollen, von referentiellen Links, die beliebige Strukturen bilden können. Die *tree items* in KMS [Akscyn, Mc Cracken, Yoder, 1988] entsprechen Conklins organisatorischen Links. Die Aggregierung von Knoten wird durch *composite nodes* [Halasz, 1987], wie z.B. *fileboxes* in NoteCards [Halasz, Moran, Trigg, 1987], ermöglicht. Um dem Leser vordefinierte Lesewege durch das Hyperdokument anbieten zu können, wurden verschiedene Arten von Pfaden entwickelt [Zellweger, 1989], wie z.B. die *guided tours* von [Trigg, 1988]. Zur integrierten Präsentation einer Menge von Knoten sind sogenannte *table tops* vorgeschlagen worden [Trigg, 1988] [Marshall, Irish, 1989].

Die oben genannten Ansätze zielen in erster Linie auf eine Verminderung von Navigationsschwierigkeiten ab, bieten jedoch kaum eine Hilfe für die Erstellung "verständlicherer" Hyperdokumente. Will ein Autor seinen Lesern verbesserte Verstehens- und Navigationsmöglichkeiten bieten, so muß er Bedingungen schaffen, die das Erkennen lokaler und globaler Kohärenz fördern. Hierzu benötigt er Strukturierungsmittel, die über eine bloße Navigationshilfe hinausgehen und die Konstruktion *kohärenter* Hyperdokumente erlauben. In Anlehnung an [Hannemann, Thüring, Streitz, 1990] sowie [Thüring, Hannemann, 1991], die einen theoretischen Rahmen zur Erfassung des Schreibprozesses bei linearen Texten vorschlagen, charakterisieren wir die Erstellung von Hyperdokumenten als **Design-Problem** und modellieren Mittel der Dokumentstrukturierung als **Design-Objekte**. Die Benutzung dieser Objekte wird durch eine Reihe von **Design-Regeln** festgelegt, die u.a. bestimmen, auf welche Weise Design-Objekte miteinander kombiniert werden können.

Die Lösung eines komplexen Designproblems wird durch die Dekomponierung in Unterprobleme erleichtert. Analog zu den drei Feldern der klassischen Rhetorik – Inventio, Dispositio und Elocutio – können bei der Erstellung von Hyperdokumenten drei derartige Unterprobleme unterschieden werden:

- die *Generierung* und die *Auswahl* relevanter Informationen unter pragmatischen Gesichtspunkten (z.B. Leserkreis und Thema),

- die *Ordnung* der selektierten Informationen bezüglich Zusammengehörigkeit (Gruppierungsaspekt) und Lesefolge (Anordnungsaspekt) sowie

- die *Präsentation* der geordneten Informationen.

Die Bearbeitung dieser Aufgabenfelder erfordert Designobjekte, die es ermöglichen, die semantischen und pragmatischen Entscheidungen bezüglich Inhalt und Strukturierung des Dokuments syntaktisch umzusetzen. Hierzu unterscheiden wir drei funktionell verschiedene Komponenten eines Hyperdokumentes:

1. Die **Inhaltskomponente** besteht aus Designobjekten, die auf die Vermittlung von Fakten abzielen. Dieses sog. Inhaltsnetz besteht aus Inhaltsknoten und Inhalts-Links (vgl. Kapitel 3.1). Die Inhaltsknoten enthalten die textuellen, graphischen etc. Anteile des Dokuments, und die Inhalts–Links zeigen Zusammenhänge an, die zwischen jeweils zwei Knoten bestehen. Damit ein Autor diese Zusammenhänge repräsentieren kann, müssen ihm Links zur Verfügung gestellt werden, die die semantischen Beziehungen zwischen den verbundenen Knoten spezifizieren und Lesern das Herstellen *lokaler* Kohärenz erleichtern.

2. Die **Organisationskomponente** enthält Designobjekte, die der Organisation des Dokuments dienen, und ermöglicht somit die Umsetzung der pragmatischen Entscheidungen, die aufgrund des Themas und in Hinblick auf einen bestimmten Leserkreis getroffen wurden. Sie besteht aus einer Hierarchie von Strukturknoten und Struktur–Links, die einen Ausschnitt der Inhaltskomponente entweder als ungeordnetes Netz oder als hierarchisch geordnete Abfolgebeziehung präsentieren (vgl. Kapitel 3.2). Durch die Hierarchisierung und Linearisierung des Inhaltsnetzes (z.B. in Form von Lesepfaden) beeinflussen die Organisationsstrukturen entscheidend den Aufbau von Makrostrukturen und steuern auf diese Weise die Bildung *globaler* Kohärenzbeziehungen.

3. Die **Präsentationskomponente** ordnet jedem Designobjekt eine adäquate Darstellungssart zu. Hyperdokumente bieten vielfältige Darstellungsarten der im Dokument repräsentierten Information (vgl. Kapitel 3.3). Hierdurch wird das klassische Feld der Elocutio erheblich erweitert.

Im weiteren Verlauf dieser Arbeit wird die Beschreibung der Designobjekte im Vordergrund stehen, während Designregeln nur beispielhaft vorgestellt werden.

3.1 *Die Inhaltskomponente*

Die *Inhaltskomponente* eines Hyperdokuments dient sowohl der Repräsentation als auch der Darstellung seiner Inhalte. Hierfür stehen als Designobjekte verschiedene Arten von **Inhaltsknoten** und **Inhalts–Links** zur Verfügung.

Jeder **Inhaltsknoten** trägt einen Namen und präsentiert Informationen in Form von Fakten, Aussagen, Behauptungen etc. Hierzu dienen einerseits **atomare Inhaltsknoten** (z.B. Text- oder Graphikknoten), die nicht weiter unterteilte, homogene Daten beinhalten, und andererseits **zusammengesetzte Inhaltsknoten**, die die Information mehrerer atomarer Knoten als Einheit darstellen (siehe z.B. die Argumentationsstruktur in Kapitel 4). Die Informationen in zusammengesetzten Inhaltsknoten stammen entweder aus atomaren Knoten, die im Hyperdokument selbst gespeichert sind, oder aus externen Informationsquellen (z.B. online DBMS). Der Zugriff auf externe Quellen und die Abbildung ihrer Datenformate auf die interne Struktur des Hypertextsystems ist Aufgabe der **atomaren Knoten mit externen Quellen**, die den von außen kommenden Informationen eine Hypertextstruktur aufprägen.

Inhalts–Links sind gerichtet und verknüpfen jeweils zwei Inhaltsknoten, indem sie von einer "Quelle" (*source*) auf ein "Ziel" (*destination*) weisen. Sie müssen durch den Leser aktiviert werden und entsprechen den *cold links* in [Catlin, Bush, Yankelovich, 1989]. Die semantische Beziehung zwischen Quelle (Q) und Ziel (Z), kann als eine *Abhängigkeit* zwischen Q und Z charakterisiert werden, wobei das Ziel in Bezug auf die Quelle eine spezifische Aufgabe erfüllt. Liefert Z beispielsweise den theoretischen Hintergrund für Q, so *erklärt* das Ziel die Quelle, enthält Z hingegen ein Resumee von Q, so wird die Quelle durch das Ziel *zusammengefaßt*. Zur Beschreibung derartiger Abhängigkeiten entwickeln wir zur Zeit eine Taxonomie von Links, die sich an der von [Mann, Thompson, 1987] vorgeschlagenen Rhetorical Structure Theory (RST) orientiert und drei unterschiedliche Abstraktionsebenen unterscheidet:

♦ Ebene 1: Auf der obersten Ebene trägt der Link keinerlei Bezeichnung und repräsentiert damit das größtmögliche Maß an Abstraktheit für eine Verbindung.

♦ Ebene 2: Auf der mittleren Ebene bilden die Namen der Links eine Reihe relativ globaler, semantischer Beziehungen in Form von Verben ab. Beispiele:
  (a) "Z diskutiert Q".
  (b) "Z illustriert Q".

♦ Ebene 3: Auf der untersten Ebene werden diese semantischen Beziehungen verfeinert, indem sie entweder durch spezifischere Verben redefiniert oder durch Attribute ergänzt werden. Beispiele:
  (a) Für Redefinition: "Z diskutiert Q" wird ersetzt durch "Z kritisiert Q".
  (b) Für Attributergänzung: "Z illustriert Q" wird ergänzt durch "graphisch".

Die Taxonomie zielt auf eine Erhöhung der lokalen Kohärenz auf der Netzebene ab, und sollte deshalb sowohl für die Verfasser als auch für die Rezipienten von Hyperdokumenten hilfreich sein. Auf Seiten des *Autors* sollte sie zu einer Verminderung der kognitiven Mehrbelastung beitragen, da sie ihn in zweierlei Hinsicht unterstützt. Die *Bezeichnungen* der Links bieten eine Hilfe bei der Analyse der semantischen Beziehungen zwischen jeweils zwei Knoten [Conklin, Begeman, 1988]. Der Autor kann sich an den vorgeschlagenen Namen orientieren und braucht lediglich zu entscheiden, welcher Link am angemessensten ist. Die *Ebenen* der Hierarchie ermöglichen ihm ein flexibles Vorgehen in Abhängigkeit von der aktuellen Arbeitssituation (vgl. hierzu ebenfalls [Conklin, Begeman, 1988]). Ist dem Autor z.B. bei der Vergabe eines Links noch nicht klar, welche der zahlreichen Beziehungen, die zwischen Quelle und Ziel bestehen mögen, er seinen Lesern mitteilen soll, so kann er zunächst eine Verbindung auf Ebene 1 herstellen, sie später durch einen Link der zweiten Ebene ersetzen und diesen zu einem noch späteren Zeitpunkt auf Ebene 3 verfeinern.

Setzen Autoren die Taxonomie zur Beschreibung semantischer Zusammenhänge ein und wählen darüberhinaus passende Knotenbezeichnungen, so führt dies zu einer Erhöhung der Lesbarkeit von Hypertextnetzen, da Einheiten der Form "Quelle – Link – Ziel" jeweils einfache Sätze bilden. Beispiel: "Searle's argument – criticized by – systems reply" (vgl. Abbildung 3). Für die *Leser* eines Hyperdokumentes sollte dies zu einer erheblichen Erleichterung beim Verstehen und Navigieren führen. Damit dieser Effekt erzielt werden kann, müssen Autoren die Inhaltskomponente ihres Dokuments so gestalten, daß das Erkennen lokaler Kohärenz vereinfacht und die Bildung einer Makrostruktur unterstützt wird. Hierzu ist es notwendig, *Designregeln* zu entwickeln, die die effektive Verwendung von Designobjekten spezifizieren, wie z.B.: "Bezeichnungen von Knoten und Links sollten so gewählt werden, daß sie den durch den Link konstituierten Zusammenhang zwischen Quelle und Ziel in Form eines einfachen Satzes möglichst genau beschreiben."

3.2 Die Organisationskomponente

Die Organisationskomponente eines Hyperdokumentes dient der Erhöhung der *globalen* Kohärenz. Hierfür stehen als Designobjekte Strukturknoten und Struktur–Links zur Verfügung. Sie unterstützen die Ordnung (Gruppierung und Anordnung von Knoten und Links) und Präsentation von Bestandteilen des Hyperdokumentes (siehe Teilaufgaben des Designprozesses von Hyperdokumenten in Abschnitt 3).

Strukturknoten fassen eine Menge von Knoten und Links des Inhaltsnetzes bezüglich einer thematischen Gemeinsamkeit, einer rhetorischen Zielsetzung und einer antizipierten Leserschaft zusammen (Gruppierungsaspekt). Sie werden als *composite nodes* im Sinne von [Halasz, 1988] realisiert, indem sie die entsprechenden Objekte referenzieren. Jeder Strukturknoten trägt einen Namen und enthält einen vom Autor definierten Inhaltsknoten als Startknoten. Jedes Hyperdokument besitzt als Einstiegspunkt einen Strukturknoten, den sog. Primärstrukturknoten. Um nach diesem Einstieg das weitere Verhalten seiner Leser zu steuern, stehen einem Autor zwei verschiedene Arten von Strukturknoten zur Verfügung:

- **Sequenzierungsknoten** sind vom Autor vorstrukturierte Lesereihenfolgen durch das Inhaltsnetz, wobei sich die Reihenfolge und Auswahl der präsentierten Inhaltsknoten am Thema und an der antizipierten Leserschaft orientiert. Jeder Sequenzierungsknoten stellt somit einen Zugang zu einem geordneten Teilnetz der Inhaltskomponente dar. Dies bedeutet, daß das Inhaltsnetz nur gemäß der im Sequenzierungsknoten definierten Anordnung traversiert werden kann. Die Anordnung seiner Elemente wird durch Sequenzierungs-Links (siehe unten) definiert. Sequenzierungsknoten können außerdem weitere Sequenzierungsknoten enthalten, so daß eine hierarchische Schachtelung möglich ist (z.B. zur Mehrfachnutzung organisierter Teilnetze in verschiedenen Exkursen). Wird ein Sequenzierungsknoten als Bestandteil eines übergeordneten Sequenzierungsknotens traversiert, so führt dies zur Einfügung seines Inhalts in den Lesepfad des übergeordneten Knotens.

- **Explorationsknoten** enthalten ebenfalls ein Teilnetz der Inhaltskomponente, welches aber nicht durch Sequenzierungs-Links geordnet ist. Es gibt also *keine* vordefinierte Lesefolge. Stattdessen ermöglichen die existierenden *Inhalts-Links* des Teilnetzes die Traversierung. Der Inhalt eines Explorationsknotens kann nur durch einen Struktur-Link von einem Lesepfad aus erreicht werden. Die Traversierung endet immer am Ausgangspunkt des Explorationsknotens im Lesepfad, so daß der Pfad an der unterbrochenen Stelle weiterverfolgt wird.

Während Sequenzierungsknoten den Leser auf eine vom Autor bestimmte Lesefolge festlegen, bieten ihm Explorationsknoten völlige Zugriffsfreiheit auf Teile des Inhaltsnetzes und ermöglichen ein selbstgesteuertes Explorieren der entsprechenden Inhaltskomponente des Hyperdokuments. Beide Knotenarten werden durch weitere Designobjekte in Form sog. **Struktur-Links** ergänzt, die die Abfolgebeziehungen in oder zwischen Strukturknoten definieren (Anordnungsaspekt). Struktur-Links sind gerichtet, ermöglichen jedoch immer das Zurückgehen zum Vorgängerknoten (*back button functionality*). Ebenso wie Inhalts–Links können sie benannt werden, wobei es dem Autor freigestellt ist, entweder bereits bestehende Namen aus dem Inhaltsnetz zu übernehmen oder die vorne erwähnte Taxonomie der Link–Bezeichnungen zu verwenden.

Wir unterscheiden zwei unterschiedliche Arten von Struktur–Links:

- **Sequenzierungs-Links** dienen dem Aufbau von Organisationsstrukturen, die dem Inhalt eines Sequenzierungsknotens eine Präsentationsabfolge zuordnen. Sie dienen zur Definition von azyklischen

Abfolgen (lineare Sequenz, Reihung, Aufsplittung eines Lesepfades in mehrere Möglichkeiten u.a.m) und können sowohl zwischen Inhaltsknoten als auch zwischen Inhalts- und Sequenzierungsknoten etabliert werden. Es handelt sich bei ihnen immer um Links von ganzen Knoten auf ganze Knoten.

♦ **Explorations-Links** dienen beim Traversieren eines Pfades dem Zugang zu einem Explorationsknoten. Sie sind immer in einen Inhaltsknoten eingebettet und verweisen auf den Startknoten des Explorationsknotens. Ihre Erzeugung führt automatisch dazu, daß aus jedem Inhaltsknoten, der im Explorationsknoten enthalten ist, zur Quelle des Explorations-Links im Sequenzierungsknoten zurückgesprungen werden kann (automatische Generierung von "back" oder "return" Links).

Tabelle 1 gibt für jede Kombination der Instanzen von Knotenklassen die Klasse der zulässigen Struktur-Links an. Leere Einträge bedeuten, daß keine Struktur-Links zwischen den entsprechenden Knoten instanziiert werden können.

Tabelle 1: Mögliche Struktur-Links zwischen Instanzen von Knotenklassen

Quelle \ Ziel	Inhaltsknoten	Sequenzierungsknoten	Explorationsknoten
Inhaltsknoten	Sequenzierungs–Links	Sequenzierungs–Links	Explorations–Links
Sequenzierungsknoten	Sequenzierungs–Links	Sequenzierungs–Links	
Explorationsknoten			

Innerhalb von Sequenzierungsknoten kann die Art der Abfolgebeziehungen von Knoten und Links, auch **sequencing model** genannt, in Anlehnung an [Zellweger, 1989] nach sequentiellen, verzweigenden und bedingten Pfaden differenziert werden. Sequentielle Pfade präsentieren eine Menge von Knoten in einer linearen Sequenz. Verzweigende Pfade enthalten Verzweigungen, an denen der Leser den weiteren Weg auswählen muß. Bedingte Pfade können u.a. andere Pfade enthalten (geschachtelte, hierarchische Pfaddekomposition) oder dynamisch aufgrund der vorherigen Leseraktionen den weiteren Pfad bestimmen. Hierbei wird die Binnenstruktur des Sequenzierungsknoten charakterisiert, ohne daß die Strukturen der über- oder untergeordneten Sequenzierungsknoten berücksichtigt werden. So kann zum Beispiel ein linearer Pfad einen anderen Sequenzierungsknoten enthalten, der wiederum als verzweigter Pfad organisiert ist.

Ein Beispiel für eine Organisationsstruktur zeigt Abbildung 1. Hier wird der Sequenzierungsknoten-3 zweimal als Modul wiederbenutzt. Ausgehend von einem Inhaltsknoten in Sequenzierungsknoten 3 ist ein Explorationsknoten über einen Explorations-Link erreichbar (und damit auch indirekt von den beiden übergeordneten Sequenzierungsknoten 1 und 2).

Die oben genannten Designobjekte stehen Autoren zur Gestaltung ihrer Dokumente zur Verfügung und ermöglichen ihnen eine Strukturierung, die über die semantischen Beziehungen des Inhaltsnetzes hinausgeht. Durch die Benutzung von Strukturknoten und –Links wird es möglich, Inhalte unter thematischen Gesichtspunkten zusammenzufassen und damit die globale Kohärenz zu steigern. Eine strukturierte Darstellung des Hyperdokuments zusammen mit sinnvollen Bezeichnungen von Knoten und Links sollte Leser beim Aufbau einer Makrostruktur unterstützen und ihr Verständnis sowie ihre Orientierungsfähigkeit erhöhen. Für Autoren erleichtert das Angebot von stärker strukturierten Objekten die Organisation komplexer Dokumente. Der Einsatz derartiger Objekte kann– ähnlich wie bei der Inhaltskomponente – durch die Entwicklung von Designregeln noch weitergehend spezifiziert werden.

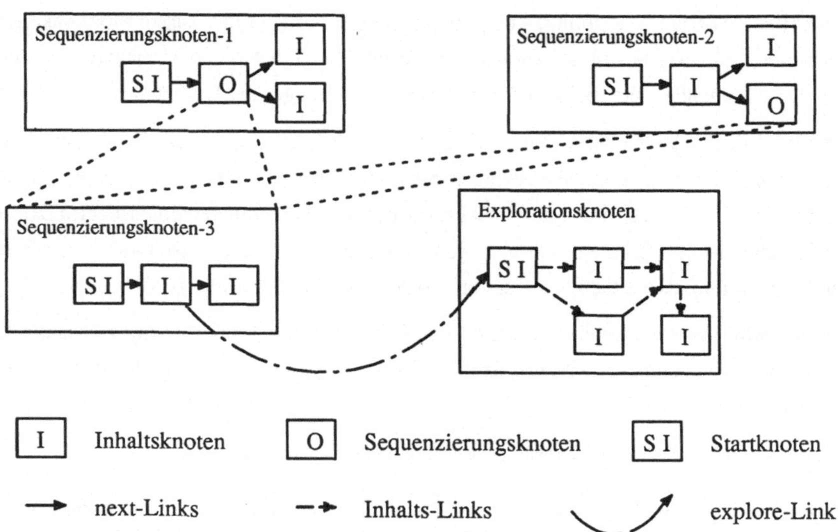

Abb. 1   Beispiel einer Organisationsstruktur. Die gestrichelten Linien verdeutlichen das Enthaltensein von Sequenzierungsknoten in übergeordneten Sequenzierungsknoten.

3.3   Die Präsentationskomponente

Die Präsentation eines Hyperdokumentes ist eine wichtige Komponente des Designs. Prinzipiell können Hypertextobjekte auf zwei Weisen dargestellt werden: Die graphische Präsentation stellt Knoten ikonisiert und Links als Kanten oder Pfeile dar, während die textuelle Präsentation den Inhalt eines Knotens mit den hierin integrierten Links (z.B. *Buttons*) anzeigt. Bei der Darstellung von Hypertextnetzen lassen sich drei Modi (**presentation models**) unterscheiden:

♦ Die **textuelle (knotenzentrierte) Darstellung** zeigt den Inhalt von Inhaltsknoten mit den von ihm ausgehenden bzw. bei ihm endenden Inhalts-Links (z.B. in Form von *Buttons*). In diesem Modus nimmt der Leser nur einen begrenzen Ausschnitt aus dem Dokument wahr, da ihm kein Überblick auf der Netzebene geboten wird.

♦ Die **graphische (graphbasierte) Darstellung** visualisiert ein Teilnetz, indem Knoten zusammen mit jenen Links angezeigt werden, deren Quelle und Ziel jeweils *vollständige* Knoten sind. Darüberhinaus signalisiert ein besonderes Knoten–Ikon, ob *eingebettete* Links von einem Knoten ausgehen bzw. an ihm enden. Diese Links sind einem Leser nur dann zugänglich, wenn er in die textuelle Darstellung wechselt.

♦ Die **kombinierte Darstellung** erlaubt die Mischung der o.g. Darstellungsformen. Es können somit gleichzeitig sowohl Teilnetze graphisch angezeigt, als auch die Inhalte von Inhaltsknoten dargestellt werden (wie zum Beispiel in *Table Top*-Knoten [Trigg, 1988]).

Ausschnitte eines Hyperdokumentes müssen bei der Traversierung von Inhaltsnetzen und von Explorationsknoten dargestellt werden. Ihnen ist keine Abfolgebeziehung zugeordnet, und sie können in allen drei o.g. Modi präsentiert werden. Auch bei Sequenzierungsknoten muß ein Teilnetz (als Inhalt) dargestellt werden, allerdings unter Berücksichtigung der Abfolgebeziehung. Die Kombination von möglichen Abfolgebeziehungen (*sequencing model*) und Präsentationsarten (*presentation model*) kann zur weiteren Klassifikation von Sequenzierungsknoten verwendet werden, woraus sich neun grundlegende Klassen ergeben, die in Tabelle 2 illustriert sind.

Tabelle 2: Beispiele für die Klassen von Sequenzierungsknoten

Sequencing m./ Presentation m.	sequentieller Pfad	verzweigter Pfad	bedingter Pfad
textuell	z.B. jeweils nur ein Knoten geöffnet oder Expansion wie in *Guide* (*replacement button*) [Brown, 1987]	z.B. ein geöffneter Knoten mit alternativen *next*-Buttons wie bei Guided Tours in *NoteCards* [Trigg, 1988]	z.B. ein geöffneter Knoten mit alternativen *next*-Buttons
graphisch	z.B. Browser für festgelegte Traversion einer Knotensequenz	z.B. Graphbrowser, d.h. graphische Netzdarstellung des Teilnetzes durch ikonisierte Knoten und deren Links	z.B. Graphbrowser mit Berechnung dynamischer Pfade
kombiniert	z.B. *Table Top* mit festgelegter linearer Lesefolge	z.B. *Table Top*-artige Darstellung von Netzstruktur und geöffneten Knoten	z.B. dynamischer *Table Top*

4   *Ein Beispiel*

Die Anwendung der im dritten Kapitel spezifizierten Designobjekte wird anhand des folgenden Szenarios erläutert: Stellen wir uns vor, daß ein Journalist einen Artikel schreibt, der sich mit der Diskussion "Können Computer denken?" befaßt, die durch [Searle, 1980] ausgelöst wurde. Das Ziel des Journalisten besteht darin, den Originalartikel, die Beiträge der anderen Diskussionsteilnehmer und Hintergrundinformationen zusammen mit einer Analyse der hierin enthaltenen Argumente dem Leser als Hyperdokument zugänglich zu machen. Einen Ausschnitt der Struktur dieses Hyperdokuments zeigt Abbildung 2, deren oberer Teil die Organisationskomponente und deren unterer Teil die Inhaltskomponente darstellt.

Der Journalist beginnt das Dokument mit einer Einführung, gefolgt von einem Überblick über die Diskussionsstruktur und einem Resümee. Die drei Knoten (*Introduction, Overview, Resume*) bilden die oberste Ebene des Dokuments und geben einem Leser eine erste, globale Übersicht. Sie werden deshalb in einem Primär-Sequenzierungsknoten zusammengefaßt, der als Startknoten des Dokuments dient. Da der Journalist sicherstellen will, daß der Leser die einzelnen Inhalte in einer sinnvollen Reihenfolge rezipiert, organisiert er den Primär-Sequenzierungsknoten als *linearen* Pfad.

Der Knoten *Overview* verdeutlicht die Diskussionsstruktur anhand eines graphischen, verzweigten Pfades. *Searle's Argument* ist der Startknoten des Pfades. Von ihm gehen drei alternative Wege aus, die jeweils einen speziellen Diskussionsstrang repräsentieren und eine sinnvolle Abfolge der Diskussionsbeiträge sicherstellen. Jeder Inhaltsknoten von *Overview* enthält den entsprechenden Originalbeitrag als Text. Von dem Inhaltsknoten *Searle's Argument* gehen im Beispiel zwei Explorations-Links aus, von denen einer zu *SHRDLU* und der andere zu *Searle's Argument Structure* führt. *SHRDLU* enthält eine Reihe strukturierter Hintergrundinformationen zu dem Programm SHRDLU (Winograd), während *Searle's Argument Structure* eine detaillierte Analyse der Argumentationsstruktur Searles repräsentiert. Zur Darstellung dieser Struktur orientiert sich der Journalist an einem von [Toulmin, 1958] vorgeschlagenen Schema und erstellt ein Teilnetz bestehend aus

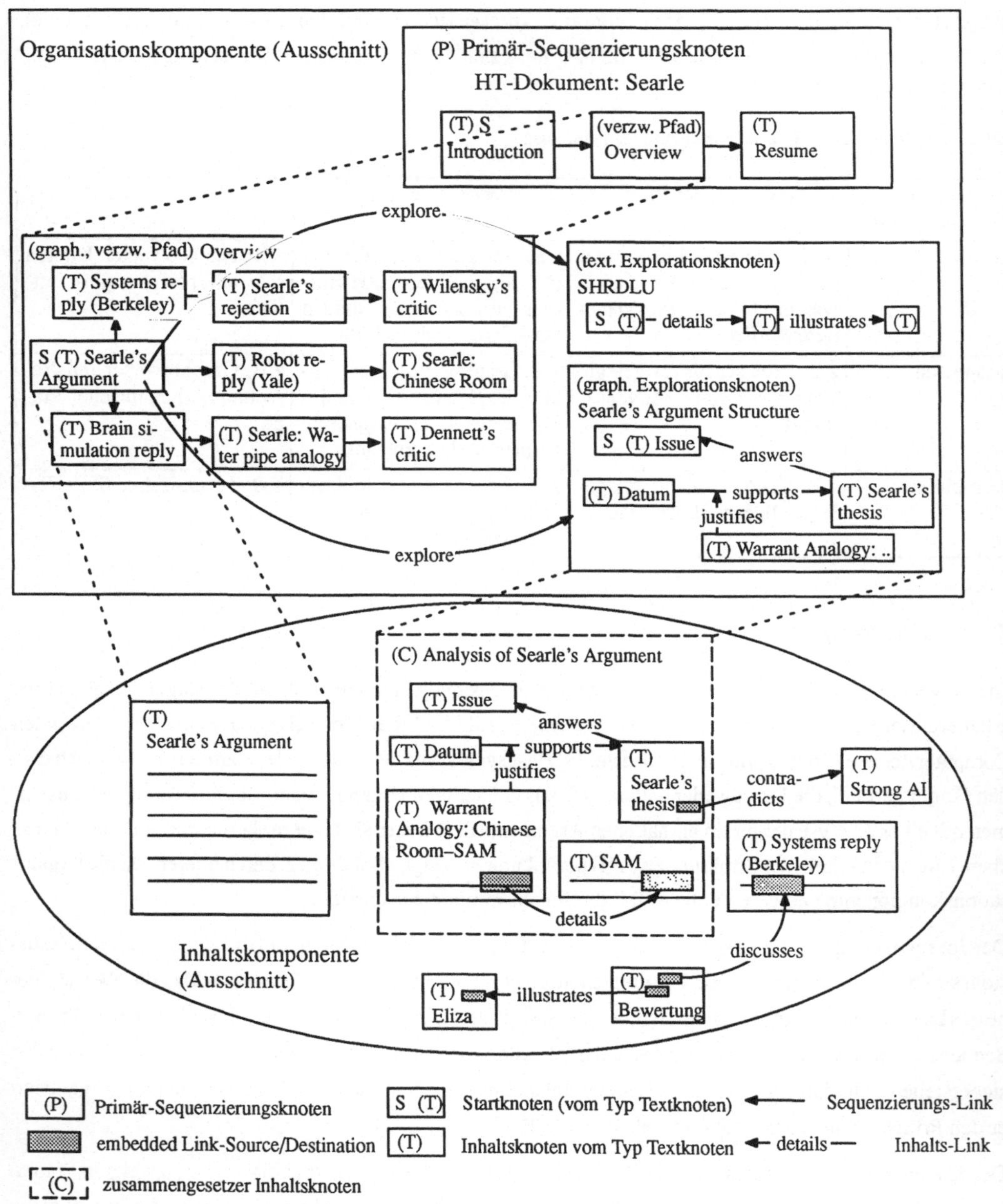

Abb. 2 Beispiel für einen Ausschnitt eines Hyperdokuments. Die gestrichelten Linien zeigen für ausgewählte Knoten die Enthaltenseins-Beziehung in Strukturknoten an.

Knoten, die Aussagen enthalten (Issue, Datum, Claim, Warrant), und Links, die diese Aussagen zueinander in Beziehung setzen (supports, justifies, answers). Da mit diesem Teilnetz keine eindeutige Lesefolge verbunden ist, entscheidet er sich, es im Organisationsanteil als graphischen Explorationsknoten *Searle's Argument Structure* zu modellieren. *SHRDLU* hingegen gestaltet er als textuellen Explorationsknoten.

Die Inhaltskomponente enthält den von Searle verfaßten Artikel (*Searle's Argument*) sowie weitere vom Journalisten selbst erstellte Knoten und Links. Hierzu zählt u.a. der zusammengesetzte Inhaltsknoten *Analysis of Searle's Argument*, dessen Inhalt in der Organisationskomponente durch den entsprechenden Explorationsknoten referenziert wird. Darüberhinaus enthält die Inhaltskomponente atomare Inhaltsknoten, die in der Organisationskomponente nicht benutzt werden (z.B. *Strong AI*, *Eliza*), vom Leser jedoch durch das Browsen im Inhaltsnetz erreicht werden können.

Abbildung 3 zeigt einen Screendump des Hyperdokumentes, dessen Struktur wir in Abbildung 2 illustriert haben. Dieses Dokument wurde auf einer Sun-Workstation mit Hilfe des HyperNeWS-Toolkits[2] erstellt. Der Screendump zeigt den Zustand des Bildschirms, nachdem ein Leser im graphischen Überblicksknoten *Overview* den Knoten *Searle's Argument* geöffnet hat und dem daraus abgehenden Explorations–Link zum Explorationsknoten *Searle's Argument Structure* gefolgt ist.

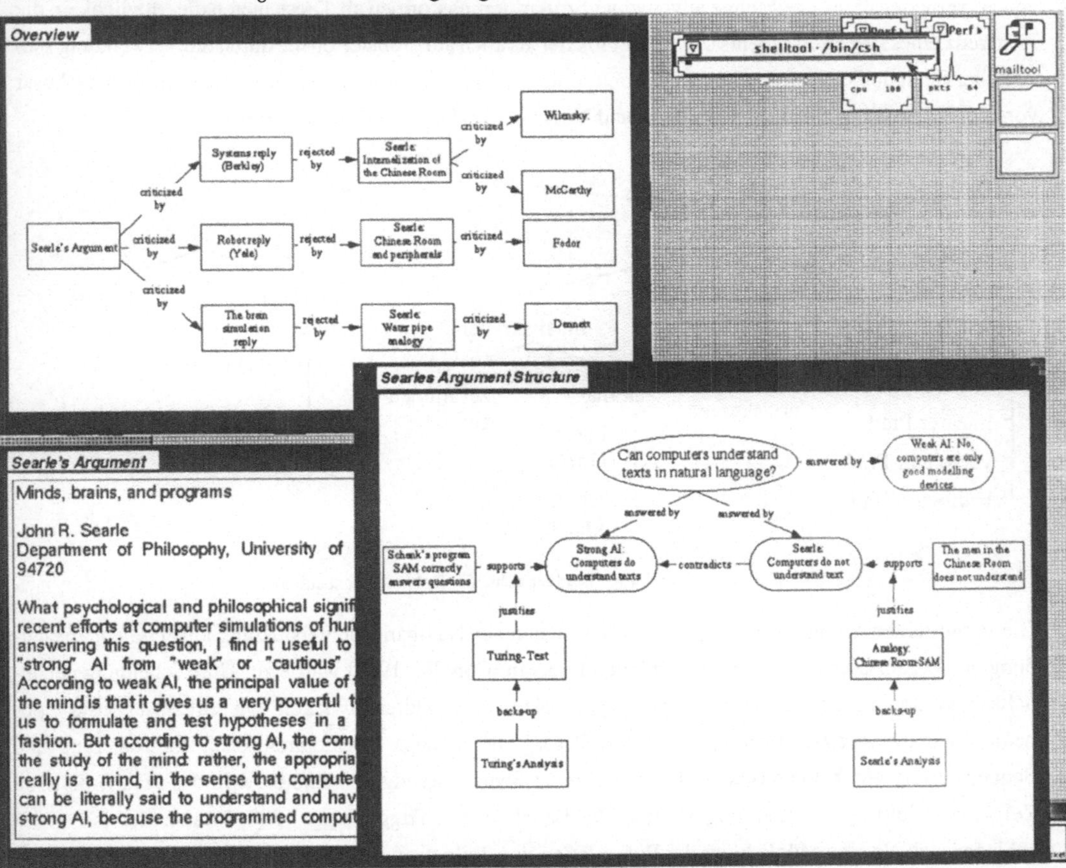

Abb. 3 Screendump eines Hyperdokuments

____

2. HyperNeWS ist ein Produkt des Turing Institute, George House, 36 North Hanover Street, Glasgow G1 2AD, UK.

5   *Zusammenfassung und Ausblick*

Die von uns vorgeschlagenen Designobjekte können in Form einer Klassenhierarchie zusammengefaßt werden (siehe Abbildung 4). Die hierarchische Ordnung drückt die Spezialisierung übergeordneter Klassen durch die ihnen untergeordneten Klassen aus. Die Eigenschaften der Oberklassen werden jeweils durch Vererbung von den Unterklassen übernommen und ggf. redefiniert oder ergänzt.

Bisher wurden keine anwendungsunabhängige Dokumentstrukturen entwickelt, die geeignet sind, die Vorteile des Hypertextkonzeptes mit der Lösung von Problemen wie *Verstehensschwierigkeiten, Desorientierung* und *Cognitive Overhead* zu verbinden. Lediglich in [de Young, 1990] wird über die Beschreibung anwendungsabhängiger Dokumentstrukturen hinaus die Identifikation globaler Strukturierungsprinzipien gefordert. Unser Ansatz stellt einen Schritt in diese Richtung dar und leitet aus Überlegungen zur Kohärenz von Hypertexten eine erste Menge allgemeiner Strukturierungsformen ab. Diese bieten die Möglichkeit, die Kohärenz eines Hyperdokuments sowohl auf lokaler als auch auf globaler Ebene durch die Verwendung spezifischer Designobjekte zu erhöhen. Hierdurch sollten nicht nur die Autoren entlastet, sondern auch die Leser von Hyperdokumenten bei der Rezeption und Navigation effektiv unterstützt werden.

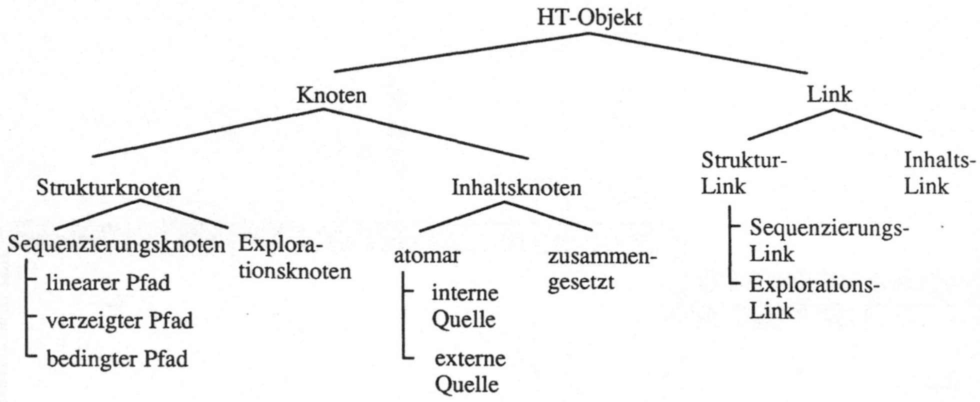

Abb. 4 Klassenhierarchie der Dokumentbestandteile

Die vorgestellten Designobjekte bauen auf Konzepten zur Navigationsunterstützung auf: Die Unterscheidung von organisatorischen und referentiellen Links in [Conklin, 1987] wurde zur Unterscheidung der Inhalts- und Organisationskomponente von Hyperdokumenten weiterentwickelt. Die Organisationskomponente nutzt *Composites* [Halasz, 1987] und Organisations-Links zur hierarchischen Aggregierung und Sequenzierung von Knoten bzw. Teilnetzen. Bei der Sequenzierung von Knoten wird das Pfadmodell von Zellweger [Zellweger, 1989] aufgegriffen. Die Tabletops von Trigg [Trigg, 1988] [Marshall, Irish, 1989] schlagen sich als eine Möglichkeit der Präsentation von Teilnetzen nieder.

Der von uns vorgeschlagene Ansatz kann als Ausgangspunkt für vier wünschenswerte Entwicklungen im Bereich Hypertext angesehen werden:

1. Es stellt die notwendigen Mittel bereit, um nicht-lineare Strukturen kohärent aufzubauen. Damit kann der Autor sein Dokument z.B. so organisieren, daß der notwendige Kontext (durch Einbettung in einen Lesepfad) für den Leser immer verfügbar ist. Der Ansatz sollte deshalb die Basis für Dokumente sein, die Problemen wie *getting lost in hyperspace* konsequent entgegenwirken.

2. Die Charakterisierung von Dokumentstrukturen ist eine Voraussetzung für das Design von Autoren-
   und Leseumgebungen. Sie ist auch die Grundlage für die Entwicklung von Unterstützungsmechanismen, die Strukturinformationen nutzen, um Autoren beim Strukturieren und Reorganisieren zu helfen.

3. In Abhängigkeit vom Anwendungsfall läßt sich die Designobjekthierarchie flexibel erweitern. Anwendungsspezifische Designobjekte können durch Redefinition oder Unterklassenbildung hinzugefügt
   werden. Diese Erweiterung beschreibt einen anwendungsspezifischen Dokumenttyp (analog zu
   SGML-Dokumenttypdefinitionen für strukturierte Dokumente [Bryan, 1988]).

4. Eine explizite Formulierung von Dokumentstrukturen erlaubt die systematische Erfassung von Eva-
   luierungsergebnissen bzgl. des Nutzens von Dokumenttypen in bestimmten Anwendungsfällen. Ein
   Vergleich des Anwendungsfalles, des Dokumenttyps und der Akzeptanz dieser Struktur bei Autoren
   und Lesern ist der Ausgangspunkt für die Entwicklung allgemeiner Strukturierungskonventionen, mit
   denen sich das Verstehen von Hypertexten verbessern läßt. Hieraus können sich Designregeln entwik-
   keln, die Autoren eine Orientierungshilfe beim Erstellen kohärenter Hyperdokumente bieten.

Im Institut für integrierte Publikations- und Informationssysteme der GMD in Darmstadt wird das Autorensystem SEPIA, das die Erstellung von Hyperdokumenten unterstützen soll, entwickelt [Streitz, Hannemann,
Thüring, 1989] [Haake, Schütt, 1990]. Im Rahmen dieses Projektes wird zur Zeit die oben vorgestellte Designobjekthierarchie formalisiert, um als Basis für Unterstützungsmechanismen zu dienen. Parallel hierzu
wird ein Modell des Autorenprozesses erarbeitet, das die Vorgehensweise von Autoren bei der Erstellung von
Hyperdokumenten beschreibt. Diese beiden Forschungsaktivitäten bilden eine zentrale Grundlage zur Realisierung eines benutzerorientierten und aufgabenzentrierten Autorensystems.

6   Literatur

[Akscyn, Mc Cracken, Yoder, 1988] R. M. Akscyn, D. L. Mc Cracken & E. A. Yoder. KMS: A distributed
    hypermedia system for managing knowledge in organizations. *Communications of the ACM*,
    31(7): 820 – 835, July 1988.

[Bryan, 1988] M. Bryan. *SGML: An author's guide to the Standard Generalized Markup Language*. Addi-
    son–Wesley. 1988.

[Brown, 1987] P. J. Brown. Turning Ideas into Products: The Guide System. In *Proceedings of the First ACM
    Workshop on Hypertext (Hypertext '87)*, pages 33 – 40, University of North Carolina at Chapel
    Hill, November 13 – 15, 1987.

[Brown, 1990] P. J. Brown. Assessing the Quality of Hypertext Documents. In A. Rizk, N. A. Streitz & J.
    André (Eds.), *Hypertext: Concepts, Systems and Applications, (Proceedings of the European
    Conference on Hypertext*, ECHT '90, Paris, France, November 1990), pages 1 – 12. Cam-
    bridge: University Press.

[Catlin, Bush, Yankelovich, 1989] T. Catlin, P. Bush & N. Yankelovich. InterNote: Extending a Hypermedia
    Framework to Support Annotative Collaboration. In *Proceedings of the 2nd ACM Conference
    on Hypertext (Hypertext '89)*, pages 365 – 378, Pittsburgh, PA, November 1989.

[Conklin, 1987] J. Conklin. Hypertext: An Introduction and Survey. *Computer Magazine*, 20(9): 17–41, Sep-
    tember 1987.

[Conklin, Begeman, 1988] J. Conklin & M. L. Begemann. gIBIS: A Hypertext Tool for Argumentation. *ACM
    Transactions on Office Information Systems*, 6(4):303–331, October 1988.

[De Young, 1990] L. De Young. Linking considered harmful. In A. Rizk, N. A. Streitz & J. André (Eds.),
    *Hypertext: Concepts, Systems and Applications (Proceedings of the European Conference on
    Hypertext*, Paris, France, November 1990), pages 238 – 249. Cambridge: University Press.

[Edwards, Hardman, 1989] D. M. Edwards & L. Hardman. 'Lost in Hyperspace': Cognitive Mapping and Navigation in a Hypertext Environment. In R. McAleese (Ed.). *Hypertext: theory into practice*, pages 105–125. Oxford: Intellect Limited, 1989.

[Haake, Schütt, 1990] J. Haake. & H. Schütt: Eine Systemarchitektur für ein wissensbasiertes Hypertext-Autorensystem. In P. Gloor & N. A. Streitz (Hrsg.), *Hypertext und Hypermedia: Von theoretischen Konzepten zur praktischen Anwendung*, Seite 65–78. Heidelberg: Springer, 1990.

[Halasz, 1988] F. G. Halasz. Reflections on Notecards: Seven Issues for the Next Generation of Hypertext Systems. *Communications of the ACM*, 31(7):836 – 852, July 1988.

[Halasz, Moran, Trigg, 1987] F. G. Halasz, T. P. Moran & R. H. Trigg. NoteCards in a Nutshell. In J. M. Caroll & P. P. Tenner (Eds.). *Proceedings of the Conference on Human Factors in Computing Systems and Graphics Interfaces*, Toronto, Canada, April 5–9, 1987.

[Halliday, Hasan, 1976] M. A. K. Halliday & R. Hasan. *Cohesion in English*. London: Longman, 1976.

[Hannemann, Thüring, Streitz, 1990] J. Hannemann, M. Thüring & N. A. Streitz. Schreiben als Designproblem: Ein integrativer Ansatz. Vortrag auf dem 37. Kongreß der Deutschen Gesellschaft für Psychologie, Kiel, 23.–27. September, 1990. Als Kurzfassung erschienen in D. Frey (Hrsg.) Bericht über den 37. Kongreß der Deutschen Gesellschaft für Psychologie, Seite 60 – 61. Göttingen: Hogrefe, 1990.

[Kintsch, van Dijk, 1978] W. Kintsch & T.A. van Dijk. Toward a model of text comprehension and production. *Psychological Review*, 85:363–394, 1978.

[Mann, Thompson, 1987] W. C. Mann & S. A. Thompson. Rhetorical structure theory: A theory of text organization. In: L.Polanyi (Ed.) *Discourse structure*, Norwood, N.J.: Ablex, 1987.

[Marshall, Irish, 1989] C. C. Marshall & P. M. Irish. Guided Tours and On-Line Presentations: How Authors Make Existing Hypertext Intelligible for Readers. In *Proceedings of the 2nd ACM Conference on Hypertext (Hypertext '89)*, pages 15 – 26, Pittsburgh, PA, November 1989.

[Schnotz, 1988] W. Schnotz. Textverstehen als Aufbau mentaler Modelle. In H. Mandl & H. Spada (Hrsg.) *Wissenspsychologie*, Seite 299–330. München–Weinheim: Psychologie Verlags Union, 1988

[Searle, 1980] J. R. Searle. Minds, brains, and programs. *The Behavioral and Brain Sciences*, (3):417–457, 1980.

[Streitz, Hannemann, Thüring, 1989] N. A. Streitz, J. Hannemann & M. Thüring. From Ideas and Arguments to Hyperdocuments: Travelling through Activity Spaces. In *Proceedings of the 2nd ACM Conference on Hypertext (Hypertext '89)*, pages 343–364, Pittsburgh, PA, November 5–8, 1989.

[Streitz, 1990] N. A. Streitz: Hypertext: Ein innovatives Medium zur Kommunikation von Wissen. In P. Gloor & N. A. Streitz (Hrsg.), *Hypertext und Hypermedia: Von theoretischen Konzepten zur praktischen Anwendung*, Seite 10–27. Heidelberg: Springer, 1990.

[Trigg, 1988] R. H. Trigg. Guided Tours and Tabletops: Tools for Communicating in a Hypertext Environment. *ACM Transactions on Office Information Systems*, 6(4): 398–414, 1988.

[Trigg, Irish, 1987] R. H. Trigg & P. M. Irish. Hypertext Habitats: Experiences of Writers in NoteCards. In *Proceedings of the First ACM Workshop on Hypertext (Hypertext '87)*, pages 89 – 108, University of North Carolina at Chapel Hill, November 13 – 15, 1987.

[Thüring, Hannemann, 1991] M. Thüring & J. Hannemann. Der Schrecken des Stils oder Schreiben ... was ist das überhaupt?. *GMD-Spiegel*, 21(1):14–21, März 1991.

[Toulmin, 1958] S. Toulmin. *The uses of argument*. Cambridge: Cambridge University Press, 1958.

[van Dijk, Kintsch, 1983] T. A. van Dijk & W. Kintsch. *Strategies of Discourse Comprehension*. Orlando: Academic Press, 1983.

[Zellweger, 1989] P. T. Zellweger. Scripted Documents: A Hypermedia Path Mechanism. In *Proceedings of the 2nd ACM Conference on Hypertext (Hypertext '89)*, pages 1–14, Pittsburgh, PA, November 5–8, 1989.

Farbmarkierungen im Hypertext als Orientierungs- und Lernhilfe

Wolfgang J. Irler und Gilberto Barbieri
Istituto di Informatica, Università di Trento
Via Inama 13, I-38100 Trento, Italia
irler@irst.uucp

Zusammenfassung

Farbig überlagerte Markierungen in einem Hypertext erweitern die Möglichkeiten einer individuellen Strukturierung und erzeugen weiterverwendbare Link-Verankerungen. Sie dienen zur visuellen Orientierung in dem Textmaterial und bieten eine Grundlage für Verzeichnisse, Anmerkungen und Auszüge.
Die prototypale Realisierung eines Hypertextes mit Markierungsmechanismus wird beschrieben. Erforderliche Objekte und Skripts basieren auf den Möglichkeiten von ToolBook.

Abstract

Coloured markings inserted in a hypertext extend the individual structuring possibilties and provide link anchors for further needs. These markings support the visual orientation in the text material and the creation of indexes, notes, and excerpts.
The prototypical realization of a hypertext with a marking feature is described. Necessary objects and scripts are based on ToolBook.

Schlüsselworte: Hypertext, Schnittstelle, Markierungen

Einführung

Die Modalitäten der Benutzung eines Hypertextes [CONK87, IRLE90a] erfordern verschiedene Paradigmen des Schnittstellendesigns [SHNE87]. Ein reines Informationssystem in einem Wissensgebiet hat den Aspekt des schnellen und präzisen Zugriffs auf Fakten und Einzelheiten zu betonen, wird also voll sein von Orientierungs- und Zugriffseinheiten in Form von Ikonen und Buttons.
Beispielhaft gehören hierzu die Mehrzahl der **HyperCard**-Stacks, die als kommerzielle Produkte oder öffentliche Auskunftsysteme angeboten werden (**FocalPoint, Glasgow Online** [HARD89], **IperMilano** [BONO90], **Oxford English Dictionary** [RAYM88].
Informationen textlicher Art hierin beschränken sich auf Kurzbeschreibungen oder Stichpunkte. Der "Hypertext"-Aspekt besteht fast ausschließlich aus "goto"-Querverweisen, ausgelöst von Mausklicks auf klar identifizierbare Buttons.

Forschungsarbeiten auf diesem Gebiet konzentrieren sich auf die Eindeutigkeit bildlicher Kommunikation und auf die Konsequenzen der Benutzererwartungen [HARD89]. Kreative Interventionen von seiten des Benutzers sind höchstens für Notizen oder Merkzeichen vorgesehen.

Ein Hypertext für Lehrzwecke kann dagegen durchaus auf einige Buttons verzichten, wenn nur das Lernmodell durchdacht angeboten wird. Die kognitive Überladung durch zu viele "Orientierungs"-Einheiten muß hier zugunsten einer didaktisch sinnvollen Verknüpfungsstrategie vermindert werden. Obwohl für computergestützten Unterricht im allgemeinen verschiedene Lernmodelle entwickelt wurden [BORK85], welche jeweils in Autorensystemen oder ähnlichen Produkten Eingang fanden, bestehen für didaktische Hypertexte noch viele Unsicherheiten bezüglich des Nutzens [RASK87]. Selbst allgemeine Qualitätskriterien zu Hypertextstrukturen [BROW90] sind häufig an einzelne Systeme gebunden.

Im Rahmen unserer Forschungsgruppe beschäftigen wir uns mit den Eigenheiten der Hypertexte, um sie in ihrer ganzen Potentialität für die Lehr- und Lernzwecke unserer Fernuniversität* zu erarbeiten. Die Grundvoraussetzung, welche zu der technologischen Wahl der Hypertexte führte, ist der Verzicht auf einen gezielten (Frontal-) Unterricht, aber auch eine gewisse Distanz zu allzu perfektem computergestützen Unterricht. Die generell vorhandene *Benutzer-Kontrolle* über die Leseschritte im Hypertext sollte zu echter *Lerner-Kontrolle* werden.

Die Ersetzung der didaktischen Einheiten durch organisierte Hypertexte bietet zusätzlich zu dem neuartigen Stoffangebot auch die Möglichkeit, das Lernen selbst einzuüben. Ein Großteil der Studenten befindet sich schon einige Zeit im Berufsleben und besitzt daher kaum Erfahrung in der systematischen Erarbeitung eines Wissensgebietes.

Somit versuchen wir, zusätzlich zu einer dosierten, hypertextartig verknüpften Wissensaufbereitung, einerseits einen individualisierten und individialisierbaren Zugang zu den Wissenselementen anzubieten [IRLE89] und andererseits ein breites Spektrum an Interventionsmöglichkeiten zur Restrukturierung des Materials zu schaffen. Das Leitmotiv hierzu wird vom Schlagwort: "Der Leser als Autor" auf den Punkt gebracht. Die beschriebenen - und in vielen Hypertextsystemen realisierten - Interventionsmöglichkeiten haben wir hierfür durch individuelle Farbmarkierungen zu erweitern versucht.

Daß damit auch eine andere visuelle Erscheinungsform des Hypertextes und ein anderes Schnittstellenmodell ("unaufdringliche Hypertext-Anker") einhergehen muß, wurde von den Autoren ausgeführt [IRLE90b]. In der heutigen Schrift versuchen wir, die Idee der Farbmarkierungen in ihren Einzelheiten auszuleuchten.

Nach einer kurzen terminologischen Klärung behandeln wir den Antagonismus Autor-Benutzer und stellen dann unsere Markierungsmethode vor. Einige wesentliche Skriptelemente der Realisierung werden angesprochen. Erste Reaktionen von Benutzern und einige selbst-kritische Betrachtungen schließen die Beschreibung des Ansatzes ab.

Hypertext-Terminologie

Wegen der Uneinheitlichkeit der Terminologie in den verschiedenen Hypertextsystemen geben wir einige, uns wesentliche Präzisierungen wieder.

---

* Centro Sviluppo Software Didattico, CUD, Rovereto, TN, Italia

Ein *Hypertext* besteht aus einer Anzahl von *Dokumenten*, welche am Computerbildschirm zu lesen sind. Die Dokumente - *Textfragmente* mit graphischen Elementen - sind untereinander durch in ihnen verankerte Verknüpfungen verbunden. Eine *Verknüpfung* - "*Link*" - wird durch einen *Mausklick* über dem *Aktivierungsort* ausgeführt, worauf das Zieldokument erscheint. Die Aktivierungsorte heißen auch "hot zones" oder aktive Zonen.

Werden die Textfragmente als *Knoten* und die Verknüpfungen als *Kanten* betrachtet, so kommt man zu der üblichen Interpretation eines Hypertextes als *Informationsnetz*. Eine optische Repräsentation dieses Netzes als "*Browser*", d.h. als graphischer *Zugangsmodus*, ist einerseits Zentrum von beschriebenen Hypertext-Systemen [FURU89], wird andererseits jedoch explizit abgelehnt [AKSC88, MARC88].

Ein Hypertext-Link ist durch seine *Link-Verankerungen* gekennzeichnet. Das Vorhandensein einer Link-Verankerung auf der Bildschirmseite wird häufig durch Form, Farbe, Umrahmung oder Etikett signalisiert, um sowohl den ostensiven Anteil, wie auch die Funktionalität zu betonen. Die *Buttons* und *Ikonen* von **HyperCard** und ähnlicher Systeme gehören hierzu.

Erst wenn jedoch eine interne "Goto"-Programmieranweisung auf einen *Zielanker* hinweist, wird aus der Button-Zone eine *Startverankerung* für einen Hypertext-Link. Ist eine Link-Verankerung ein editierbarer Textteil, hat man aktive Textelemente oder "hotwords". Als Zielanker dient häufig ein ganzes Zieldokument.

Konzeptuell sollte die virtuelle Verankerung einer Hypertext-Verknüpfung von ihrer optischen Präsentation (z.B. als Button) getrennt werden, und letztere wiederum von der eigentlichen Funktionalität der Link-Definition. Nur so ist ein Hypertext "ohne" ablenkende Buttons [IRLE90b], aber mit ausgeprägter Link-Struktur, bzw. generalisierten Verknüpfungen [MYLO90] denkbar. Kein kommerzielles Hypertextsystem führt diese Trennung konsequent durch.

In **Guide** [BROW87] wird die Funktionalität von dem *Link-"Typ"* bestimmt und die Verankerung mit der Aktivierungszone identifiziert: ein Querverweis-"Button" (*Reference*) verweist starr auf einen Zieltext, ein Ersetzungs-Text (*Expansion*) strukturiert hierarchisch in Outline-Gliederung, eine Anmerkungsnote (*Note*) läßt ein Textfenster aufblitzen. Nur die Kommando-Definition (*Command*) erlaubt in der neuen Version einen limitierten Zugang zu inneren Zustandsgrößen und damit eine gewisse Flexibilität und etwas "rechnerische Komplexität" [HALA88]. Da die optischen Hinweise auf die Stelle der Guide-Buttons das Hauptcharakteristikum dieses Systems sind, hilft nicht einmal die Möglichkeit, diese Visualisierung eventuell auszuschalten. Auch **Hyperties** und **BlackMagic** trennen die Link-Definition nicht von der Formatierung des Textes.

Wie ein Textelement durch eine *Markierung* zu einer individuellen Link-Struktur werden kann, beschreiben wir weiter unten. Vorher versuchen wir den Antagonismus Autor-Benutzer zu analysieren.

Der Autor als Benutzer und der Benutzer als Autor

Betrachten wir den Gebrauch eine Hypertextsystems, so entdecken wir, daß auch der *Autor als Benutzer* seines Hypertexts eine Rolle spielt. Nach dem eigentliche Schreiben des Textes und den ersten Link-Definitionen muß auch er den passiven Teil des Systems mitbenutzen, um sich in der schon bestehenden Netz-Struktur zurechtzufinden und Präzisierungen anzubringen.

Tabelle I. Tätigkeiten von Autor und Benutzer

Autor	Autor=Benutzer	Benutzer=Autor	Benutzer	OBJEKT
schreibt	präzisiert	**markiert**	liest	WORTE
verfaßt	interpretiert	**kopiert**	perzepiert	TEXT
zeichnet	beschreibt	kommentiert	betrachtet	GRAPHIK
segmentiert	bezieht ein	**exzerpiert**	studiert	DOKUMENTE
charakterisiert	ordnet an	**kennzeichnet**	überfliegt	BEGRIFFE
benennt	umschreibt	assoziiert	durchforscht	KONZEPTE
trägt ein	gliedert	**vervollständigt**	**blättert**	VERZEICHNIS
eröffnet	ordnet	hakt ab	geht durch	LISTE
kennzeichnet	gruppiert	**kommentiert**	visualisiert	VERANKERUNG
plant	realisiert	**kritisiert**	verfolgt	VERKNÜPFUNG
bildet	plaziert	verschiebt	drückt	KNOPF/BUTTON
entwirft	präzisiert	ersetzt	erkennt	IKONE
programmiert	implementiert	modifiziert	startet	SCRIPT
-	-	**erzeugt**	**springt an**	MARKIERUNG
positioniert	verbindet	fügt hinzu	besichtigt	KNOTEN
zieht	verwirft	verschiebt	verifiziert	KANTE
skizziert	ordnet an	ergänzt	durchstreift	NETZ
gestaltet	verfeinert	**individualisiert**	überfliegt	ORIENTIERUNG
eröffnet	erleichert	erweitert	verwendet	ZUGANG

Wegen der Schnittstellenmodalitäten ist der Leser des Resultats ein Benutzer. Der *Benutzer als Autor* erscheint dann, wenn er aktiv am Hypertext mitwirkt. Auf schematische Weise sind die Tätigkeiten von Autor und Benutzer in ihrer jeweils doppelten Rolle in Tabelle I aufgelistet.

Wenn auch im einzelnen hier nur einige unterstrichene Tätigkeiten interessieren, so soll die Liste dafür sensibilisieren, wieweit die Hypertext-Technologie den Unterschied zwischen Autor und Benutzer zu verwischen imstande ist. Die Realisierung derartiger Möglichkeiten bedarf jedoch noch einiger Forschungs- und Entwicklungsanstrengungen. In ähnlicher Weise wie das Fertigstellen eines Hypertextes kann die Bearbeitung eines fertigen Produktes seitens des Endbenutzers gesehen werden. Durch Umordnen und Feinstrukturierung [TRIG88] soll sich der - interessierte - Benutzer eine eigene Version des Materials erzeugen, nicht primär für andere, sondern als Selbsthilfe für optimales Lernen. Wir erkennen hierin Analogien zur "physischen" Beschäftigung mit einem Wissensmaterial.

Beim Studieren schlagen wir ein Buch auf, spüren das Gewicht, die Dicke (des Inhalts?), blättern die Seiten, knicken die Ecken, stecken Buchzeichen und Orientierungshilfen hinein, unterstreichen, markieren mit Farbmarkern, kritzeln Anmerkungen, kopieren Zitate, photokopieren Seiten, reißen womöglich Teile heraus und kleben sie neu zusammen, malen graphische Beziehungenlinien, schreiben uns Merksprüche und Spickzettel, kurzum bringen den Inhalt in andere Form.

Diese physischen Begleithandlungen beim Lernen, welche das Lernmaterial bis zur Unkenntlichkeit verändern können, unterstützen sicherlich die kognitiven Funktionen. In seinem Wissenschafts-Krimi "Il labirinto della memoria" - "das Labyrinth des

Gedächtnisses" - weist Roberto Vacca gar auf die antike Tradition des Lernens von Konzepten anhand der Orientierung in einem Gebäude oder Theater hin [VACC88]. Ähnliches müssen wir für obige Hilfsmittel und Begleithandlungen annehmen und versuchen, sie in das Schnittstellenangebot zu übernehmen.

In der "künstlichen Realität" des Hypertextes [POLI90] bleibt der Kontakt etwas steif und eingeschränkt, wenn die einzige Intervention ein kurzes Anfahren mit der Maus mit darauffolgenden Klicks ist. Wir plädieren in unserem Modell für eine breite Palette von Bewegungen und Aktionen, sowie das Anbringen von farbigen Markierungspunkten, die die Artifizialität der Schnittstellenproblematik relativieren.

Die letzten Widerstände gegen einen alltäglichen Gebrauch des Computers als "elektronisches Buch" werden sicher erst dann hinfällig, wenn Gestalt und Benutzermodalitäten sich konventionellen "physischen" Gegebenheiten angleichen: der in der Hand gehaltene Flach-Bildschirm, mit einem kabellosen Stift als Zeige-, Schreib- und Markiergerät, wie es schon Alan Kay forderte [KAY77], und was jetzt als "ActiveBook" oder "notebook computer" angeboten wird [RYAN91].

Neuere Operationssysteme, wie **PenPoint**, oder das "electronic paper project" [BROC91] konzentrieren sich auf die Steuerung von Programmen vermittels Eingabestift. Für die obigen Benutzertätigkeiten müssen ebenfalls entsprechende virtuelle Analogien entwickelt werden. Eine davon ist das farbige Markieren von Text und die darauf aufbauenden Manipulationen.

Farbige Textmarkierungen

Wie schon ersichtlich, haben Farbmarkierungen im Hypertext verschiedene Implikationen, erfordern aber auch einige Vorkehrungen in Bezug auf das Erscheinungsbild und die Planung der Bildschirmseiten. Wenn auch unsere radikale Ablehnung der optischen Präsentation einer Link-Verankerung nicht geteilt werden sollte, so muß doch wenigstens akzeptiert werden, daß die Rhetorik der Textformatierung vordringlich ihrem Verständnis zu dienen hat. Hinweise auf die Existenz von aktiven Regionen im und um den Text lenken nur ab; weder Form der Buchstaben, noch Farbe oder sonstige Hinweise sollten funktionellen, d.h. hyper- textlichen Charakter haben. Auch das Mauszeiger-Flackern über aktiven Zonen (**Guide**, **KMS**) stört ein konzentriertes Lesen und überlädt die Kognition durch die andauernde Dekodierung. Trotz einiger Schnittstellentests für Hypertexte [NIEL90] hat noch keine Untersuchung diese vorgebichen Orientierungshilfen mit dem Verständnis des Inhalts konfrontiert.

Nur wenn der Text nicht schon mit Link-Buttons "zugekleistert" ist, kann man noch sinnvolle Farbmarkierungen anbringen, deren kognitive Funktion allein in der Hervorhebung des darunterliegenden Textes besteht.

Technisch läßt sich eine Farbmarkierung durch eine Farbüberdeckung über der inter- essierenden Textstelle realisieren. Zusätzlich zu dem (durchsichtigen) Farbrechteck soll aber auch der unterstrichene Text selbst weiterverarbeitet werden. Dieser muß voll- ständig kopier- und editierbar sein. Die daraus folgende Konstruktionsvorschrift für den Hypertext verträgt weder überlappende Textfelder, noch überlagerte Text-Buttons (wie z.B. in der HyperCard-Bearbeitung "Hypertext on Hypertext" der ACM Edition von Hypertext '87) und natürlich auch keinen graphischen Bitmap-Text.

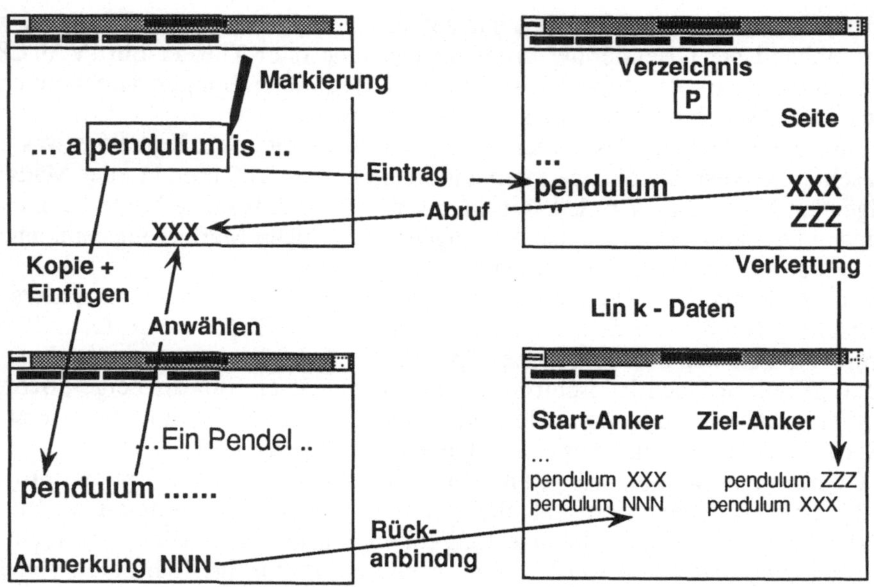

Bild 1. Markierung mit nachfolgendem Eintrag in Stichwortverzeichnis
und Einfügung der Kopie in eine Anmerkung.

Generell sollte jeglicher Text in einem einheitlichen Textfeld stehen, auch die Bezeichnungen einer (evt. überlagerten) Graphik; nur so ist Kopieren und folglich Markieren
von Textteilen garantiert.
Das Umschalten von *Navigationsmodus* auf *Markierungsmodus* kann per Menü-
Auswahl oder durch eine Tastenkombination initiiert werden. In unserem Vorschlag
wird hierfür die zweite (die rechte) Maustaste verwandt. Die kognitive Belastung durch
die Dualität:

linke Taste = Navigation,
rechte Taste = Markieren,

scheint uns vertretbar.
Bild 1 veranschaulicht die Abfolge während der Markierung, wie sie durch geeignete
Skript-Kombinationen programmiert wurde. Nach Drücken der rechten Maustaste
nimmt der Mauszeiger eine Bleistiftform an und beginnt, sowohl ein Farbrechteck zu
malen, als auch den ausgewählten Text zu speichern. Ein Weiterziehen der Maus folgt
der Selektionsmetapher aus Textverarbeitungsprogrammen.
Nach Lösen der Taste steht der selektierte Text im Kopierspeicher und ist auf der
Originalseite farbig gekennzeichnet. Ein Eintrag in ein alphabetisches Schlüsselwort-
verzeichnis erfolgt über eine Menü-Auswahl. Die Einfügung in ein geeignetes An-
merkungsfeld (*Paste Text*) oder in eine andere Liste wird automatisch durch eine
Rückanbindung mit der Originalstelle verbunden (Bild 1, unten). Natürlich kann eine
Text-Weiterverwendung auch entfallen.
Das graphische Rechtecks-Object speichert auf jeden Fall den angestrichenen Text. Es
wird somit zu einem Ziel-Anker für die geordneten Schlüsselworte aus dem
Verzeichnis, für die entsprechenden Textstellen in den Anmerkungen und für Abfragen
der Art: "wo taucht in einer Markierung das Wort *pendulum* auf".

Eine Aneinanderreihung der miniaturisierten Seiten, die - ähnlich wie die *recent*-Anweisung aus **HyperCard** - einen Überblick über die Markierungs-Struktur liefert, unterstützt visuell orientierte Leser beim Wiederauffinden der Seiten.

Durch eine Menü-Selektion lassen sich verschiedene Farben der Markierungen ein- und ausschalten, sowie auch eventuell löschen. Eine Zuordnung einer bestimmten Farbe zu einem Benutzer oder zu einer Bedeutung ermöglicht eine kooperative Erarbeitung eines Hypertexts.

Prototypale Programmierung

Die programmtechnische Realisierung des eben Beschriebenen stellt einige Anforderungen an das zugrundeliegende System. Ein objekt-orientierter Ansatz in Art der **Smalltalk**-Programmierung ist unerläßlich. Wegen der Farbe und der Forderung nach aktiven Textteilen ließe sie sich effizient nur in **HyperPAD**, **SuperCard** oder **ToolBook** ausführen. **HyperCard** wäre teilweise erst in der Version 2.0 dazu in der Lage.

Wir beschränken uns auf die Beschreibung der **OpenScript**-Elemente von ToolBook und weisen nur kurz auf die entsprechenden Nuancen in den anderen System hin.

In ToolBook haben wir die Möglichkeit, sogenannte *HotWords* zu definieren, im Text liegende aktive Zonen, welche wiederum ein Skript tragen können, folglich als Link-Verankerung fungieren. Als (fast) vollständige Objekte empfangen sie die Palette der internen Meldungen (z.B. Mausklicks) und können sie weitergeben. Ein "unsichtbares" Objekt (die einzige Möglichkeit hierfür in HyperPAD und HyperCard 1.) erfüllte den gleichen Zweck, ist aber nicht an den Text geheftet. Die Hotwords, wie ja auch die Buttons von **Guide**, lassen sich leider nicht einfach farblich hinterlegen, weswegen wir eine graphische Überlagerung vornehmen.

Der wesentliche Teil der Markierung wird von einem *ButtonStillDown*-Handler abgewickelt. Ein Auszug ist in Ablistung 1 abgedruckt.

Da sich der Text in einem *RecordField* des Hintergrunds befindet und das durchsichtige Rechteck auf der Vordergrund-Seite, liegt das letztere als Markierung vor dem Text, also auch vor einem eventuellen Hotword. Dessen Skript muß durch geeignete Meldungsweiterleitung zugänglich bleiben.

Ablistung 1:

```
..
to handle buttonStillDown loc, isShift, isCtrl
..    -- the selection = Farbrechteck mit bounds b --
      -- TextBeg = Beginn der Markierung --
if mark is true then
    set the bounds of the selection to\
    (the first item of b), (the second item of b),\
    (the first item of loc), (the fourth item of b)
  put the textFromPoint(loc) of recordField "Text" into textEnd
    select chars (item 2 of textBeg) to (item 2 of textEnd)\
      of textLine (item 1 of textBeg) of text of recordField \
      "Text" of this page
else ...
..
```

Alle Markierungs-Skripts liegen außerdem in einem *System-Book* und lassen sich in eine entsprechende Anwendung einbinden.

Die erzeugten Verknüpfungen - in Verzeichnis und Anmerkungen - werden in einer rudimentären Link-Datenbank gespeichert und verarbeitet: als sukzessive Einträge und Abrufe aus Recordfields. Eine Organisation der Markierungs-Verankerungen in einer relationalen Link-Datenbank [BARB91] ist der nächste Schritt.

Vergleichbare Ansätze

Verschiedene Systeme ermöglichen eine zusätzliche Kennzeichnung der Link-Verankerungen in Form von umrahmenden Rechtecken oder Stilelementen, jedoch nicht in Farbe. In **Guide** kann ein Button-Text einen bestimmten Buchstabenstil annehmen; **HyperCard** besitzt die Control-Command-Kombination zur Visualisierung der Button-Rechtecke; **ToolBook** hat eine *Show-Hotwords*-Option, ähnlich wie **Hypergate**.

Hypergate erlaubt (auch in der Lese-Version) Anmerkungen, benamte Buchzeichen, Ergänzungen des Inhaltsverzeichnisses, und bringt während der Lese-Session "Brotkrumen" neben den Verweisen auf schon gelesene Seiten an [BERN88].

Intermedia sieht generelles Kopieren und Einfügen von Link-Ikonen vor und macht keinen Unterschied zwischen Autoren- und Lese-Fassung [YANK88].

Der **Guide**-*Reader* der neuen Version erlaubt das Kopieren von Text, jedoch nicht das Einfügen innerhalb von *Guidance*-Dokumenten.

BlackMagic speichert nummerierte Buchzeichen von einer Session zur anderen, die dann farbig aufleuchten.

Da **Hyperties** im Grunde als Enzyklopädie-System entworfen wurde [MARC88], hinterlassen Benutzer keine Spuren. Ähnliches gilt für alle Konsultations-Systeme.

Als verteilte Hypertext-Datenbank ist **KMS** geignet zur kooperativen Bearbeitung gemeinsamer Dokumente [AKSC88]. Es gibt nur eine Vollversion. Kennzeichnungen können als Querverweis-Ikonen eingefügt werden. In einigen Systemen steht der Autoren-Aspekt total im Vordergrund (**WE** [SMIT87]), immer konzentriert auf die abstrakte Konstruktion des Hypertext-Netzes.

Systeme aus dem Forschungsbereich unterscheiden im allgemeinen nicht zwischen Autor und Leser, mit der Konsequenz, daß die gesamten Schnittstellenkommandos von beiden beherrscht werden müssen.

Die Wiederauffindungsmodalitäten in **SuperBook** [REMD87] heben auf allen Seiten die gesuchten Worte hervor, die als aneinandergekettete Hypertext-Anker fungieren. Auch die Text-Datenbank **AskSam** besitzt diese Möglichkeit.

Kritische Diskussion

In unseren Betrachtungen fehlen einige Aspekte. Die Markierungsmethode ist als individuelles Hilfsmittel konzipiert. Mehrfachzugriff auf ein Hypertext-Buch, konkurrierende Markierungen oder der Gebrauch während einer Vorlesung sind noch nicht ausgearbeitet und benötigen eine modifizierte Grundsoftware. Eine Verwendung zur Beurteilung von Hypertext-Strukturen, als Ersatz einer "low-tech" Zettel-Kommunikation [BROW90], scheint zwar theoretisch machbar, müßte aber ausgetestet werden.

Benutzereindrücke (aus dem akademischen Bereich) lassen Zweifel aufkommen, ob die aktuelle Tendenz der allgegenwärtigen Buttons und Ikonen in Hypertexten noch aufzuhalten ist. Das "ernsthafte" Lesen eines Hypertextes ist schlecht von oberflächlichem Überfliegen zu trennen. Dem Rechnung zu tragen, gelten unsere Bemühungen, einen geeigneten Test durchzuführen.

Eine Individualisierung des Hypertextes durch Farbmarkierungen verändert diesen ähnlich wie die Untersteichungen in einem Schulbuch: nach dem Schuljahr kann man es wegwerfen, da kein anderer sich mehr darin zurechtfindet.

Das Benutzer-Modell hinter unserem Ansatz bedarf noch einiger empirischer Untermauerung. Uns ist z.B. keine wissenschaftliche Erhebung zu der "Rhetorik" der weitverbreiteten Farbmarker für Textbücher bekannt. Die kontrastierenden Meinungen bezüglich ihrer Funktion gehen - nach unseren Erkenntnissen - vom Unterstreichen unbekannter Ausdrücke bis zur systematischen Einfärbung des Textes. Eine Beurteilung der Qualität (und Quantität?) der Markierungen könnte in einem Unterrichtsrahmen in eine Gesamtnote einfließen, leidet jedoch am Fehlen geeigneter Kriterien. Eine ausgewogene Markierungs-Struktur könnte prämiert und späteren Studenten zur Verfügung gestellt werden.

Da ein Hypertext für didaktische Zwecke auch Elemente aus der Forschung über "intelligente Tutorensysteme" [PSTO88, MÜHL90] aufweisen sollte, müßten diese und ausgewählte CAI-Methoden mit der Markierung koordiniert werden.

Eine Einbettung des Hypertextes in ein allgemeines Informations-Systems hat dafür Sorge zu tragen, daß Hervorhebungen auf dem Text nicht kontraproduktiv eine neue Verständnis-Barriere aufbauen.

Schlußfolgerungen

Die Machbarkeit der Textmarkierungen hat die Möglichkeiten erweitert, mit einem Hypertext "herumzuspielen". Eine allgemeine Nützlichkeit dieser Idee ist zu erwarten, denn jedes Mittel muß recht sein, einen Studierenden zur kreativen Beschäftigung mit dem Lehrmaterial zu stimulieren. Der Aspekt der Einbeziehung des Lesers in die Produktion des Hypertextes kann zu neuen, auch für Autoren überraschenden Ergebnissen führen.

Bibliographie:

[AKSC88] Akscyn R, McCracken D, Yoder E (1988), KMS: A distributed hypermedia system for managing knowledge in organizations. *Comm. ACM*, Vol. 31, n.7, 820-835.

[BERN88] Bernstein M (1988), The bookmark and the compass: orientation tools for hypertext users. *ACM SIGOIS Bulletin*, Vol.9, n.4, Oct.1988, 34-45.

[BARB91] Barbieri G, Colazzo L, Molinari A (1991), Relational back-ends in the management of large hypertexts. In: Proc. Hypertext/Hypermedia, Graz, May 1991 (vorliegender Band).

[BONO90] Bonomi M, Logli M (1990), HyperMilan. Note di Software, Bull-Italia: Milano, No. 48/49, Jun.-Oct.1990, 51-62.

[BORK85] Bork A (1985), Personal Computers for Education. Harper & Row Pub.: New York.

[BROC91] Brocklehurst E R (1991), The NPL electronic paper project. *Int.J.Man-Machine Studies*, Vol.34, n.1, Jan.1991, 69-95.

[BROW87] Brown P J (1987) Turning ideas into products: The Guide System. In: Hypertext 87 Papers, Univ.of North Carolina, Chapel Hill NC, ACM: New York, 33-40.

[BROW90] Brown P J (1990), Assessing the quality of hypertext documents. In: Rizk A, Streitz N, André J (eds.), Hypertext: Concepts,Systems, and Applications (Proc. of ECHT'90), Cambridge Univ.Press: Cambridge, UK, 1-12.

[CONK87] Conklin J (1987),Hypertext: a survey and introduction. *IEEE Computer,* Vol. 20, 9,17-41.
[POLI90] Polillo R (1990), Interacting with artificial realities. Note di Software, Bull-Italia: Milano, No. 48/49, Jun.-Oct.1990, 7-28.
[FURU89] Furuta R, Stotts P D (1989), Programmable browsing semantics in Trellis. In: Proc. Hypertext 89, Pittsburgh, PA, Special Issue *SIGCHI Bulletin*, ACM: New York, 27-42.
[HALA88] Halasz F G (1988), Reflections on NoteCards: Seven issues for the next generation of hypermedia systems. *Comm. ACM*, Vol. 31, n.7, 836-852.
[HARD89] Hardman L (1989), Evaluating the usability of the Glasgow Online hypertext. *Hypermedia*, Vol.1, n.1, Spring 1989, 34-63.
[IRLE89] Irler W J, Colazzo L, Barbieri G (1989), Implementing access modes to instructional hypertext. Text iV, AICA Text Processing Conference, Milano, Dec.1989, AICA: Milano, 211-220.
[IRLE90a] Irler W J, Colazzo L (1990), Hypertext systems and computer-supported learning. *Education in Computing Newsletter*, Vol.2, n.1, Jan.-Apr-1990, 39-58..
[IRLE90b] Irler W J, Barbieri G (1990), Non-intrusive hypertext anchors and individual colour markings. In: Rizk A, Streitz N, André J (eds.), Hypertext: Concepts,Systems, and Applications (Proc. of ECHT'90), Cambridge Univ.Press: Cambridge, UK, 261-274..
[KAY77] Kay A, Goldberg A (1977), Personal dynamic media. *IEEE Computer*, Vol.10, n.3, Mar.1977, 31-41.
[MARC88] Marchionini G, Shneiderman B (1988), Finding facts vs. browsing knowledge in hypertext systems. *IEEE Computer*, Vol.21, 1, pp. 70-80.
[MÜHL90] Mühlhäuser M (1990), Hyperinformation in instructional tool environments. In: Norrie D H, Six H W (eds.), Computer Assisted Learning, (Proc. of ICCAL'90), Springer: New York, 245-264.
[MYLO90] Mylonas E, Heath S (1990), Hypertext from the data point of view: paths and links in the Perseus project. In: Rizk A, Streitz N, André J (eds.), Hypertext: Concepts,Systems, and Applications (Proc. of ECHT'90), Cambridge Univ.Press: Cambridge, UK, 324-336.
[NIEL90] Nielsen J, Lyngboeck U (1990), Two field studies of hypermedia usability. In: Jonassen D H, Mandl H (1990, eds.), Designing Hypermedia for Learning. NATO ASI Series F, Vol. 67.
[PSTO88] Pstoka J (1988, eds.), Intelligent Tutoring Systems: Lessons Learned. Erlbaum: Hillsdale, NJ.
[RASK87] Raskin J (1987), The hype in hypertext: a critique. In: Hypertext 87 Papers, Univ.of North Carolina, Chapel Hill NC, ACM: New York, 325-330.
[RAYM88] Raymond D R, Tompa F W (1988), Hypertext and the new Oxford English dictionary. *Comm. ACM*, Vol.31, n.7, Jul.1988, 871-879.
[REMD87] Remde J R, Gomez L M, Landauer T K (1987), SuperBook: An automatic tool for information exploration - hypertext? In: Hypertext 87 Papers, Univ.of North Carolina, Chapel Hill NC, ACM: New York, 175-188.
[RYAN91] Ryan B (1991), Dynabook revisited with Alan Kay. *BYTE*, Feb.1991, 203-208.
[SHNE87] Shneiderman B (1987), User interface design for the Hyperties electronic encyclopedia. In: Hypertext 87 Papers, Univ.of North Carolina, Chapel Hill NC, ACM: New York, 189-194.
[SMIT87] Smith J B, Weiss S F, Ferguson G (1987), A hypertext Writing Environment and its cognitive basis. In: Hypertext 87 Papers, Univ.of North Carolina, Chapel Hill NC, ACM: NewYork, 195-214.
[TRIG88] Trigg R (1988), Guided tours and tabletops: tools for communicating in a hypertext environment. In: Proc. of CSCW '88, Portland, OR, ACM: New York, 216-226.
[VACC88] Vacca R, Ambrosetti C (1988), Il Labirinto della Memoria. Bompiani: Milano.
[YANK88] Yankelovich N, Haan B, Meyrowitz N, Drucker S M (1988), Intermedia: The concept and the construction of a seamless information environment. *IEEE Computer*, Vol.21, n.1, Jan.1988, 81-96.

Optimale Startpunkte zur Navigation in Hypermediasystemen - ein entscheidungstheoretischer Ansatz

Wolfgang H. Janko, Alfred Taudes, Wolfgang Faber
Abteilung für Angewandte Informatik, insbesondere Betriebsinformatik
Institut für Informationswirtschaft und Informationsverarbeitung
Wirtschaftsuniversität Wien
A-1090 Wien, Augasse 2-6

0. Abstract

Dieser Beitrag stellt ein Verfahren zur Bestimmung optimaler Startpunkte zur Navigation in Hypermediasystemen auf Basis der Theorie des optimalen Stoppens und Testens vor. Ausgangspunkt unserer Betrachtungen ist das Verfahren von Frisse. Dabei wird das "Browsing" in einem Hypermediasystem durch einen Algorithmus ergänzt, der auf Basis der Relevanz eines Knotens und seiner Nachfolger einen oder mehrere optimale Startpunkte für den Beginn dieses Prozesses bestimmt. Wir zeigen, daß unter Verwendung eines entscheidungstheoretischen Modells der hierzu notwendige Rechenaufwand erheblich verringert werden kann und die Anzahl der dem Anwender präsentierten Einstiegspunkte in das Hypermediasystem a priori begrenzt werden kann.

1. Einleitung

Hypermediasysteme werden i.A. definiert als Netz von Knoten, die Informationen enthalten und die durch Kanten ("Links") miteinander verbunden sind (vgl. hierzu z.B. Carlson[88]). Jeder Benutzer eines solchen Informationsnetzes kann sich von einem Startpunkt aus über die vorhandenen Links unter Zuhilfenahme von Navigationshilfen wie z.B. Linkbeschreibungen, "Landkarten" der näheren Umgebung etc. von Informationsknoten zu Informationsknoten bewegen ("Browsing"). Welche Richtung er bei Existenz mehrerer Links wählt, ist dabei nur von seiner Interessenslage abhängig. Diese Art der Informationsbeschaffung durch den Benutzer entspricht zwar der assoziativen Art und Weise, in der das menschliche Gehirn Informationen speichert und verarbeitet, ist aber auch mit einigen Problemen behaftet. Insbesondere kann es speziell in größeren Hypermediasystemen sehr zeitaufwendig sein, mit Hilfe dieses Suchmechanismus alle Knoten, die die gesuchten Informationen enthalten, zu durchqueren. Es ist daher üblich, diesen Navigationsmechanismus durch Verfahren, die zum traditionellen Information-Retrieval entwickelt wurden, zu ergänzen (ein Beispiel dafür ist der Hypertalkbefehl "find"). Diese haben jedoch den Nachteil, daß sie aus allen Informationseinheiten nur auf die direkt relevanten Einheiten zuückgreifen, d.h. sie vernachlässigen die Links und damit die inhaltlichen Beziehungen zwischen den Informationseinheiten. Gerade diese semantischen Informationen sind aber ein sehr wichtiger Unterschied zwischen Hypermedia- und herkömmlichen Informationssystemen. So kann z.B. ein Knoten dadurch sehr relevant für eine Abfrage sein, daß er die Wurzel eines Baumes von Knoten, die relevante Informationen enthalten ist, obwohl er selbst keine relevanten Informationen enthält. Für größere Hypermediaanwendungen sind deshalb **leistungsfähige Verfahren des Information-Retrieval unumgänglich.**

Der unbefriedigende gegenwärtige Stand der Informationsfindung in Hypermediasystemen ist ein häufig angeführter Kritikpunkt; für Halasz ist die Forderung nach besseren Verfahren eine der sieben Schlüsselanforderungen an zukünftige Hypermediasysteme (Halasz[88]). Die oben angeführten Probleme bilden den Ausgangspunkt für eine Reihe von Forschungsansätze wie z.B. die Ansätze zum Content Based Information Retrieval von Croft[89] oder graphische Abfragesprachen, die die Suche nach bestimmten Teilgraphen im Hyperspace erlauben (vgl. z.B. Consens[89]). Basis unseres Ansatzes zur Verbesserung der Navigationsmöglichkeiten in Hypermediasystemen sind die Arbeiten von Frisse (Frisse[88], Frisse[89]). Frisse argumentiert, daß in einem Hypermediasystem ein traditioneller Information Retrievalalgorithmus nicht dazu benutzt werden sollte, alle Knoten, deren Inhalt für eine Abfrage relevant ist, zu finden, sondern dazu, einen oder mehrere **optimale Startpunkte für die weitere Suche durch Browsing unter Berücksichtigung der im Hypermediasystem enthaltenen semantischen Beziehungen** aufzufinden, also eines Knotens, der entweder selbst einige der gesuchten Informationen enthält oder aber direkt über eine unmittelbare Verbindung zu Informationseinheiten verfügt, die diese Informationen enthalten . Man beachte, daß die zweite Variante bei einfacher Volltextsuche entfallen würde. Frisse betrachtet hierarchisch strukturierte Hypermediasysteme und geht von folgenden vier Annahmen aus, um optimale Startpunkte zur Navigation zu finden:

1. Der Nutzen eines Knotens (= Informationseinheit) für eine bestimmte Abfrage kann aus ihrem **"inneren Wert"** und ihrem **"äußeren Wert"** berechnet werden.

2. Der innere Wert einer Informationseinheit wird durch die Auftretenshäufigkeit der Abfrage-Terme innerhalb der Informationseinheit und (umgekehrt proportional) durch die Anzahl der Informationseinheiten, die diesen Term beinhalten, bestimmt .

3. Der äußere Wert einer Informationseinheit wird durch die Anzahl der unmittelbar nachfolgenden Informationseinheiten (unabhängig vom Auftreten eines Abfrage-Terms) bestimmt, wobei weniger Nachfolger sich in einem höheren Wert ausdrücken.

4. Der optimale Startpunkt zur Beantwortung einer Abfrage ist dann diejenige Informationseinheit mit dem höchsten Gesamtgewicht. Der nächstbeste Startpunkt ist diejenige Informationseinheit mit dem nächsthöchsten Gewicht, die kein Nachfolger einer Einheit mit höherer Gewichtung ist. Wenn dieser nächstbeste Startpunkt unmittelbarer Nachfolger irgendeines

anderen Startpunktes ist, sollte die Startpunktrolle der nächstbesten Informationseinheit auf diesen Vorgänger übergehen.

Aus diesen Annahmen leitet Frisse folgende Formel zur Berechnung des Gewichts eines Knotens bezüglich einer Abfrage her[1]:

$$T_i \; = \; \sum_j G_{ij} + \frac{1}{y} \sum_d T_d \quad \text{mit}$$
$$G_{ij} \; = \; k \cdot F_{ij} \cdot \left[\log \frac{n}{N_j} + 1 \right]$$

Dabei bedeutet n die Anzahl der Knoten im System, T_i das Totalgewicht von Knoten i, G_{ij} das innere Gewicht von Knoten i bezüglich Abfrageterm j, F_{ij} die Auftretenshäufigkeit von Term j in Knoten i, N_j die Anzahl der Knoten, die Abfrage-Term j enthalten, y die Anzahl der i unmittelbar nachfolgenden Knoten und k ist eine Konstante.

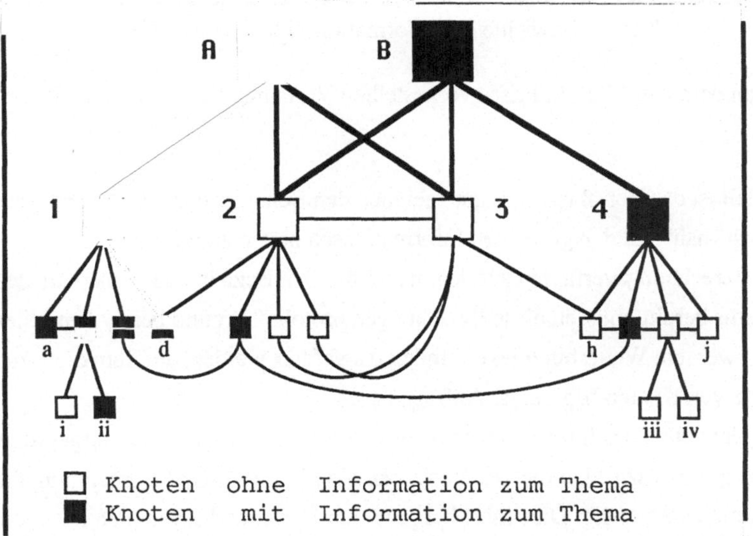

Abb. 1: Information-Retrieval in einem hierarchischen Hypermediasystem

Wir wollen dieses Verfahren anhand eines in Abbildung 1 dargestellten hypothetischen Hypermediasystems demonstrieren. Dabei wird ein Startpunkt für eine Abfrage gesucht, die aus ei-

---

1 In Frisse[89] wird das innere Gewicht jeder Karte auf eine andere Art bestimmt. Es hängt ab vom sog. "degree of belief" (einer Schätzung, wie nützlich eine unter einem bestimmten Begriff klassifizierte Informationseinheit als Antwort auf eine bestimmte Query ist), der durch User-Feedback einer ständigen Änderung unterliegt. Der Ansatz Totalgewicht = inneres plus äußeres Gewicht bleibt jedoch erhalten.

nem Term besteht, der in jedem schwarz gekennzeichneten Knoten genau einmal enthalten ist (also $k = 1$, $n = 21$, $N_j = 10$ und $F_{ij} \in \{0;1\}$ $\forall$ i). Daraus ergeben sich die in Tab. 1 abgebildeten Gewichte der einzelnen Knoten (die Punkte auf der untersten hierarchischen Ebene sind von links nach rechts durchnumeriert von a bis o). Der optimale Startpunkt unter Verwendung dieses Algorithmus ist demnach Knoten (1) mit einem Informationswert von 2,81, nächstbester Startpunkt ist Knoten (A) mit einem Informationswert von 2,40.

Knoten	inneres Gewicht	äußeres Gewicht	Gesamtgewicht
i, iii, iv	0	0 (kein Nachfolger)	0
ii	1,32	0 (kein Nachfolger)	1,32
a, c, d, i	1,32	0	1,32
b	1,32	0,66	1,98
f, g, h, i, j, k	0	0	0
1 mit y = 4	1,32	1,49	→ 2,81 ←
2 mit y = 3	0	0,44	0,44
3 mit y = 0	0	0	0
4 mit y = 4	1,32	0,33	1,65
A	1,32	1,08	2,40
B	1,32	0,70	2,02

Tab. 1: Gewichte der Informationseinheiten aus Abb. 1

Die Kritik an dem von Mark E. Frisse vorgestellten Verfahren läßt sich folgendermaßen zusammenfassen:

1. Prinzipiell ist das Verfahren sehr gut geeignet, den Benutzer nach der Eingabe einer Abfrage möglichst "nah"[2] zu den gesuchten Informationseinheiten zu bringen.

2. Da das Berechnungsverfahren auf den hierarchischen Beziehungen innerhalb des Hypermediasystems beruht, müssen diese Beziehungen protokolliert und bei dynamischen Systemen gepflegt werden. Weiterhin muß ein Index o.ä geführt werden, auf dem die Berechnung der Relevanz von Knoten bzgl. einer Abfrage beruht.

3. Da das Gewicht einer Informationseinheit von seinen hierarchisch untergeordneten Einheiten abhängig ist, wird bei diesem Verfahren eine "Bottom-Up"-Berechnung der Gewichte aller Knoten notwendig. Dies führt bei größeren Hypermediasystemen zu einem sehr grossen Rechenaufwand. Ebenso kann es passieren, daß viele Knoten als Startpunkte in Frage kommen. In diesem Fall würden entweder alle präsentiert, wodurch der Informationsgehalt für den Benutzer fällt, oder nur die "besten", wodurch der Rechenaufwand, der für die Bestimmung der Gewichte der anderen Knoten aufgewendet wurde, vergeudet ist.

4. Das Verfahren kann nur bei hierarchischen Hypermediasystemen angewandt werden.

---

2 Unter "Nähe" soll in diesem Zusammenhang z.B. die Anzahl der über Links zwischengeschalteten Informationseinheiten verstanden werden.

2. Navigation in Hypermediasystemen durch Optimales Stoppen und Testen

Wir wollen Kritikpunkt 3 als Ausgangspunkt nehmen, um dieses Verfahren unter Verwendung von Erkenntnissen der Entscheidungstheorie zu verbessern. Ziel ist es, den Rechenaufwand zur Bestimmung eines optimalen Startknotens zu verringern und die Anzahl der dem Benutzer präsentierten Startpunkte a-priori zu begrenzen. Ausgangspunkt ist die Theorie des optimalen Stoppens und Testens (dargestellt in MacQueen[64], Janko[85]). Gegensatnd der Theorie ist folgender in Abb. 2 graphisch dargestellter **Entscheidungsprozeß**: einem Entscheidungsträger wird eine Reihe von Alternativen präsentiert, aus denen er diejenige wählen möchte, die für ihn den höchsten Nutzen hat. Allerdings kann er diesen nicht direkt beobachten, sondern erhält nur eine Information x darüber, die ihm probabilistische Aussagen über den wahren Nutzen u liefert. Hat der Entscheidungsträger x für eine bestimmte Alternative beobachtet, kann er

- die Alternative akzeptieren und den Suchvorgang stoppen,
- die Alternative verwerfen und weitersuchen oder
- die Alternative testen, um eine genauere Information y über den wahren Nutzen zu erhalten und auf dieser Basis entscheiden, ob die Alternative akzeptiert werden soll oder nicht.

Weiterhin wird angenommen, daß die Beobachtung von x mit konstanten Suchkosten c_s und daß das Testen einer Alternative mit konstanten Testkosten c_t verbunden ist. Die Lösung eines derartigen Stopp- und Testproblems ist eine stationäre Strategie, die auf Basis der Wahrscheinlichkeiten, mit der bestimmte Werte von x,y und u auftreten, angibt, unter welchem Wert x_1^* eine Alternative verworfen, ab welchem Wert x_2^* eine Alternative ohne Test akzeptiert und ab welchem Testergebnis v^* eine getestete Alternative akzeptiert werden soll.

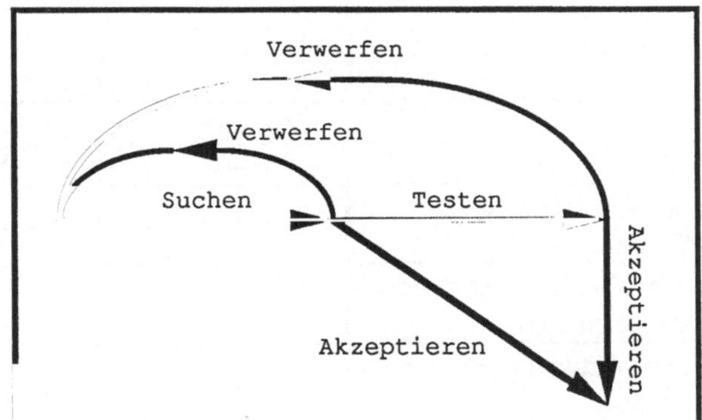

Abb. 2: Graphische Darstellung des Suchen-Testen-Stoppen

Für derartige Entscheidungsprozesse gibt es eine ganze Reihe von Beispielen aus dem täglichen

Leben.: jemand will einen Gebrauchtwagen kaufen, wobei er selbst den Wert des Wagens nicht genau bestimmen kann; er entscheidet also unter Unsicherheit. Er beginnt sein Handeln mit der Suche nach einem geeigneten Kaufobjekt (verbunden mit Suchkosten wie z.B. Kosten für Zeitungsannoncen, Fahrtgeld oder Opportunitätskosten für den Zeitaufwand). Hat er ein solches gefunden, dann kann er so begeistert sein, daß er es gleich kauft. Oder es mißfällt ihm so sehr, daß er es gleich ablehnt. Ist er sich über den Wert des Wagens nicht sicher, so kann er zu einem Sachverständigen gehen, dort den Wagen schätzen lassen (verbunden mit Kosten) und aufgrund der Schätzung eine Entscheidung treffen. Lehnt er den Wagen ab, muß er seine Suche von Neuem beginnen. Ein derartiges **Stopp- und Testproblem** ist lösbar, wenn

1. für die Zufallsvariablen X, Y und U eine gemeinsame Verteilung existiert und bekannt ist,
2. der Erwartungswert E(U) existiert und endlich ist und
3. $F(z|x)$, $z=E(U|X=x, Y)$ stochastisch geordnet ist, d.h. es gilt { $x_1 < x_2 \Rightarrow F(z|x_1) \geq F(z|x_2)$ }!

Anhand eines Gleichungssystems[3] lassen sich die Werte x_1^*, x_2^* und v^* berechnen und man erhält so die Entscheidungsregeln für die Suche sowie den Test des Ergebnisses der Suche:

A.1.	$x \leq x_1^*$	$\Rightarrow$	**Verwerfen**
A.2.	$x \geq x_2^*$	$\Rightarrow$	**Akzeptieren**
A.3.	$x \in (x_1^*, x_2^*)$	$\Rightarrow$	**Testen**
B.1.	$y < v^*$	$\Rightarrow$	**Verwerfen**
B.2.	$y \geq v^*$	$\Rightarrow$	**Akzeptieren**

Tab. 2: Übersicht über die möglichen Entscheidungsfälle

Die Werte von x_1^* und x_2^* können so variieren, daß genau fünf verschiedenen Politiken möglich sind:

Politik	x_1^*	x_2^*
Nie testen	$x_1^* = x_2^*$	$x_2^* = x_1^*$
Immer testen	$x_1^* = -\infty$	$x_2^* = +\infty$
Testen für einen x-Wert größer einem bestimmten Vergleichswert	$-\infty < x_1^* < +\infty$	$x_2^* = +\infty$
Testen für einen x-Wert kleiner einem bestimmten Vergleichswert	$x_1^* = -\infty$	$-\infty < x_2^* < +\infty$
Testen für einen Wert von x in einem bestimmten Intervall	$-\infty < x_1^* < +\infty$	$-\infty < x_2^* < +\infty$

Tab. 3: Mögliche Entscheidungspolitiken für das Testen

---

[3] Eine genauere formale Beschreibung der Vorgehensweise findet sich in MacQueen[64] und Janko[85].

Wir wollen dieses entscheidungstheoretische Modell verwenden, um für eine an ein Hypermediasystem gestellte Abfrage eine optimalen Startpunkt zu bestimmten. Dabei gehen wir davon aus, daß den Alternativen im Modell bestimmte Knoten des Hypermediasystems entsprechen, die sequentiell durchsucht werden. Den Suchkosten c_s entspricht daher die CPU-Zeit, die notwendig ist, um zum nächsten Knoten dieser Ebene zu gelangen und dessen Relevanz für die Abfrage zu bestimmen. Die dabei möglichen Werte entsprechen den möglichen Beobachtungen x. In Abhängigkeit dieses Wertes kann nun sofort zum nächsten entsprechenden Knoten. weitergegangen werden oder dieser Knoten näher untersucht werden, indem seine Nachfolgeknoten untersucht werden. Den Testkosten c_t entspricht hier wiederum die hierfür notwendige CPU-Zeit. Nun wird auch der Zusammenhang zum Verfahren von Frisse deutlich. Der "Suchschritt" zur Beobachtung von x entspricht der Berechnung des inneren Gewichtes, der "Testschritt" zur Beobachtung von y der Bestimmung des Gesamtgewichts.

Wir wollen dieses Verfahren wiederum anhand des in Abb. 1 vorgestellten Hypermediasystems demonstrieren. Für die Zufallsvariablen X,Y und U soll gelten: $x \in \{0,1,2,3\}$, $y \in \{0,1,2,3\}$ und $v \in \{0,1,2,3\}$ (siehe auch Abb. 4). Dies bedeutet, daß für jeden der in Frage kommenden Knoten die Relevanz bezüglich einer Abfrage 0, 1, 2 oder 3 sein kann. Ebenso soll das Ergebnis des Tests eines Knoten nur die Ergebnisse 0, 1, 2 oder 3 liefern und wir wollen annehmen, daß das Testergebnis die Relevanz, d.i. den Nutzen eines Knotens perfekt wiederspiegelt. Dies hat zur Folge, daß für die in untenstehender Abbildung dargestellten gemeinsamen Verteilung

Vektor X:	.000	1.000	2.000	3.000
$\Rightarrow R = E(U\|X=x,Y)$	.050	.550	1.300	2.500
Vektor Y:	.000	1.000	2.000	3.000
Vektor U:	.000	1.000	2.000	3.000
$h_{xyu} =$	0.665	0	0	0
	0	0.035	0	0
	0	0	0	0
	0	0	0	0
	0.0975	0	0	0
	0	0.03	0	0
	0	0	0.015	0
	0	0	0	0.0075
	0.03	0	0	0
	0	0.03	0	0
	0	0	0.02	0
	0	0	0	0.02
	0	0	0	0
	0	0.005	0	0
	0	0	0.015	0
	0	0	0	0.03

Tab. 4: Gemeinsame Verteilung von X,Y und U

von X,Y und U gilt: $h_{ijk} = 0 \; \forall \; j \neq k$. In Analogie zum obigen Beispiel wollen wir auch hier x als inneres Gewicht und y als äußeres Gewicht gemäß der Formel von Frisse bestimmen, wobei wir die Formeln durch einfaches Runden dahingehend modifizieren, daß sie nur Ergebnisse im angegebenen Wertebereich liefern.

Auf Basis dieser Verteilung ergibt sich bei Suchkosten $c_s = 0{,}05$ und Testkosten $c_t = 0{,}1$ z.B. folgende optimale Entscheidungspolitik, wobei der gesamte erwartete Ertrag v* 2,3 beträgt :

Suchkosten	Testkosten	X	0	1	2	3
.050	.100	T(R,V0)	1.400	1.525	1.800	2.450
		Politik	Verwerfen	Testen	Testen	Akzept.

Tab. 5: Entscheidungspolitik für $c_s = 0{,}05$ und $c_t = 0{,}1$

Dies bedeutet, daß Knoten mit Relevanz (innerem Gewicht) 0 keinesfalls als Startpunkt in Frage kommen. Wird ein Knoten mit Relevanz (innerem Gewicht) 1 oder 2 beobachtet, soll dieser "getestet" werden, indem sein Gesamtgewicht bestimmt wird. Ist dieses kleiner als 2,3, soll dieser verworfen werden. Anderenfalls ist dies der optimale Startpunkt, ebenso wie Knoten mit Relevanz (innerem Gewicht) 3. Angewandt auf unser Beispiel würde man also folgendermaßen vorgehen: man beginnt mit Knoten a und berechnet sein inneres Gewicht als 1. Für diesen Wert ist die optimale Entscheidung ein Test, also die Berechnung des Gesamtgewichts. Dieses beträgt 1 - der Knoten wird abgelehnt. Für die Knoten b, c, d und i wird ebenfalls mit einem negativen Ergebnis getestet. Für Knoten b beträgt das getestete Gesamtgewicht zwar 2, ist aber immer noch kleiner als v*. Die Knoten f, g, h, i, j, k, l, n und o werden aufgrund ihres inneren Gewichts von 0 sofort verworfen. Anschließend wird Knoten 1 bei einem inneren Gewicht von 1 getestet. Dies ergibt ein Gesamtgewicht von 3 und führt zur Annahme von Knoten 1 als optimalem Startpunkt.

Informationseinheit	inneres G.	Entscheidung	Gesamtgew.	Entscheidung
a, c, d,i	1	Testen	1	Verwerfen
b	1	Testen	2	Verwerfen
f, g, h, i, j, k	0	Verwerfen	---	---
1 mit y = 4	1	Testen	3	Akzeptieren

Tab. 6: Suche eines optimalen Startpunkts mit Suchen-Testen-Stoppen bei den Werten $c_s = 0{,}05$ und $c_t = 0{,}1$ sowie v* = 2,3

Wir haben also bei 21 Knoten für 12 Knoten die inneren Gewichte und für 6 Knoten die äußeren Gewichte bestimmt. Wären wir nur analog zur oben aufgezeigten Methode nach Frisse vorgegangen, hätten wir für alle 21 Knoten die inneren und äußeren Gewichte bestimmt. Man sieht anhand dieses Vergleichs die durch Verwendung der Theorie des optimalen Stoppens und Testens erzielbare **Verringerung des zur Bestimmung eines optimalen Startpunkts notwendigen Rechenaufwands.**

Es ist interessant zu studieren, wie sich die optimalen Politiken verändern, wenn die Such- und Testkosten variiert werden. Für obige Verteilung ergeben sich z.B. die in Tabelle 7 aufgelisteten optimalen Entscheidungspolitiken:

Suchkosten	Testkosten	X	0.000	1.000	2.000	3.000
		$R = E(V|X=x)$	0.050	0.550	1.300	2.500
.010	.100	$T(R,V_0)$	2.200	2.235	2.340	2.620
		Politik	Verwerfen	Verwerfen	Testen	Testen
.010	.200	$T(R,V_0)$	2.100	2.135	2.240	2.520
		Politik	Verwerfen	Verwerfen	Verwerfen	Testen
.010	.300	$T(R,V_0)$	2.000	2.035	2.140	2.420
		Politik	Verwerfen	Verwerfen	Verwerfen	Akzept.
.050	.100	$T(R,V_0)$	1.400	1.525	1.800	2.450
		Politik	Verwerfen	Testen	Testen	Akzept.
.050	.200	$T(R,V_0)$	1.300	1.425	1.700	2.350
		Politik	Verwerfen	Verwerfen	Testen	Akzept.
.050	.300	$T(R,V_0)$	1.200	1.325	1.600	2.250
		Politik	Verwerfen	Verwerfen	Testen	Akzept.
.050	.400	$T(R,V_0)$	1.100	1.225	1.500	2.150
		Politik	Verwerfen	Verwerfen	Verwerfen	Akzept.
.100	.100	$T(R,V_0)$	.933	1.128	1.520	2.403
		Politik	Verwerfen	Testen	Testen	Akzept.
.100	.200	$T(R,V_0)$	.833	1.028	1.420	2.303
		Politik	Verwerfen	Verwerfen	Testen	Akzept.
.100	.300	$T(R,V_0)$	.733	0.928	1.320	2.203
		Politik	Verwerfen	Verwerfen	Testen	Akzept.
.100	.400	$T(R,V_0)$	.633	0.828	1.220	2.103
		Politik	Verwerfen	Verwerfen	Akzept.	Akzept.
.200	.100	$T(R,V_0)$	.385	.748	1.338	2.400
		Politik	Verwerfen	Testen	Testen	Akzept.
.200	.200	$T(R,V_0)$	.285	.648	1.238	2.300
		Politik	Verwerfen	Testen	Akzept.	Akzept.
.200	.300	$T(R,V_0)$	.185	.548	1.138	2.200
		Politik	Verwerfen	Akzept.	Akzept.	Akzept.
.300	.100	$T(R,V_0)$	.069	.531	1.238	2.400
		Politik	Verwerfen	Akzept.	Akzept.	Akzept.

Tab. 7: Entscheidungspolitiken bei verschiedenen Such- und Testkosten

Man erkennt an dieser Tabelle zweierlei: zum einen bewirkt eine Erhöhung der Testkosten, daß die Politik "Testen" durch die Politiken "Verwerfen" oder "Akzeptieren" ersetzt wird, zum anderen bewirkt eine Erhöhung der Suchkosten eine schnellere Entscheidung für die Politik "Akzeptieren".

Zusammenfassung

In diesem Beitrag wurde der von Frisse entwickelte Ansatz zur Bestimmung eines oder mehrerer optimaler Startpunkte zur Navigation in Hypermediasystemen verfeinert, indem mit Hilfe der Theorie des optimalen Stoppens und Testens Schranken für die inneren Gewichte bestimmt werden, unter denen das Bestimmen des entsprechenden Gesamtgewichts unterbleiben kann. Als wichtigste Kritikpunkte an der Kombination der beiden vorgestellten Modelle als Algorithmus zur Startpunktsuche sei zusammenfassend folgendes angemerkt:

1. Prinzipiell wird die Grundidee des Frisse-Verfahrens beibehalten: der Wert eines Knotens wird durch dessen eigenen Wert (= "inneres Gewicht") und den Wert der ihm untergeordneten Knoten (= "äußeres Gewicht") bestimmt.

2. Gegenüber dem Verfahren von Frisse ergibt sich durch die Einführung eines Such-Test-und-Stop-Verfahrens ein erheblich verminderter Rechenaufwand, da nicht mehr die Gewichte aller Informationseinheiten bestimmt werden, sondern die Gewichte der unteren hierarchischen Ebenen nur im Bedarfsfall "getestet" werden.

3. Durch die Einführung des Such-Test-und-Stop-Verfahrens ergibt sich kein erhöhter Pflegeaufwand für das Hypermediasystem, da auch das Frisse-Verfahren zur Bestimmung der Gewichte der Informationseinheiten Kenntnis über die Auftretenshäufigkeit der Abfrage-Terme im Hypermediasystem benötigt und diese Kenntnis in der Praxis nur durch das Führen eines Index ermöglicht wird.

Literatur

Carlson[88]
Carlson, Patricia Ann: Hypertext: A Way of Incorporating User Feedback into Online Documentation, in: Barrett, Edward (Ed.): Text, ConText and HyperText, S. 93-110

Consens[89]
Consens, Mariano P.; Mendelzon, Alberto O.: Expressing Structural Hypertext Queries in GraphLog, in: Association for Computing Machinery (Hrsg.): Hypertext '89 Proceedings, S. 269-292

Croft[89]
Croft, Bruce W.; Turtle, Howard: A Retrieval Model Incorporating Hypertext Links, in: Association for Computing Machinery (Hrsg.): Hypertext '89 Proceedings, S. 213-224

Frisse[88]
Frisse, Mark E.: Searching for Information in a Hypertext Medical Handbook, in: Communications of the ACM, 1988 (Vol 31), Heft 7, S. 880-886

Frisse[89]

Frisse, Mark E.; Cousins, Steve B.: Information Retrieval from Hypertext: Update on the Dynamic Medical Handbook Project, in: Association for Computing Machinery (Hrsg.): Hypertext '89 Proceedings, S. 199-212

Halasz[88]

Halasz, Frank G.: Reflections on NoteCards: Seven Issues for the Next Generation of Hypermedia Systems, in: Communications of the ACM, 1988 (Vol 31), Heft 7, S. 836-852

Janko[85]

Janko, Wolfgang H.; Hartmann, Joachim: Flexible Informationsbeschaffung in Alternativensuchproblemen, in: Ballwieser, Wolfgang; Berger, Karl-Heinz (Hrsg.): Information und Wirtschaftlichkeit, S. 199-228

MacQueen[64]

MacQueen, James B.: Optimal Policies for a Class of Search and Evaluation Problems, in: Management Science, 1964 (Vol 10), Heft 4, S. 746-759

HyperAuthor—An Authoring Tool Based on Hypertext

Hermann Kaindl and Holger G. Ziegeler
Siemens AG Österreich, Gudrunstraße 11, A—1100 Vienna, Austria
e-mail: hgz@siegud.at

Summary

This paper describes an approach to use hypertext to support authoring of linear text in the sense of conventional (technical) literature like books, papers, reports, etc. We try to model and treat such authoring as an explicit process. It makes excellent use of hypertext, satisfying the need for external representations in the course of authoring. We found indications that this process can also help for authoring hypertext systems themselves. A prototypical implementation of a system based on this approach has been used to write this paper.

Introduction

While the basic idea of *hypertext* is old, only recently has its implementation on cheaper hardware become practicable (for an introduction and survey see for instance [4]). Nevertheless, the publication of conventional books, papers, etc. based on "linear" text will prevail for quite a while. For this reason, several attempts have been reported which support authoring of linear text with hypertext. Engelbart [5] intended to generally *augment* the human intellectual capabilities with hypertext, specifically supporting authorship. Trigg and Irish [12] reported on the experiences of users of a (general) hypertext system, who built their own extensions to support various aspects of authoring linear text. Psychological investigations by Neuwirth and Kaufer [9] showed the relevance of external representations in the course of authoring and their potential support by hypertext. Streitz *et al.* [11] describe an approach for the active support to cognitive processes involved in authoring. Smith *et al.* [10] base their authoring tool on a cognitive model.

Our approach is along these lines and aims to design a practical tool, which supports all phases of the authoring of documents. Besides helping the professional author by automating routine tasks, it is meant to helpfully guide less experienced writers, since it makes the entire process more explicit (Neuwirth and Kaufer [9] detected a correspondence between more structuring and better results). In the near future, hypertext may become very useful for supporting the process of authoring books or papers. In the following, we describe an approach in this direction, and a prototypical authoring tool for technical literature based thereon. This paper itself has been written by using this authoring tool (hence there is some kind of self-reference).

Our approach emphasizes the use of hypertext, first of all for building a kind of informal "knowledge base" about the domain of the intended publication(s).* Hence, this approach includes aspects of *authoring hypertext* as well. Since hypertext itself is the domain of this and other papers, as well as of reports about more general hypertext issues, in our case this informal knowledge base represents descriptions of hypertext (again, a self-reference). We also built a small "tutorial" component in our hypertext system which uses the knowledge base to inform the ever increasing number of interested people about the key ideas and concepts of hypertext. Its users simultaneously *read about* hypertext and *navigate through* hypertext, in essence reinforcing the learning process (see [6]).

In the following sections, we first try to treat authoring (linear text) as an explicit process, in order to find out how hypertext can be of use to support it. After identifying and sketching such possibilities, we describe our approach for an authoring tool based thereon and a prototypical implementation. Finally, we discuss the advantages and the remaining open problems of this approach.

The Authoring Process of a Technical Paper

Most of the people experienced in writing (technical) papers will agree that a major portion of this process hinges upon developing and organizing ideas. Only thereafter a detailed planning/design of the document and finally the writing of text takes place. The psychological studies by Neuwirth and Kaufer [9], the cognitive model described by Smith *et al.* [10], as well as the experiences reported by Trigg and Irish [12] serve as evidence for this view. There is also an analogy to the development of (traditional) software (see also Walker [14]), where it has become more and more evident that the actual coding should be done only after serious specification and design phases.

In the following, we try to sketch this process by identifying several important steps. In this description we make use of terms coined in AI. As stated above, one of the purposes is to find out to what extent hypertext can actually be useful in supporting this process. We interpret authoring in a broad sense, including initiation and carrying out of underlying research.

First of all, let us assume a starting point, and identify it as the "birth of a basic idea". This may induce brainstorming, intended to discover more about the idea and to find related ones (Trigg and Irish [12] report on attempts in this direction). When this is successful, steps to develop and structure these ideas are necessary, possibly intertwined with each other and performed repeatedly. Depending on the kind of research, experiments and/or analyses can be involved in developing the ideas, and this part of the process is

---

*Note, that this notion of a knowledge base has to be distinguished from the one coined in the field of *Artificial Intelligence* (AI), where the knowledge must be represented in a machine-interpretable form. Nevertheless, due to its explicit representation of links, the method of text structuring in a hypertext system is more akin to *knowledge representation* than any other form of current "non-AI" data processing.

potentially long and also difficult to describe. Naturally, there is a need for structuring (usually in a hierarchy), which can be solved by introducing a taxonomy of concepts. (We even see a certain resemblance to *knowledge engineering* for *knowledge-based (expert) systems*.)

Up to this point, no specific document is necessarily in the mind of the author(s) (though they can already have a certain vision), and due to our experience also the process of *authoring hypertext* may start in the same way. On such an "edifice of ideas", the planning/design of one or more document(s) can be based. This involves yet another ordering of selected ideas/concepts, since in conventional publishing the final text has to be linear. (There is an analogy to the concept of a *linear plan* in AI.) In this stage, however, it has been found that partial ordering, which results in hierarchical structures, is useful. These hierarchical structures for the planned document need not necessarily coincide with those of the underlying knowledge base (as described in the previous paragraph). An experienced author tends to begin with more abstract items first, and adds more and more details by elaborating them (*hierarchical planning*). Although this argumentation suggests a strict top-down procedure, we are aware that humans sometimes gain from the use of bottom-up processes, i.e., the early formulation of small portions of text may make sense (for the immediate processing of an intuition).

Only after all this work has been done—taking place (partially) just in the authors' heads—the actual writing of the linear text can be done successfully. Besides the linguistic aspects, cognitive work is also involved in formatting the text and in preparing it for high-quality printing. While especially these final steps are supported by various tools today, support for the even more important earlier steps can rarely be found (apart from pencil and paper).

Authoring with Hypertext

In the following analysis, we attempt to describe *how* hypertext can support the process described above (in particular, which of its steps), and *to what extent*. For this purpose, we work out the various steps. We also address the issue of integration with other tools, which is necessary here.

Although hypertext cannot directly support the birth of a basic idea, the following steps could be subsumed via the notion of *idea processing*, which is often associated with hypertext. Basically we suggest to create a hypertext node for each idea and to sketch it informally first by means of short textual phrases. Related ideas (as discovered by brainstorming, for instance) should be treated in the same way, and their mutual relationships can and shall be represented explicitly by hypertext links between the corresponding nodes.

Once there exists a network of nodes representing ideas and concepts, further structure can be posed on it by establishing a hierarchy (which is often considered distinct from links for cross-references in hypertext [2]). In particular, we suggest to organize the ideas/concepts "from general to specific" in *taxonomies* (which play a major role in *object-oriented programming* and in *knowledge representation* within AI). As an example, Fig. 1

```
Idea Processing
        Conventional Idea Processing
        Idea Processing with Hypertext
                Representing Ideas and Relations
                Ideas Guiding in Hypertext
Structuring
        Structuring of Text
                Conventional Structuring
                        Table of Contents
                        Indices
                Structuring Using Hypertext
                        Structuring via Nodes/Links
                        Structuring by Contexts
        Structuring of Knowledge
                Structuring via AI Frames
                Semantic Nets
Possibilities of Hypertext
        Construction
                Authoring Hypertext
                Design with Hypertext
        Information Access
                Reading Hypertext
                        Complete Reading
                        Selective Reading
                Searching
                        Navigational Access
                        Text Search
                        Retrieval from Hypertext
Integration of Hypertext and AI
        Reasoning about Structured Text
        Documentation of Knowledge Bases
        Support for Knowledge Engineering
Applications of Hypertext
        Pure Text Hypertext
                Publishing with Hypertext
                        Authoring Hypertext
                        Authoring Linear Text
                        Combined Authoring
        Software Hypertext
                HAISE
        AI Hypertext
                HAISE
HCI Support for Hypertext
        Graphic Design
        Overview Diagrams
        Path Recording
        Marking Visited Nodes
        History List
Critical Features of Hypertext Systems
        Navigation
        Environment
                Integration
                Portability
                Tools
        Authorship
                Quality
                Collaboration
        Changes
                Structural Changes
                Version Control
Implementation of Hypertext
        Conventional Approach
        Based on KE Tools
```

Figure 1: Taxonomy of Ideas and Concepts

shows such a taxonomy of ideas and concepts related to hypertext, which represents the basic structure of our informal hypertext knowledge base.

Up to this point, we think this approach may be equally useful for authoring a hypertext system intended for readers of hypertext. In fact, our own prototypical tutoring system about hypertext has originated from such a process. First experience with our system suggests that the taxonomy supports navigation.

When continuing to write a conventional linear document, one can base its design on the web of ideas represented in hypertext. We suggest to represent explicitly all aspects involved. As described in the previous section, the resulting hierarchy for the document is not necessarily the same as for the underlying knowledge base. Since we see an analogy to the process of developing software, this can be tried along the same lines. (Nelson [8] had already proposed how to use hypertext for supporting program development, and for instance Bigelow [1] described a CASE system based on hypertext.) For the design of a paper, in particular, nodes with elaborations of ideas can be created and appropriately connected to the nodes representing the text which sketches the ideas.

The actual writing of linear text can of course be supported by this approach in the sense that everything of importance is explicitly available through hypertext. The typing, however, just needs a good text editor, as usual. Since the nodes of hypertext contain text, there should be one integrated in the system, in any case. Issues of formatting and printing may require an extra tool, and this must be integrated with the hypertext system.

A significant part of work in the course of scientific projects may stem from the necessity to deal with related literature. We suggest integrating literature references on the study field in the knowledge base. Two ways of access can be realized. On the one side, there is a global direct access by the list (or topic related lists) of references. On the other side, one creates cross links from nodes of related ideas/concepts to literature references. The representation of the bibliography entries shall be formalized in order to make it machine interpretable (especially for automatic handling in the actual text of a document).

An Authoring Tool Based on Hypertext

The authoring tool *HyperAuthor* on PC which we built as a prototypical realization of the ideas of the preceeding section is the document authoring component of our present hypertext system. It works with the informal knowledge base (in our case on hypertext), which serves as a reservoir of ideas. It contains also a bibliography of related publications (references from the documents are treated automatically), and a document management system for different types of technical publications, such as books, papers, or reports. HyperAuthor can be described along three dimensions: the static view, the dynamic view, and the analytic view.

Statically, HyperAuthor is a tool built as an integration of an application developed with the hypertext system HyperShell [13], the document preparation system $\text{\LaTeX}$ [7], and an integrating environment. The hypertext application consists of two major parts standing side by side which we call authoring and printing interface. The *authoring interface* provides the user interface with support in all areas pertaining to input. It is subject to control by the author, but must (semi-)automatically propagate all changes and keep the information consistent. HyperAuthor provides organizational support, such as a skeleton and templates. (In the description of WE by Smith *et al.* [10] we could not find reference to such facilities.) The *printing interface* deals with the generation of printable output for the used publishing system which is a backend of HyperAuthor. Here, the user is concerned with the format and lay-out of the text. In order to again save the user as much effort as possible, we choose LaTeX as actual output component of this backend, since it provides the unprofessional author with a comprehensive capability of automatic formatting. Basic parameters for the layout are automatically generated by HyperAuthor from templates.

Dynamically, HyperAuthor offers three *phases* of the authoring process. First, the *IDEAS* phase supports the early activities when ideas are collected. This is done by creating nodes for ideas/concepts and links between them in the hypertext knowledge base within the HyperShell application. Second, in the *PLAN* phase, collected ideas are arranged to determine the structure of the document. This task consists of finding a linear order of ideas and planning the refinement of ideas for their presentation. Third, during the *TEXT* phase the skeleton of the document, which is the result of the second phase, is finally filled with linear text. While HyperAuthor offers these three phases, it is possible to use each of them alone. E.g. in the case of a paper on completed research (in the domain of machine learning), we skipped the *IDEAS* phase.

The third dimension of HyperAuthor describes the analytical model in the mentioned phases. In the *IDEAS* phase the hypertext system provides the means to collect ideas. They are described in nodes (mostly in brief terms), and their connections are explicitly represented by links between the nodes. In addition, they are organized hierarchically. As seen in Fig. 1, we establish the ordering concept "general-to-specific" by special links to build a taxonomy of ideas/concepts.

In the *PLAN* phase, we deal with the design of a specific document. This will reference certain concepts of the underlying hypertext knowledge base. The resulting hierarchy possibly contains sub-trees of the taxonomy (chosen by judging the potential relevance for the document in work). It will, however, in general be different from the taxonomy. The designed structure is the document's skeleton of sections and subsections. The necessary activities are basically modelled as top-down design, allowing for exceptions of bottom-up work. Within a level of design, the collection of ideas is converted into a chain of (yet empty) blocks, which will eventually contain the related text. If applicable, these blocks can be refined on a deeper level.

When writing linear text in the last phase (*TEXT*), the vertical structure is mainly used (and not expanded further) as a constant reminder for the author. It helps to determine which elementary step of elaboration is presently performed, where in the document's structure the step can be found, and which references to other parts are intended. Filler elements can also be inserted, which are small portions of text that serve as transitions between adjacent elaboration steps. At the end of the third phase, the document will explicitly be represented in the system as the complete linear text with all information on its structure and also on the phase-based development. In the printout all vertical structure can be explicitly found only in the visible order of sections and subsections. The conceptual logic, however, is only implicit in the printed linear text, but it is still represented in the authoring system.

As suggested in the previous section, our application features options to handle literature references of related work. The entries are collected in a separate part of the knowledge base and grouped according to user specified areas. The application provides helpful features like guided creation of new entries, checks for ambiguity, or automatic sorting of entries. The entries can be accessed as text via links in all three authoring phases. Moreover, they can be cited in the actual text with following automatic generation of a bibliography in the printout, since they are represented in a coded form (we choose the BIBTEX format [7]).

Conclusion

Our approach of treating linear text authoring as an explicit process points to excellent possibilities to support such an activity with hypertext. In part, this process can also help for authoring hypertext systems intended for readers of hypertext. A prototypical implementation of a system based on this approach has been described, which has successfully been used to write this paper, as well as other papers and reports. While our approach originated from the desire to support technical writing, its scope of applicability is possibly even larger.

At the time of this writing, we are working on the reimplementation of HyperAuthor by use of another hypertext tool, taking our current prototypical version as a basis. We plan to provide more support for handling multiple related documents, version management, and collaborative authoring. (For instance, Catlin *et al.* [3] support extended handling of annotations.) As a first major application of HyperAuthor besides writing reports and papers, requirement analysis for *Software Engineering* is to be supported, hopefully leading to better user requirement documents. In the long run, we would like to use hypertext as a basis for a whole CASE system.

Hypertext as an electronic medium could and should have the effect to reduce the current paper explosion. One might think that our approach will even increase the production of printed paper, since it supports the authoring of linear text. We believe that hypertext in itself may be an excellent means for publishing technical results, and we envision a possible substitution of the current technical reports by some medium based on hypertext. Since, however, printed text will continue to be used for quite a while, we suggest publishing just short versions of technical papers in printed proceedings and journals, combining this with electronic reports using hypertext. Our approach of supporting idea processing can be useful for combined authoring of both media. Anyway, this may be a currently more realistic step towards the universal and world-wide literature system envisioned by Nelson [8].

References

[1] J. Bigelow. Hypertext and CASE. *IEEE Software*, 23–27, March 1988.

[2] P. J. Brown. Linking and searching within hypertext. *Electronic Publishing— Origination, Dissemination, and Design*, 1(1):45–53, April 1988.

[3] T. Catlin, P. Bush, and N. Yankelovich. InterNote: Extending a hypermedia framework to support annotative collaboration. In *Proceedings of Hypertext'89*, pages 365–378, ACM, Pittsburgh, PA, November 1989.

[4] J. Conklin. Hypertext: An introduction and survey. *IEEE Computer*, 20(9):17–41, September 1987.

[5] D. C. Engelbart. Authorship provisions in AUGMENT. In *Proceedings of Compcon'84*, pages 465–472, IEEE, 1984.

[6] H. Kaindl and H. G. Ziegeler. HIS—An information system about hypertext on hypertext. 1991. Submitted for publication.

[7] L. Lamport. LaTeX, *A Document Preparation System, User's Guide and Reference Manual*. Addison-Wesley, 1985.

[8] T. H. Nelson. Replacing the printed world: A complete literary system. *Information Processing*, 1013–1023, 1980.

[9] Ch. M. Neuwirth and D. S. Kaufer. The role of external representations in the writing process: Implications for the design of hypertext-based writing tools. In *Proceedings of Hypertext'89*, pages 319–341, ACM, Pittsburgh, PA, November 1989.

[10] J. B. Smith, S. F. Weiss, and G. J. Ferguson. A hypertext writing environment and its cognitive basis. In *Proceedings of Hypertext'87*, pages 195–214, ACM, Chapel Hill, NC, November 1987.

[11] N. A. Streitz, J. Hannemann, and M. Thüring. From ideas and arguments to hyperdocuments: Travelling through activity spaces. In *Proceedings of Hypertext'89*, pages 343–364, ACM, Pittsburgh, PA, November 1989.

[12] R. H. Trigg and P. M. Irish. Hypertext habitats: Experiences of writers in NoteCards. In *Proceedings of Hypertext'87*, pages 89–108, ACM, Chapel Hill, NC, November 1987.

[13] *HyperShell Hypertext Control System*. Text Technology, Macclesfield, Cheshire, 1990.

[14] J. H. Walker. Authoring tools for complex document sets. In E. Barrett, editor, *The Society of Text: Hypertext, Hypermedia, and the Social Construction of Information*, pages 132–147, MIT Press, 1989.

Spezielle Eigenschaften
großer Hypermedia-Systeme

Frank Kappe

Institut für Grundlagen der Informationsverarbeitung
und Computergestützte neue Medien,
Technische Universität Graz

Institut für Multi-Mediale Informations-Systeme (IMMIS),
Forschungsgesellschaft Joanneum

Zusammenfassung

Dieser Artikel basiert auf Überlegungen zum Design eines sehr großen Hypermedia-Systems (Hyper-G) und beschreibt einige spezielle Systemeigenschaften, die sich aus der Anforderung, große Datenmengen verwalten zu können, ergaben. Es zeigt sich, daß gewisse Konzepte (im speziellen in Bezug auf User Interfaces und Link-Verwaltung), die bei kleineren Hypermedia-Systemen gute Ergebnisse liefern können, für große Systeme völlig unbrauchbar sind. Umgekehrt ergeben sich neue Ansätze, die speziell auf große Hypermedia-Systeme zugeschnitten sind und bei kleineren nicht den gewünschten Erfolg liefern würden.

Nach einer kurzen Einleitung beschreibt der Artikel die Auswirkungen großer Datenmengen auf Implementation, System Design, User Interface, Autor und System-Administration. Dabei liegt der Schwerpunkt auf dem System Design.

1 Einleitung

So widersprüchlich es klingt, so begegnen uns doch im täglichen Leben immer wieder Beispiele einer neuen (oft schlechteren) Qualität durch höhere Quantität (z.B. Straßenverkehr, Überbevölkerung etc.). Verschärfend kommt noch hinzu, daß es nicht immer leicht einzusehen ist, warum ein 'mehr desselben' die Qualität des 'selben' beeinflussen soll.

Auch im Bereich der Softwareentwicklung und -anwendung sehen wir immer wieder, wie Programmsysteme, die für kleinere Anwendungen konzipiert sind, bei größeren Datenmengen zusammenbrechen. Einerseits werden die Antwortzeiten unzumutbar, weil die verwendeten Algorithmen nicht für große Datenmengen verwendbar sind; aber viel entscheidender ist, daß sie sehr oft einfach unbedienbar werden.

Auf früheren Erfahrungen mit Bildschirmtext [8, 9, 10] aufbauend, wird derzeit an der Technischen Universität Graz ein großes Hypermedia-System – *Hyper-G* – entwickelt. Rückgrat des Systems werden vor allem mehrere große Enzyklopädien (Allgemein- und Spezialwissen, mit Abbildungen) sowie eine große Anzahl von Bildern (mehrere 10.000, vor allem aus den Bereichen Wissenschaft, Kunst und Geographie) sein. Zusätzlich gibt es noch einige Film- und Tonstücke sowie Spezial-Exponate. Insgesamt ist das System auf Mega-Quantitäten von Dokumenten und Terra-Quantitäten von Bytes ausgelegt [6].

Welche Auswirkungen hat nun die Forderung nach großen Datenmengen auf Implementation, System Design, User Interface, Autor und System-Administration?

2   Implementations-Aspekte

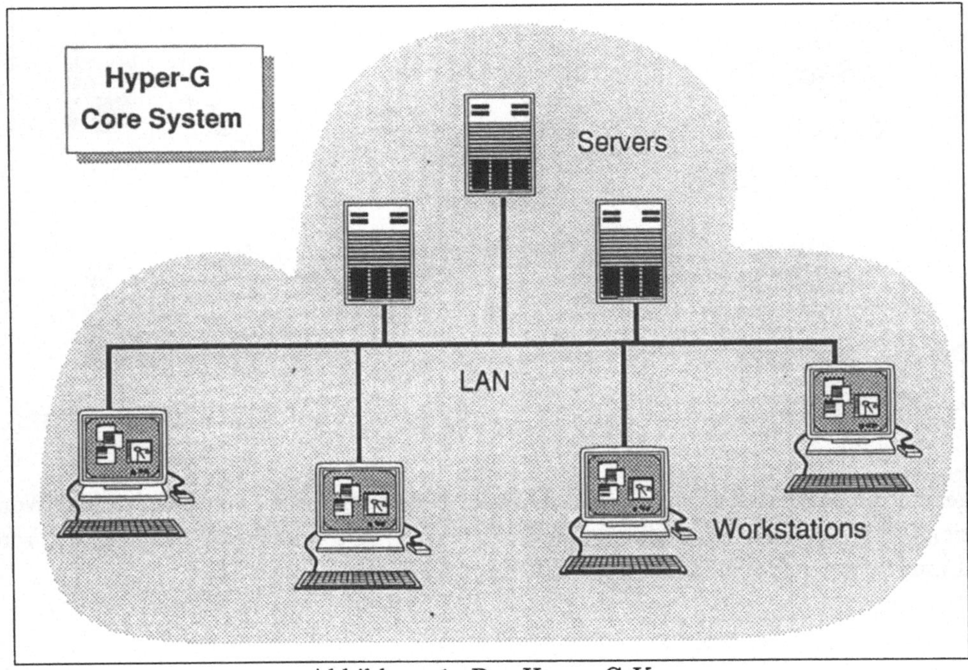

Abbildung 1: Der Hyper-G Kern

Die unmittelbaren Auswirkungen auf die Implementation liegen klar auf der Hand. Um große Datenmengen zu speichern und darauf schnell zugreifen zu können, werden große Speichermedien benötigt. Die Verwendung von Servern mit großen Speichermedien und hohem Datendurchsatz einerseits und Workstations mit schneller Grafik andererseits bietet sich an. Es entsteht ein verteiltes System (Abbildung 1).

Hyper-G wird aber nicht nur auf einem lokales Netz von Servern und Workstations laufen, sondern dieses Konzept wird in zwei Richtungen erweitert. Einerseits sollen auch weiter entfernte Benutzer die Möglichkeit haben, über langsamere Übertragungswege (z.B. Telefonleitungen) mit einfacheren (billigeren) Terminals die Möglichkeiten von Hyper-G wenigstens eingeschränkt zu nutzen.

Auf der anderen Seite wird es nicht möglich bzw. sinnvoll zu sein, alle Daten lokal zu halten; beispielsweise Flugpläne, Telefonbücher etc. Für diese Anwendungen ist eine Verbindung zu anderen (bereits existierenden) Datenbanken vorgesehen. Diese "Durchschaltung" wird jedoch vor dem Benutzer versteckt, d.h. mit einem Hyper-G-konformen User Interface versehen.

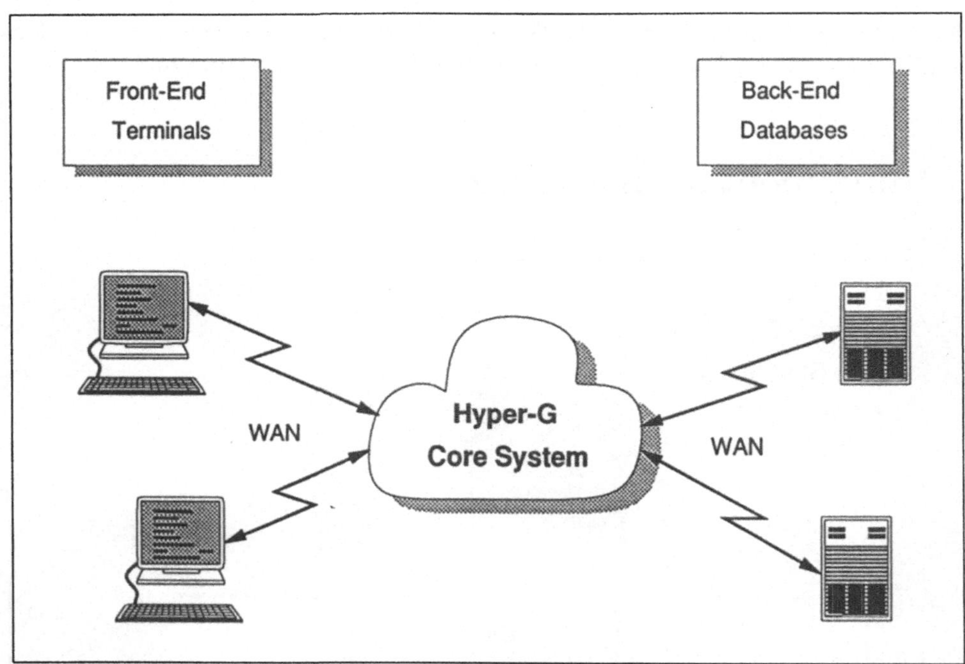

Abbildung 2: Hyper-G und der Rest der Welt

Insgesamt präsentiert sich Hyper-G also lokales Netzwerk (LAN) von Servern und Workstations, eingebettet in ein wide area network (WAN) mit einfachen Terminals als Front-End und externen Datenbanken als Back-End (Abbildung 2).

3   System Design

Wesentlich dramatischer sind die Auswirkungen auf das Design und auch die Funktionalität des Systems, insbesondere auf die Darstellung und Funktionen von Links.

3.1 Automatische Wartung von Links

Millionen von Dokumenten bedeuten Abermillionen von Links. Dabei sind Links keineswegs statisch, sondern ändern sich. In Hyper-G kann prinzipiell jeder Benutzer (durch Zugriffsrechte gesteuert) Dokumente einbringen, verlinken („Annotation") oder löschen. Wenn beispielsweise ein Dokument gelöscht wird, müssen alle Links, die es als Quelle oder Ziel referenzieren, ebenfalls entfernt werden. Dadurch werden eventuell andere Dokumente unerreichbar und müssen dann ebenfalls entfernt oder woanders angebunden werden, wodurch wiederum einige Links ungültig werden...

Jedenfalls ist die Wartung der Links keine triviale Angelegenheit, besonders wenn sehr viele Dokumente und Links existieren. Daher ist es notwendig, daß die Wartung der Links automatisch erfolgt. In obigem Beispiel muß das System selbständig bemerken, daß durch Löschen eines Dokuments weitere Anpassungen in der Datenbank notwendig werden und diese soweit sinnvoll selbständig durchführen. Allenfalls muß das System den Benutzer vor der Löschung von möglicherweise unbeabsichtigten Konsequenzen in Kenntnis setzen.

Ein weiteres Problem ist die Überladung der Datenbank mit veralteter oder uninteressanter Information. Dieses Problem wird in Abschnitt 6 behandelt.

3.2 Automatische Generierung von Links

Bei kleinen Hypermedia-Systemen ist die Erzeugung von Querverweisen direkt durch den Autor des Dokuments kein Problem. Um jedoch alle sinnvollen Querverweise anlegen zu können, muß der Autor potentiell alle anderen Dokumente des Systems kennen, was bei großen Systemen unzumutbar ist.

Daher wird Hyper-G selbstverständlich dem Autor erlauben, Querverweise (also Links) zu erzeugen, jedoch darüber hinaus automatisch Links generieren. Wir bauen dabei auf unseren Erfahrungen mit – der Öffentlichkeit zugänglichen – Lexika auf. So wurden beispielsweise in „Meyer's 10-bändigem Lexikon" mit 51300 Eintragungen ('Dokumente') und 13000 Querverweisen weitere 266200 Links automatisch erzeugt [13].

Dabei wurde zunächst einfach für jedes Wort im Text, für das eine Eintragung existiert, ein Link erzeugt. Natürlich treten bei einem so einfachen Algorithmus allerlei Unzulänglichkeiten auf (z.B. „Man" erhält einen Querverweis auf die Insel Man etc.), die sich aber durch kleine Verbesserungen des Algorithmus teilweise beheben lassen.

Im allgemeinen sind jedoch in Hypermedia-Systemen zuviele Links nicht so schädlich wie in konventionellen Informationssystemen. Der Benutzer kann sie ja einfach ignorieren (oder darüber lachen)!

3.3 Dynamische Links

Wenn ein Hypermedia-System auch den Duden samt Synonymlexika, Fremdwörterlexika etc. (bzw. im englischsprachigen Raum z.B. das Oxford English Dictionary[2, 14]) enthält, ist schon einigermaßen garantiert, daß zu jedem Wort ein entsprechendes Dokument existiert, das zumindest die Bedeutung des Wortes erklärt. Durch die oben angedeutete automatische Linkgenerierung ist auch sichergestellt, daß dann ein Link dorthin existiert.

Wenn aber ohnehin fast von jedem Wort ein Link ausgeht, hat es eigentlich gar keinen Sinn mehr, diesen Link irgendwie speziell zu kennzeichnen. Der Benutzer kann einfach prinzipiell jedes Wort, das er als Teil eines Dokuments am Schirm sieht, selektieren (z.B. „anklicken"). In den meisten Fällen bekommt er auch ein entsprechended Dokument, in dem dieses Wort näher erläutert wird.

Schnellen Datenbankzugriff vorausgesetzt, müssen diese Links auch gar nicht generiert sein, bevor der Benutzer das bewußte Wort anklickt. Erst bei der Auswahl des Wortes durch den Benutzer wird eine Datenbank-Abfrage durchgeführt und zum gefundenen Dokument verzweigt. Diese *dynamischen Links* bieten folgende Vorteile:

- Reduktion der Anzahl der (statischen) Links. Dadurch wird nicht nur Speicherplatz eingespart, sondern auch die Wartung der Links vereinfacht. Wird (vergleiche Beispiel bei Abschnitt 3.1) ein Dokument gelöscht, so wird es nicht mehr in der Datenbank gefunden, sodaß ab sofort auch keine dynamischen Links dorthin existieren. Umgekehrt können die im speziellen Dokument enthaltenen Wörter nicht mehr angeklickt werden, sodaß auch keine „ausgehenden" Links zerstört werden müssen. Der Wartungsaufwand verringert sich also.

- Der Benutzer muß auch nicht immer in allen Datenbanken suchen, sondern kann eine Menge von „aktiven Datenbanken" definieren, die seinen Anforderungen genügen. Dadurch kann die Zahl der richtigen, aber unsinnigen Links reduziert werden (*link filtering*). Das ist bei statischen Links nicht so elegant möglich.

- Die in Abschnitt 2 erwähnten externen Datenbanken mit möglicherweise variablen Daten (z.B. Adressen, Fahrpläne, Kurse etc.) sind nur über solche dynamischen Links anbindbar, da eine statische Linkgenerierung und -wartung nicht möglich ist.

- Bei entsprechender Datenbank können auch alle Dokumente gesucht werden, die das aktuelle Dokument referenzieren (*"associative link following"*), bzw. in denen ein bestimmtes Wort vorkommt (entspricht einer Volltextsuche).

Hyper-G unterstützt also eine automatische, dynamische Linkgenerierung und -wartung. Darüber hinaus gibt es natürlich benutzerdefinierte Links, insbesondere bei Bild-, Film- und Tondokumenten, wo eine automatische Generierung (noch?) nicht möglich ist. Zusätzlich sind auch automatisch generierte, aber statische Links vorgesehen, die mit aufwendigeren Algorithmen als es zur Laufzeit möglich wäre gefunden werden können.

Man beachte auch, daß dieses Konzept sich nur für große Datenbestände eignet, und bei kleinen Hypermedia-Systemen nur Frustrationen des Benutzers wecken würde, weil er viele Worte anklicken muß, um einen Link zu finden.

3.4 Link-Priorität

Durch die vielen Möglichkeiten der Link-Erzeugung ergeben sich unterschiedliche „Qualitäten" von Links. Dabei soll gute Qualität für den Benutzer bedeuten, daß er durch den Link mit hoher Wahrscheinlichkeit dorthin gelangt, wo für ihn relevante Informationen gespeichert sind.

Es ergibt sich folgende Hierarchie von Link-Qualitäten (nach abnehmender Qualität sortiert):

1. **Benutzerdefinierter Link**

    (a) Vom Benutzer selbst generierter Link (z.B. Annotation)

    (b) Vom Autor des Dokuments generierter Link

    (c) Von der System-Administration generierter Link

    (d) Von anderem Benutzer generierter Link

2. **Automatisch generierter Link**

    (a) Statischer Link

    (b) Dynamischer Link

Wenn an einer Stelle mehrere Links wegführen, erhält der Benutzer zunächst den mit der höchsten Qualität. Somit wird eine Link-Priorität definiert. Es ist auch nur dann notwendig, einen dynamischen Link zu suchen, wenn keine Links höherer Priorität existieren oder der Benutzer damit nicht zufrieden ist.

4 Die Sicht des Benutzers

Für den Benutzer eines großen Hypermedia-Systems stellen sich vor allem dieselben Probleme wie bei kleineren Systemen [3]: Sich im „Hyper-Space" zu verirren, keinen Überblick zu erhalten, Wiederfinden von Informationen, Abschätzung der verfügbaren Menge von Information zu einem bestimmten Thema, usw.

Viele Ideen zur Lösung dieser Probleme versagen bei großen Datenmengen völlig, z.B. das Konzept *graphischer Browser* (siehe Abbildung 3). *User Interface Metaphors* helfen, dem unbedarften Benutzer eine Vorstellung vom System zu geben[4]. Es gibt aber noch andere Möglichkeiten, dem Benutzer den Zugang zur gewünschten Information zu erleichtern.

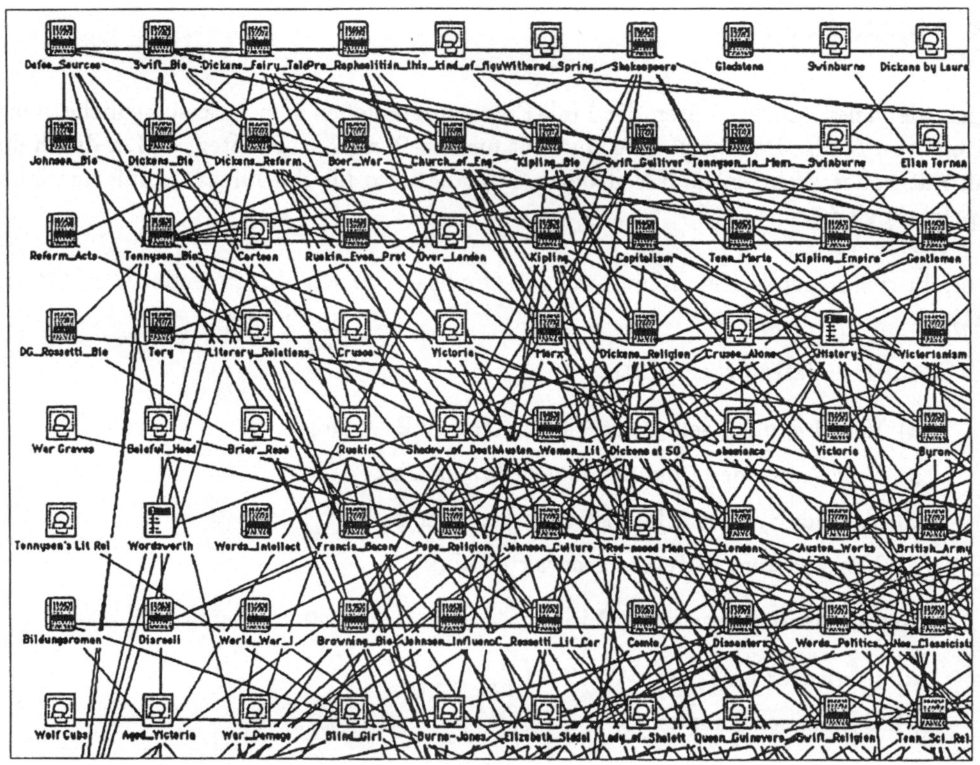

Abbildung 3: Graphischer Browser von InterMedia; aus [3]

4.1 User Interface Metaphors

Sogenannte *User Interface Metaphors* helfen dem unbedarften Benutzer beim Umgang mit komplexen Programmsystemen, indem sie einen ihm schon bekannten Ausschnitt der Wirklichkeit simulieren [4]. Für Hyper-G, dessen Anwendungen vom (Universitäts-) Informationssystem bis zum virtuellen Museum ("Viewseum" [12]) reichen [7], und das daher mit einer Vielzahl an Eingabemedien und Voraussetzungen über den Wissensstand des Benutzers arbeiten muß, ist es wichtig, sich nicht auf eine bestimmte Metapher festzulegen, sondern mehrere anzubieten.

Für Hypermedia-Systeme wurden bereits eine Reihe von Metaphern vorgeschlagen, wie etwa die "Desk-Top" Metapher von Xerox' *Star* [5], HyperCard's "Stack" [15], Benest's "Buch"-Metapher [1], die Erweiterung davon ("Bücherei") und die "Reise" durch die Informationslandschaft. In Hyper-G wird es möglich sein, auf dieselben Daten über unterschiedliche Benutzungsmetaphern zuzugreifen.

4.2 Collections

Die Datenbasis von Hyper-G ist in sogenannte *Collections* gegliedert, also Sammlungen von Wissen / Informationen zu einem bestimmten Thema. Diese Collections sind hierarchisch angelegt (es gibt also Unter-Collections), allerdings nicht als Baum, sondern nur als zyklenfreier, gerichteter Graph. Das heißt, eine Collection kann gleichzeitig Unter-Collection mehrerer übergeordneter Collections sein. Zum Beispiel kann das Wissensgebiet „Biochemie" sowohl Teilgebiet von „Chemie" als auch „Biologie" sein. Die Blätter des Collection-Pseudobaumes sind die einzelnen Dokumente, z.B. in der Collection „Lexika", Unter-Collection „Meyer's Lexikon" wäre das ein einzelner Lexikon-Eintrag.

Dieser Pseudo-Baum ist nicht sehr tief, sodaß dem Benutzer jederzeit ein graphischer Überblick über seine augenblickliche Position in der Hierarchie gegeben werden kann. Man kann dann in dieser Hierarchie hinauf- oder herabsteigen, um benachbarte Wissensgebiete zu erforschen.

4.3 Touren

Darüber hinaus gibt es „Touren", die von einem Autor (kann prinzipiell jeder Benutzer sein), zusammengestellt wurden. Diese Touren brauchen sich um die hierarchische Collection-Struktur nicht zu kümmern, sondern verlinken irgendwelche Dokumente (z.B. zu einer linearen Liste). Typische Titel von Touren wären etwa „Impressionistische Bilder", „Bilder von van Gogh", „Kappes Lieblingsbilder", wobei durchaus Überschneidungen möglich sind. Wenn der Benutzer auf seinem Weg durch die Tour eine andere Tour kreuzt, hat er die Möglichkeit, „umzusteigen". Touren müssen auch nicht streng linear sein, sondern der Autor kann alle Möglichkeiten eines Hypermedia-Systems voll ausschöpfen. So entstehen auch „Lektionen" zu einem bestimmten Thema als Tour.

Innerhalb von Touren (die typischerweise höchstens 100 Dokumente umfassen), ist eine komfortablere Navigation möglich. So gibt es z.B. eine (vom Autor der Tour erstellte) graphischen Übersicht über die Tour, und das System unterstützt den Benutzer im Auffinden von noch nicht gesehenen Teilen der Tour, bietet tour-spezifische Hilfe an, etc.

4.4 Datenbankabfragen

Weiters hat der Benutzer die Möglichkeit, Datenbankabfragen zu formulieren. Vor allem beim Einstieg in das Hypermedia-System sind *key queries* von Bedeutung. Dabei handelt es sich um einfache Präfix-Abfragen aus einer (benutzer-konfigurierbaren) Liste von aktiven Datenbanken. Kleine Tippfehler werden vernachlässigt. Durch diese Form von Abfragen kann sehr schnell herausgefunden werden, was es alles zu einem bestimmten Thema in verschiedenen Datenbanken (Collections) gibt.

Für genauere Abfragen gibt es Collection-spezifische *form queries*, es ist also ein Formular auszufüllen. In der Collection „Bilder alter Meister" könnte so ein Formular die Felder *Maler, Name des Bildes, Jahr, Stil, Motiv, Museum...* haben, die aber nicht alle ausgefüllt werden müssen. So findet man z.B. alle Bilder von Leonardo da Vinci, die im Louvre hängen.

5 Autor

Natürlich muß auch der Autor von Dokumenten (der wie erwähnt auch jeder Benutzer sein kann), vom System besonders unterstützt werden. Neben mehreren Dokumenten-Editoren (je nach Typ des Dokuments) unterscheidet sich besonders der Link-Editor eines großen Hypermedia-Systems von dem kleinerer Systeme.

Da es für den Autor unzumutbar ist, alle möglichen Querverweise selbst herauszusuchen, muß ihm das System Vorschläge für die Erzeugung von Links geben können. Dabei bedient sich Hyper-G den in den Abschnitten 3.2 und 3.3 beschriebenen Verfahren.

6 System-Administration

Von der System-Administration muß einiges getan werden, um ein unkontrolliertes Wachsen der Informationsmenge und ein Verfilzen der Link-Struktur zu verhindern.

Um das System vor veralteten oder unwichtigen Beiträgen von Benutzern zu schützen, altern Beiträge, d.h. neben Eröffnungsdatum und Modifikationsdatum erhält jedes Dokument ein Verfalldatum (typischerweise 6 Monate, kann vom Systemadministrator hinaufgesetzt werden). Etwa 2 Monate vor Verfall wird der Autor per E-Mail oder beim Login verständigt und kann das Verfallsdatum verlängern.

Tut er das nicht, wird das Dokument gelöscht. Damit müssen auch alle Links von und zu diesem Dokument gelöscht werden. Die Autoren dieser Dokumente werden ebenfalls verständigt, ihre Dokumente gegebenenfalls zu überarbeiten. Erfolgt keine Bestätigung, werden nach einiger Zeit auch diese Dokumente entfernt.

Die Systemadministration durchforscht auch Logfiles, die ergebnislose Suchen protokollieren. Wenn notwendig, werden dann entsprechende Links halbautomatisch erzeugt. Ebenso können statische Links, mit denen die Benutzer nicht zufrieden sind (d.h. sie gehen gleich wieder zurück) automatisch lokalisiert und gegebenenfalls entfernt werden.

Inwieweit ein individueller Benutzer das Hypermedia System modifizieren kann, ist von einem komplexen System von Zugriffsrechten abhängig.

Literatur

[1] BENEST I. D. : "A Hypertext System with Controlled Hype". In *Proc. of the Hypertext II Conference, York*, 1989.

[2] BOWERS R. A. : "The Oxford English Dictionary on Compact Disc". *Electronic and Optical Publishing Review*, 8(2):88–91, June 1988.

[3] CONKLIN J. : "Hypertext: An Introduction and Survey". *IEEE Computer*, 20(9):17–41, September 1987.

[4] DAVIES G., MAURER H., and PREECE J. : *Presentation Metaphors for a very large Hypermedia System*. IIG Report 282, IIG, Graz University of Technology, Austria, April 1990. Also to appear in: Journal of Micro Computer Applications 2 (1991).

[5] JOHNSON J., ROBERTS T. L., VERPLANK W., SMITH D. C., IRBY C., BEARD M., and MACKEY K. : "The Xerox Star: A Retorospective". *IEEE Computer*, 22(9):11–26, September 1989.

[6] KAPPE F. : *Aspects of a Modern Multi-Media Information System*. PhD thesis, Technical University Graz, Austria, 1991.

[7] KAPPE F. : "Unorthodoxe Anwendungen von Hypermedia-Systemen". In WALL-MANNSBERGER J. (editor), *Hypertext - State of the Art*, R. Oldenbourg, Vienna, Munich, 1991. In German. To appear.

[8] MAURER H. : *Bildschirmtext muß ein Erfolg werden*. IIG Report B42, IIG, Graz University of Technology, Austria, February 1984. In German.

[9] MAURER H. : *Bildschirmtextähnliche Systeme*. IIG Report B11, IIG, Graz University of Technology, Austria, 1981. In German.

[10] MAURER H., ROSZENICH N., and SEBESTYEN I. : "Videotex without Big Brother". *Electronic Publishing Review*, 4:201–214, 1984.

[11] MAURER H. and TOMEK I. : "Hypermedia Bibliography". To appear in: Journal of Micro Computer Applications 2 (1991).

[12] MAURER H. and WILLIAMS M. : "Hypermedia Systems and other Computer Support in Museums". To appear in: Journal of Micro Computer Applications 2 (1991).

[13] MÜLNER H. : "A System of Inter-Active Encyclopaedias". In *Proc. 4th Austrian-Hungarian Informatics Conference, Budapest*, pages 181–190, John von Neumann Society for Computing Sciences, Hungary, 1989.

[14] RAYMOND D. R. and TOMPA F. W. : "Hypertext and The Oxford English Dictionary". *Communications of the ACM*, 31(7):871–879, July 1988.

[15] WILLIAMS G. : "HyperCard". *Byte*, 12(14):109–117, December 1987.

Every interactive system evolves into hyperspace:
The case of the Smart Game Board

Anders Kierulf, Ralph Gasser, Peter M. Geiser, Martin Müller, Jurg Nievergelt, Christoph Wirth
Informatik, ETH, CH-8092 Zurich

Abstract. Although an interactive system may be dedicated to a specific application, if it aims at a heterogeneous user community it must provide many application-independent functions, such as: User interface, an explanatory and communications component, and data base functions for data structuring and visualization. In other words, *every* user-friendly interactive application evolves into a hypermedia system. We present a case study of this phenomenon for an esoteric application: The Smart Game Board evolved from a computerized board and a programmer's workbench into a powerful tool that supports game fans in the many functions they normally perform using a wooden board and paper: playing, analyzing, annotating, organizing and storing game collections. The special nature of these documents is reflected in highly specialized support functions, such as searching for patterns in a collection of Go games.

Contents

1   The functions of an interactive system: General vs. application dependent

Early interactive systems, such as text editors, tended to be monoliths with ad hoc constructions for every function provided [BN 82]. Operations on text, such as 'insert'; for viewing and printing, such as 'scroll' and 'format'; for dialog control, such as 'undo' or 'quit': These were all tossed into one big amorphous "command language", often with hundreds of commands. The most significant achievement in the field of man-machine communication was the gradual emerging, in the late seventies and early eighties, of integrated interactive systems: Systems whose application-independent operations, such as dialog control, are universal, i.e. provided once-and-for-all, and always active. Thus the different applications that run on an integrated interactive system need not replicate these general functions. The most beneficial effect for the user is the perception that 'all applications talk the same language', as they share a common set of application-independent operations (e.g. [Ni 82]). Today, for example, we take it for granted that an application uses the window system of the host, along with all viewing and dialog control operations that come with it; but as recently as a decade ago, user interfaces were designed to be independent of the operating system.

What has happened to user interfaces is about to happen to the complex of facilities and operations we associate with the term 'hypertext': Building structures that link items from the same or from different data collections, providing aids to visualization of such structures, and navigation therein. Naturally, structure building, visualization, and navigation are not unique to hypermedia systems. Systems for computer-assisted instruction, computer-aided design, computer-aided software engineering, data management systems, expert system shells - these are just examples of dedicated interactive systems that become more useful when they let the user organize data and access it through visualization and navigation. Can you think of *any* class of interactive systems that can do without?

Structure building, visualization, and navigation are application-independent functions that *any* interactive system should provide as universal operations, as modern systems provide user interface functions. From this point of view, hypertext and hypermedia are not so much systems in their own right, as they are components essential to any interactive system.

We present an example of an interactive system that is increasingly developing towards hypermedia. The Smart Game Board [Ki 90, KCN 90] has two major functions: 1) A programmer's workbench for implementors of game-playing programs; 2) A special-purpose 'document handling system' to manage games. The second function is the focus of this paper. We describe the Smart Game Board's hypertext features, some enhancements under development, and the structure that makes them possible.

2 Functions, surface, and structure

Functions. The Smart Game Board evolved from a computerized board and a programmer's workbench into a powerful tool used by hundreds of game fans in the many functions they normally perform using a wooden board and paper: Playing, analyzing, annotating, organizing and storing game collections. In these functions it is similar to game data bases that have appeared on the market in recent years, in particular for chess (e.g. ChessBase). But the Smart Game Board provides data base and hypermedia functions *independently of any specific game*: So far it handles chess, Go, Othello, Go-Moku, and Nine-Men's Morris (Mühle). It achieves this generality by carefully separating game specific aspects (such as the rules of a game and graphical appearance of the board) from general features common to many board games, such as: two players that move alternatingly; the course of a game, and variations analyzed but not played, can be represented as a game tree; etc.

Surface. Most of the Smart Game Board's user interface is embodied in a control panel common to all games (the figure below shows it in a window at the top left of the screen). Game-independent operations are defined as motions on a game tree. Game-specific operations (e.g. setting up positions in chess, entering marks for annotating Go games) and status information (e.g. castling status in chess) are provided in a menu specific for each game.

#	Game ID	Opening	White	Black	Result	Date
21			0	0		
7	07 Duras-Rubins	4 Knights	Duras	Rubinstein, Akib	0:1	1907
8	07 Janowski-Ru	4 Knights	Janowski	Rubinstein, Akib	0:1	1907
9	Rubinstein's Imm		Rotlewi	Rubinstein, Akib	0:1	190.
10	11 Rubinstein-B		Rubinstein	Bernstein	1/2	1911
11	11 Rubinstein-C.		Rubinstein	Capablanca	1:0	1911
12	07 Salwe-Rubins		Salwe	Rubinstein, Akib	0:1	1907

Structure. The structure of the Smart Game Board is designed to separate game-specific from game-independent aspects. It provides slots where each game plugs in its specific routines for the rules (legal move recognition and execution), the user interface (board display, move input, menu functions), and an optional playing algorithm. A search engine provides depth-first search and iterative deepening based on game-specific routines for move generation, position evaluation, and time control. A programmer must provide one or two game-specific modules to add another game to the Smart Game Board. A straightforward module to implement the functions: Execute and undo legal moves, display the board, and track move input. And a module as sophisticated as he can realize to generate strong moves. The Smart Game Board is written in an object-oriented version of Modula-2 under MPW (Macintosh Programmer's Workshop), and runs on the Apple® Macintosh™.

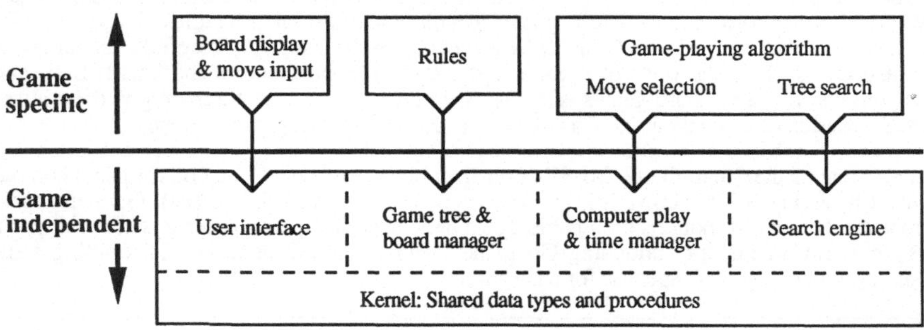

3 Structure building, visualization, and navigation

The important functions for structure building, visualization, and navigation are all game-independent: Each new game added to the Smart Game Board inherits these functions for free.

Structure building. The Smart Game Board supports structures on three levels: 1) a move and events associated with it are organized as a list of properties; 2) property lists are organized as a game tree; 3) game trees are organized as a game collection.

The *property list* stores the move and associated information: Textual comments, shorthand comments like "!" or "??", marks to display on the board, time left after playing this move, and more.

The *game tree* preserves the entire history of all the moves played, including all variations explored. The root contains a game info record describing who played the game, when and where it was played, the outcome, and more. The game tree can be edited, with subtrees being permuted or deleted.

The *game collection* organizes a set of games. Depending on the desired function, it can be organized in two ways: 1) As a list of individual game trees: This makes it easy to select a subset of games in response to a query such as "all games by Takemiya playing White since 1986". 2) As a multi-game, where several game trees are merged into one, with the game info inserted at the nodes where the games diverge. This is ideal for opening studies, where a line is usually studied in the context of other openings, with full games to illustrate possible plans and continuations.

In addition to the collection of our own amateur games, our library includes several thousand master games in chess, several hundred professional Go games, and more than 3000 Othello games.

Visualization. The current state of the game is shown in several linked views (see the screen figure above); a modification in one view is immediately reflected in all other views. The *board view* shows the current state of the board; the *game record view* shows an extract of the annotated game tree, with the property list of at least the current and the next nodes, and comments associated with the current move. The *overview* function shows a sequence of board positions throughout the game; these snapshots quickly reveal the character of a game. *Game collections* are shown in a separate window as a list of games with player names and outcome. The *tree view* is a graphical overview of all the alternative move sequences analyzed. As an example, the following diagram of Rubinstein's game shown above hints at the explosion of tactics that starts at move 22. Clicking anywhere in this tree activates the corresponding position in all other views.

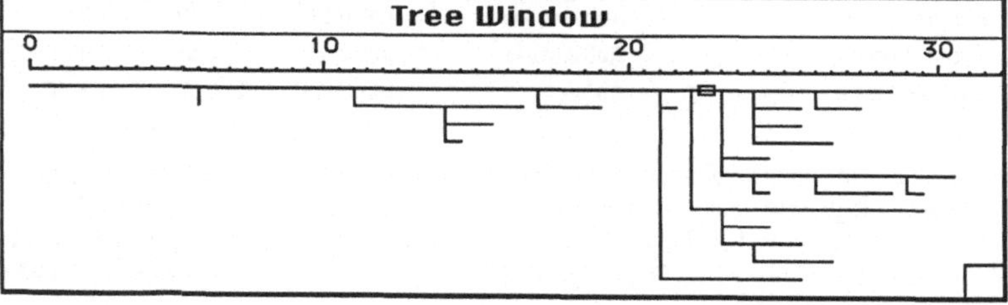

Navigation. The user has various ways to move around the game tree, with commands such as: To next/previous move or branch point, to a specific move number, back to the main branch after exploring some variations, or searching for text or other specific properties. Using the tree view, he can point to any node to go to that position, or drag the mouse around the tree to browse quickly through the game.

4 The importance of efficient search in accessing a game-base

The Smart Game Board has certainly not yet reached the limits of useful hypertext functions that a game data base should provide (neither have the various chess data bases available on the market). Our design of a consistent set of functions of moderate complexity is guided by the feedback from a growing user community; and is made considerably harder by trying to meet the occasionally contradictory conventions already established for different types of games. The following features are among those being implemented now, planned or, at least, on our wish list for the near future:

- Producing documents. Game annotation is a special brand of literature with its own conventions and standard of excellence. The conventions differ drastically from game to game, as illustrated by the entirely different styles used to present an annotated Go game or chess game. The Smart Game Board has good facilities to support the production of annotated board figures for chess and Go, but not yet for tying figures to the corresponding text. If the label attached to a point on the Go board changes from 'b' to 'c', for example, one would obviously want all references to 'b' changed to 'c'. This is not trivial, however, as the label 'b' in one diagram is an independent entity from 'b' in another diagram, and thus it becomes necessary to identify the portion of text that 'belongs' to each diagram.

- Links between arbitrary nodes and games (not necessarily merged into a multi-game). When annotating a game, for example, one would like to refer to similar positions that occurred in other games, so the reader can quickly switch to the corresponding position, check out what happened in that game, and return to the original position. Given the structures already supported by the Smart Game Board, such dynamic links are easily added.

But the single most important function a game base with a rich interconnection network must provide for the dedicated game player is support for searches of the most varied kinds. The Smart Game Board offers the following search functions:

- Search for nodes in a game tree: Find all nodes with a specified property, such as a specific comment-string; provide boolean operations on such sets of nodes.
- Search for games in a game collection, according to player, date, color of player, result of game.
- Pattern-directed search comes in two main versions:
  - Given a pattern library and one position, find all occurrences of library patterns in this position.
  - Given a game library and one pattern, find all games where the pattern occurs at some time during the course of the game.

An open-ended endeavor to enhance these functions involves computer searches for "similar" positions. "Similarity" is a game-specific concept whose definition ranges from straightforward to profound. We have implemented some of the straightforward similarity searches, for example in Go openings, where 'similarity' might mean an exact pattern match in a corner of the board, equating all positions that differ only through symmetry transformations (described in the next section). In chess endgames, one might look for positions with bishops on squares of opposite color, and a given number of white and black pawns. Once the game-specific procedure identifies similar positions, game-independent links between these positions can be established, and the user can navigate between these positions.

Applications of pattern-directed search are manifold:
- A game-playing program may retrieve locally good moves from a pattern library.
- As a tool for study: Retrieve master games which exhibit a particular local position, and compare their moves with our own moves.
- Statistical study of the success ratio of a particular opening.

5 Pattern matching for hypertext access: Go as an example

In the game of Go, the shape of local configurations of stones on the board are important. Human expertise is often expressed in relation to small **patterns**. We can define a pattern as the status of all points in a bounded region of the board, typically a rectangle. To support users of a game database and to use pattern knowledge in a game-playing program we need tools to create, store and find patterns.

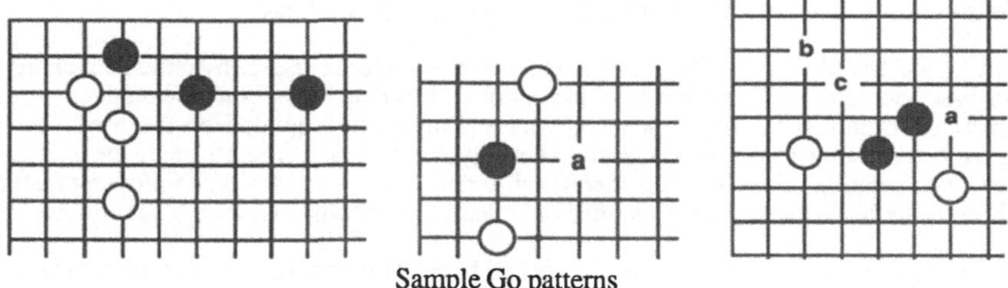

Sample Go patterns

Many Go books concentrate on pattern-related knowledge. A typical example is [Is 77]. For each pattern, the book gives moves to play and moves to avoid, an evaluation of the pattern, and sometimes a full board position from a reference game where the pattern appears in a game context. A hypermedia tool can provide all this information much faster and more completely than the biggest stack of books.

Pattern matching can be used in Go-playing programs. First, each game position is matched against a large pattern library. Then, possible moves and precomputed parts of the position evaluation are retrieved from the library.

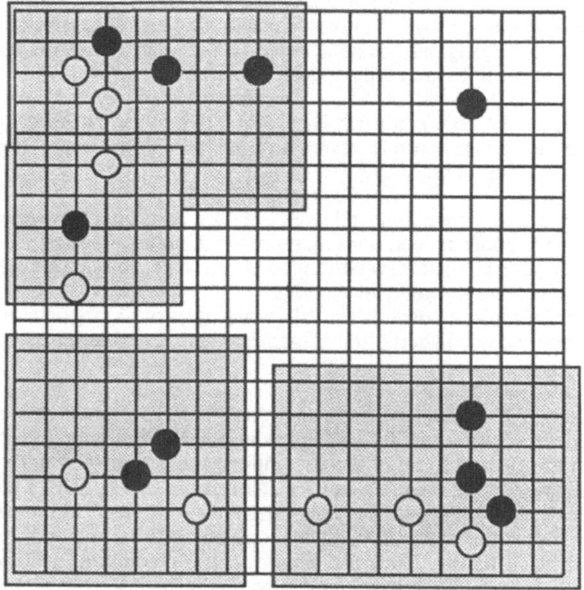

Finding patterns in a full-board position.

Given a library of local patterns and the current full-board position, a fast pattern matching procedure finds all local patterns that occur in the position, even if the patterns are shifted, rotated, mirrored, or their colors are reversed [Ge 91]. [Ma 84] discusses methods of describing and encoding Go patterns. For efficient access, our pattern matching algorithm is based on an encoding proposed by Gonnet: A two-dimensional pattern is linearized along a spiral that starts in the center, as shown in the figure below. The string that encodes the pattern is concatenated with its associated information (such as recommended moves) into a pattern descriptor. All descriptors are concatenated into a long string that represents the pattern library. The library is indexed by PAT trees [Go 88] so that access time is logarithmic in the number of patterns - time does not depend on the sizes or contents of the patterns.

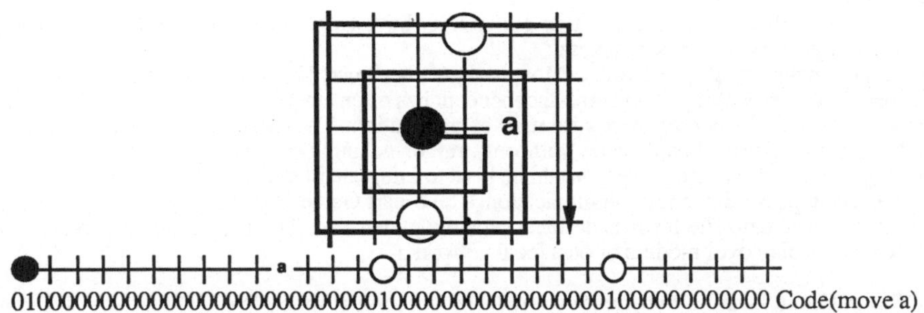

A pattern, its linearization, and its descriptor:
2 bits for every point on the board, followed by associated information.

There are several other useful pattern-matching functions we plan to implement:
- Access to a game database by local pattern: Given a local pattern, find all games in a large collection in which the pattern occurs at least once during the game. In theory this function could be implemented by explicitly storing all positions of all games as full board patterns in a library, and access them using the method above. But this naive method wastes too much memory to be practical. Given that most pairs of consecutive positions in a game differ by only one stone (on one of the 361 points of the Go board), many data compression schemes come to mind. The problem is to find one that compresses effectively and is compatible with fast pattern matching.

- Approximate pattern matching: A player often searches for patterns that need not match the query exactly, but are "similar" in some way. As a first extension, we plan to allow don't-care points in the pattern, and a limited number of mismatches. A more radical extension is to design a feature space and to compare feature vectors that describe a pattern, instead of comparing actual patterns.

6 What is the conclusion ?

We have argued that hypertext functions are becoming an integral part of any interactive system. Thus it is important to explore the boundary between application-dependent and application-independent aspects of hypertext. The Smart Game Board is a hypertext system for applications where the collections of objects to be stored have an unusually rich structure, where elaborate conventions are already established on how to present these structures, and where conventions differ from game to game. Thus its continued evolution provides some insight into the question: What application-independent hypertext features can be extracted from the various applications and dealt with in a common kernel system?

Experience with the Smart Game Board suggests the answer: Structure building and navigation are quite application-independent, whereas visualization and search are mostly application-specific. The following reasons support this conclusion:
1) The structures used to organize complex materials depend more on the user's thinking habits than on the subject-matter - libraries and data management systems have perhaps invented all the classifications systems the human mind can cope with.
2) Navigation means moving around a structure, so if the structure is general-purpose, so will the navigation commands be.
3) Visualization and search come in two versions: The easy one is visualization of the organizing structures, and search with respect to those structures (e.g. alphabetic search in an ordered tree). But general-purpose structural visualization and search is merely a weak support for the user to find his way around a large collection of documents of a special nature. Pattern-directed search is much more powerful, in particular if the patterns have a visual representation familiar to the user. This is the case for all board games, where experts have developed a highly trained eye for instant recognition of relevant patterns, as de Groot's famous experiments about recalling chess positions show [dG 65]. Relevant patterns, of course, are highly application-specific, and so are pictures and specifications of patterns used in search algorithms.

The Smart Game Board and its active user community have taught us other lessons that may apply to the design of hypertext systems in general:
• Gain functionality by generalization. Most tools of the Smart Game Board were first designed for one specific game. Making them game-independent has often simplified and improved them.
• Choose a reasonably homogeneous domain of application. The Smart Game Board can probably handle any two-person board game with only minor adaptations, but games of chance or many-person games, such as card games, would be hard to integrate in the present structure.
• Provide many possibilities for communication. The Smart Game Board can read and write games in text form, in standard file formats defined by game player associations, and in compressed form. It can be used to play over modem or on a local network.

Is the Smart Game Board a hypertext system? The question is moot. We feel that any well-designed interactive system qualifies to the extent that it supports the user's desire to organize, see, and explore his data the way he likes. General-purpose hypertext systems will not serve the needs of the user community nearly as well as dedicated application systems that stand out in two ways:

• First and foremost, they provide *powerful application-specific functions* (such as search and visualization).
• Second, they have *a general-purpose hypertext component* for building and depicting organizational structures, and browsing therein.

References

[BN 82]   H. Burkhart, J. Nievergelt: The development of editors: From utility program to the integrated interactive system. In Textverarbeitung und Bürosysteme (A. Endres, ed), 93-114, Oldenbourg Verlag, 1982.

[dG 65]   A.D. de Groot: Thought and choice in chess, Mouton, The Hague, 1965.

[Ge 91]   P. M. Geiser: Recognizing and using patterns in the game of Go. Diploma Thesis ETH Zürich, 1991.

[Go 88]   G. H. Gonnet: Efficient Searching of Text and Pictures, Extended Abstract. Tech. Report OED-88-02, Univ. of Waterloo Centre for the New Oxford English Dictionary, June 1988.

[Is 77]   Y. Ishida: Dictionary of Basic Joseki. 3 Vols., Ishi Press, Tokio, 1977.

[Ki 90]   A. Kierulf: Smart Game Board: A Workbench for Game-Playing Programs, with Go and Othello as Case Studies. Diss. ETH Zurich, 1990.

[KCN 90]   A. Kierulf, K.H. Chen, J. Nievergelt: Smart Game Board and Go Explorer: A study in software and knowledge engineering. Comm. ACM, Vol 33, No 2, 152-166, Feb 1990.

[Ma 84]   Y. Mano: An Approach to Conquer Difficulties in Developing a Go Playing Program. Journal of Information Processing 7, 2 (1984), 81-88.

[Ni 82]   J. Nievergelt: Errors in dialog design and how to avoid them. In Nievergelt, Coray, Nicoud, Shaw: Document Preparation Systems. North Holland, 1982.

CHAOS, ein Ansatz zur Modellierung von Informationssystemen

Thomas A. Landolt
Schweizerische Bankgesellschaft
UBILAB (UBS Informatics Lab)
CH–8033 Zürich
E–mail: landolt@ulab.ubs.ubs.arcom.ch

Die vorliegende Zusammenfassung beschreibt den Versuch, das Hypertext–Konzept nicht mehr nur zur Gliederung grosser Dokumentationsmengen, sondern auch zur Gestaltung ganzer Informationssysteme mit Abfrage– und Bearbeitungskomponenten zu verwenden. Diese Idee wird mit dem realisierten Prototypen CHAOS (C+ + Hyperdokument Administrations– und Organisations–System) einer Anwendung in einem grossen Rechenzentrum illustriert.

1.   Einleitung

Ein grosser Teil der heutigen Hypertext–Anwendungen dient zur Organisation und Verwaltung von statischen Informationen, sei es im Bereich der technischen Dokumentation, im Bereich der Lernsysteme oder in der Verwaltung eines Archivs. Die Hauptarbeit des Benutzers beschränkt sich auf die Navigation im System und auf die Suche nach der gewünschten Information. Diese ist dabei typischerweise in einzelnen Blökken abgelegt, seien das Karten in *HyperCard* [Go 87] oder Dokumente in *Intermedia* [Me 86].

Es existieren heute noch wenig Anwendungen, die in den einzelnen Dokumenten eigene Funktionalität anbieten und damit das Link–Konzept quasi als Integrationsinstrument verschiedener Applikationen verstehen (vielleicht mit Ausnahme einiger *Hyper-Card*-Systeme). Gerade hier scheint aber eine grosse Chance dieses Konzeptes zu liegen. Häufig benötigt man bei der Erfüllung irgendwelcher Arbeiten mit einem bestimmten Werkzeug detailliertere Informationen. Oder man möchte während der Navigation durch Dokumente mit darin gefundenen Daten verschiedene Auswertungen machen können. Nicht zuletzt können Links dazu dienen, nicht nur die abgelegte Information zu organisieren, sondern auch die zu erledigenden Arbeiten in geeigneter Form zu gliedern.

Das vorgestellte System baut auf einem weitergefassten Dokumentbegriff auf: Ein Dokument wird nicht nur als eine statische Darstellung von Information aufgefasst, sondern bekommt auch eigene Verarbeitungseigenschaften. Damit bietet ein Dokument die Möglichkeit, neben der reinen Bearbeitung auch Abfragen und Auswertungen vorzunehmen. Die vorhandene Funktionalität hängt dabei von der jeweiligen Klasse ab, zu der ein Dokument gehört. Dem Entwickler soll eine derartige Gliederung in Klassen dazu dienen, durch eigene spezifische Erweiterungen in Unterklassen einfach neue Applikationsarten zu formulieren (zum Beispiel ein spezielles Analysedokument, welches auf einem Standard–"Spreadsheet"–Dokument aufbaut).

Die Dokumente werden durch verschiedene Referenzier– und Aktivierungsmechanismen ergänzt:

- "Referenz–Links" ermöglichen die Navigation in einer vorhandenen Dokumentstruktur.

- Der Aufruf bestimmter Dokumentfunktionen kann durch sogenannte "Methoden–Links" realisiert werden. Mittels Methoden–Links können auch Werte aus einem Dokument in ein anderes Dokument übernommen werden.

- "Action–Links" führen schliesslich bei ihrer Aktivierung einen Betriebssystem–Befehl aus.

Diese Konzepte, eine Dokumentklassenhierarchie und verschiedene Linkmechanismen, bauen auf einem "Application Framework" in einer objekt–orientierten Umgebung auf. Damit soll ein Grundgerüst zur Modellierung des Systems via Dokumenten und zur Verwaltung der dazu notwendigen Informationen realisiert werden. Ein Systementwickler in der Nähe des Benutzers soll später die Feinmodellierung mit der Einfachheit eines Instrumentes wie *HyperCard* und mit der Offenheit einer klassischen Programmierumgebung vornehmen können.

Konkret wurde mit diesen Ideen ein Prototyp für eine Supportorganisation innerhalb den Rechenzentren unserer Bank entwickelt. Realisiert wurde das System auf einer *SUN–3* mit $C++$ [St 87] und dem "Application Framework" $ET++$ [We89].

2.   Situation und Bedürfnisse der Benutzer

Aus den Gesprächen mit den Benutzern liessen sich drei verschiedene Bedürfnisse an das System formulieren:

- Sicherstellung der Verwaltung sämtlicher relevanter Dokumente,

- Erhalt der Informationen über die aktuelle Software–Konfiguration auf einem bestimmten Rechner,

- Erhalt der Informationen über bestehende Abhängigkeiten zwischen verschiedenen Software–Arten, um damit diverse Tests durchführen zu können.

2.1.   Dokumentverwaltung

Momentan existiert eine Reihe verschiedener Dokumente mit unterschiedlicher Form und Struktur und mit verschiedener Lebensdauer, die an diversen Orten erstellt werden. Gewisse Dokumente werden bei den Benutzern selbst gebildet, aufgrund von anderen Dokumenten und Informationen. Gewisse Dokumente erreichen die Organisation von aussen oder werden an bestimmte Stellen ausserhalb weitergegeben. Es gibt Dokumente, die nur elektronisch abgelegt sind und solche, die zumindest elektronisch erstellt und verschickt werden. Gewisse Dokumente werden aber auch innerhalb der Bank mit einem Textsystem erfasst und dann ausgedruckt, worauf sie unsere Benutzer in Papierform erreichen.

Für diese Vielfalt an Dokumenten wurde folgende Gliederung definiert:

- Handbücher: Dokumente mit Referenz–Charakter, die über eine längere Zeit hinweg gültig bleiben.

- "Release–Notes": Diese Dokumente werden für einen neuen Software–Release erstellt. Sie beschreiben die im Release enthaltenen Änderungen und die zur Installation notwendige Konfiguration. Ideal wird ein einziges Mal für die Installation darauf zugegriffen.

- Installations–Checklisten: Mit Hilfe der Release–Notes werden durch den Support zuhanden des Betriebspersonals Punkt–für–Punkt–Anleitungen zur Installation neuer Software erstellt.

- Software–Lieferpläne: Der zeitliche Ablauf, auf welcher Maschine welcher Software–Release installiert wird, ist im Software–Lieferplan festgehalten.

- "Problem"–Dokumente: Tritt auf einer Maschine ein Fehler auf, so wird darüber eine Notiz erstellt, der "Incident Report" (IR). Unter Umständen kann ein Fehler nicht sofort behoben werden, sondern muss temporär durch eine Umgehungslösung vermieden werden. Falls dies beim Betrieb besondere Massnahmen in der Bedienung erfordert, muss eine sogenannte Weisung erstellt werden, die zwingend zeitlich beschränkt ist. Es gibt Zehntausende von IRs, die heute in einer Datenbank verwaltet werden.

- Allgemeine Informationen: Diverse Bulletins, die in der einen oder anderen Art relevante Informationen für den Betrieb der Rechenzentren enthalten können.

Bei all diesen Dokumenten gibt es eine Reihe von Querbeziehungen und Referenzen. Diese sind zum Teil explizit erwähnt. So enthalten beispielsweise Weisungen einen Hinweis auf den IR, der den aufgetretenen Fehler beschreibt. Manche dieser Beziehungen bestehen allerdings vage und sind erst mit steigendem Wissen formulierbar. In einem Informationssystem sollen diese Dokumente sinnvoll verwaltet werden können und zwar derart, dass jederzeit ein einfacher Zugriff auf die interessierende Information möglich ist.

2.2. Lieferplan

Neue Software wird auf den verschiedenen Grossrechnern (13 Maschinen) je nach Software–Art nach einem vorgegebenen Prozedere installiert. Sämtliche Installationen werden zuerst auf den Entwicklungsmaschinen, danach auf den Testmaschinen und erst zuletzt auf den produktiven Rechnern durchgeführt. Aus Risikoüberlegungen werden sämtliche Installationen zudem auf den einzelnen Systemen gestaffelt vorgenommen.

Der Lieferplan stellt dabei das Instrument dar, mit welchem sämtliche Installationen örtlich und zeitlich festgehalten werden und anhand dem die gesamte Integration der Software–Arten koordiniert werden kann. Er wird von der mit der Integration beauftragten Organisation in Papierform erstellt. Unsere Benutzer formulierten für den Plan eine Reihe von Wünschen:

- Der Plan soll einfach aktualisierbar sein, damit er nicht nur als Planungshilfmittel dient, sondern auch Auskunft über den aktuellen Zustand geben kann.

- Er muss vertiefte Informationen bieten: Nicht nur die Einträge der einzelnen Releases sind von Interesse, sondern auch, was diese Releases enthalten.

- Er soll ein Ausweis darüber sein, welche Releases an einem bestimmten Tag auf den Systemen installiert sein werden.

- Er muss Auskunft geben, welche Installationsaktivitäten an einem bestimmten Tag auf den verschiedenen Maschinen durchzuführen sind.

2.3. Abhängigkeiten

Innerhalb eines organisierten "Change–Managements" ist den Abhängigkeiten zwischen den einzelnen Software–Arten grösste Aufmerksamkeit zu schenken. Gegenseitige Beziehungen existieren in der Art "Software x benötigt eine Routine der Software y, die erst mit Release Nr. z zur Verfügung steht" und umgekehrt "die Installation von Release z der Software y ist die Voraussetzung zum Betrieb der Software x". Diese Art von Information ist zwingend nötig für eine Planung der Lieferung und für das Treffen der richtigen Massnahmen im sogenannten "No Go"–Fall (installierte Software muss, z.B. wegen zuvieler Fehler, wieder zurückgezogen werden). Mit dem Wissen um die Abhängigkeiten können die nötigen Massnahmen bei einem "No Go" bereits geplant und vorbereitet werden.

Es lassen sich 3 Abhängigkeitsrelationen unterscheiden (im Beispiel auf Software–Release x bezogen):

- "Voraussetzung ist": Rückwärtsabhängigkeit ("Voraussetzung für Rel. x ist Rel. y")

- "Gleichzeitigkeit": symmetrische Abhängigkeit ("Rel. x und Rel. y müssen gleichzeitig installiert werden")

- "Voraussetzung für": Vorwärtsabhängigkeit ("Rel. x ist Voraussetzung für Rel. y")

Abhängigkeiten können zwischen allen Schichten des Systemes existieren und können sich auf Hardware, systemtechnische Software, applikatorische Software, spezielle Parameter und andere Rechner beziehen. Es gibt zwei Spezialfälle der gleichzeitigen Abhängigkeit:

- Synchrone Abhängigkeit: Ein Software–Release, meist Kommunikations–Software, muss auf mehreren Maschinen gleichzeitig installiert werden.

- Bandabhängigkeiten: Die zu installierende Software wird für die einzelnen Maschinen physisch auf Magnetbändern geliefert. Eine komplette Software–Lieferung kann mehrere Bänder umfassen.

Wünsche im Rahmen der Abhängigkeiten sind:

- Das Berechnen sämtlicher zurückzuziehender Bänder, falls ein bestimmtes Band zurückgezogen werden muss (transitive Hülle).

- Die Ausgabe sämtlicher Abhängigkeiten über eine ganze Kette von Software–Releases (die Abhängigkeitsbeziehung ist transitiv).

- Abklärung, ob gewisse Software–Konfigurationen aufgrund der Abhängigkeiten überhaupt "legal" sind.

Als grosses Problem bei der Behandlung der Abhängigkeiten stellten sich nicht nur die bis anhin fehlenden Abfragemöglichkeiten heraus, sondern vor allem die fehlende Information darüber. Sehr viele Abhängigkeiten werden stillschweigend vorausgesetzt und treten unter Umständen erst nach einer gewissen Zeit in Erscheinung. Aus diesem Grund muss die Möglichkeit, Abhängigkeiten zu formulieren, sehr flexibel und einfach sein, um auch später auftretende Beziehungen erfassen zu können.

3. Die Basiskomponenten von CHAOS

3.1. "Hyper–Dokumente" mit verschiedenen Link–Mechanismen

Das "innerste" Element des Systems sind die einzelnen Dokumente (Informationsträger) in einem Beziehungsnetz (ausgedrückt durch Links). Alle erwähnten Anforderungen wurden für den Benutzer mittels unterschiedlichen Dokumentklassen realisiert (vgl. Bild 1). Die Basisklasse enthält die gesamte Linkfunktionalität. Darauf ist die Klasse der normalen Textdokumente, der Tabellendokumente und weiterer Dokumente aufgebaut. Darüber werden spezielle Klassen, wie Inhaltsverzeichnis oder Software–Installations–Plan, zur Verfügung gestellt. Durch Vererbung besitzen spezifische Dokumente die Funktionalität ihrer Basisklasse, z.B. enthalten alle erwähnten Dokumente die Linkfunktionalität.

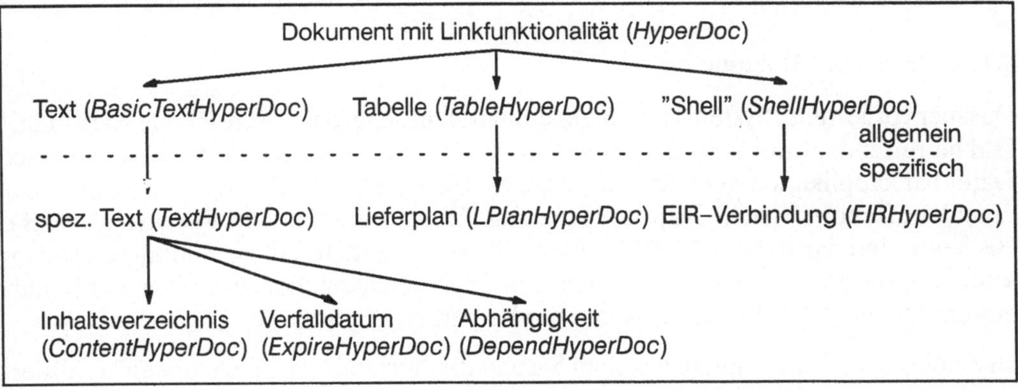

Bild 1: Realisierte Dokument–Hierarchie

Die Referenz–Links wurden, *Intermedia*–ähnlich [Me 86], durch Block– und Linkklassen realisiert. Ein Linkobjekt, verankert im Ausgangsdokument, enthält dabei die Referenz auf einen Block in einem Zieldokument. Dieser Block kann irgendeine Stelle im Dokument markieren. Es gibt zwei Arten von Referenz–Links: Die "see also"–Beziehung für normale Querverweise und die Unterkapitel–Beziehung zur hierarchischen Gliederung.

Zur Aktivierung verschiedener Dokumentfunktionen dienen die "Action"– und die Methoden–Links. Ihr Aufruf bewirkt das Ausführen eines bestimmten Betriebssystem–Befehles oder einer Methode. Die Methoden sind die in der jeweiligen Dokumentklasse realisierten Funktionen. Derselbe Mechanismus wird auch von den einzelnen Dokumenten verwendet, um weitere Methoden auf anderen Dokumenten aufzurufen, z.B. kann ein Inhaltsverzeichnis–Dokument einen bestimmten Test auf allen in seinem Verzeichnis eingetragenen Dokumenten ausführen.

3.2. Navigation

Es sind verschiedene Hilfsmittel vorhanden, um innerhalb der Dokumentstruktur aus einer globalen Perspektive heraus zu navigieren:

* ein Inhaltsverzeichnisbaum: gebildet durch die erwähnten Referenz–Links des Typs ”Unterkapitel”, sowohl lokal als auch global bildbar,

* ein Schlüsselwortverzeichnis: gebildet durch ”Schlüsselwort”–Links, einschränkbar durch Filter–Ausdrücke,

* eine Liste der bereits verfolgten Links.

4. Spezifische Erweiterungen

Neben den ”normalen” Dokumentklassen wie Text– und Tabellenkalkulations–Dokument, die im Sinne bekannter Werkzeuge vorhanden sind, wurden einige für das Anwendungsgebiet spezifische Dokumentklassen zur Verfügung gestellt. Diese Klassen bauen komplett auf den vorhandenen allgemeinen Dokumentklassen auf.

4.1. ”Externe” Dokumente

Das hier vorgestellte System wird kaum einmal sämtliche, das beschriebene EDV–Umfeld betreffende, Informationen enthalten. Verschiedenes wird bereits heute mit einer Datenbankapplikation verwaltet. So existiert für Erstellung, Ablage und Zugriff der ”Incident Reports” (siehe Kap. 2.2.) das sog. ”Electronic Incident Reporting” (EIR). Bis heute sind darin etwa 30'000 Problemfälle registriert. Auf diese umfangreiche Dokumentation muss das System natürlich den Zugriff sicherstellen, ohne dass der Benutzer die Quelle der Information kennen oder bemerken muss.

In einer ersten Phase musste aus dem System die Verbindung ”nach aussen” realisiert werden. Dazu wurde die Dokument–Klasse *ShellHyperDoc* gebildet: Anstelle von normalem Text enthält das Dokument eine Verbindung zu einer UNIX–”Shell”. Damit können Befehle und Programme von einem Dokument aus gestartet werden. Gibt ein solches Programm Text aus, erscheint dieser im Dokument. Der Benutzer hat die Möglichkeit, einen Startbefehl zu formulieren. Dieser wird ausgeführt, sobald man ein solches Dokument öffnet.

Aufbauend auf dem ”Shell”–Dokument konnte nun eine Demonstration des ”Electronic Incident Reporting” (EIR) realisiert werden. Mittels der Benutzer–Methode ”show_IR” kann ein bestimmter ”Incident Report” aus der Datenbank abgefragt werden. Diese Methode kann auch aus anderen Dokumenten durch einen Methodenlink an das EIR–Dokument geschickt werden. Für den Benutzer zeigt sich damit beim ”Verfolgen” eines Links kein Unterschied zu einem lokal abgelegten Dokument.

4.2. Abhängigkeitsdokumente

Die Klasse der Abhängigkeitsdokumente (*DepHyperDoc*) behandelt die Abhängig-
keitsproblematik zwischen verschiedenen Software–Schichten (vgl. Bild 2). Die Dokumentklasse ist auf Text aufgebaut, enthält aber zusätzliche "Abhängigkeitsobjekte".
Diese stellen eine formale Definition der bestehenden Abhängigkeiten dar. Die Definition kann vom Benutzer mit einem einfachen Dialog vorgenommen werden. Zu jedem
Software–Release gehört ein derartiges Abhängigkeitsdokument. Es enthält jeweils
vier Abschnitte (entsprechend Kap. 2.4.): "Voraussetzung ist", "Gleichzeitigkeit" mit
dem Spezialfall "synchrone Installation", "Voraussetzung für" und "Bandabhängigkeiten".

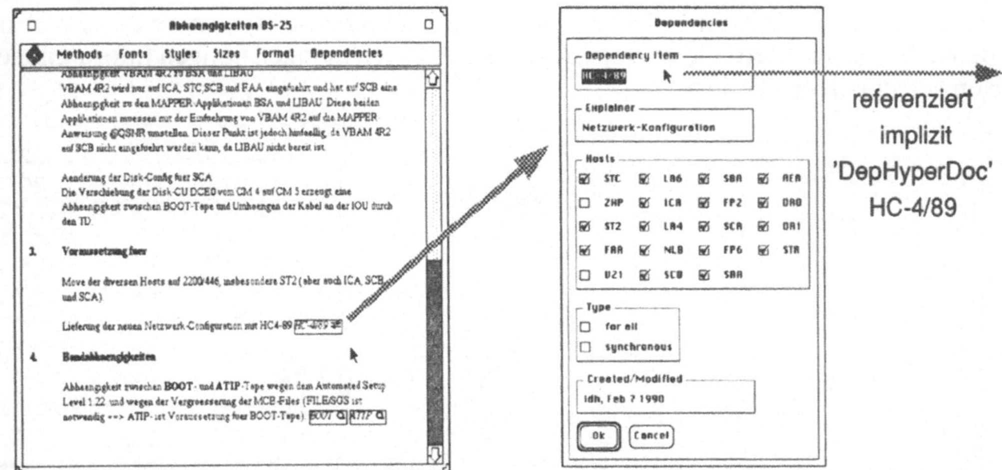

Abhängigkeiten Basis-Software Nr. 25 (BS-25)   **Abhängigkeit zu Hyperchannel-Release 4/89**
('DepHyperDoc' BS-25)   ('Dependency' HC-4/89)

Bild 2: Abhängigkeits–Dokument

Folgende Abfragen sind anhand der formulierten Abhängigkeitsobjekte möglich:

- Ein bestimmtes Band aus dem Lieferumfang muss zurückgezogen werden: Welche
  anderen, abhängigen Bänder sind ebenfalls zurückzunehmen? ("Tape–No Go")

- Ein bestimmter Software–Release muss zurückgenommen werden: Welche Software
  mit welchen Bändern ist davon abhängig und muss gegebenenfalls auch zurückgenommen oder auf eine spezielle "No Go–Version" umgeschaltet werden? ("Release–
  No Go")

Für den Band–Rückzug sind die Angaben aus den Bandabhängigkeiten nötig. Aus diesen Daten wird die transitive Hülle gebildet. Die Software–Abhängigkeiten werden innerhalb des "Release–No Go" verwendet: Im zurückzunehmenden Release werden alle
Software–Releases der Abschnitte "Gleichzeitigkeit" und "Voraussetzung für" in eine
Liste aufgenommen. Damit enthält diese Liste die bei einem Rückzug zu beachtende
Software. Der entsprechende "No Go"–Test wird bei der referenzierten Software im
entsprechenden Abhängigkeitsdokument rekursiv in derselben Art durchgeführt, bis
so der gesamte "Abhängigkeits–Baum" berechnet ist. Beim Aufbau wird ein Ast dann

abgebrochen, wenn entweder im referenzierten Release keine Abhängigkeiten mehr vorhanden sind, wenn das Abhängigkeitsdokument des Releases fehlt oder wenn eine bereits erwähnte Softwareart mit einer neueren Releasenummer erreicht wird.

4.3. Lieferplandokumente

Das Lieferplandokument (*LPlanHyperDoc*) dient als Hilfsmittel zur Planung der verschiedenen Software–Installationen. In einer Tabelle werden die Software–Installationen für die verschiedenen Grossrechner zu bestimmten Zeitpunkten nach vorgegebenen Regeln eingetragen (vgl. Kap. 2.3.). Mit Referenz–Links kann von jedem Eintrag aus die Dokumentation zur entsprechenden Software–Version erreicht werden ("Release–Notes"), resp. können Details einer Installation betrachtet werden. Die vorhandenen Benutzer–Methoden beziehen die für die Berechnungen nötigen Informationen von verschiedenen Seiten:

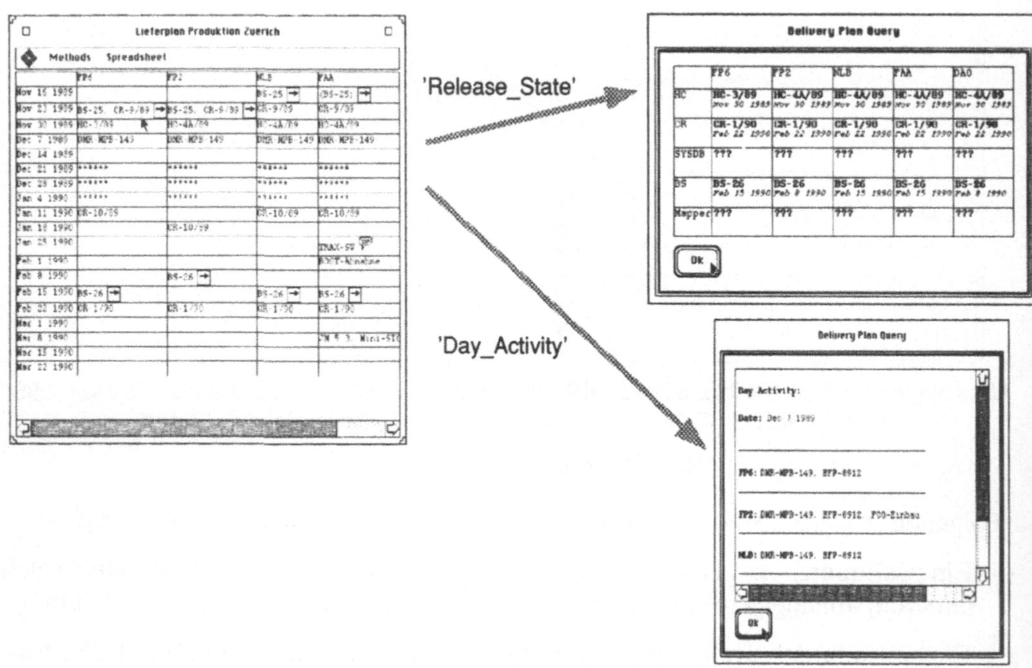

Bild 3: Lieferplan–Dokument mit zwei möglichen Abfragen

* Aus dem vorliegenden Lieferplan: Die Abfrage "Show Release State" (aktueller Lieferzustand) gibt zu allen bestehenden Software–Arten den an einem bestimmten Datum aktuellen Releasezustand auf jeder im Plan erwähnten Maschine heraus.

* Aus anderen Lieferplänen: Die Abfrage "Day Activity" (gesamte Installationstätigkeit an einem Tag) fasst sämtliche Einträge zu einem bestimmten Datum aus einer Reihe von Lieferplänen zusammen, aufgeteilt auf die verschiedenen Maschinen. Die verschiedenen Lieferpläne können zum Beispiel Hardware–Installations–Pläne, System–Software–Lieferpläne, Applikatorische Lieferpläne, etc. umfassen.

- Aus den Abhängigkeits–Dokumenten: Die Abfrage "Check Configuration" (legale Konfiguration) testet zu einem bestimmten Datum, ob die aufgrund der formulierten Abhängigkeiten bestehenden Bedingungen im aktuellen Lieferzustand erfüllt sind. Bei illegalen Zuständen wird eine Fehlermeldung ausgegeben, zum Beispiel in der Art "Falscher Level Basis–Software BS–25 für Hyperchannel–Software HC–4/89 auf Host FP6 (BS–26 nötig)" oder "Synchrone Installation von Communication Release CR–9/89 nötig (Fehler auf Host AEA)".

5.   Diskussion

Mit dem Prototypen wurde primär die Abfragekomponente des Systems realisiert. Die Erfassungsseite wurde völlig vernachlässigt. Ein derartiges System ist immer davon abhängig, wie gut die damit erhältliche Information bewirtschaftet wird. Den Möglichkeiten, Informationen in das System zu übernehmen, muss genügend Aufmerksamkeit geschenkt werden. Die Datenbank–Schnittstelle, sei es für die in den Dokumentklassen beschriebenen Objekte oder für die Ablage der Dokument– und Linkstruktur, fehlt ebenfalls. Des weiteren wurde die Navigation und die Suche nur rudimentär realisiert. Gerade hier stellten die Benutzer wesentliche Anforderungen an das System.

Dennoch konnten anhand des Prototypen einige Punkte gezeigt werden. Links scheinen in diesem Umfeld, vernünftig und unter Einhaltung gewisser Strukturvorschriften verwendet, sinnvoll zu sein. Auch wenn ein normaler Benutzer dieses Konzept nicht durchschaut und er zuweilen staunt, wenn gewisse in einer anderen Umgebung bereits gelesene Dokumente nach der Verfolgung eines Links schon wieder auftauchen. Die freie Definierbarkeit von Links durch den Benutzer muss vorsichtig angegangen werden [Ra87]. Im vorliegenden Kontext scheint diese Möglichkeit allzu grosse Anforderungen zu stellen.

Links sind als Idee generell genug, um bereits auf Betriebssystem–Ebene zur Verbindung "applikationsartiger" Dokumente realisiert zu werden (entspricht [Me 89]). Die Gliederung in verschiedene Dokumente, die sehr spezifisch auf die Behandlung von Teilproblemen angepasst sind, scheint dabei vielversprechend zu sein. In der "Kommunikation" dieser Dokumente auf Referenz– und Methoden–Link–Ebene wurde ein interessantes Integrationskonzept gefunden.

Ein objekt–orientiertes "Framework" mit genügend mächtigen Basisklassen (Text, Grafik, Tabelle, etc.) kann eine geeignete Basis zur Realisation eines derartigen Informations– und Dokumentationssystems bieten. Zusammen mit den erwähnten Linkmechanismen hätte man eine sehr komfortable Realisationsgrundlage.

Mit weiteren Arbeiten versuchen wir, das vorgestellte Konzept weiter zu formulieren. Mit dem neuen System, einem Arbeitsplatz für einen spezifischen Bankmitarbeiter, wird zusätzlich die Verbindung zu operationellen Daten wesentlich wichtiger. Zudem tritt die Informationsbearbeitung gegenüber der reinen Abfrage in den Vordergrund. Eine bessere Trennung von Dokumenten und Links wird notwendig sein (etwa durch einen Link–Server in der Art von [Pe 89]). Die bereits durchgeführten Arbeiten scheinen den vorgestellten Ansatz auch für das neue System zu bestätigen.

Literatur

[Ga 86]   Garrett L.N. and Smith K.E.: Building a Timeline Editor from Prefab Parts, *Proceedings OOPSLA '86*, ACM SIGPLAN, 1986, pp. 202–213.

[Go 87]   Goodman D.: *The Complete HyperCard Handbook*, Bantam Books, New York, 1987.

[Ha 88]   Halasz F.G.: Reflections on NoteCards: Seven Issues for the Next Generation of Hypermedia Systems, *Comm. of the ACM 31*, Nr. 7, 1988, pp. 836–852.

[Me 86]   Meyrowitz N.: Intermedia: The Architecture and Construction of an Object–Oriented Hypermedia–System and Applications Framework, *Proceedings OOPSLA '86*, ACM SIGPLAN, 1986, pp. 186–201.

[Me 89]   Meyrowitz N.: The Missing Link: Why We're All Doing Hypertext Wrong, In: Barret E. (ed.): *The Society of Text: Hypertext, Hypermedia and the Social Construction of Information*, MIT Press, Cambridge MA, 1989, pp. 107–114.

[Pe 89]   Pearl A.: Sun's Link Service: A Protocol for Open Linking, *Proceedings Hypertext '89*, ACM, 1989, pp. 137–146.

[Ra 87]   Raskin J.: The Hype in Hypertext: A Critique, *Proceedings Hypertext '87*, ACM, 1987, pp. 325–330.

[St 87]   Stroustrup B.: *The C + + Programming Language*, Addison Wesley, Reading MA, 1987.

[We 89]   Weinand A., Gamma E. and Marty R.: Design and Implementation of ET + +, a Seamless Object–Oriented Application Framework, *Structured Programming 10*, Nr. 2, 1989, pp. 63–87.

[Ya 88]   Yankelovich N. et al.: Intermedia: The Concept and the Construction of a Seamless Information Environment, *IEEE Computer 21*, Nr. 8, 1988, pp. 81–96.

Konzepte eines verteilten Hypertextsystems

Dieter Meiser
Universität des Saarlandes, FB 14 Informatik
Im Stadtwald 15, D-6600 Saarbrücken

1. Einleitung

Wir stellen in diesem Artikel die Konzeption eines verteilten Hypertextsystems vor. Die Verteilung von Hypertext bietet dabei sowohl die Möglichkeit des entfernten Zugriffs auf einen Hypertext über ein Rechnernetz, als auch den gleichzeitigen Zugriff auf verschiedene Hypertexte durch einen Benutzer.

Durch den Einsatz verteilter Hypertextsysteme kann der Benutzer auf Hypertexte zugreifen, deren Existenz er kennt, deren physikalischer Ort jedoch transparent gehandhabt wird. Der transparente Zugriff auf einen Hypertext kann ergänzt werden durch die Möglichkeit des Verfolgens "externer Kanten". Externe Kanten sind dabei als Verweise zu anderen Hypertexten zu verstehen. Sie entsprechen also etwa Literaturverweisen, wie sie aus der herkömmlichen Literatur bekannt sind. Auch das Folgen externer Kanten kann für den Benutzer transparent behandelt werden.

Zunächst beschreiben wir die Architektur des verteilten Hypertextsystems anhand funktioneller Gesichtspunkte und gehen dann näher auf den Kern des Systems, die Hypertextmaschine, ein.

Erste Ansätze zur Verteilung von Hypertext finden sich z.Bsp. in [Del86], [Meis88]. Im Januar 1990 wurden erste Schritte in Richtung Hypertextstandardisierung unternommen. [Nist90]

Diese Arbeit wurde gefördert durch das BMFT Projekt TK 558-VA011 mit Unterstützung des DFN-Vereins.

2. Das funktionale Modell

Das funktionale Modell beschreibt die Integration des verteilten Hypertextystems in seine Umgebung und seine Zerlegung in Subkomponenten (funktionale Objekte). Diese Zerlegung wird auf Grund funktionaler Aspekte durchgeführt.

Die folgende Figur verdeutlicht die funktionale Aufteilung des verteilten Hypertextsystems:

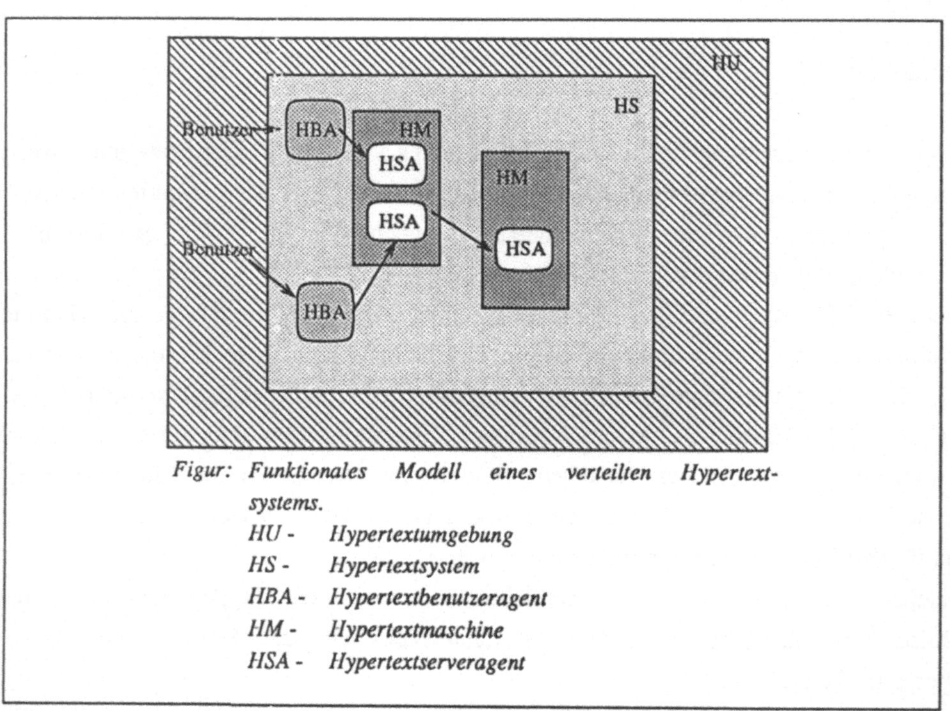

Figur: Funktionales Modell eines verteilten Hypertextsystems.
HU -   Hypertextumgebung
HS -   Hypertextsystem
HBA - Hypertextbenutzeragent
HM -   Hypertextmaschine
HSA - Hypertextserveragent

Die oberste Ebene des verteilten Hypertextsystems wird als *Hypertextumgebung* (HU) bezeichnet. Sie integriert alle Komponenten des Systems. Wir verstehen unter Komponenten dabei sowohl Hardware- als auch Softwarekomponenten.

Die Hypertextumgebung wird gebildet aus den *Benutzern* sowie aus dem *Hypertextsystem* (HS). Benutzer können dabei sowohl menschliche Endbenutzer als auch Anwendungsprogramme sein. Das Hypertextsystem setzt sich aus den *Hypertextbenutzeragenten* (HBA) sowie aus den *Hypertextmaschinen* (HM) zusammen. Die Hypertextbenutzeragenten repräsentieren die Benutzer innerhalb des Hypertextsystems. Die Hypertextmaschinen verwalten die Hypertexte und stellen Funktionen (Hypertextfunktionen) zur Manipulation, insbesondere zum Blättern, bereit.

Die Durchführung der Hypertextfunktionen wird von den *Hypertextserveragenten* (HSA) übernommen.

Durch diese Vorgehensweise erhalten wir eine Klient/Serverarchitektur eines verteilten Hypertextsystems. Die Klienten sind dabei die Benutzer bzw. ihre HBAs, die Server sind die Hypertextmaschinen HM, die die Hypertexte verwalten und den HBAs Dienste in Form von Hypertextfunktionen anbieten. Der Kern des verteilten Hypertextsystems wird durch die Hypertextmaschinen HM gebildet.

3. Die Hypertextmaschine

Eine abstrakte Hypertextmaschine besteht aus einem *Interface*, einer Datenstruktur, dem *Hypertextgraphen* und einer aktiven Instanz, dem *Hypertextserveragenten*. Die Hypertextmaschinen bilden die Einheiten der Verteilung und sind immer vollständig auf einer realen Maschine implementiert. Es können mehrere Hypertextmaschinen auf einem Rechner existieren. Das Interface der Hypertextmaschine erlaubt dem Benutzer den Zugriff auf den Hypertextserveragenten. Die Hypertextmaschine nimmt Berechtigungsüberprüfungen vor, erstellt Abrechnungen und koordiniert die, in ihrem Innern, konkurrent ablaufenden Hypertextserveragenten. Der Hypertextserveragent führt Operationen auf dem Hypertextgraphen aus. Der Agent bietet diese Operationen nach außen hin an, so daß sie vom Benutzer oder von einem Anwendungsprogramm in Anspruch genommen werden können.

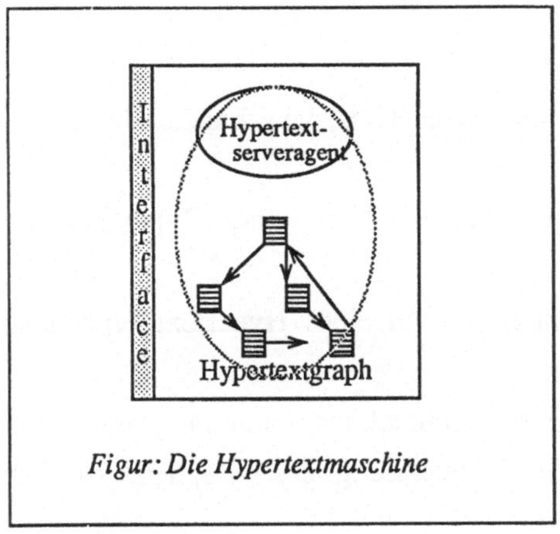

Figur: Die Hypertextmaschine

3.1 Der Hypertextgraph

Die Datenstruktur, die vcn der Hypertextmaschine verwaltet wird, nennen wir den *Hypertextgraphen*. Formale Ansätze zur Beschreibung des Hypertextgraphen können in der Literatur etwa in folgenden Aufsätzen nachgelesen werden: [Stotts89], [Tompa89], [Garg88].

Diese Ansätze stellen jeweils einen bestimmten Aspekt von Hypertext in den Vordergrund. Wir legen ein graphbasiertes Modell für Hypertext zu Grunde, das wir im Folgenden in formaler Weise einführen.

Def.: Hypertext:

Ein Hypertext G ist ein 5-Tupel $\langle K, E, F, I, A \rangle$ mit

K = endliche Menge von Knoten

$E \subseteq K \times K \times A$ endliche Menge von gerichteten, markierten Kanten

I = endliche Menge von Teilinformationen (Karten)

$F: K \to I$ ordnet jedem Knoten eine Teilinformation zu.

A = endliche Menge von Linktypen (Attributen oder Markierungen).

3.2 Links

Da wir uns auf die Verteilung von Hypertext konzentrieren, unterscheiden wir zwei wichtige Klassen von Links:

- *Interne Links* verweisen von einem Knoten eines Hypertextgraphen auf einen Knoten des gleichen Graphen und

- *Externe Links,* die von einem Knoten eines Hypertextgraphen auf einen Knoten eines anderen Graphen verweisen.

Externe Links werden in unserer Darstellung dadurch gekennzeichnet, daß dem Knoten auf den verwiesen wird, die Bezeichnung des Graphen, zu dem der Knoten gehört, vorangestellt wird.

Beispiel:

Sei G1 = <K1, E1, F1, I1, A1> mit

$K1 = \{k_{11}, k_{12}, k_{13}, k_{14}\}$

$A1 = \{a_{11}, a_{12}, a_{13}\}$

$E1 = \{<k_{11}, k_{12}, a_{11}>, <k_{12}, k_{13}, a_{12}>,$
$\quad <k_{13}, k_{14}, a_{13}>, <k_{14}, k_{11}, a_{12}>$
$\quad <k_{13}, G2.k_{23}, a_{14}> \}$

$I1 = \{i_{11}, i_{12}, i_{13}, i_{14}\}$

$F1(k_{1i}) = i_{1i}$ mit $k_{1i} \in K1$ und $i_{1i} \in I1$

Sei G2 = <K2, E2, F2, I2, A2> mit

$K2 = \{k_{21}, k_{22}, k_{23}\}$

$A2 = \{a_{21}, a_{22}\}$

$E2 = \{<k_{21}, G1.k_{12}, a_{21}>, <k_{21}, k_{22}, a_{22}>,$
$\quad <k_{22}, k_{23}, a_{21}>, <k_{23}, k_{21}, a_{21}> \}$

$I2 = \{i_{21}, i_{22}, i_{23}\}$

$F2(k_{2i}) = i_{2i}$ mit $k_{2i} \in K2$ und $i_{2i} \in I2$

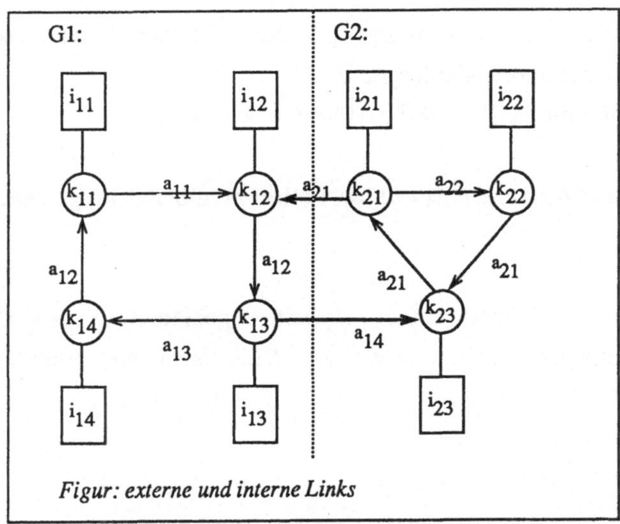

Figur: externe und interne Links

3.3 Hypertextopertionen

Zur Beschreibung von Hypertextoperationen führen wir den Begriff *aktueller Knoten* bzw. *Zustand eines Hypertextes* ein.

Def.: Hypertextzustand

Einen Hypertext G = <K,E,F,I,A> ergänzt um einen *aktuellen Knoten k_i* nennen wir einen *Hypertextzustand* G_z = <K,E,F,I,A,k_i>. Die Operationen, die auf dem Hypertext ausgeführt werden, erzwingen dann einen Zustandsübergang $G_z \rightarrow G_z'$.

Bem.:Wenn keine Mißverständnisse auftreten können, schreiben wir im Folgenden G statt G_z.

Def.: Allgemeiner Hypertextzustand

Ein *allgemeiner Hypertextzustand* G_{z*} wird dadurch definiert, daß mehrere aktuelle Knoten erlaubt sind. $G_{z*} = <K,E,F,I,A,k_1, \ldots ,k_n>$ mit $k_1, \ldots ,k_n \in K$; $1 <= n <= |K|$

Wir können die Operationen, die auf einem Hypertext angewendet werden, in zwei große Gruppen einteilen:
- Browsing- und Filteroperationen
- Editieroperationen

Neben den Operationen, die sich auf die Knoten und Kanten eines Hypertextes beziehen, erlauben wir auch Operationen, die sich auf die den Kanten zugeordneten Attributen beziehen.

In diesem Artikel stellen wir die Browsingoperation und ihre Funktionsweise im Falle verteilter Hypertextsysteme in den Vordergrund.

Weitere Operationen werden in [Meis91] ausführlich behandelt.

Die Funktion, die wir hier betrachten ist *Follow*. Follow erlaubt das Folgen einer Kante.

- *Follow*:
  Durch Folgen von Links kann in einem Hypertext geblättert werden. Die Inhalte der dabei erreichten Knoten, können etwa am Bildschirm des Benutzers dargestellt werden.

```
Sei G = <K,E,F,I,A,k_i> und (k_i,k_j,a_r) ∈ E.
Follow( (k_i,k_j,a_r))   führt zu G' = <K,E,F,I,A,k_j>
```

Im Folgenden betrachten wir die Funktionsweise der Hypertextmaschine und die Behandlung des Folgen externer Kanten.

3.4 Zugang zur Hypertextmaschine

Ein Benutzer, der Dienste einer Hypertextmaschine in Anspruch nehmen möchte wird im Hypertextsystem durch einen *Hypertextbenutzeragenten HBA* repräsentiert (vgl. Kap.2). Dadurch erreichen wir, daß der Benutzer und die Hypertextmaschine auf unterschiedlichen realen Maschinen lokalisiert sein können und abstrahieren gleichzeitig von den physikalischen Gegebenheiten einer zu Grunde liegenden Architektur eines verteilten Systems.

Der Zugang zur Hypertextmaschine wird über sogenannte *access-points* durchgeführt. Jede Hypertextmaschine besitzt einen *login-access-point*, über den die Benutzer sich anmelden müssen. Nach dem Anmelden wird ein *Hypertextserveragent* für den Benutzer installiert, der die gewünschten Dienstleistungen erbringt.

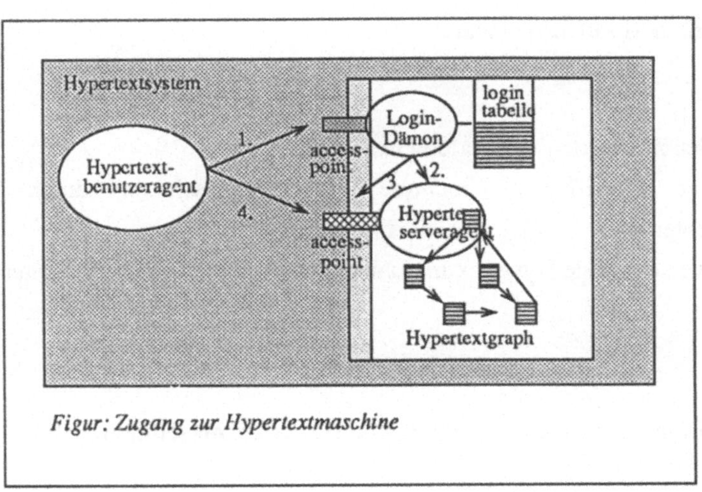

Figur: Zugang zur Hypertextmaschine

Schematisch läßt sich der Zugang zur Maschine wie folgt darstellen:

1. Jeder berechtigte Benutzer wird in einer *login-tabelle* eingetragen. Diese Tabelle enthält als Einträge die Benutzernamen und die ihnen zugeordneten Benutzerkennworte.

2. Der Benutzer wendet sich über den login-access-point an einen sogenannten "Login-Dämon" und teilt ihm seine Benutzerkennung und sein Passwort mit.

3. Der Login-Dämon überprüft die Zugangsberechtigung des Benutzers anhand der "Login-tabelle". Kann dem Benutzer der Zugang zur Hypertextmaschine gewährt werden, richtet der "Login-Dämon einen "Hypertextagenten" ein (2) und teilt dem Agenten einen "access-point" (3) zu.

4. Der Benutzer erhält als Antwort auf seinen Auftrag an den Login-Dämon den access-point mitgeteilt und kann nun über diesen Point mit dem Hypertextagenten kommunizieren. (4)

3.5 Der Startknoten

Der HSA realisiert die in 3.3 angesprochenen Hypertextfunktionen. Nachdem ein Hypertextagent eingerichtet wurde, benötigt er zum Arbeiten einen aktuellen Knoten. Den ersten aktuellen Knoten eines Hypertextagenten bezeichnen wir als den

Startknoten. Wir ordnen jedem Benutzer einen individuellen Startknoten zu, der vom Benutzer verändert werden darf.

3.6 Verteilter Zugriff auf Hypertexte

Wir unterscheiden zwei Arten von verteiltem Zugriff:

1. Gleichzeitiger Zugriff auf mehrere Hypertextmaschinen durch verschiedene Benutzeragenten
2. Zugriff auf verschiedene Hypertextmaschinen durch Folgen externer Kanten.

3.6.1 Gleichzeitiger Zugriff auf verschiedene Hypertextmaschinen

Ordnen wir beispielsweise jedem Benutzeragenten ein Fenster einer Workstation zu, so kann ein Benutzer gleichzeitig mit mehreren Benutzeragenten und damit mit mehreren Hypertextmaschinen arbeiten:

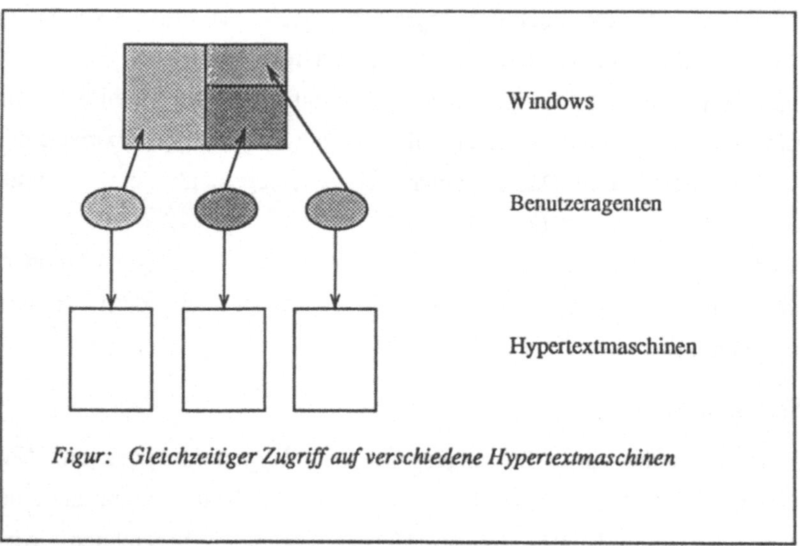

Figur: Gleichzeitiger Zugriff auf verschiedene Hypertextmaschinen

Gleichzeitiger Zugriff auf mehrere Hypertexte ist insbesondere dann interessant, wenn in einem Quelltext geblättert wird und gleichzeitig in Referenzdokumenten verglichen wird.

3.6.2 Behandlung externer Referenzen

Betrachten wir hierzu 2 Hypertexte G1 und G2 (vgl etwa Beispiel, Seite 4). Jeder Hypertext wird von einer Hypertextmaschine verwaltet.

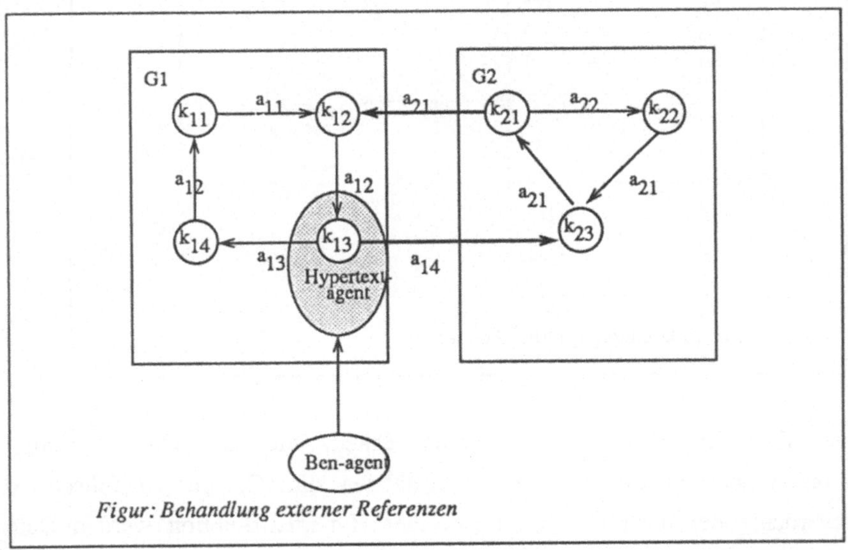

Figur: Behandlung externer Referenzen

Der Benutzer greift momentan auf Knoten k_{13} zu. Möchte der Benutzer nun der externen Kante $\langle k_{13}, k_{23}, a_{14}\rangle$ folgen, so ist die Vorgehensweise wie folgt:

Der Hypertextagent in G1 übernimmt die Rolle eines "stellvertretenden" Benutzeragenten. Er übernimmt die Anmeldung an G2 , und reicht im Folgenden die Benutzereingaben an den Hypertextagenten in G2 weiter, nimmt dessen Antworten entgegen und reicht sie an den Benutzeragenten weiter.

Durch diese Vorgehensweise erreichen wir einen transparenten Wechsel von Hypertextmaschinen, wenn externen Links gefolgt wird.

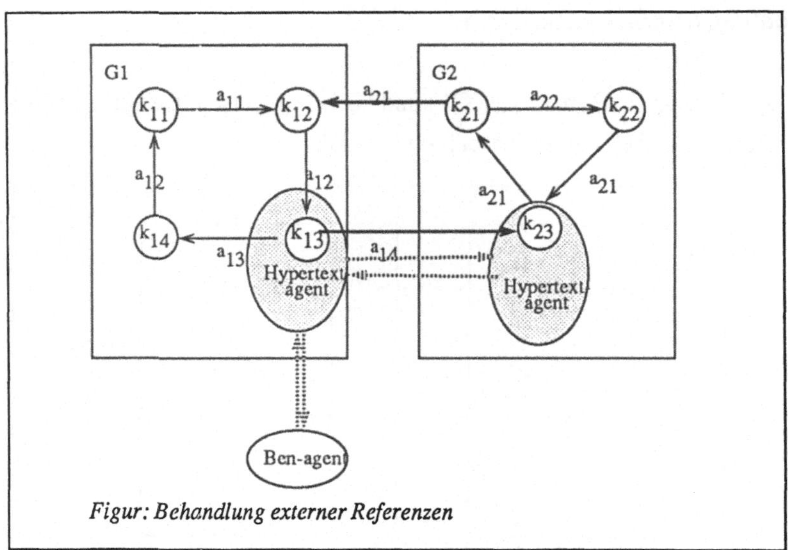

Figur: Behandlung externer Referenzen

Im Fall verteilter Hypertextsysteme müssen Daten, die zur Durchführung einer Hypertextfunktion benötigt werden, unter Umständen zum Ort der Ausführung (HSA) übertragen werden, oder nach Durchführung einer Hypertextfunktion werden Daten als Ergebnis zum Aufrufer (HBA) übertragen. Wir unterscheiden deshalb zwischen einem lokalen und einem globalen Kontext.

3.7 Globaler Kontext/ Lokaler Kontext

3.7.1 Globaler Kontext

Unter dem "globalen Kontext" verstehen wir den globalen Hypertextgraphen, der von einer oder mehreren Hypertextmaschinen verwaltet wird. Auf den globalen Kontext kann von den HBAs unter Verwendung der HSAs zugegriffen werden.

3.7.2 Lokaler Kontext

Unter einem lokalen Kontext verstehen wir private Daten eines Benutzers. Sie werden von den HBAs verwaltet. Es handelt sich hierbei etwa um Anmerkungen zu globalen Hypertextkarten oder um Teile des Hypertextgraphen, die lokal editiert wurden.
Zur Präsentation von Daten des globalen Kontexts, am Bildschirm des Benutzers, müssen diese in den lokalen Kontext übertragen werden. Daten des lokalen Kontexts werden zum globalen Kontext bei der Ausführung von Editieroperationen übertragen.

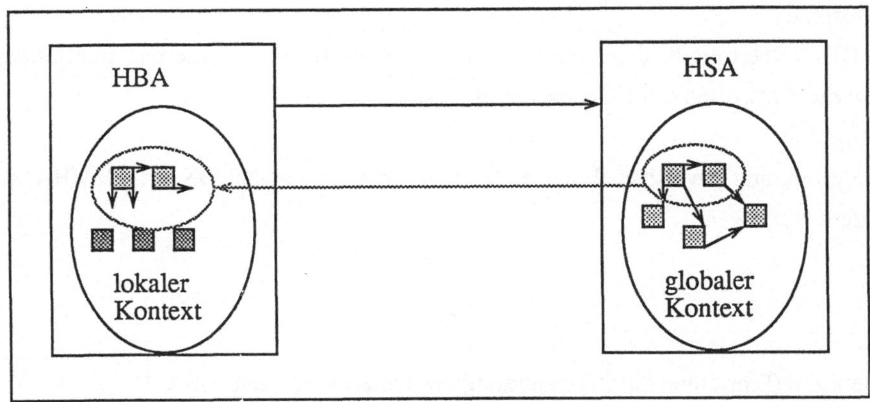

Figur: Globaler/lokaler Kontext

Betrachten wir nun die Browsingfunktion und die Auswirkung ihrer Ausführung auf die Übertragung von Daten zwischen lokalem und globalem Kontext.

Die Hypertextfunktionen "Follow" führt einen Wechsel des aktuellen Knotens herbei. Sollen die Inhalte der Knoten angezeigt werden, so werden sie in den lokalen Kontext des HBA übertragen werden.

Diese Datenübertragung wird von Protokollen, den Hypertextprotokollen, gesteuert.

3.7.3 Hypertextprotokolle

Wir können prinzipiell zwei Protokolle betrachten:

- HAP (Hypertextaccessprotokoll):   Dieses Protokoll beschreibt die Interaktion zwischen HBA und HSA.
- HSP (Hypertextsystemprotokoll):   Beschreibt die Interaktion zwischen HSAs.

HAP:

a. Bindephase (Einrichten einer Verbindung zwischen HBA und HSA)
   Zuerst muß eine Verbindung zwischen HBA und HSA hergestellt werden. Anschließend muß der Benutzer sich identifizieren und kann dann mit der Hypertextmaschine arbeiten.

b. Aktionsphase

Der HBA übermittelt dem HSA Aufträge (Aufrufe von Hypertextfunktionen) und nimmt die Antworten des HSA entgegen.

c. Abbauphase

Die Verbindung zwischen HBA und HSA wird abgebaut. HSA und HBA werden beendet.

HSP:

a. Bindephase (Einrichten einer Verbindung zwischen HSA 1 und HSA 2)

Nachdem eine Verbindung zwischen den beteiligten HSAs hergestellt ist wird HSA1 sich stellvertretend für den zugeordneten HBA identifizieren.

b. Aktionsphase

Der HSA1 übermittelt Aufträge (Aufrufe von Hypertextfunktionen), die er von einem HBA erhalten hat an HSA2, nimmt die Antworten von HSA2 entgegen und reicht sie an den HBA weiter.

c. Abbauphase

Die Verbindung zwischen HSA1 und HSA2 wird abgebaut. HSA2 wird beendet.

Zum Abschluß wollen wir an einem kleinen Beispiel demonstrieren, wie die Konzepte unter Verwendung vorhandener Dienste realisiert werden können. Die Durchführung der verteilten Funktionalität kann mit Remote Procedure Call (RPC) und Filetransfer (z.B FTAM) realisiert werden.

3.8 Beispiel: Hypertext, RPC und FTAM

Die Aufrufe der Hypertextfunktionen werden mit Hilfe eines RPC durchgeführt. Zur Übertragung von Daten vom globalen Kontext zum lokalen Kontext und umgekehrt wird ein Filetransfer (FTAM) eingesetzt.

Wir wollen die Funktionsweise nun am Beispiel der Funktion Follow demonstrieren:

Sei $G = <K, E, F, I, A>$ mit

$K = \{k_1, k_2, k_3, k_4\}$

$A = \{ a_1, a_2, a_3 \}$

$E = \{ <k_1,k_2,a_1>, <k_2,k_3,a_2>, <k_3,k_4,a_3>, <k_4,k_1,a_2> $

$I = \{i_1, i_2, i_3, i_4\}$

$F(k_j) = i_j$ mit $k_j \in K$ und $i_j \in I$ $1 <= j <= 4$ und sei

$G_z = <K, E, F, I, A, k_1>$

Der HBA gibt beim Aufruf der Funktion *Follow* als Parameter einen Link und einen Dateinamen an.

HBA: Follow(e1, Dateiname) mit e1 = <k1,k2,a1>

Der HSA führt die Funktion aus und wir erhalten einen neuen Hypertextzustand $G_{z'} =$

$<K, E, F, I, A, k_2>$

Anschließend legt der HSA die Informationen, die zum lokalen Kontext des HBA übertragen werden sollen (aktueller Knoten, Links und Informationseinheit) in einer Datei auf dem Rechner, auf dem der HSA läuft, ab.

Als Ergebnis der Durchführung der Funktion Follow erhält der HBA den Namen der Datei, in der die Informationen abgelegt sind, vom HSA als Antwort zurück.

Anschließend stößt der HBA einen Filetransfer an und kopiert sich so die Daten in seinen lokalen Kontext.

4. Zusammenfassung

Die vorgestellten Konzepte erlauben uns ein verteiltes Hypertextsystem zu realisieren. Insbesondere sollte es möglich sein, Zugang zu Hypertextdokumenten über ein öffentliches Netz (z.B. WIN) zu realisieren. Wir haben eine ausführliche Spezifikation des Hypertextgraphen und der Hypertextfunktionen erarbeitet, deren Darstellung jedoch den Rahmen dieses Artikels sprengen würde. Wir sind im Begriff, prototypische Realisierungen der Konzepte für verschiedene verteilte Systeme vorzunehmen (vgl. [Schw]).

5. Literatur

[Del86]   Delisle, N and Schwartz, M "Neptune: A Hypertext System for CAD Applications." Proc ACM SIGMOD'86, Washington DC May 28-30, ACM SIGMOD Record, 15:2, June 1986 132-143

[Garg88]   Garg, P: "Abstraction Mechanisms in Hypertext" in Comm. of The ACM, Vol 31, Nr 7 Juli 1988

[Meis88]   Meiser, Nilam, Prinz, Scheidig, "Das verteilte Hypertextsystem DHS", in Proceedings III-Forum, Saarbrücken Oktober 1988, Seite 101 - 113, Informatik Fachberichte, Springer Verlag.

[Meis90]   Meiser, D.: "Die verteilte abstrakte Hypertextmaschine DAHM" in Proceeding of IiI, Tuczno 1990, S 248-265

[Meis91]   Meiser, D: "Verteilte Anwendungen im DFN"; Studie des DFN Vereins, März 1991

[Nist90]   Proceedings of the Hypertext Standardization Workshop Jan 16-18, 1990, NIST Special Publication 500-178

[Schw]   Schweizer, M: "Implementierung eines verteilten Hypertextsystems" Diplomarbeit Universität des Saarlandes, FB 14 Informatik, in Vorbereitung

[Stotts89]   Stotts P, Furuta R: "Petri-Net-Based-Hypertext: Document Structure with Browsing Semantics" in ACM Transactions on Information Systems, Vol 7, Nr. 1 Jan 1989, Seite 3 - 30

[Tompa89]   Tompa, F. WM "A Data Model for Flexible Hypertext Database Systems" in ACM Transactions on Information Systems, Vol 7, Nr. 1 Jan 1989, Seite 85-100

Strukturierung von hypertext-basierten Bedienungsanleitungen im Prototyp "FAXUAL"

H. Möller & J. Schiff
Siemens AG, ZFE IS INF 32
Otto-Hahn-Ring 6, D-8 München 83

1 Einführung

Ein wirtschaftlich besonders interessantes Anwendungsfeld für Hypertext ist technische Dokumentation: Hypertext-Systeme können dort den Nutzungskomfort wesentlich erhöhen, z.B. bei Reparaturanleitungen mit direktem Zugriff auf Ersatzteilkataloge. Ebenso bieten sie ein Potential zur Senkung hoher Dokumentationskosten (z.B. im Anlagenbau typisch ca. 7% der Gesamtkosten! [Rose89]), etwa indem durch entsprechende Verknüpfung bestimmte Dokumentteile mehrfach genutzt werden.

Um mit heutigen Systemen große Hyperdokumente zu erstellen, ist allerdings ebenfalls noch ein (zu) hoher Aufwand nötig. Zum Beispiel muß der Autor alle elektronischen Verbindungen einzeln definieren, sie bei inhaltlichen Änderungen auf evtl. Konsistenzverletzungen prüfen und gegebenenfalls auch einzeln entsprechend korrigieren. Auch kann die Vielfalt der Verbindungen zu einem "Vernetzungs-Spaghetti" führen, in dem der Leser leicht die Orientierung verliert; vgl. das bekannte Bild des unüberschaubaren Intermedia-Browsers in [Conk87].

Ein Einsatz wissensbasierter Techniken verspricht hier deutliche Verbesserungen. Mit Hilfe geeigneter Repräsentationsmechanismen könnten Hyperdokumente nämlich entsprechend der Anwendungs-Semantik strukturiert werden und nicht nur wie bei heutigen Systemen auf der anwendungs-unspezifischen Ebene der einfachen Knoten und Verbindungen. Eine solche semantische Strukturierung könnte dann als Basis sowohl für mächtige, arbeitssparende Editier-Operationen dienen als auch für eine "intelligente" Filterung der jeweils relevanten Information.

In diesem Beitrag stellen wir unsere ersten Schritte in Richtung zu semantisch strukturiertem Hypertext anhand unseres Prototypen "FAXUAL" dar. Dabei wurde ein Teil der Bedienungsanleitung für ein Telefaxgerät auf der Basis eines kommerziellen Hypertext-Systems als elektronisches Manual aufbereitet. Hier stellte sich eine Strukturierung nach Handlungspfaden als wichtiges Prinzip heraus. Die Erfahrungen aus diesem Prototypen gehen in unsere weitere Arbeit ein, die wir zum Schluß des Beitrags skizzieren.

2 Der Prototyp FAXUAL

2.1 Hintergrund

Im Rahmen eines zweimonatigen Werkstudenten-Einsatzes bei der Siemens AG wurde Anfang 1990 eine Studie zum Thema "Technische Dokumentation und Hypertext (HT)" durchgeführt. Als Ziel wurde die Realisierung eines Prototypen angestrebt, um die Eignung von HT für die Technische Dokumentation zu demonstrieren und auftretende Probleme zu identifizieren.

Dazu wurde ein kostengünstiges und kommerziell verfügbares HT-System unter MS-DOS gesucht. Es sollte minimale HT-Funktionalität mit annehmbaren Graphik-Eigenschaften verbinden. Wichtig war die Anforderung, beliebige Graphik-Bereiche sensitiv machen zu können. Es wurde das Programm OPUS I der Firma Roykore Software Inc. ausgewählt, das die geforderten Kriterien erfüllt, obwohl es nur in zweiter Linie ein HT-System ist.

Im Rahmen der Studie mußte aus dem weiten Feld der Technischen Dokumentation eine überschaubare und doch hinreichend komplexe Anwendung gefunden werden. Dabei wurde ein allgemein verfügbares Siemens-Produkt gesucht, um ein halbwegs realistisches Test-Szenario zu ermöglichen. Die Wahl fiel schließlich auf den Fernkopierer HF 2305. Daß die Verwendung eines PCs zur Beschreibung eines Telefaxgerätes wenig realistisch erscheint, wurde wegen der überwiegenden Vorteile des Testbetts "Telefaxgerät" bewußt in Kauf genommen.

Da aus Zeitgründen nur für eine Funktion des Telefaxgeräts die Bedienungsanleitung als Hyperdokument exemplarisch implementiert werden konnte, war es wichtig, einen nichttrivialen, selten durchgeführten Vorgang auszuwählen. Damit konnten einerseits typische Probleme identifiziert werden und andererseits stand eine ausreichende Anzahl von in dieser Funktion ungeübten Testpersonen zur Verfügung.

Die Entscheidung fiel hier auf die Funktion "Rundbrief senden". Mit dem Fernkopierer kann man einen Rundbrief an verschiedene Adressaten senden, eine Funktion, die zwischen 4 und 30 Bedienschritten erfordert, je nach "Szenario" (Adressen bereits gespeichert oder nicht etc.). Die Vielfalt an Verzweigungen und Ausnahmen waren ein weiterer Grund für die Wahl dieser Funktion.

2.2 Funktionalitäts-Diagramm (FD)

In der Original-Bedienungsanleitung [SIEMoJ] wird das Rundbrief-Senden unter dem Aspekt der Funktionalität beschrieben. Das heißt, es wird beschrieben, welche Zustände des Geräts beim Rundbrief-Senden auftreten können und welche Bedienschritte dann jeweils auszuführen sind. Der Fokus der Bedienungsanleitung ist somit die Funktionalität des Geräts und nicht die Handlungsabsicht des Benutzers.

Diese Vorgehensweise liegt nahe, da eine Bedienungsanleitung alle Fähigkeiten des Gerätes beschreiben muß und die Strukturierung nach Geräte-Funktionalität auf dem Papier eine möglichst geringe Redundanz erlaubt. Die Anleitung kann somit auf einen minimalen Umfang reduziert werden. Diese Struktur wurde zunächst für FAXUAL übernommen. Dazu wurde in Anlehnung an [Haag81] eine graphische Symbolsprache entwickelt, die einem Autor von HT-Bedienungsanleitungen die konsistente Erfassung der Geräte-Funktionalität erleichtern sollte.

Die Bedienung eines beliebigen Systems läßt sich nach [Haag81] auf das folgende einfache zyklische Schema reduzieren: Zustand des Systems, Entscheidung und Aktion des Benutzers, Entscheidung und Reaktion des Systems, wieder Zustand des Systems usw.

Durch Erweiterung des von [Haag81] vorgeschlagenen "Allgemeinen Zustands- und Funktionsdiagramms" entstand eine verschachtelbare Notation. Ein Oval stellt den Zustands eines Systems dar und ein Rechteck sowohl die Aktion des Benutzers als auch die Reaktion des Systems. Dabei können einzelne Rechtecke, also "Funktionen", selber wieder eine komplexe Struktur repräsentieren. Die Entscheidungen werden durch ein Rechteck mit verschiedenen "Ausgängen" symbolisiert. Speziell für die Beschreibung einer Funktionalität im Hinblick auf eine HT-Bedienungsanleitung wurde ein abgerundetes Rechteck als Symbol für einen "button" eingeführt. Diese bilden Konnektoren zu der bei HT leicht zugänglichen kontextabhängigen Zusatzinformation (Bild 1).

Mit dieser Symbolsprache konnte die Funktionalität des Fernkopierers innerhalb kurzer Zeit aus der vorliegenden Original-Bedienungsanleitung konsistent und übersichtlich extrahiert werden.

Als einen weiteren Vorteil des FD erwies sich die Möglichkeit, schon bei der Beschreibung der Funktionalität eine Benutzer-Modellierung vorzunehmen: Ein geübter Benutzer des FAX-Gerätes kann z.B. aufgrund der Funktionsbezeichnung „Telefax-Nummern speichern" die nötigen Aktionen durchführen, die dem sporadischen Benutzer detaillierter erklärt werden müssen.

Nicht zuletzt wäre es möglich, aus einem FD automatisch ein fertiges Bildschirm-Layout zu erzeugen, das anschließend vom Autor nur noch mit Inhalt "gefüllt" werden müßte.

2.3 Empirische Ergebnisse und Lösungsansätze für die identifizierten Probleme

Verschiedene Testpersonen wurden gebeten, mit Hilfe von FAXUAL einen Rundbrief zu versenden. Die unrealistische Situation, als Bedienungsanleitung für das FAX-Gerät einen PC zu benutzen, stellte anfangs eine große Schwierigkeit dar. Als eigentliches Problem zeichnete sich darüber hinaus eine starke Verwirrung der Testpersonen ab, die sich auf drei Gründe zurückführen ließ:

● Die Gestaltung des Bildschirm-Layouts erwies sich als ungünstig, da zuviel Information auf einmal angeboten wurde.

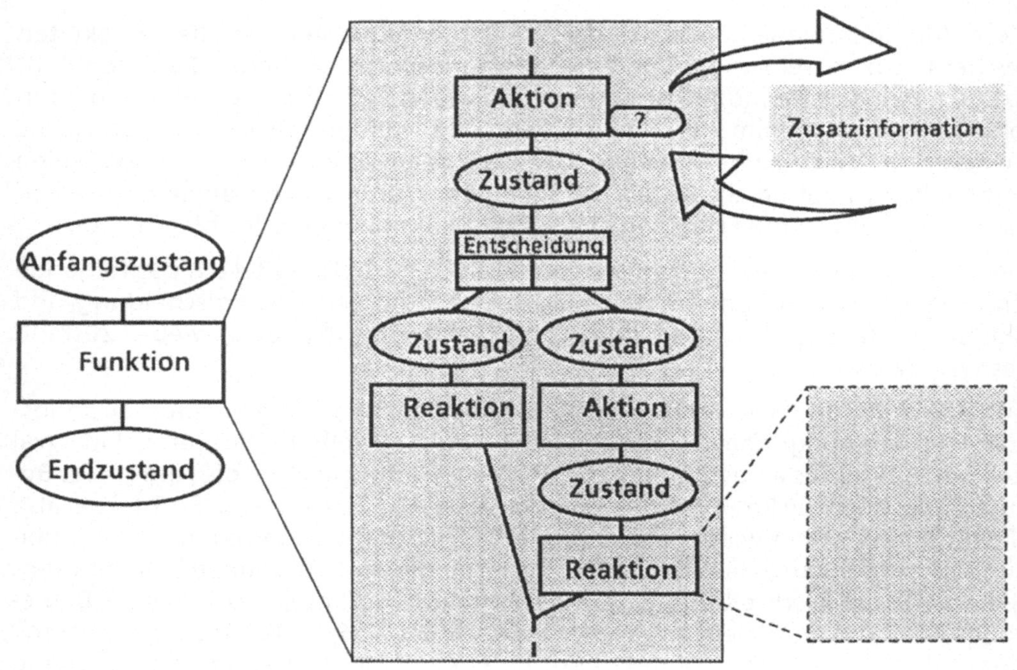

Bild 1: Erweitertes "Allgemeines Zustands- und Funktionsdiagramm"

- Weiterhin war der Versuchung nicht widerstanden worden, zuviel Zusatzinformation über Links anzubieten. Außerdem schuf das Überangebot an Navigationsmitteln ("Weiterblättern", "Zurückblättern", "Inhaltsangabe", "Störungsmeldungen", "History", etc.) erhebliche Probleme.

- Am gravierendsten erwies sich jedoch die Desorientierung des Benutzers durch die Vielzahl der zu treffenden Entscheidungen, welcher Teil der Funktionalität erklärt werden sollte.

Auf Grund der empirischen Ergebnisse wurde die Bedienungsanleitung fast völlig neu konzipiert:

Das Layout-Problem ließ sich am einfachsten verbessern: Beispielsweise wurde die Anzahl der Bedienschritte auf drei bis vier pro Bildschirm reduziert, die Farbgebung dezenter gestaltet, Formulierungen überarbeitet und anderes. Prinzipiell ist die Layout-Gestaltung aber kein theoretisches Problem.

Schwieriger dagegen war es, den Mittelweg zwischen Überangebot und damit Verwirrung des Benutzers und dem gänzlichen Verzicht auf Zusatzinformation zu finden: "Wozu dann noch HT?" Durch Beschränken auf die allernotwendigste Zusatzinformation und durch eine geschicktere graphische Aufbereitung konnte auch dieses Problem entschieden entschärft werden.

Das Überangebot an zu treffenden Entscheidungen aber konnte auf zwei tieferliegende Gründe zurückgeführt werden.

- Zum einen richtet sich das Angebot an Funktionalität bei elektronischen Geräten (z. B. Kopierer, Telephonanlagen, etc.) oftmals nach dem technisch Machbaren und nicht nach dem vom Benutzer tatsächlich gewünschten. Doch soll in diesem Zusammenhang darauf nicht weiter eingegangen werden.

- Der andere Grund betrifft die für die Bedienungsanleitung gewählte Strukturierung: Der normale Benutzer bringt für sein Telefaxgerät wenig Interesse auf. Wichtig ist es, daß das Gerät beispielsweise einen Rundbrief versendet, und das möglichst schnell und ohne daß der Benutzer viel nachdenken muß. Was das Gerät alles kann, ist nützlich für den häufigen Benutzer, dessen tägliche Arbeit dadurch erheblich vereinfacht wird.

Als Konsequenz wurde die Strukturierung nach Funktionalität aufgegeben und die Bedienungsanleitung nach Handlungspfaden gegliedert. Das heißt, das primäre Strukturierungsprinzip für die Bedienungsanleitung ist jetzt eine logische Abfolge von Handlungen, die den Benutzer möglichst direkt zum Ziel führen (z.B. Versenden eines Rundbriefs). Im Unterschied zur funktionalen Strukturierung wird hier vom Autor eine Bewertung der möglichen Gerätezustände und Operationen vorgenommen, z.B. "Normalfall / Ausnahmefall", "einfache Operation für Gelegenheitsbenutzer / mächtige komplexe Operation für Geübte". Der Haupt-Handlungspfad bei FAXUAL wurde für den "Normalfall" für Gelegenheitsbenutzer ausgelegt. "Ausnahmen" und "komplexe Operationen für Geübte" sind aber über elektronische Verknüpfungen im Hyperdokument leicht und schnell zugreifbar, ebenso wie Erläuterungen für absolut ungeübte Telefax-Benutzer (z.B. "Wo ist die Taste INFO/KOPIE ?"), vgl. Bild 2.

Die überarbeitete Version von FAXUAL mit der klaren Strukturierung nach Handlungspfaden erzielte in einer erneuten Versuchsreihe deutlich bessere und ermutigendere Resultate. Zu dem gleichen Ergebnis kamen auch [Simo90], die als Studie unter anderem eine "Bedienungsanleitung für Drehtorantriebe" auf HT realisierten. Im Gegensatz zur funktionalen Strukturierung konnte für die Strukturierung nach Handlungspfaden aber noch keine explizite Strukturierungssystematik mit zugehöriger graphischer Notation ausgearbeitet werden.

3 Weitere Arbeiten

Die bei FAXUAL gewonnenen Erfahrungen gehen in unsere weitere Arbeit im Rahmen eines neu beginnenden Esprit-Projekts ein. Der Kern dabei wird die Definition eines "semantischen Datenmodells" [PeMa88] für Hyperdokumente oberhalb der Ebene einfacher Knoten und Verbindungen sein. Die spezifische Struktur eines Dokumentations-Sachgebiets kann dann als "Schema" (im Datenbank-Sprachgebrauch) formuliert werden. Die konkreten Ausprägungen dieser Struktur, d.h. in unserem Fall das Netz der einzelnen Knoten und Verbindungen des Hyperdokuments, sind schließlich "Instanzen" des Schemas.

SENDEN   **RUNDBRIEF**

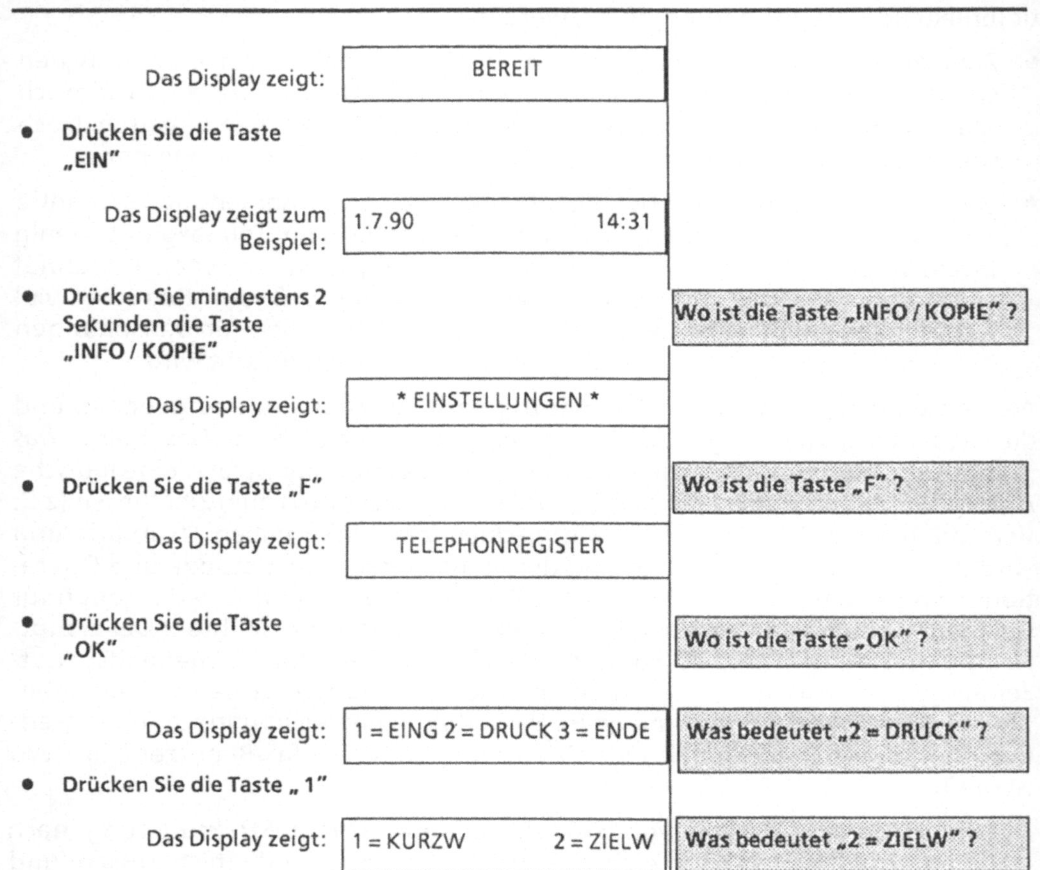

Bild 2: Auszug aus der Bedienungsanleitung (Buttons grau hinterlegt)

Um ein geeignetes semantisches Datenmodell zu definieren, müssen wir klären, welche Art von struktureller Information wir damit ausdrücken wollen, etwa Handlungspfade für Bedienungsanleitungen. Dazu müssen Handlungspfade aber noch geeignet formalisiert werden. Zum Beispiel könnte man Handlungspfade aus einzelnen "Aktionen" aufbauen, wobei jede Aktion durch Attribute wie "notwendige Voraussetzungen", "Ergebnis", "Randbedingungen", "Parameter", "geeignet-für-Benutzerkategorie" usw. gekennzeichnet sein könnte.

Mit einer derartigen semantischen Modellierung von Bedienungsanleitungen würden automatische Überprüfungen von Manuskripten möglich. Zum Beispiel könnte bei der Beschreibung einer Aktion wie "Verteiler bestimmen" geprüft werden, ob die vorher auszuführenden Aktionen ("Adressen eingeben") schon beschrieben wurden. Wir müssen aber noch in Zusammenarbeit mit Autoren - in unserem Fall technischen Fachredakteuren - untersuchen, wie weit solche automatischen Überprüfungen sinnvoll sind, d.h. von den Autoren genutzt und angenommen werden.

Bei der Definition des semantischen Datenmodells und der Funktionalität unseres Autorensystems werden wir allerdings in mehreren Hinsichten sorgfältig abwägen müssen:

- Mächtigkeit und Allgemeinheit: Ein Datenmodell kann umso mächtiger sein, je spezifischer es auf eine bestimmte Anwendungsklasse zugeschnitten wird; es verliert damit umgekehrt aber an Allgemeinheit.

- Mächtigkeit und Komplexität: Die Formulierung von Sachgebiets-Strukturen mit einem mächtigen Datenmodell könnte unter Umständen so komplex werden, daß wir damit an Akzeptanz bei den Autoren verlieren.

Um solche Fragen zu entscheiden wollen wir pragmatisch vorgehen und sehr stark anwendungsgetrieben anhand einer realistischen Pilotanwendung arbeiten.

4 Literatur

[Conk87] Conklin, J.: Hypertext: An Introduction and Survey. IEEE Computer, Vol. 20, No. 9, pp.17-41, September 1987.

[Haag81] Haag, W.: Dokumentation von Anwendungssystemen aus der Sicht der Benutzer. Darmstadt: Toecher-Mittler 1981.

[PeMa88] Peckham, J. & Maryanski, F.: Semantic Data Models. ACM Computing Surveys, Vol.20, No.3, pp.153-190, September 1988.

[Rose89] Rose, B.: Notstand in der technischen Dokumentation - Auf die Industrie rollt eine Kostenlawine zu. VDI-Nachrichten, 15.12.89, S.4.

[SIEMoJ] SIEMENS AG: "Wie Sie den Fernkopierer HF 2305 bedienen können - Bedienungsanleitung". Ohne Jahresangabe.

[Simo90] Simon, L.: Wissensbasierte Erstellung und Benutzung handlungsorientierter Anweisungs„texte". FORWISS, Erlangen: 1990.

Allgemein zugängliche und private Objekte im Hypertextsystem CONCORDE

H.Peyn[2]   M.Hofmann[1]   H.Langendörfer[1]   T.Töpperwien[2]

[1] TU Braunschweig
Inst. f. Betriebssysteme und Rechnerverbund
Bültenweg 74/75
D-3300 Braunschweig
Tel.: [+49] 531 391 3249
FAX: [+49] 531 391 4577
UUCP: unido!infbs!hofmann
EARN: hofmann@dbsinf6.bitnet

[2] Telenorma
EVO 3
Kleyerstr. 94
D-6000 Frankfurt/Main 1
Tel.: [+49] 69 266 3048
FAX: [+49] 69 266 3315
UUCP: unido!tnevo!peyn

1   Motivation

Die Mehrzahl aller Veröffentlichungen, die sich mit Hypertext beschäftigen, haben die Schnittstelle zum Benutzer als Schwerpunkt. Das liegt einerseits daran, daß Oberflächengestaltung immer ein dankbares Thema darstellt, andererseits daran, daß die Zugriffs- und Navigationsthematik sicher ein Problem ist, bei dem überzeugende Lösungsvorschläge die Akzeptanz eines Hypertextsystems merklich erhöhen. Wie jedoch schon in [AYM88] festgestellt wird, bestimmt die dem System zugrunde liegende logische Struktur, das Datenmodell, wesentlich die Gestaltung der Benutzungsoberfläche.

Wir wollen uns in diesem Papier deshalb mit den Objekten des CONCORDE–Hypertextsystems beschäftigen und dabei besonders auf die Kommunikation zwischen den verschiedenen Moduln eingehen. Diese wird bei bestimmten Benutzeraktionen wie etwa dem Löschen eines Knotens im Hypertext nötig. Gerade die Kommunikation macht die Zusammenhänge und Besonderheiten unseres Ansatzes deutlich und nutzt die Vorteile der von uns verwendeten objektorientierten Umgebung Smalltalk-80 [GoRo89].

Der Aufbau des Papiers ist weiter wie folgt: Zunächst wird in Abschnitt 2 ein kurzer Abriß der Konzepte gegeben, die CONCORDE zugrunde liegen. Ausgehend von den hier

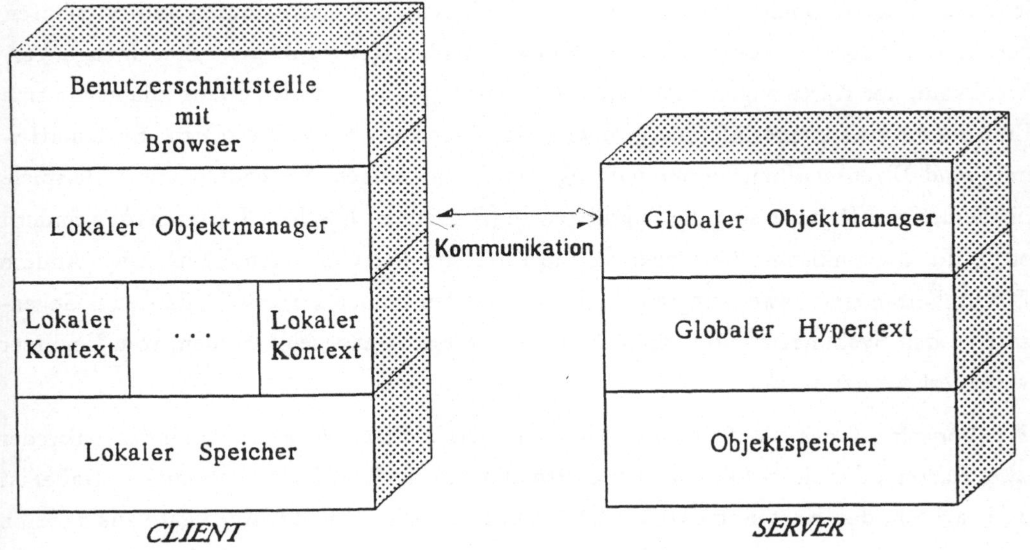

Bild 1: Softwarearchitektur des CONCORDE-Prototypen

definierten Begriffen wird in Abschnitt 3 das Szenario einer typischen Benutzeraktion gebildet; die dabei auftretenden Problemstellungen werden analysiert. Abschnitt 4 enthält dann eine Definition der Objekte und eine Beschreibung der Kommunikation, die bei der Behandlung der Benutzeraktion abläuft. In Abschnitt 5 wird schließlich der Stand des Projekts kurz beleuchtet.

2 Konzept und Aufbau von CONCORDE

CONCORDE ist ein seit Frühjahr 1988 laufendes Projekt des Instituts für Betriebssysteme und Rechnerverbund der TU Braunschweig. Ziel dieses Projekts ist die Entwicklung eines Hypertextsystems für aktive Anwender. Die Softwarearchitektur des Systems gliedert sich in zwei separate Bereiche: in eine Datenbasis, die allgemein zugängliche Information enthält, den **globalen Hypertext**, sowie in die **lokalen Kontexte** (siehe Bild 1). Der globale Hypertext wird vom Globalen Objektmanager verwaltet, die lokalen Kontexte von einem Lokalen Objektmanager.

Ein lokaler Kontext enthält eine aus dem globalen Hypertext kopierte Teilmenge der dort gespeicherten Information und zusätzlich private Informationen, die nicht in den globalen Hypertext geschrieben werden. Jedem lokalen Kontext ist ein Benutzer zugeordnet; dieser kann die CONCORDE-Objekte nur im lokalen Kontext manipulieren.

Das Basisobjekt von CONCORDE ist die **Karte**. Eine Karte besteht aus Inhalt der Datentypen Text, Graphik oder Bitmap, einer Reihe von Systemattributen und Attributen der Anwendung. Sie besitzt einen systemweit eindeutigen Schlüssel. Eine Menge Verweise kann der Karte zugeordnet sein. Der Begriff „Karte" wurde gewählt, da er für eine Einheit, die eine kleine Informationsmenge repräsentiert, passend erschien. Systemattribute sind Eigenschaften, die unabhängig von der jeweiligen Anwendung sind. Beispiele für derartige Attribute sind die Zugriffsrechte (Schreiben, Löschen, Eigenschaften_ändern etc.), die Kartenklasse, die Ikone, die die Karte im Browser symbolisiert usw. Andere Eigenschaften sind anwendungsabhängig. Sie werden immer dargestellt, da sie im Gegensatz zu den Systemattributen, die nur auf Anforderung angezeigt werden, vom Benutzer verändert werden dürfen.

Ein **Verweis** ist das zweite Basisobjekt von CONCORDE. Verweise verbinden entweder zwei Karten oder einen Bereich einer Karte und eine andere Karte miteinander. Dabei ist zu beachten, daß Karten in CONCORDE auch komplexe Objekte (Aggregate aus anderen Karten) repräsentieren können. Verweise, die von Karten ausgehen, liefern auf Anforderung eine Verweisinformation („info"), die u.a. eine Erklärung ihrer Bedeutung enthält. Verweise, die von Bereichen ausgehen, dienen als Anmerkungen. Wir unterscheiden zwei Kategorien von Verweisen: individuelle Verweise und vordefinierte Verweise.

Vordefinierte Verweise sind typisierte Verweise, die im globalen Hypertext definiert sind. Typisiert bedeutet in diesem Fall, daß das System in der Lage ist zu kontrollieren, ob das Setzen des Verweises oder eine andere Operation im konkreten Fall erlaubt ist. Für jeden Verweistyp sind daher zwei Mengen von Kartenklassen definiert. Die eine Menge enthält die Klassen, deren Instanzen erlaubte Quellen des Verweises sind, die andere Menge die Klassen der erlaubten Ziele. Zusätzlich können noch explizite Constraints definiert werden. Letzteres erfordert im Prototypen derzeit noch direktes Programmieren in Smalltalk; die Entwicklung eines Struktureditors zur Eingabe von Constraints ist aber geplant. Jeder Verweis besitzt ebenfalls einen systemweit eindeutigen Schlüssel. Der Typ des Verweises wird dem Benutzer als Name des Verweises dargestellt und soll daher die Semantik der Anwendung ausdrücken. In einem Beispiel, das während der Entwicklung des Prototypen dem Testen diente, wurden Kartenklassen und Verweistypen angelegt, die das Schreiben eines Drehbuchs unterstützen (siehe auch die folgenden Beispiele).

Individuelle Verweise besitzen keinen Typ. Sie können zwar mit einem Namen versehen, aber beim Setzen nicht kontrolliert werden. Im Gegensatz zu den vordefinierten Verweisen werden sie nur in den lokalen Kontexten gehalten und dort im lokalen Speicher abgelegt, auch wenn die Karten, zu denen sie gehören, in den globalen Hypertext zurückgeschrieben („freigegeben") werden. Wir sehen in dieser Trennung der beiden Verweiskategorien folgende Vorteile:

Zunächst ist es möglich, private Verweisstrukturen gegen den Zugriff anderer Anwender zu schützen. Durch das Halten in einem lokalen Kontext garantieren wir die Privatheit der individuellen Verweise. Zweitens bietet CONCORDE zusätzlich die spezielle Kartenklasse „PrivateNotiz" in jedem Kontext an; die Instanzen dieser Klasse werden ebenfalls nicht in den allgemein zugänglichen Hypertext geschrieben, sondern lokal gehalten. Karten dieser Klasse werden über individuelle Verweise mit anderen Karten verknüpft. Derart werden private Bemerkungen ermöglicht. Drittens können durch individuelle Verweise Beziehungen, die nur einem Benutzer wichtig sind, lokal und unkontrolliert ausgedrückt werden; dies vermeidet die Existenz von irrelevanten Verweisen im globalen Hypertext.

Um das folgende Beispiel zu verstehen, muß die Struktur einer Karte und eines Verweises näher erläutert werden. Jede Karte ist von einem bestimmten Typ (z. B. „Textstelle"), hat einen Schlüssel (z. B. K1) und zwei Listen, in denen die zu der Karte hinführenden bzw. von der Karte wegführenden Verweise als Schlüssel gespeichert sind. Jeder Verweis ist ebenfalls von einem Typ, z. B. „Spricht", hat einen Schlüssel (z. B. L2) und zwei Instanzvariable zur Aufnahme der beteiligten Kartenschlüssel. Hier werden der Schlüssel der Karte, von der der Verweis ausgeht, und der Schlüssel der Karte, zu der der Verweis hinführt, eingetragen. Obgleich sowohl in Karten als auch in Verweisen auf die jeweils andere Objektkategorie Bezug genommen wird, sind beide Arten von Objekten voneinander unabhängig. In CONCORDE sind Verweise also *first class objects*.

Wie oben beschrieben, arbeitet der Lokale Objektmanager mit Kopien der CONCORDE-Objekte aus dem globalen Hypertext, um eine private Manipulation zu ermöglichen und direkte Änderungen auf dem „Originalobjekt" zu vermeiden. Diese Kopien werden in sog. **Hüllen** verwaltet. Für jede Kartenkopie wird eine Hülle erzeugt; auf ihr werden die für den lokalen Kontext wichtigen Informationen eingetragen. Als wichtigste Information enthält eine Kartenhülle die Schlüssel der individuellen Verweise.

Der Lokale Objektmanager legt für jeden lokalen Kontext mehrere Verzeichnisse an, in denen die vorhandenen Karten- und Verweishüllen gespeichert werden. Die erzeugten Hüllen werden unter dem Schlüssel des CONCORDE-Objektes gespeichert. Private Karten und individuelle Verweise werden mit einem Schlüssel versehen, der nur im Bereich des jeweiligen Lokalen Objektmanagers eindeutig ist. Der Globale und Lokale Objektmanager verwenden jeweils disjunkte Schlüsselräume.

Grundsätzlich befinden sich für jede Kartenkopie alle abgehenden und ankommenden Verweise als Kopien im lokalen Kontext. Der Lokale Objektmanager fordert auf Grund der Informationen auf der Kartenkopie die beteiligten Verweise in einer Art *prefetching* an.

Der Zusammenhang zwischen zwei CONCORDE-Karten, die durch einen vordefinierten und einen individuellen Verweis verbunden sind, soll an einem Beispiel veranschaulicht werden. Das folgende Bild 2 zeigt eine „Charakter"-Karte K2 und eine „Textstellen"-Karte K1, die durch einen vordefinierten „Spricht"-Verweis und einen individuellen Verweis („Wiederholung") verbunden sind.

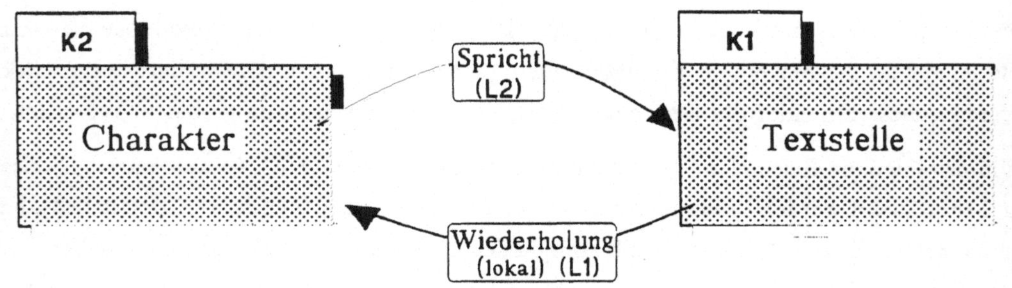

Bild 2: Beispiel für Kartenverbindungen zwischen zwei Karten

Diese einfache, intuitive Darstellung wird im lokalen Kontext durch zwei Karten in Kartenhüllen verwaltet. Bild 3 auf Seite 6 zeigt die Darstellung des Beispiels der Kartenverbindungen im lokalen Kontext. Die beiden Verweise werden in Verweishüllen gespeichert. Der vordefinierte „Spricht"-Verweis (mit dem Schlüssel L2) wird auf der Karte K2 als abgehende und auf der Karte K1 als hinführende Verbindung eingetragen. Der individuelle Verweis (mit dem Schlüssel L2) wird auf der Kartenhülle K1 als abgehende und auf der Kartenhülle K2 als hinführende lokale Verbindung eingetragen. Man sieht auf dem Bild, daß auf den Karten die Verweisschlüssel gespeichert sind. Wenn man von einer Karte ausgeht, kann man nur feststellen, daß diese Karte über Verweise mit anderen Karten verbunden ist. Wohin diese Verweise führen bzw. woher sie kommen, läßt sich erst feststellen, wenn über den auf der Karte bzw. Kartenhülle eingetragenen Verweisschlüssel der Verweis angefordert wird.

3   Szenario einer typischen Benutzeraktion

Das im Bild 4 zu sehende Szenario zeigt eine typische Situation. Es existieren zwei Benutzer, die verschiedene CONCORDE-Objekte, also Karten und Verweise, in ihrem Kontext haben.

Der Kontext A enthält die Karte K1, eine „Textstelle", die von einem „Charakter" (K3) gesprochen wird, was durch den Verweis L2 dargestellt wird. Der „Charakter" wird von dem „Schauspieler" K2 dargestellt (Verweis L6). Die Verweise L2 und L6 sind typisiert (vordefiniert) [HoLa90]. Der Benutzer A hat die Karten „Schauspieler" (K2) und „Textstelle" (K1)

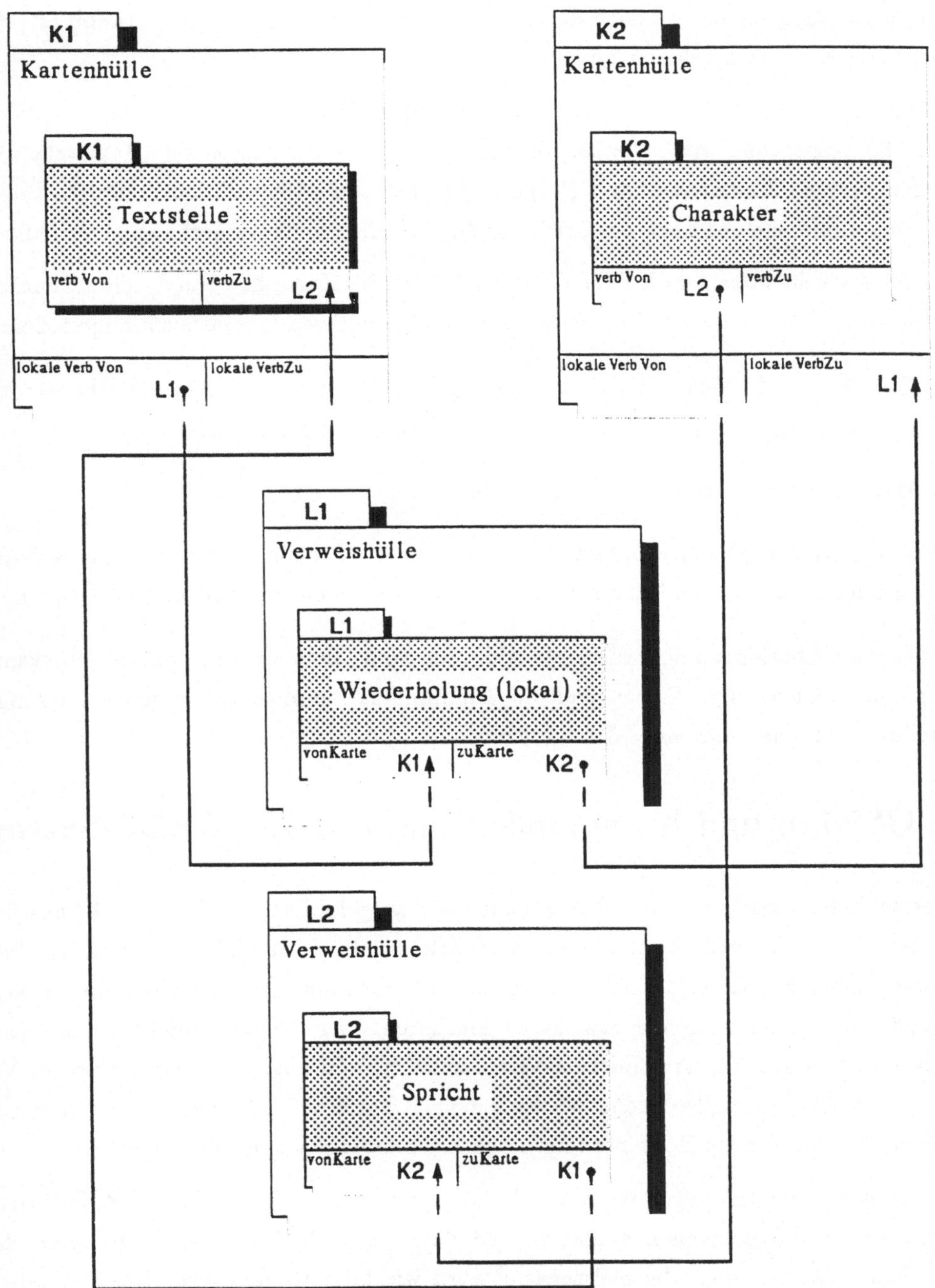

Bild 3: Beispiel für Kartenverbindungen zwischen zwei Kartenhüllen

über einen individuellen Verweis verknüpft, in diesem Fall durch „spricht mit verstellter Stimme" (L7). Weiterhin existiert eine private Karte K6, die als Notiz verwendet wird („muß noch überarbeitet werden" L3). Der Punkt neben der Karte K1 zeigt an, daß diese

Karte im globalen Hypertext noch durch Verweise mit anderen Karten verknüpft ist, die nicht in den Kontext A geladen sind.

Der Kontext B enthält ebenfalls eine Kartenkopie der „Textstelle" K1, die von dem „Charakter" K3 gesprochen wird, wie der Verweis L2 zeigt. Weiterhin ist die „Textstelle" K1 über den Verweis „Textstellenfolge" (L5) mit der „Textstelle" K5 verbunden. Der Benutzer B hat die „Textstelle" K1 noch mit der Notiz K4 als individuelle Anmerkung L4 verknüpft.

Benutzer A löscht in seinem lokalen Kontext A jetzt die Karte K1. Durch diese Benutzeraktion werden vom Lokalen Objektmanager eine Menge von Operationen angestoßen:

- Es müssen alle Verweise zwischen den Karten K1 und K2, K3, K6 gelöscht werden, um keine ins Nichts zeigenden Verweise (*dangling links*) zu haben.

- Danach kann die Karte K1 gelöscht werden.

- Als drittes muß der Kontext des Benutzers B aktualisiert werden, da nach der Löschaktion die Karte K1 sowie die umliegenden Verweise nicht mehr existieren.

Der folgende Abschnitt zeigt, wie diese Aktionen vom Globalen und Lokalen Objektmanager umgesetzt werden. Dabei spielt die Kommunikation miteinander sowie die Aufgabenteilung untereinander eine wichtige Rolle.

4 Objekte und Kommunikation im CONCORDE-System

Als erste Aktion wird der Globale Objektmanager aufgefordert, die Textstelle K1 aus dem globalen Hypertext zu löschen. Dieser überprüft, ob durch das Löschen der Karte Integritätsbedingungen verletzt werden. Wenn keine Verletzung vorliegt, werden die Verweise gelöscht, die von K1 ausgehen bzw. zu K1 hinführen. Der Globale Objektmanager kann dabei natürlich nur die vordefinierten Verweise löschen, in unserem Beispiel also der Verweis L2 zwischen der „Textstelle" K1 und dem „Charakter" K3; Bild 4 zeigt in seinem unteren Teil den für die Kontexte relevanten Ausschnitt des globalen Hypertexts.

Der Globale Objektmanager verwaltet die allgemein zugänglichen CONCORDE-Objekte unter ihrem Schlüssel in einem speziellen Feld, dem sog. CONCORDE-Array. Beim Löschen einer Karte (K1 aus dem Beispielszenario) wird wie folgt vorgegangen. Zuerst wird der Verweis L2 aus den beteiligten Karten ausgetragen. Dazu wird auf der „Charakter"-Karte K3 der Schlüssel des „Spricht"-Verweises L2 in der Liste gelöscht, die die Schlüssel der abgehenden Verweise aufnimmt. Danach wird der „Spricht"-Verweis aus dem CONCORDE-Array gelöscht. Analog dazu wird der Verweis L5 aus der Karte K5 ausgetragen und gelöscht. Bei dem Löschen des Verweises L5 handelt es sich um eine Folgeaktion,

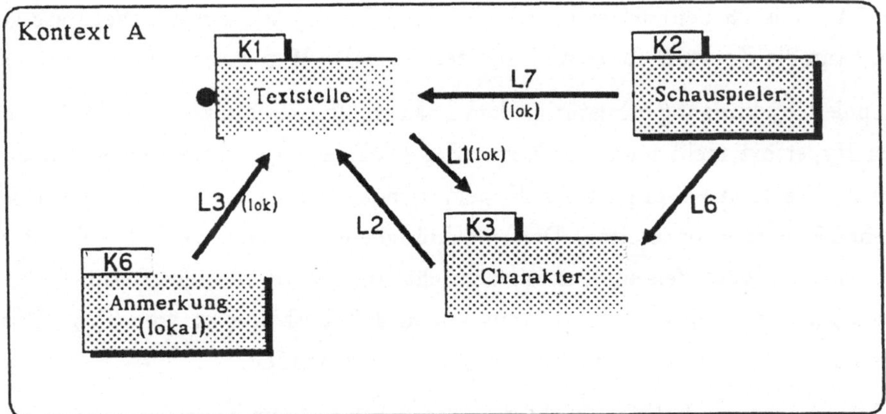

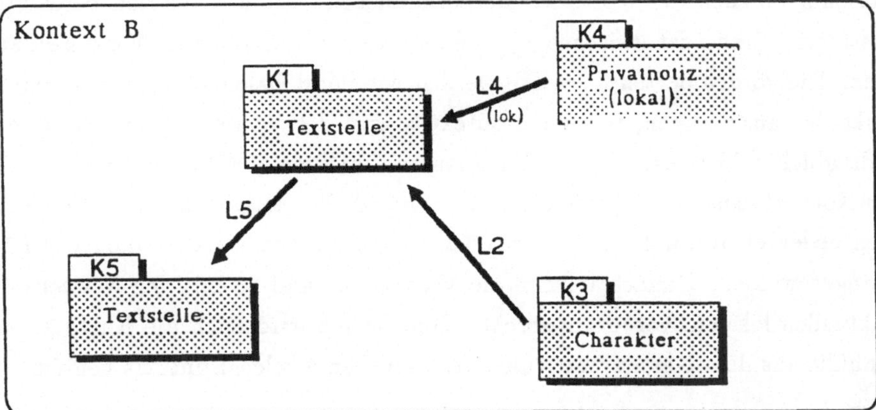

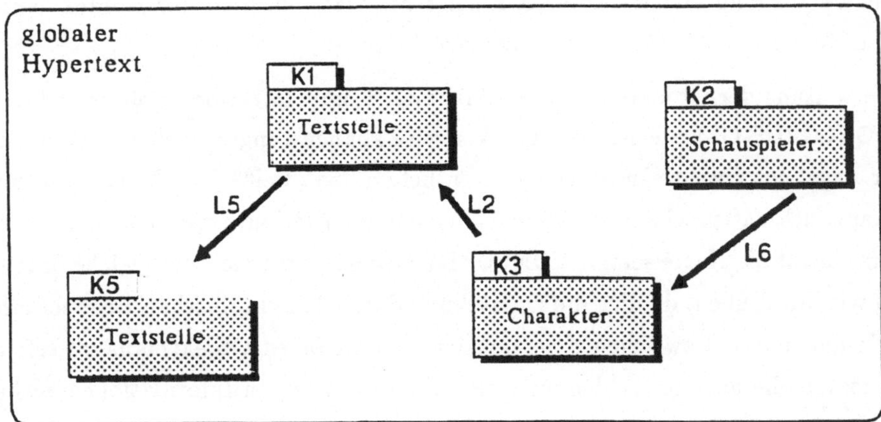

Bild 4: Ein Szenario lokaler Kontexte

denn der Verweis L5 befindet sich nicht im Kontext A. Nachdem alle Verweise gelöscht wurden, kann die Karte K1 insgesamt aus dem globalen Hypertext gelöscht werden.

Der Globale Objektmanager bestätigt dem Lokalen Objektmanager, daß die Karte K1 im globalen Hypertext nicht mehr existiert. Der Globale Objektmanager muß neben dem Löschen der Karte aus dem globalen Hypertext noch das Aktualisieren der vom Löschen betroffenen Kontexte vorbereiten. Dazu wird für alle Kontexte, die vom Löschen der Karte und der Verweise betroffen sind, eine Nachricht erzeugt. In unserem Beispiel enthält die Nachricht für den Kontext B die Informationen, daß die Karte K1 vom Typ „Textstelle" und die Verweise L2 und L5 vom Benutzer A gelöscht wurden.

Daraufhin beginnt der Lokale Objektmanager mit der Bereinigung der lokalen Kontexte. Er muß zum Löschen der Karte K1 die vorhandenen Verweise aus den beteiligten Karten austragen. Dabei ist zwischen vordefinierten und individuellen Verweisen zu unterscheiden. Die vordefinierten Verweise werden wie im globalen Hypertext direkt auf den Kartenkopien ausgetragen; für den Kontext A wird der Verweis L2 auf K3 ausgetragen. Die individuellen Verweise, die zu den privaten Objekten gehören und nur in dem einen lokalen Kontext existieren, werden auf den Kartenhüllen ausgetragen. Auf unser Beispiel bezogen bedeutet das, daß die Verweise L1 und L3 auf den Kartenhüllen von K6 und K2 ausgetragen werden. Danach werden die Verweise L1 und L3 mit den Verweishüllen aus dem aktuellen lokalen Kontext gelöscht. Zum Schluß wird auch die Karte K1 mit ihrer Kartenhülle aus dem Kartenverzeichnis des aktuellen lokalen Kontexts gelöscht.

Wenn Benutzer B zu arbeiten beginnt, werden die Nachrichten für den für ihn neu geladenen Kontext abgerufen und ausgewertet. Die Karte K1 wird mit den Verweisen L5, L2 und L4 aus dem lokalen Kontext B gelöscht. Dadurch wird der Kontext aktualisiert und die Konsistenz des Gesamtsystems gewährleistet.

Die Verwaltung der Objekte und der Ablauf der Kommunikation erfolgt objektorientiert. Die CONCORDE-Objekte Karten und Verweise können „angesprochen" werden und sind in der Lage, gewünschte Informationen zu liefern. So „weiß" jede Karte von ihrem Typ und kann sich entsprechend verhalten. Zusätzliche Attribute wie das Alter eines „Charakters" kennt die Karte selbst. CONCORDE-Objekte verstehen das gleiche Smalltalkprotokoll wie ihre Hüllen, da dies die Darstellung durch den graphischen Browser erleichtert. Die Kommunikation zwischen dem Lokalen und Globalen Objektmanager erfolgt durch Nachrichten, die nur die für den weiteren Ablauf benötigten Informationen enthalten.

5 Projektstatus

Im bisherigen Verlauf des Projekts wurde ein Prototyp entwickelt, der auf den in [HoLa89] beschriebenen und in Abschnitt 2 zusammengefaßten Konzepten beruht. Diese erste Prototypversion wurde auf dem Workshop Hypertext/Hypermedia [GlSt90] im April 1990 in Darmstadt vorgestellt. In dieser Version des Prototypen sind bereits die in diesem Papier beschriebenen Objekte und Strukturen realisiert.

Obwohl die Implementierung eines Prototypen meist nur der Bestätigung eines Konzepts dient, sind wir der Auffassung, daß sich auch prototypische Hypertextsysteme nicht durch „Spielanwendungen" evaluieren lassen, sondern ihre Gebrauchsfähigkeit in ernsthaften Anwendungen unter Beweis stellen müssen. Der bestehende Prototyp wird daher im Vergleich zur in Darmstadt vorgestellten Version erweitert:

- Die Funktionalität des Browsers ist bereits erweitert worden (Filtermöglichkeiten bei der Darstellung; stärkere Parametrisierung).

- Der bisher verwendete Graph-Layoutalgorithmus ist ersetzt worden; der Benutzer hat jetzt auch stärkeren Einfluß auf die Erstellung der Hypertext–Netzdarstellung [HLLL90].

- Die Kartenklassen und Verweistypen werden an die neue Anwendung – Unterstützung von Wissensakquisition und Verwaltung einer Wissensbasis – angepaßt [HSL90]. Ferner wird das System um aktive Elemente [LMY88] angereichert.

Wüschenswert ist ferner der Anschluß einer Datenbank für die Verwaltung der persistenten Objekte sowie die Implementierung eines Suchmoduls. Beides soll beim weiteren Ausbau von CONCORDE realisiert werden.

6 Literatur

[AYM88] **R.Akscyn, E.Yoder, D.McCracken**, The Data Model is the Heart of Interface Design; in: Proc. CHI'88, Washington (D.C.), 1988, pp.115–120

[GlSt90] **P.Gloor, N.Streitz (eds.)**, Proceedings der Hypertext/Hypermedia–Tagungen in Basel und Darmstadt 1990; Springer, 1990

[GoRo89] **A.Goldberg, D.Robson**, Smalltalk-80 — The Language; Addison-Wesley, Reading (MA), 1989

[HLLL90] **M.Hofmann, H.Langendörfer, K.Laue, E.Lübben**, Attempts to Draw Nice Graphs by an Interactive Hypertext Browser; CONCORDE-Forschungs- und Entwicklungsdokument Nr. 4, Braunschweig, September 1990

[HoLa89] **M.Hofmann, H.Langendörfer**, Konzept eines Informationssystems zur Schaffung einer individuellen Arbeitsumgebung durch spezielle Hypertext–Verweise; in: Proc. GI–Fachtagung Interaktive Schnittstellen für Informationssysteme, Clausthal–Zellerfeld, Notizen zu Interaktiven Systemen, Heft 18, November 1989, pp.113–132

[HoLa90] **M.Hofmann, H.Langendörfer**, User Support by Typed Links and Local Contexts in a Hypertext System; in: Proc. Intelligente integrierte Informationssysteme (IiI), Schloß Tuczno (Polen), September 1990, pp.106–124

[HSL90] **M.Hofmann, U.Schreiweis, H.Langendörfer**, An Integrated Approach of Knowledge Acquisition by the Hypertext System CONCORDE; in: Proc. ECHT'90, Paris, November 1990, pp.166–179

[LMY88] **K.-Y.Lai, T.W.Malone, K.-C.Yu**, Object Lens: A „Spreadsheet" for Cooperative Work; in: ACM ToOIS, Vol.6, No.4, Oktober 1988, pp.332–353

MATHBANK: Mathematisches Fachwissen als Hypertext

Uwe Quasthoff
Universität Leipzig
Sektion Mathematik
D-O-7010 Leipzig

ABSTRACT: Beschrieben wird das Projekt MATHBANK. Ziel
ist die Erstellung eines Hypertext-Systems, mit dem der
Zugriff   auf   das   Wissen   aus   einer   größeren   Hand-
bibliothek mathematischer Fachbücher möglich ist. Diskutiert werden speziell die Nutzung der in der Mathematik vorhandenen Struktur zur Erstellung von Karten
sowie die Möglichkeiten der automatischen Sprachverarbeitung zur Analyse mathematischer Texte bei der Erzeugung von Verweisen.

1. Einleitung

Das Projekt MATHBANK der Sektion Mathematik der Universität
Leipzig stellt sich zum Ziel, die Grundlagen für eine MATHematische
DatenBANK zu untersuchen, in der mathematisches Fachwissen in großem
Umfang zugänglich ist.
Die Auswahl des Wissensgebiets Mathematik steht in engem Zu-
sammenhang mit der Organisation der Datenbank: Die klare hierarchische Struktur innerhalb der Mathematik (trotz der vielen Querverbindungen) ermöglicht den Einsatz eines Hypertextsystems in natürlicher Weise.
Weiterhin ist die Mathematik als Wissensgebiet ein in sich
relativ abgeschlossenes Gebilde (das trifft ebenso auf einzelne
Teilbereiche der Mathematik zu), so daß es möglich erscheint, mit
Mitteln der automatischen Sprachverarbeitung die Karten des Hypertextsystems und die Verweise zwischen ihnen aus vorhandenem Lehrbuchtext automatisch zu erstellen. Bei der automatischen Analyse wirkt
sich die im Vergleich zur Alltagssprache häufig einfachere sprachliche Struktur solcher Fachtexte besonders positiv aus.
Hauptziel der gegenwärtigen Anstrengungen ist die automatische
Verarbeitung mathematischer Fachtexte, um die Bereitstellung einer
großen Datenmenge für das Hypertextsystem zu ermöglichen.

2. Hintergrund

Bei der Alltagsarbeit des Mathematikers tritt häufig das Problem auf, daß Wissen aus Randgebieten des eigentlichen Spezialgebie-
tes beschafft werden muß. Dabei wird in der Regel viel Zeit mit
Suchen verbracht, wobei ein großer Teil dieser Zeit darauf entfallen
kann, zunächst geeignete Quellen zu finden. Dies entspricht einer
Suche in Katalogen (oder Referateorganen). Als zweiter Schritt wird
in der ausgewählten Literatur nach dem Gewünschten weitergesucht.
Ziel der Suche kann dabei eine vorher im Prinzip vollständig bekannte Aussage sein (beispielsweise zur Bestätigung von vagem Wissen). Es kann aber auch nach einer erwünschten Aussage gesucht

werden, bei der nicht alle notwendigen Bedingungen bekannt sind
oder nach Zusammenhängen zwischen verschiedenen Aussagen.

Hat man in einem längeren Text eine interessante Aussage gefunden, so ist man in der Regel am Zusammenhang interessiert:
Man sucht von dieser Stelle aus rückwärts, um Definitionen der
verwendeten Begriffe zu haben (diese können sich für verschiedene
Quellen unterscheiden) und vorwärts, um weitere damit zusammenhängende interessante und möglicherweise nützliche Aussagen zu
finden.

Diese Arbeiten sollen von MATHBANK unterstützt bzw. selbständig
durchgeführt werden. Neben einem Sachkatalog in Hypertextform (vgl.
etwa HYPERCAT [4]) enthält MATHBANK auch mathematisches Wissen.

Alle Aussagen sollen in einer möglichst einheitlichen Form vorliegen, die folgende Bedingungen erfüllt: Erstens muß die Form so
flexibel sein, daß sich praktisch alle mathematischen Lehrsätze,
Definitionen usw. ohne großen Aufwand in diese Form bringen lassen.
Zweitens soll das Datenformat auch für den Erstbenutzer sofort ver-
ständlich sein, die Aussagen also in natürlicher Sprache vorliegen.

Die Auswertung der Datensätze erfolgt durch ein spezielles
Programm, dieses ermöglicht eine komfortable Suche zum Auffinden von
Aussagen

- bestimmter Struktur,
- mit bestimmten Stichworten,
- aus bestimmten Gebieten und
- mit bestimmten Formeln.

Ist der Nutzer nicht in der Lage, vor der Suche diejenigen
Angaben zu machen, die den gewünschten Effekt liefern (d.h. es
erfüllen zu viele oder gar keine Karten die gestellten Bedingungen),
dann bietet das Programm durch vorhandenes Wissen über begriffliche
Zusammenhänge in der Mathematik umfangreiche Unterstützung an:

- Einschränkung oder Erweiterung des Gebiets
- Einschränkung der Stichworte in ihrer Bedeutung
- Angebot verwandter Stichworte
- Bevorzugung bestimmter Quellen (Autoren, Bücher,
  Jahre,...)

Der Leistungsschwerpunkt von MATHBANK soll nicht darin liegen,
daß das Programm bei einer überschaubaren Menge von mathematischen
Aussagen wirklich jede Frage vollständig beantwortet, sondern wir
wollen bewußt zulassen, daß ein kleiner Teil des vorhandenen Wissens
durch Fragen nur schwer als Antwort zu erhalten ist (da die gesuchten Aussagen nicht richtig "verstanden" wurden und das Programm
den Zusammenhang mit der Frage nicht erkennt). Dafür soll die Menge
des zur Verfügung stehenden mathematischen Wissens praktisch beliebig groß sein.

3. Organisation der Datenbank

Für unser Problem bietet sich als Grundgerüst die Datenstruktur von Hypertext an. Dabei sollen in der Datenbank nur
mathematische Lehrsätze und Definitionen (im Folgenden mathematische
Aussagen genannt) gespeichert werden, nicht aber die Beweise sowie
erläuternder Text. Damit bleibt der Dateiumfang geringer, der Nutzer

kann aber durch eine Quellenangabe bei Bedarf trotzdem in der Literatur nachschlagen.

3.1. Hierarchische Struktur

In der Mathematik sind auf natürliche Weise Beziehungen zwischen einzelnen Begriffen gegeben, die eine klare hierarchische Struktur liefern:

Zunächst wird der gesamte Bereich der Mathematik aus gegenwärtiger Sicht relativ einhellig in ca. 20 Teilgebiete gegliedert, siehe etwa die Gliederung der höheren Mathematik in 18 Sektionen auf dem Internationalen Mathematikerkongresses 1990.

Für jedes solche Fachgebiet läßt sich mit Hilfe von Inhaltsverzeichnissen von Standardwerken eine sinnvolle weitere Untergliederung bis hin zu einzelnen mathematischen Spezialdisziplinen angeben. Dabei entsteht zwischen den einzelnen mathematischen Teildisziplinen eine hierarchische Struktur. Der von diesen mathematischen Begriffen erzeugte Graph ist zwar kein Baum, aber die Baumstruktur ist nur durch relativ wenige Kanten verletzt.

Verfügt MATHBANK erst einmal über ein grundlegendes System von solchen Fachbegriffen, so lassen sich neu auftretende Begriffe automatisch einordnen: Wir gehen davon aus, daß eine größere Menge von Aussagen etwa aus einem Lehrbuch in der Reihenfolge ihres Auftretens in unsere Datenbank aufgenommen werden sollen. Neue Begriffe sind dadurch charakterisiert, daß sie durch Definitionen explizit als neu gekennzeichnet werden. Sie werden dort eingeordnet, wo sich das System bei Behandlung des Kapitels (oder Unterabschnitts) des betrachteten Buches gerade befindet. Querverweise von dem neuen Begriff zu bereits bekannten Begriffen lassen sich automatisch dadurch erzeugen, daß man die in der betrachteten Definition vorkommenden bekannten Begriffe als Kandidaten wählt.

3.2. Form von Karten

A) Daten-Karten. Unter Daten-Karten wollen wir hier diejenigen Karten verstehen, die mathematische Aussagen enthalten, nicht aber solche, die wie Inhaltsverzeichnisse, Überschriften usw. zur Strukturierung beitragen.

Bei der Umwandlung von sequentiellem Text in Hypertext steht man gewöhnlich vor dem Problem, den Gesamttext durch relativ willkürliche Schnitte auf einzelne Karten zu verteilen [2]. Da der MATHBANK-Text aus einzelnen mathematischen Aussagen besteht, ist sofort eine natürliche Unterteilung des Textes gegeben.

Jede Daten-Karte enthält eine mathematische Aussage sowie eventuell Bemerkungen. Dabei überschreitet eine typische Karte nicht die Größe eines Bildschirms. Sowohl Definitionen als auch Lehrsätze haben folgende Struktur: Sie bestehen aus einer Anzahl von Voraussetzungen und einer oder mehreren Behauptungen. Diese Behauptungen können in unterschiedlicher Relation zueinander stehen, die wichtigsten Fälle sind die Gültigkeit aller Behauptungen bzw. die Äquivalenz mehrerer Behauptungen. Die folgenden Beispiele zeigen die Zerlegung von Lehrbuchtext in diese Form:

Beispiel: Lehrbuchtext:
    Lehrsatz: Jede differenzierbare Funktion f ist stetig.
äquivalente Hypertext-Karte:
    LEHRSATZ:
    Voraussetzung: f differenzierbare Funktion
    Behauptung: f ist stetig

Lehrbuchtext:
    Definition: Die Folge $\{x_n\}$ heißt konvergent, falls es
        eine Zahl g gibt, so daß $\{x_n-g\}$ eine Nullfolge ist.
äquivalente Hypertext-Karte:
    DEFINITION:
    Voraussetzung: Es gibt eine Zahl g, so daß $\{x_n-g\}$ eine
    Nullfolge ist.
    Behauptung: $\{x_n\}$ ist konvergent.

Die hier sichtbare gleiche logische Struktur (Voraussetzung / Behauptung) bei Lehrsätzen und Definitionen ist dabei nicht die Folge eines Verlustes an Information, sondern hat den folgenden Grund: Der Begriff der Konvergenz läßt sich auf andere Art auch mittels sogenannter Cauchyfolgen definieren, diese Definition ist unserer äquivalent und die in unserer Definition getroffene Aussage läßt sich dann als Lehrsatz formulieren.

B) Übersichts-Karten. Diese Sorte von Karten enthält keine mathematische Information im engeren Sinne, sondern dient ähnlich dem Sachkatalog einer Fachbibliothek zunächst der Heranführung an die gesuchte Information. Solche Übersichten reichen von einer allgemeinen Gliederung der Mathematik bis hin zu Inhaltsverzeichnissen von Fachbüchern. Durch Querverweise ist es wieder einfach möglich, zu relevanten Informationen aus benachbarten Teildisziplinen zu gelangen.

Diese Information ist dem Nutzer beim Blättern in der Datenbank zugänglich, kann aber auch vom System bei der automatischen Suche genutzt werden.

3.3. Suchverfahren:

Innerhalb der Datenbank kann nach mehreren Verfahren gesucht werden, um verschiedene Vorgehensweisen zu ermöglichen. Speziell sollen folgende Suchverfahren unterstützt werden:

- mit Inhaltsverzeichnissen (ähnlich in Büchern)
- graphisch mit Browser und Filtern (typisch Hypertext)
- durch Indizierung nach Fachbegriffen (wie in Dateiprogrammen)
- durch Zeichenketten-Suche (wie in Text-Programmen)
- wissensbasiert (d.h. nach logischen Zusammenhängen)

Durch längeres Arbeiten mit MATHBANK erhält jeder Nutzer sein eigenes Nutzerprofil, in dem seine Suchstrategien, die von ihm bevorzugten Quellen, das vorhandene Grundwissen (das ergibt sich aus den gestellten Fragen und den Rückfragen nach Definitionen usw.) verzeichnet sind. Ein bekanntes Nutzerprofil kann den notwendigen Dialog wesentlich verkürzen. Weiter lassen sich erfolgreiche Nutzerprofile (nach Freigabe) auch von anderen verwenden.

3.4. Dateiumfang

Eine solche Datenbank ist nur sinnvoll, wenn sie über einen großen Datenumfang verfügt und alle Suchvorgänge so angelegt sind, daß mit wachsender Dateigröße die Suchzeiten nur logarithmisch wachsen.

Für Bücher mit großer Informationsdichte (z.B. Dieudonné [1]) sind bei der gewählten Datenstruktur etwa 5 Karten je Buchseite nötig, bei etwa 400 Seiten/ Buch also etwa 2000 Karten.

Auf einer CD-ROM ist damit die Speicherung von mehreren tausend Büchern möglich. Wegen der klaren hierarchischen Struktur kann gesichert werden, daß der Suchvorgang noch im Minutenbereich liegt.

3.5. Erstellung der Datenbank

Sinnvoll ist nur die automatische Eingabe von gedrucktem Text, d.h. graphische Eingabe über Scanner mit Zeichenerkennung (OCR) oder direktes Einlesen von Computer-Satzbändern. Dann müssen aber aus dem fortlaufenden Text die aufzunehmenden mathematischen Aussagen erkannt und auch die dazugehörigen Verweise automatisch erstellt werden. Dazu muß der Text inhaltlich "verstanden" werden. Die bisher einzige brauchbare Methode, Verständnis zu prüfen, ist die Beantwortung von Fragen durch den Computer. Wir können aber die Nutzung unserer Datenbank als Beantworten von Fragen betrachten, wobei zwar die Möglichkeiten bei der Formulierung der Fragen eingeschränkt sind, aber die inhaltlichen Anforderungen bei der Beantwortung dadurch nicht berührt werden.

Die Analyse der eingegebenen Texte erfolgt mit Mitteln der automatischen Sprachverarbeitung, die für unser Problem besonders gut einsetzbar sind.

4. Automatische Sprachverarbeitung für mathematische Texte

Die automatische Verarbeitung von umgangssprachlichem Text ist gegenwärtig noch mit sehr vielen Problemen behaftet, die hauptsächlich aus dem nicht-eindeutigem Gebrauch der Sprache und dem außerordentlich wichtigem Wissen des Menschen "über die Welt", welches dem Computer kaum zur Verfügung steht, entstehen. Siehe z.B. [3].

Bei der Analyse mathematischer Texte befinden wir uns in unvergleichlich einfacherer Situation als bei der Verarbeitung von Alltags-Sprache:

Einige formal-grammatische Strukturen treten kaum oder nur in einfacher Form auf:
- kaum eine andere Zeitformen als die Gegenwart ist von inhaltlicher Bedeutung,
- nur wenige Verben treten auf,
- fast alle Aussagen lassen sich passivisch formulieren.

Die logisch-inhaltliche Struktur ist einfacher als in der Alltags-Sprache:
- es wird kein Hintergrund-Wissen außerhalb der Mathematik benötigt, d.h. der gesamte Alltagskontext ist ohne Bedeutung,
- logisch klare Struktur, z.B. kaum mehrdeutige Rückbezüge,
- Fachsprache funktioniert (fast) ohne Mißverständnisse,
- keine handelnden Personen, keine Veränderung von Zuständen,
- keine zeitliche Struktur,
- keine räumliche Struktur (außer in Geometrie),

- der Gebrauch von Artikeln (allgemein/speziell) ist klarer,
- alle Aussagen sind deklarativ, keine Aufforderung zum Handeln, keine Emotionen oder Dialoge.

Die Wortbedeutung ist klarer als in der Umgangssprache.

Trotzdem ist die mathematische Fachsprache nicht trivial zu bearbeiten, da prinzipiell fast jede Schwierigkeit, die überhaupt bei der Analyse natürlichsprachiger Texte auftreten kann, auch in einen mathematischen Text vorstellbar ist. Der Unterschied zur Alltagssprache ist jedoch, daß diese Schwierigkeiten in viel geringerer Häufigkeit auftreten. Dementsprechend hatte unser Ziel von vornherein zugunsten einer großen Datenmenge einen kleinen Teil "unverstandenen" Text zugelassen.

5. Schlußfolgerung

Die logisch klare Struktur der Mathematik und die sprachliche Einfachheit der mathematischen Fachtexte ermöglicht den automatischen Aufbau eines Hypertextsystems als Datenbank mathematischer Aussagen.

Literatur

1. Dieudonné, J.: Grundzüge der modernen Analysis, Bd.1, VEB Dt. Verlag der Wissenschaften, Berlin 1972
2. Frisse, M. From Text to Hypertext, Byte Oct. 1988, 247-253
3. Görz, G.: Strukturanalyse natürlicher Sprache, Addison-Wesley 1988
4. Hjerppe, R.: Project HYPERCATalog, in: Intell. Syst. for the Infomation Siciety, B. Brookes (Ed.), North Holland 1986

Technisches Informationssystem für computergestützten Fahrzeugservice

Dieter Roller
Hewlett Packard GmbH, Herrenberger Straße 130
D-7030 Böblingen

Zusammenfassung

In diesem Beitrag wird ein Systemkonzept vorgestellt, welches die Flut von technischen Informationen, die heute und insbesondere in der Zukunft in Fahrzeugservicebetrieben handzuhaben ist, computergestützt bewältigt. Es wird zunächst gezeigt, wie ein durchgehender Informationsfluß von der Fahrzeugannahme über die Serviceausführung bzw. Fahrzeuginstandsetzung bis zur Rechnungsstellung realisiert werden kann. Die auf hybriden Medien gespeicherten Informationen werden dabei für den Anwender transparent verwaltet. Hypertextfunktionen realisieren die Verknüpfungen von Informationen wie Ersatzteile und Einbaupläne und sind eine Grundlage für das integrierte technische Informationssystem. Das vorgestellte Konzept wurde in wesentlichen Teilen bereits realisiert und zeichnet sich durch eine signifikante Effizienzsteigerung in Fahrzeugservicebetrieben aus.

Einleitung

Fahrzeuge, insbesondere Automobile, werden in ihrem Aufbau zunehmend komplexer. Bereits heute sind in Fahrzeugen der oberen Leistungsklassen eine Vielzahl von hochentwickelten Baugrupen mit zugeordneten elektronischen Steuergeräten enthalten. Die Folge dieses Trends ist, daß technische Informationen, die zur Wartung und Instandsetzung der Fahrzeuge notwendig sind, in ihrer Menge rasant zunehmen [1, 2]. Solche technischen Informationen werden derzeit in erster Linie in Papierform als Handbücher und/oder auf Mikrofilmen bereitgestellt. Die besonderen Probleme dabei sind, daß Daten in Servicebetrieben häufig nicht vollständig in aktueller Form vorliegen und außerdem das Auffinden von benötigten Informationen sehr zeitraubend ist. Dabei sind Suchzeiten von bis zu einer viertel Stunde für eine bestimmte Informationsseite keine Seltenheit. Dies führt in der Praxis oft dazu, daß versucht wird Service- und/oder Instandsetzungsarbeiten ohne die offizielle Information auszuführen, was wiederum zu länger dauernden Arbeitsgängen oder gar zu inkorrekt durchgeführten Arbeiten führen kann. Zur Lösung dieser Problematik und letztlich einer Steigerung der

Kundenzufriedenheit ist ein effizientes computergestütztes technisches Informations-system erstrebenswert. Die Ziele für die Einführung eines solchen Systems sind:

- Erhöhung der Aktualität von technischen Informationen,
- Verbesserung der Rückmeldung in die Fertigung / Entwicklung,
- Verbesserung der Qualität des Reparaturvorganges,
- Reduzierung der Reparaturzeiten und -kosten.

Technische Informationen werden an verschiedenen Arbeitsplätzen innerhalb eines Fahrzeugservicebetriebes benötigt. Beispiele hierfür sind Informationen wie Lagerbestände und Teilespezifikationen im Teilelager und Einbauanleitungen, Meßvorschriften, Einstellwerte usw. am Reparaturplatz in der Werkstatt. Es besteht daher die Forderung nach einem integrierten Gesamtsystem. Da aus wirtschaftlichen Gründen ein derartiges Gesamtsystem kaum in einem Schritt realisierbar ist, sollte die Lösung aus einem modularen Konzept bestehen, in dem Einzelkomponenten, wie zum Beispiel ein elektronischer Teilekatalog, voll funktionsfähig als Einstiegslösung installiert werden können. Es ist dabei jedoch erforderlich, daß die einzelnen Applikationsmodule so konzipiert sind, daß sie zu einem integrierten Gesamtsystem ausbaubar sind. Die Konzeption muß daher folgende Merkmale aufweisen:

- Erweiterbare zukunftsorientierte Architektur
- Einzelkomponenten vorbereitet für optimale Integration in Gesamtsystem
- Geringe Einstiegskosten
- Modulare Softwarekonfiguration
- Flexible Systemkonfiguration für verschieden große Servicebetriebe
- Einbindung existierender Lösungen

In diesem Beitrag wird das Konzept eines integrierten technischen Informationssystems vorgestellt, welches den oben genannten Zielen und Hauptanforderungen gerecht wird.

Integriertes Informationskonzept für Fahrzeugservicebetriebe

Die in einem Fahrzeugservicebetrieb handzuhabenden technischen Informationen werden in dem hier vorgestellten Ansatz durch ein System von vernetzten Applikationsmodulen, breitbandig abgedeckt (vergleiche Abb. 1). Im folgenden wird der Fluß von technischen Informationen in diesem Applikationsnetz kurz beschrieben und typische Aufgaben der einzelnen Komponenten aufgezeigt.

Zunächst erfolgt bei der Annahme eines instandzusetzenden oder zu wartenden Fahrzeugs die Aufnahme der Fahrzeugkenndaten wie Type, Leistung, Baujahr usw., sowie gegebenenfalls von Symptomen, die das Fehlverhalten beschreiben (Modul *Fahrzeugannahme*). Entsprechende Reparaturaufträge werden in die Werkstatt gegeben, wo die Planung und Ausführung der entsprechenden Aufträge erfolgt (Modul

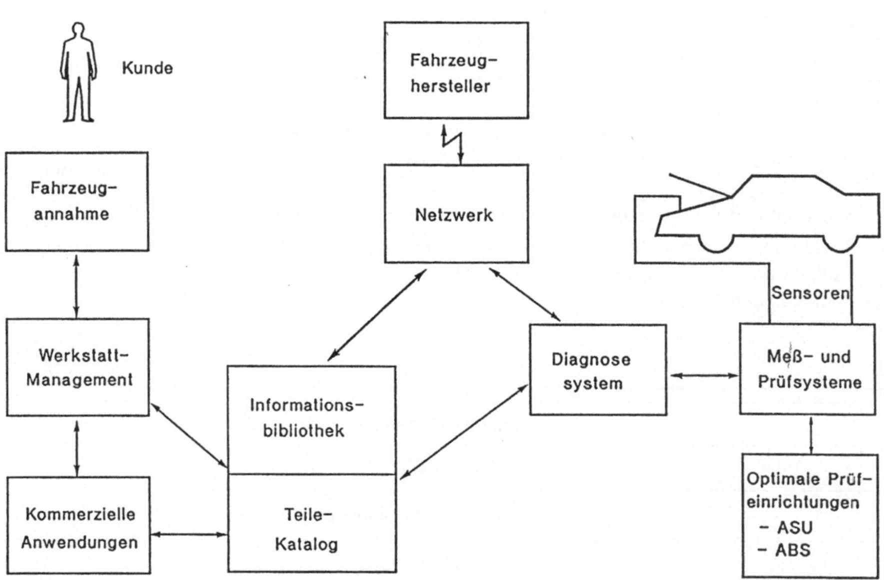

Abb. 1: Vernetzte Applikationen im Fahrzeugservicebetrieb

Werkstattmanagement) Bei der Auftragsausführung werden typischerweise Informationen wie Prüfplane, Schaltdiagramme, Reparaturpläne (Modul *Informationsbibliothek*) und Ersatzteilbeschreibungen (Modul *Teilekatalog*) benötigt. Aus Effizienzgründen ist außerdem eine Verbindung zu kommerziellen Applikationen wie Ersatzteilbestellung - z. B. vom hausinternen Teilelager - oder Fakturierung - z. B. Übergabe von Arbeitswerten - gefordert (Modul *Kommerzielle Anwendungen*). Im Rahmen der rechnergestützten Diagnose (Module *Meß- und Prüfsysteme* und *optionale Prüfeinrichtungen*) werden automatisch Einstellwerte, Graphiken zur Aggregatverbauung usw. aus der Informationsbibliothek angezeigt. Die technischen Informationen, die in der Informationsbibliothek, im Teilekatalog und im Diagnosesystem gehalten werden, werden typischerweise vom Fahrzeughersteller zentral zur Verfügung gestellt. Um kurzfristig Datenaktualisierungen vornehmen zu können, ist eine Datenverbindung zu dieser zentralen Stelle gefordert.

Abb. 2 zeigt die Basisarchitektur für das integrierte Gesamtsystem. Die Applikationsmodule, inklusive eines Moduls, der die Verwaltung des Systems unterstützt, haben eine gemeinsame konsistente Benutzeroberfläche. Der Datenaustausch der einzelnen Module untereinander erfolgt über ein Kommunikationssoftwaremodul. Hardwaretechnisch setzt sich das Gesamtsystem aus vernetzten Rechnerstationen bzw. Terminals zusammen.

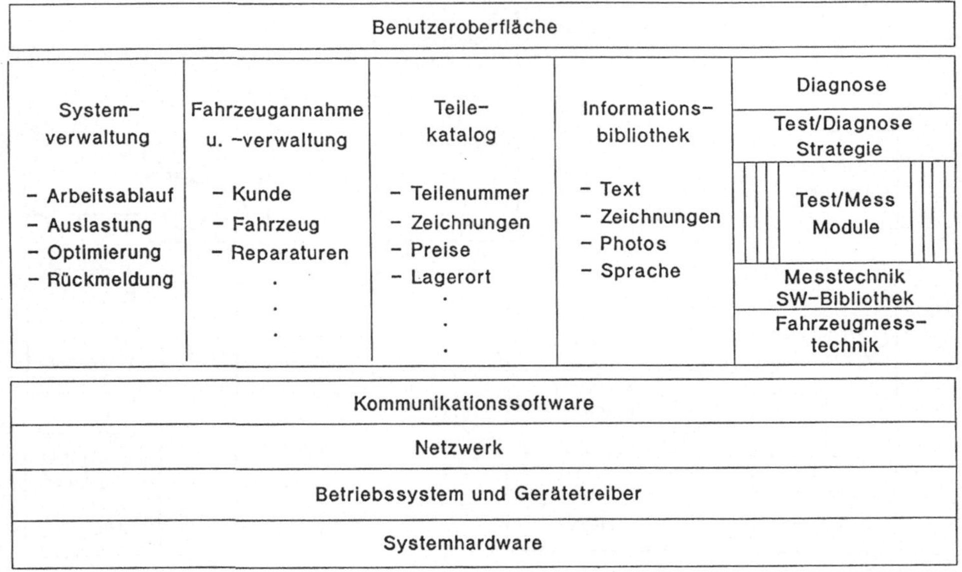

Abb. 2: Basisarchitektur für integriertes Gesamtsystem

Technologische Realisierung

In diesem Abschnitt fokussieren wir uns auf die Applikationen Informationsbibliothek und Teilekatalog und stellen ein Konzept vor, welches beide Anwendungen in einer besonders effizienten integrierten Form ermöglicht. Ein voll funktionsfähiger Prototyp wurde bereits nach diesem Konzept für einen europäischen Automobilkonzern realisiert und zeigte bei ersten Tests hervorragende Resultate. Die Menge an Informationen, die in der Informationsbibliothek und im Teilekatalog gehalten werden muß, bewegt sich im Bereich von hunderten Megabyte bis zu einigen Gigabyte (konventionell in der Größenordnung von 100 000 Handbuchseiten). Es stellt sich daher zunächst die Frage nach einem geeigneten Speichermedium. Da auf diese Informationen nur lesend zugegriffen werden muß, bietet sich hier die CD-ROM-Technologie (Compact Disk - Read Only Memory) an [3]. CD-ROMs zeichnen sich durch ein besonders günstiges Preis/Speichervolumenverhältnis aus und haben eine Kapazität von 550 MB (im High-Sierra-Format). Sie können den Inhalt (Text und Illustrationen) von ca. 10 bis 20 herkömmlichen Handbüchern aufnehmen. Um einen Zugriff auf die Information von verschiedenen CD-ROMs ohne Disk-Wechsel zu ermöglichen, sind mehrere Laufwerke im Parallelbetrieb vorgesehen.

Die hardwaretechnische Ausstattung eines Arbeitsplatzes besteht zusätzlich aus Rechner, Festplatte, Monitor, Drucker und Diskettenlaufwerk. Der Ausbau zu mehreren Arbeitsplätzen basiert auf dem Client-Server-Prinzip und erfolgt durch

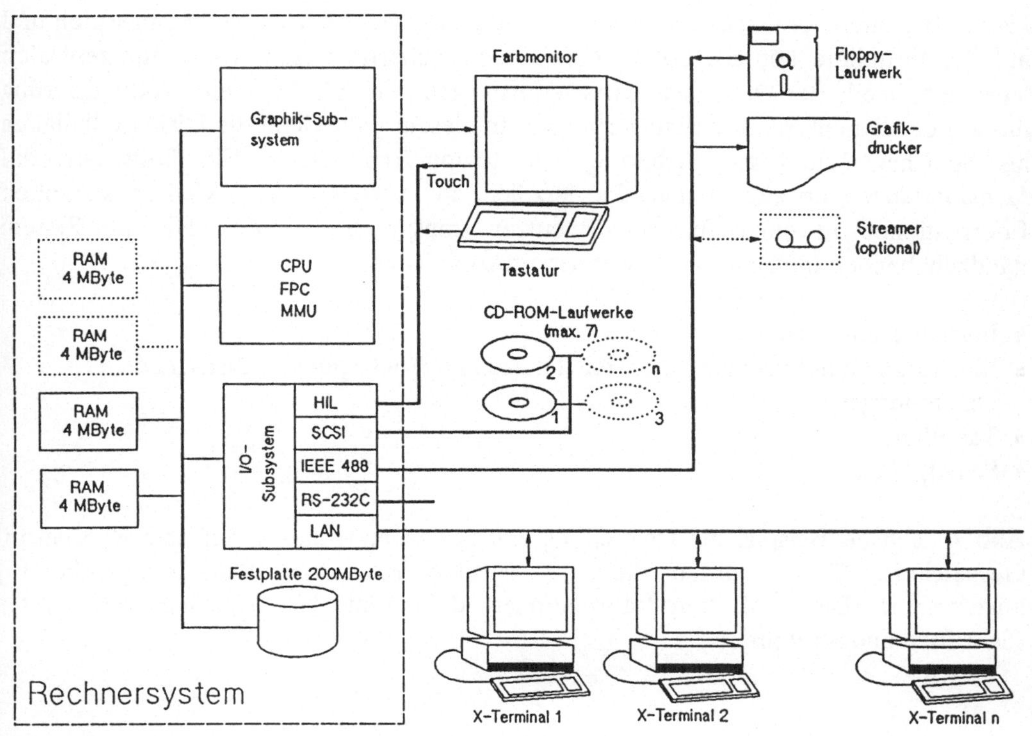

Abb. 3: Konfigurationsschema für technisches Informationssystem

Anschluß von zusätzlichen Terminals. Abb. 3 zeigt schematisch den Aufbau eines solchen Systems. Die Festplatte wird dabei zur Haltung des Betriebssystems, sowie als Speichermedium für temporäre Daten (z. B. Benutzerkennung, Fahrzeugkenndaten) verwendet. Eine weitere wichtige Funktion der Festplatte ist die Pufferung von CD-ROM-Daten nach dem Cache-Prinzip. CD-ROMs haben eine mittlere Zugriffszeit von typischerweise ca. 500 ms, die hauptsächlich durch die Positionierung des Lesekopfes bestimmt ist. Um die Anzahl der Zugriffe zu minimieren, werden bei jedem Zugriff mehr Daten als unmittelbar durch eine Benutzereingabe angefordert ausgelesen und auf die Festplatte übertragen. Die zusätzlich gelesenen Daten sollen dabei eine gewisse Verwandschaft mit den angeforderten Daten aufweisen, in der Form, daß sie mit einer bestimmten Wahrscheinlichkeit in unmittelbar nachfolgenden Operationen benötigt werden. Dies impliziert eine wichtige Anforderung an den Autorenprozeß, in dem die Datenstruktur der CD-ROM festgelegt wird [4].

Um zu vermeiden, daß bei jeder Aktualisierung des auf einer CD-ROM gehaltenen Datenbestandes die komplette CD-ROM ausgetauscht werden muß (Kosten und Produktionszeit für CD-ROM!) wird die Änderungsinformation (in der Regel ein kleiner Bruchteil der Gesamtinformation) mittels Diskette in das System eingespielt und auf die Festplatte kopiert. Sofern ein Datenfernübertragungsanschluß zur zentralen Verteilungsstelle der Daten sich wirtschaftlich vertreten läßt, kann eine Aktualisierung direkt über Datenfernübertragung erfolgen. In diesem Falle dient die Diskette lediglich als Speichermedium zur Sicherung von temporären Daten. Ein Softwaremodul *Mediamanager* verwaltet dabei die letztlich auf verschiedenen Medien verteilten Informationen in einer für den Benutzer transparenten Form. Die im System handzuhabenden Informationen bestehen prinzipiell aus

- Formatierten Texten,
- Illustrationen in Form von Strichzeichnungen und/oder photorealistischen Darstellungen,
- Tabellen,
- Schaltplänen.

Abb. 4 zeigt als Beispiel die Darstellung eines Servicedokuments auf dem Bildschirm. Gespeicherte Texte werden durch Konstrukte aus einer Mark-up-Sprache [5] angereichert. Diese Mark-up-Informationen definieren das Aussehen des Textes (Schrifttyp und Struktur).

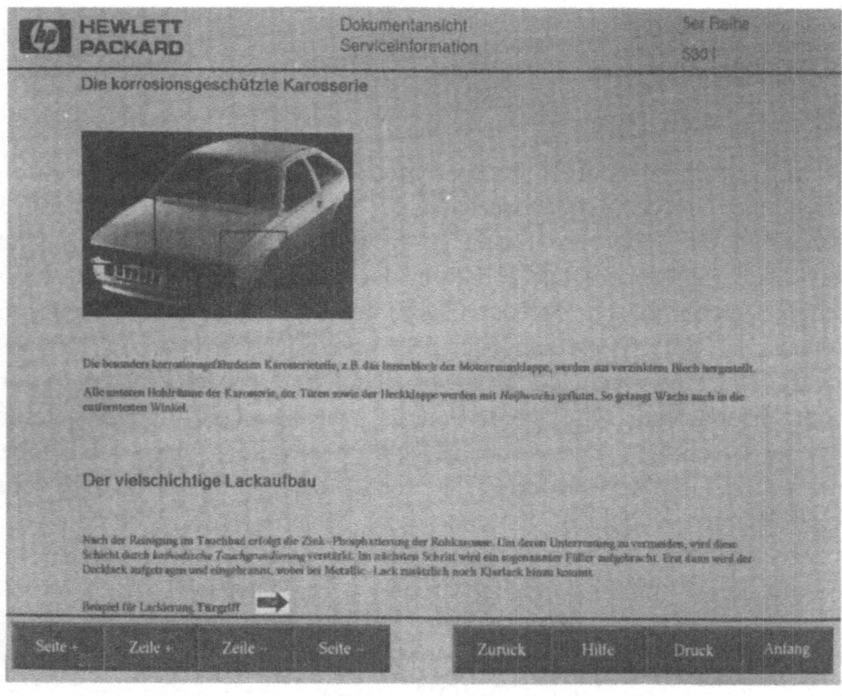

Abb.4 : Beispiel einer Dokumentdarstellung

Neben der übersichtlichen Darstellung auf dem Bildschirm ist es für den Benutzer des Systems in der Praxis besonders wichtig, eine einfache und schnelle Zugriffsmöglichkeit auf die jeweils relevante Information zu haben. Dabei kommt es häufig vor, daß je nach Situation und/oder Fachkenntnis des Anwenders kontextbezogene Zusatzinformation benötigt wird. Zum Beispiel kann zum Verständnis der Einbaubeschreibung für ein Ersatzteil Dokumentation über ein Sonderwerkzeug oder die Beschreibung der Baugruppe, zur der das Ersatzteil gehört, notwendig sein.

Andererseits kommen in der Praxis in verschiedenen Servicedokumenten gleiche Graphiken vor (z. B. Skizze eines Verteilersteckers im Ersatzteilkatalog sowie in der Beschreibung von Zündungseinstellung und in der Reparaturanleitung). Ebenso sind bestimmte Textstellen in verschiedenen Dokumenten identisch. Offensichtlich ist daher die Forderung nach der Konsistenz der jeweiligen Informationen zu stellen.

Die hier beschriebene Lösung für das skizzierte Problem einer Informationsbibliothek und eines Teilekatalogs für Fahrzeugservice basiert auf dem Hypertextkonzept [6, 7]. Für die von der Problematik her ähnlich gelagerte Situation von Dokumentation bzw. On-line-Hilfe für Computersoftware wurde Hypertext in neueren Arbeiten bereits untersucht [8, 9].

Nach diesem Ansatz können sich Dokumente aus verschiedenen der oben genannten Informationstypen zusammensetzen (Compount Documents). Die einzelnen Informationssätze werden dann bei der Speicherung eines Dokumentes über Zeiger referenziert. Dadurch ergibt sich zunächst die geforderte Datenkonsistenz, da gleiche Teile nur einmal gespeichert werden. Ein weiterer unmittelbar sichtbarer Vorteil ist die auf diese Weise erreichte kompakte, bzw. redundanzfreie Datenhaltung. Um dem Benutzer bei der Informationsabfrage direkt aus dem jeweils momentanen Kontext heraus Sprünge zu beliebigen relevanten
weiteren Informationen zu ermöglichen, muß bei der Dokumentationsaufbereitung bereits das Aufsetzen einer umfassenden Verzeigerung, das heißt, Definieren von Verknüpfungen, erfolgen. Insbesondere sind hierbei auch Verknüpfungen zu berücksichtigen, die für eine spätere Einbindung der Dokumentation in ein System zur Feherdiagnose wichtig sind [10].

Folgende Hypertextfunktionen sind implementiert:

- Bidirektionale Verknüpfungen zwischen Dokumenten aktivierbar durch Auswahl-
  listen, Ikone und Hotspots
- Verknüpfungen zwischen systematisch geordneten Teiledaten und Dokumenten
- Hotspots definierbar für Text und Graphik
- Ein- und Entfalten von Dokumentteilen

Dabei sind Hotspots markierte Stellen in einem Dokument (Text oder Graphik), die bei Anwahl einen Sprung zu einem anderen Dokument oder das Auslösen von anderen

Aktionen bewirken. Hierbei ist für zukünftige Versionen z. B. das Abspielen einer Ton- oder Videosequenz vorgesehen (Hypermedia [11]). Abb.5 zeigt die Verknüpfung von Informationen wie sie sich bei der Benutzung des Systems darstellt. Dabei ist schematisch eine Folge vom Bildschirminhalten dargestellt. Die Rechtecke mit dunklem Querbalken und dreieckigen Pfeilmarkierungen nach oben und unten stellen Rollfenster (scroll boxes) dar, die eine tabellarische Auswahl ermöglichen. Im einzelnen sind folgende Zugriffsmethoden zum Abrufen von Informationen implementiert:

- Volltextsuche,
- mehrstufige Suche über Hierarchie von Baugruppen bzw. Überschriften,
- von der Indizierung für Volltextsuche unabhängige Schlüsselsuche,
- Suche mittels quasi-natürlichsprachlicher Problembeschreibung.

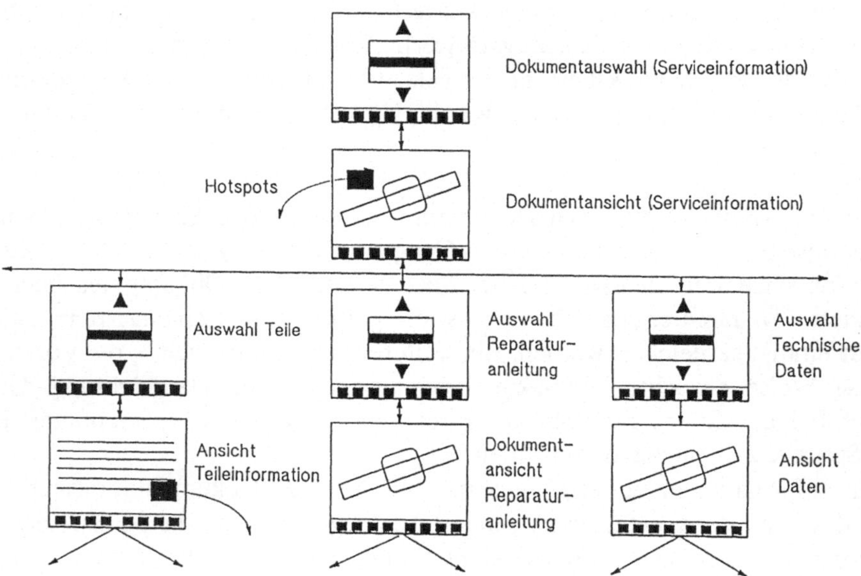

Abb.5 : Dokumentauswahl über Verknüpfungen

Der Zugriff auf Information durch eine quasi-natürlichsprachliche Problembeschreibung basiert auf Synonymtabellen, die verschiedene Phrasen auf einen einheitlichen Schlüssel zurückführen (Bsp.: Lampe - Birne - Licht - LED). Da der typische Anwender eines solchen technischen Informationssystems keinerlei Computererfahrung hat, ist die Konzeption der Benutzerschnittstelle besonders kritisch. Die im Rahmen dieser Arbeit entwickelte Benutzerschnittstelle ist fensterorientiert (konform zu OSF Motif) und benutzt Ikone zur Markierung von Funktionen soweit sinnvoll.

Eine Implementierung des in diesem Beitrag beschriebenen Systems hat gezeigt, daß zumindest rein technisch gesehen, sich gegenüber der herkömmlichen Informationsverwaltung für den Fahrzeugservice markante Vorteile ergeben. Insbesondere führt der schnellere Zugriff auf aktuellere und vollständigere Information zu einer qualitativen Verbesserung im Betriebsablauf. Um eine genaue Rentabilitätsaussage für einen konkreten Anwendungsfall machen zu können, müssten allerdings eine Reihe weiterer Parameter, wie z. B. Kosten für Systemanschaffung, Systemwartung und Benutzerschulung, mitberücksichtigt werden.

Schlußfolgerung und Ausblick

Es wurde ein Konzept für ein computergestütztes technisches Informationssystem für Anwendungen im Fahrzeugservice vorgestellt, das sich insbesondere durch seinen integrierten Ansatz auszeichnet. Durch die schnelle Verfügbarkeit von aktuellen Daten in der Informationsbibliothek und des Teilekataloges wird ein signifikant verbesserter Ablauf in einem Servicebetrieb erreicht. Die Realisierung der Integration von Informationsbibliothek und Teilekatalog mit dem Diagnosesystem als Weiterentwicklung der vorgestellten Arbeit birgt eine vielversprechende zusätzliche Effizienzsteigerung.

Literaturhinweise

[1] Schulmeyer, G.: Automobilelektronik im Umbruch; Datenkommunikation in fahrzeuggestützten Systemen. Elektronik 17 (Aug. 1989) pp. 74 - 79

[2] Schwaiger, K., Weishaupt, W.: Die Vielfalt der Daten bündeln. Elektronik 17 (Aug. 1989) pp. 93 - 96

[3] Stammeier, R., Lennartz, B.: CD-ROM in Industrieanwendungen. Design & Elektronik, Ausgabe 20, (Oct. 1989) pp. 62 - 63

[4] Cichocki, E. M., Ziemer, S. M.: Design considerations for CD-ROM retrieval software. Journal of the American Society for information science (1988) pp. 303 - 312

[5] Thomas, H.: Internationaler Standard für Textdateien. c't Magazin für Computertechnik, Heft 2 (1990) pp. 48 - 56

[6] Gloor, P. A., Streitz, N.A (eds): Hypertext und Hypermedia, Springer-Verlag (1990)

[7] Brockmann, R. J.: Writing better Computer Documentation: From Paper to Hypertext, John Wiley&Sons (1990)

[8] Brown P. J.: Making UNIX On-line Documentation more effective Microprocessors and Microsystems 9 (1985) pp. 346 - 349

[9] Campagnoni, F. R., Ehrlich, K.: Information Retrieval using a Hypertext-Based Help System. ACM Trans. Off. Inf. Syst. 7, 3 (July 1989), pp. 271 - 291

[10] Delfs, H.: Diagnose-Expertensysteme brauchen Hypertext. In: Gloor, P.A., Streitz, N.A (eds): Hypertext und Hypermedia, Springer-Verlag (1990) pp. 171 - 184

[11] Ambrom, S., Hooper, K. (eds.): Interactive Multimedia: Visions of Multimedia for Developers, Educators and Information Providers. Microsoft Press (1988)

Natürliche Sprache und Computer-Animation -
Eine multi-mediale Dialogoberfläche

Ch. Rumpf, U. Harke, U. Leiner, M. Niemöller
Siemens AG
Zentralabteilung Forschung und Entwicklung
W-8000 München 83, Otto-Hahn-Ring 6
Fax.:   + 49 - 89 - 636 - 40512

Zusammenfassung

In dem Multi-Media-Projekt der Siemens Zentralabteilung Forschung und Entwicklung wird
ein interaktives Computeranimationssystem mit einer um die Eingabe natürlicher Sprache
erweiterte Bedienoberfläche erstellt. Ausgehend von der Analyse der heutigen Situation
wird die Forderung nach besserer Bedienbarkeit insbesondere der Werzeuge der Computer-
Animation begründet. Der erste Prototyp besteht aus einer virtuellen Welt, die verschiedene taktile Eingabewerkzeuge kennt, und aus einem fortgeschrittenen Spracherkennungs-
system. Die Objekte der virtuellen Welt folgen physikalischen Bewegungsgesetzen und können interaktiv manipuliert werden.

Abstract

The objectives of the multi-media project currently carried out at Siemens Corporate R&D
laboratories are outlined. The longterm goal is to develop a computer animation system
with a speech dialog interface. We sketch the experiences made in a production of an
animation with tools available today. Based on that experience research was done on the
extension of animation tools by physics-based models and on the improvement of the user
interface by providing a command-word recognizer leading to a first prototype. Objects in a
virtual world can be manipulated interactively and follow physical laws in their kinematical
behaviour.

Einleitung

Die traditionellen Eingabemittel bei Computern sind Tastatur und Maus. Nicht nur im
Hinblick auf Multi-Media Systeme ist diese Beschränkung unzureichend. Mit der Erwei-

terung der Einsatzfelder für die elektronische Datenverarbeitung steigen die Anforderungen an die Bedienoberflächen für Rechner im Hinblick auf Benutzungsfreundlichkeit und problemgerechte Bedienoberfläche. Der Dialog mit dem Rechner ist den menschlichen Interaktionsformen anzupassen. Neben dem Sprachdialog sind fotorealistische Festbilder und Bewegtbildsequenzen zur Darstellung komplexer Objekte und deren Dynamik in Bedienoberflächen als Interaktionsformen einzubringen. Die zwischenmenschliche Kommunikation basiert hauptsächlich auf Sprache und visueller Information, die insbesondere beide simultan wahrgenommen werden können. Beim Entwurf zukünftiger Bedienoberflächen sollte daher dem natürlichen Bedürfnis des Menschen, Dinge durch Zeigen, Berühren und Bewegen zu identifizieren und Anweisungen „einfach auszusprechen", entgegengekommen werden.

Auf drei Gebieten lassen die Kommunikationsfähigkeiten der meisten Rechner heute noch besonders viel zu wünschen übrig:

- Verstehen von kontinuierlich gesprochener Sprache
- Verarbeitung und Erstellung von visueller 3D-Information (Handskizzen, Bilder, Filme etc.)
- Ergonomische und standardisierte Bedienoberflächen.

Auf diesen drei Gebieten wurden in den letzten Jahren erhebliche Fortschritte gemacht. Sie werden jedoch jedes für sich und getrennt von den anderen bearbeitet.

Ein grundlegendes Anliegen unseres Projektes ist die Zusammenführung dieser Techniken, wobei in einem ersten Prototypen Überlegungen zur Standardisierung nicht im Vordergrund standen. Das Fernziel ist es, eine interaktive Animationsumgebung mit taktilen Eingabemitteln und mit Hilfe von fließend gesprochener Sprache bedienen und steuern zu können.

Auf dem Weg dahin haben wir bisher folgende Stationen erreicht: Zunächst wurde eine anspruchsvolle Animation (Videofilm) erstellt. Dabei wurden heutige Animationssysteme im Gebrauch erprobt und der gesamte Erstellungsprozeß studiert. Im nächsten Abschnitt werden die dabei erkannten Probleme und gewonnenen Erfahrungen besprochen. Im zweiten Schritt entwickelten wir ein kleines Animationssystem, das es erlaubt, eine virtuelle Welt zu erzeugen und mit den Objekten zu arbeiten. Dies ermöglicht uns, zwei wesentliche Probleme der heutigen Computer-Animation anzupacken: die Simulation von dynamischem Verhalten der virtuellen Körper sowie die Verbesserung der Bedienoberflächen.

Zukünftige Arbeiten werden es ermöglichen, Animation auf Task-Level und somit auf hohem semantischem Niveau zu steuern. Dies betrifft insbesondere die Steuerung von simulierten menschlichen Bewegungen (human animation) über Sprache. Dabei werden Befehle in Form von ganzen Sätzen gegeben, die in Inhalt und Art Anweisungen in zwischenmenschlichen Dialogen ähnlich sind. Typische Beispiele hierfür sind: „Lege Schalter XY auf Stellung 5." oder „Gehe durch den Raum zur Werkbank".

Heutige Erstellung von Computer-Animation

Im technisch-wissenschaftlichen Bereich ist die Anwendung von Computer-Animation noch relativ neu. Eine virtuelle Kamera, die den Betrachter z.B. durch das Innere eines virtuellen Hauses führt, oder die Beobachtung der komplizierten Bewegungen eines ebenfalls simulierten Montageroboters, bieten neue Möglichkeiten zur Optimierung technischer Systeme. Unsere Arbeiten zielen auf dem Gebiet der Computer-Animation vor allem auf die Simulation der Bewegungsabläufe von Menschen und Robotern (human animation). Damit wird es möglich sein, neue Arbeitsplätze im voraus ergonomisch günstig zu gestalten, oder die technische Realisierbarkeit von Arbeitsabläufen zu prüfen. Heute ist die Bedienung solcher Systeme noch recht kompliziert. Neue Interaktionsformen, insbesondere die Kommunikation in natürlicher Sprache, versprechen hier, neue Dimensionen zu erschließen.

Vor der technischen Erstellung einer Animation, muß ein Dokument vorliegen, das in der Informatik als Spezifikation und Pflichtenheft bezeichnet würde. Es handelt sich um das Drehbuch, welches den Inhalt, zeitlichen Ablauf und die Choreographie der Animation vorschreibt. Zum Produkt führen von da aus die drei technischen Schritte:

- Modellierung der Objekte,
- Bewegungsdefinition,
- Rendering.

Daran schließt sich die Nachbearbeitung (postprocessing) an, die das Produkt in das gewünschte Format, z.B. Videoband, bringt.

Modellierung

Modellieren in diesem Zusammenhang bedeutet die Eingabe, Beschreibung, Strukturierung, Verknüpfung und visuelle Darstellung von dreidimensionalen Objekten. Bei komplexen und fein strukturierten Objekten ist der Aufwand an Manpower hierfür erheblich. Solid Modelling erzeugt starre, nichtverformbare Objekte mit geschlossenen Oberflächen. Rotationssymmetrische Objekte sind leicht durch ein Polygon, welches das Profil beschreibt, zu definieren. Beim Sweeping definiert man eine 2-D Fläche, die, entlang einer geraden oder gekrümmten Strecke bewegt, einen 3-D Körper definiert. Das Constructive Solid Modelling baut komplexe Objekte aus mathematisch einfach zu beschreibenden Elementen, wie Block, Zylinder, Kugel und Kegel, durch deren Verküpfung mit booleschen Operationen auf. Anspruchsvoller wird die Technik zur Beschreibung von Freiformflächen. Dies kann man z.B. dadurch erreichen, daß man den Querschnitt beim Sweeping verändert. Zur Behandlung weicher Gegenstände und in der Medizin gemessener 3-D Daten, setzt man sogenannte "Voxels" ein. Diese stellen ein Volumenelement (in Anlehnung an pixel - picture element) mit Eigenschaften wie Farbe, Transparenz etc. dar. Es existieren erst wenige Lösungen, die bei der Darstellung von Gasen und Flüssigkeiten benötigt werden, wie z.B. particle based animation.

Bewegungsdefinition

Man unterscheidet die drei elementaren Arten der dreidimensionalen Animation: Keyframes [Gom 85], parametrisierte Keyframes und Algorithmen, auf die dann höhere Stufen aufbauen (Task-Level Animation). Die zweite Art, also die parametrisierte Interpolation zwischen Keyframes, ist für die Darstellung der Bewegungen des menschlichen Körpers geeignet. Ein simplifiziertes Skelett definiert dabei die Gelenke und deren Freiheitsgrade. Um aber Kommandos der Art „Gehe zur Tür" verarbeiten zu können, ist Task-Level Animation notwendig. Hier sind Aufgabenplanung und mögliche Interruptbehandlungen zu berücksichtigen. Derzeit gibt es hierfür in nur wenigen Instituten [Bad87] Ansätze. Zeltzer [McK89] verfolgt einen verwandten Ansatz mit „autonomous agents", die quasi aus eigenem Antrieb einem Ziel zusteuern.

Die heute verbreiteste Animationsart ist die Keyframe-Animation. Der Mensch muß dabei in mühseliger, handwerklicher Arbeit Details festlegen. Eine gewisse Entlastung ist die Interpolation (inbetweening), so daß nicht jedes einzelne Bild neu erstellt werden muß. Von einem Keyframe zum nächsten können Parameter, wie Positionen, Lage, Formen und Farben der Objekte verändert werden. Lichtquellen können ein- oder ausgeschaltet, ihre Position und Lichtstärke verändert werden. Die Hauptaufgabe des Animators ist es festzulegen, innerhalb welcher Framesequenz und somit zu welcher Zeit die Änderungen stattfinden sollen. Schließlich gehört auch die Animation der virtuellen Kamera dazu. Dies bedeutet, Position, Blickwinkel und Blickpunkt (Fokus) der Kamera in der zeitlichen Abfolge zu beschreiben.

Eine weitere algorithmische Animationsmethode benutzt kinematische Regeln, sowie inverse Kinematik zusammen mit Randbedingungen (Beschränkungen) in einem Simulationssystem. Die Bewegungen von Körpern werden durch Lösung der physikalischen Bewegungsgleichungen beschrieben. Dies führt zu Bewegungen, die für den Beobachter natürlich erscheinen. Hinzu kommt hierbei noch die Kollisionsvermeidung, eine Methode, die in der Robotik viel eingesetzt wird.

Rendering

Rendering ist das Erstellen eines am Bildschirm sichtbaren Bildes für einen Rahmen (Frame). Hier kann die Berücksichtung von Eigenschaften wie Schattierung, Transparenz von Objekten, und Spiegelungseffekte die Bildqualität wesentlich beeinflussen.

Die Animation oder Bewegungdefinition eröffnet neben den 3 räumlichen Dimensionen beim Modellieren die vierte Dimension, die Zeit. Um bei der interaktiven Erstellung einer Animationssequenz das Ergebnis, nämlich die schnelle Abfolge von Frames und damit den Bewegungseffekt zu sehen, enthalten solche Animationssysteme einfache "Renderer".

Diese sind deshalb sehr schnell, da sie sich darauf beschränken, bunte Drahtmodelle der Objekte zu zeigen. Bestenfalls werden die Oberflächen der Objekte mit sehr simplem sogenannten "Solid Rendering" ausgefüllt. Dadurch bekommt der Anwender schon einen guten Eindruck über die Lage der Objekte zueinander.

Diese recht bescheidene Qualitätsstufe des Renderns ist in den Arbeitsprozessen der Modellierung und der Bewegungsdefinition ausreichend. Anspruchsvoller ist man bei dem Rendern des Endergebnisses. Hier kann man bei gegebener Auflösung und Farbqualität des Monitors bis zur Qualität von fotorealistischen Bildern gelangen. Dieser Schritt findet i. a. in länger laufenden Hintergrundprozessen statt. Jeder Rahmeninhalt muß einzeln gerendert werden. Bei längeren Sequenzen ist dies nicht nur sehr CPU-intensiv, sondern produziert auch Daten von enormer Menge.

Begründet in dieser Notwendigkeit, zwischen Geschwindigkeit und Qualität zu wählen, liegt die Forderung an moderne Animationssysteme, einerseits interaktives Previewing in niedriger Auflösung und andererseits hochauflösendes Rendering in der Stapelverarbeitung anzubieten.

Postprocessing
In der Regel kann weder das Rendern selbst noch das Lesen der gerenderten Daten von einer Festplatte in Echtzeit geschehen. Deshalb ist das Übertragen der Daten in ein Videoformat, und zwar Rahmen für Rahmen, unumgänglich.
Durch die geeignete Vertonung mit Text, Musik und / oder Umweltgeräusche kann die Aussagekraft eines Filmes wesentlich ergänzt werden. Dies ist in der Regel unverzichtbar.

Trip to the Insights

Um den Status Quo der Computer-Animation zu beurteilen und Schwächen der heutigen Werkzeuge aufzudecken, haben wir eine kurze Animation "Trip to the Insights" erstellt. Der Inhalt des Filmes zeigt eine Projektion der langfristigen Ziele unseres Vorhabens. Eine Anwenderin arbeitet mit einem futuristischen, sehr komfortablen Animationssystem. Die interaktive Konstruktion eines Hauses beginnt mit 2D-Grundrißzeichungen und wächst Stockwerk um Stockwerk in die Höhe. Durch natürlichsprachliche Eingaben können Objekte geändert oder ausgetauscht werden, der Blickwinkel verändert werden. Man kann in das Haus eintreten und sich darin umschauen. Durch diesen Film können wir die dargestellte Zielumgebung mit der heutigen Arbeitsumgebung anschaulich vergleichen. Darüberhinaus regt das Projekt fruchtbare Diskussionen zwischen Fachleuten auf den drei Gebieten Sprachverarbeitung, Bedienoberflächen und Computer-Animation an. Nicht zuletzt demonstriert der Film die Nutzbarkeit der Computer-Animation in Architektur, Produktion, Simulation und vielen anderen Bereichen.

Für den etwa dreiminütigen Film wurden mehr als 3000 Frames in VHS-Qualität erzeugt. Auf Workstations war die durchschnittliche Rendering-Zeit ca. 3 Minuten je Rahmen, was sich zu 150 Stunden aufaddiert. Die höhere UMATIC-Highband-Qualität erfordert einen etwa sechsfachen Rechenaufwand. Es ist unbestritten, daß Rendern außerordentlich teuer ist, wenn fotorealistische Qualität erreicht werden soll. Auch mit sehr leistungsfähigen Rechnern der Zukunft wird Echtzeit-Rendern für interaktive Arbeit nur bei reduzierter Qualität möglich sein.

Mit Ausnahme des Renderns sind alle Arbeitsgänge der Animationserstellung sehr interaktiv und fordern erheblichen Aufwand an Arbeitskraft. Während einige Modellierer bereits graphische Bedienoberfächen haben und die Maus als Eingabegerät kennen, gestatten die meisten Animationssysteme lediglich Eingaben über die Tastatur. Der Anwender, insbesondere der Neuling, bekommt zu wenig Orientierungshilfen und verliert sich leicht im virtuellen dreidimensionalen Raum. Die Verbesserung der Bedienoberfächen würde zu erheblich besseren Produkten führen und die Technik der Computer-Animation, die heute noch einer relativ kleinen Gruppe von Experten vorbehalten ist, einer breiteren Anwendung zuführen. Die Spezifizierung von Bewegung durch Keyframe-Animation bedarf gut ausgebildeter Leute mit einem ausgeprägten räumlichen Vorstellungsvermögen und Sinn für natürliche Bewegungsabläufe und Effekte. Besonders schwierig ist es, Bewegungsabläufe nicht kantig sondern natürlich aussehen zu lassen, als ob die Körper physikalischen Gesetzen gehorchten. Hierzu bedient man sich am besten der Simulation, deren Algorithmen aber ihrerseits wieder sehr CPU-intensiv sein können.

Die softwaretechnische Aufteilung der drei oben beschriebenen Schritte auf drei unterschiedliche Softwarepakete ist historisch bedingt und muß überwunden werden. Die Kommunikation zwischen den Paketen geschieht über Datenfiles. Dies impliziert eine strenge Trennung der Arbeitschritte und hohen Zeitaufwand beim Wechsel von einer Phase in eine andere. Mit einem integrierten System kann der Benutzer effektiver arbeiten, da Iterationsschritte leichter durchführbar sind und keine Wiederholungen implizieren.

Prototyp für ein Animations-System mit Spracheingabe

Angeregt durch die im vorangegangenen Abschnitt diskutierten Erkenntnisse, wurden Arbeiten auf den drei Gebieten Simulation von Bewegungsdynamik, Darstellung und Interaktion mit einer virtuellen Welt, sowie Integration von Sprache in die Bedienoberfläche begonnen, die alle in einem gemeinsamen Prototypen mündeten. SESAM (Siemens Environment for Speech controlled AniMation) ist der erste Prototyp einer angestrebten, interaktiven Animationsumgebung mit einer multimedialen Bedienoberfläche.

Virtuelle Welt und Bewegungssimulation

SESAM enthält eine einfache 3D-Welt, in der verschiedene vorgefertigte Objekte erzeugt werden können, indem auf deren Beschreibungen in einer Datenbasis zurückgegriffen wird. Neben den üblichen geometrischen Strukturen, die durch Eckpunkte und Polygone beschrieben werden, haben unsere Objekte auch physikalische Eigenschaften, die durch Massenpunkte und Randbedingungen oder Beschränkungen von Freiheitsgraden definiert sind [Nie90]. Den Objekten können Attribute wie Elastizität, Anfangsgeschwindigkeit, Gravitation und die Art der Darstellung zugeordnet werden, die vom Animator während der Sitzung interaktiv verändert werden können. Die freie Bewegung der Körper wird durch die Lagrangefunktion der pysikalischen Bewegungsgleichungen beschrieben, die die Einschränkungen und Randbedingungen mitberücksichtigt. Die Lösung dieser Gleichungen erfolgt durch einen neuen approximativen, iterativen Algorithmus [Nie90]. Dadurch, daß in der Approximation nur diejenigen Parameter berücksichtigt werden, die einer Veränderung unterliegen, wird der Algorithmus echtzeitfähig. Die Bewegungen akzeptiert der Beobachter als vollkommen natürlich, wenn auch, um das Echtzeitverhalten zu erreichen, z. B. der Drehimpulserhaltungssatz nicht immer vollständig erhalten ist.

Benutzungsoberfläche

Die Funktionalität des Animationssystems für die virtuelle Welt in SESAM ist soweit möglich getrennt gehalten von Funktionen des Dialogteiles. Der Dialog kann interaktiv durch den Benutzer geführt werden, oder durch Lesen von Skriptdaten aus einer Datei selbständig ablaufen. Seine Aufgabe ist es, die Dialogoberfläche (s. Bild1) aktuell zu halten. Dies

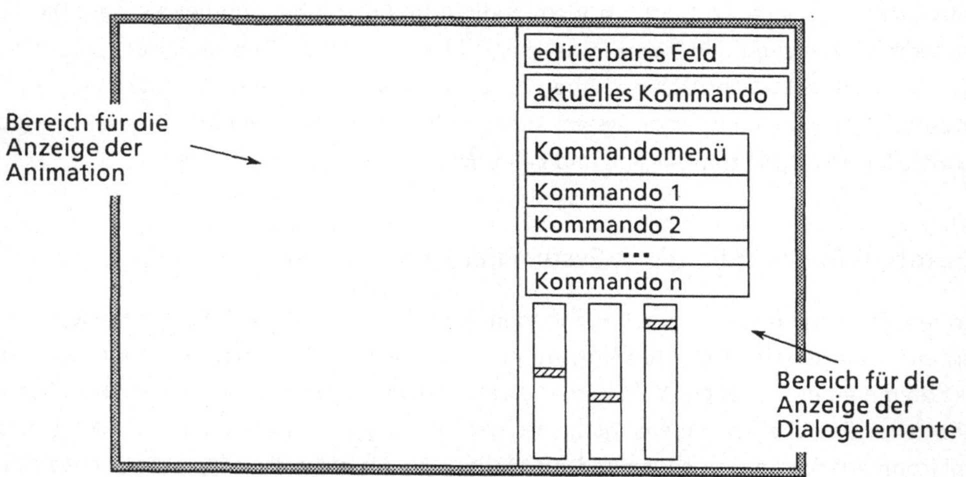

Bild 1: Bedienoberfläche des Systems

beinhaltet, Feedback nach erfolgten Eingaben zu geben, indem die dann gültigen Kommandos, das zuletzt ausgewählte Kommando und Fehlermeldungen angezeigt werden. Neben Menüs stehen auch andere interaktive Eingabemöglichkeiten zur Verfügung, wie editierbare Felder, Schieberegler (slider), 3D-Kraftmoment-Sensor (Geometry Ball) und, wie weiter unten noch ausgeführt wird, die natürliche Sprache. Unabhängig davon, mit welchem Interaktionsmedium ein spezielles Kommando eingegeben wurde, reagieren der Dialogteil und das Animationssystem in identischer Weise.

Unsere Oberfläche erlaubt die simultane Eingabe über verschiedene Eingabekanäle. Der Animator kann zu jedem Zeitpunkt die für ihn und die Situation optimale Methode benutzen: Tastatur, Menüauswahl und der Wechsel der Sliderfunktionalität durch Mausclick. 3D-Eingabegeräte wie die Sensor-Kugel erleichtern die Orientierung und die Bewegung von Objekten im virtuellen Raum. Die natürlichere und ergonomische Kommunikationsform ist die Sprache. Die hier vorgestellte Verknüpfung von verschiedenen Eingabegeräten mit der Eingabe in natürlicher Sprache wertet die Bedienoberfläche erheblich auf, da die Interaktion mit dem Animationssystem dadurch wesentlich verbessert wird.

Spracheingabe

Im ersten Prototypen unserer multi-medialen Bedienoberfläche ist ein sprecherunabhängiger Worterkenner integriert, der kontinuierliche Hidden-Markov-Modelle für Phoneme benutzt. Jedes erkannte Wort ist mit Hilfe eines Aussprachelexikons aus einer Sequenz von Phonemen zusammengesetzt. Der Worterkenner kann zu mehreren alternativen Sequenzen (Hypothesen) kommen und wählt daraus diejenige aus, die die Wahrscheinlichste ist und keinen speziellen Kriterien widerspricht. Die Erkennungsrate ist in gewissem Maße abhängig von dem konkreten Kommandovorrat und liegt bei 98%. Mit speziellen HW-Boards kann der Erkennungsprozeß in Echtzeit ablaufen. Es handelt sich dabei um zwei Boards mit A/D-Wandler, drei Signalprozessoren und einem ASIC-Chip für das vector-matching. Diese Boards sind als Teil des Projektes SPICOS [Zue90] für das Erkennen von kontinuierlicher Sprache entstanden. Durch das Hinzufügen eines dritten Boards wird man in der näheren Zukunft Echtzeit für das Erkennen kontinuierlich gesprochener, natürlicher Sprache erreichen.

Software- und Hardwaretechnische Aspekte

Die Dialogkomponente ist der Monitor für die Ein-/Ausgaben. Sie wurde mit den Standard-Werkzeugen LEX und YACC in UNIX erstellt. Die Eventschleife prüft ständig ab, ob Eingaben vorliegen (s. Bild 2). Diese Eingaben können derzeit über die physikalischen Geräte Tastatur, Maus oder Geometry-Ball sowie über Spracheingabe ausgelöst werden. Sie werden interpretiert und in eine geräteunabhängige Form gebracht. Die der Dialog-Grammatik entsprechenden Kommandosequenzen werden in Aktionen des Animationssystems übersetzt. Diese Sequenzen sind die einzige Schnittstelle zwischen dem Dialogpaket und dem Animations-

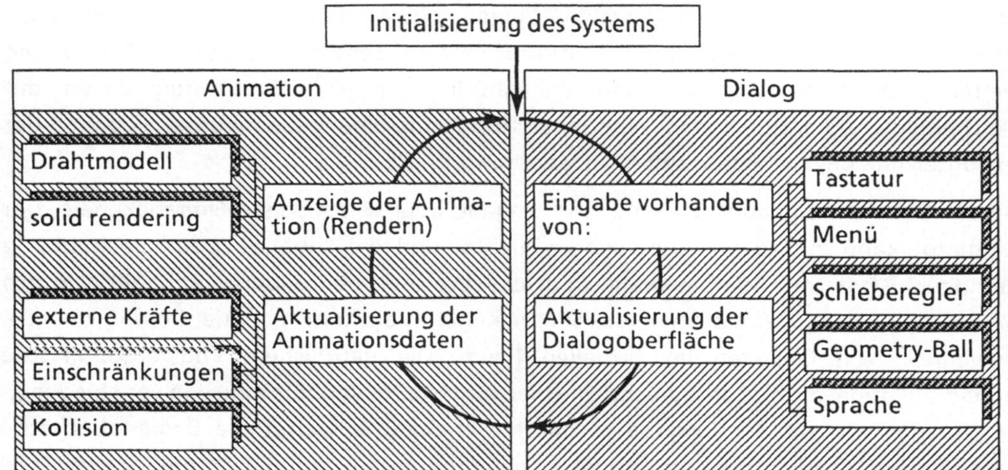

Bild 2: Ablaufdiagramm

system. Liegen keine Eingaben vor, fährt das Animationssystem in der Berechnung der laufenden Prozesse ohne Einfluß von außen fort.

Der Prototyp ist innerhalb der letzen zwölf Monate entstanden. Die verwendete Programmiersprache ist C. Die Animation und die Kontrolle des Benutzerdialoges laufen auf einer Silicon Graphics 4D 50G unter Verwendung der Graphikbibliothek ab. Der Spracherkennungsteil läuft auf einer Sun 4 Workstation, die mit den beiden speziellen Sprachboards am VME-Bus ausgestattet ist. Die Sun 4 und die Silicon Graphics sind über TCP/IP gekoppelt.

Die Trennung des Dialogteils von der eigentlichen Anwendung sowie die Verwendung des UNIX Werkzeugs LEX für die Interpretation der Eingaben haben erwiesen, daß eine Integration von neuen Eingabewerkzeugen innerhalb des Systems leichter möglich ist als bei herkömmlicher Programmierung. Die Realisierung der Dialog-Grammatik innerhalb von YACC ermöglicht zusäztlich eine schnelle Erweiterung und Umstellung der Dialoggestaltung.
Der Dialogteil kann nicht nur die über Tastatur eingegebenen Daten interpretieren, sondern auch Inhalte aus Dateien lesen. Daher ist es möglich, z.B. selbstablauffähige Demonstrationen aus Dateien abzurufen.

Erste Erfahrungen im Gebrauch der integrierten Oberfläche
Es hat sich gezeigt, daß die Spracheingabe die Handhabung des komplexen Systems beschleunigt, insbesondere dann, wenn ein Wechsel der Hand von einem Gerät zum anderen (etwa von Maus zu Tastatur) dadurch vermieden werden kann. Die Bedienung des Geometry-Balls wird anfangs als gewöhnungsbedürftig betrachtet. Anwender sind jedoch schon nach kurzer Zeit mit dem Gerät vertraut. Es bietet eine besonders gute Möglichkeit, sich innerhalb eines Raumes zu orientieren, sowie die Lage von Objekten im Raum zu verändern.

Eine gute Rückmeldung von Informationsdaten (etwa Koordinaten, Drehachse) an den Benutzer würde den Einsatz dieses Geräts noch mehr unterstützen. Als positiv hat sich das Angebot der Schieberegler herausgestellt. Da diese für unterschiedliche Aktionen (z.B. Ändern von Farbe, Drehen eines Objektes) verschiedene Wertebereiche liefern, geben sie durch zusätzliche Anzeige der aktuellen Werte eine gute Rückkopplung für den Anwender. Die Kombination verschiedener Eingabemedien innerhalb einer Dialogoberfläche kommt sowohl dem unerfahrenen Anwender als auch dem Experten zugute.

Zukünftige Arbeiten

In Zukunft werden Forschungsarbeiten bezüglich der Animation selbst und der multimedialen Benutzungsoberfläche fortgesetzt. Im Animationsbereich werden wir die Funktionalität von SESAM durch die konventionelle Keyframe-Technik erweitern. Sowohl die Simulation der Bewegungsdynamik als auch die Key-Frame-Methode haben ihre Vorteile und Anwendungsgebiete. Die Zusammenführung wird dem Anwender beides anbieten.

Animation auf dem bisher diskutierten recht elementaren Niveau genügt nicht den Anforderungen für verschiedene Anwendungen wie z.B. der Human Animation. Hierbei handelt es sich um Task-Level Animation auf hohem Niveau [Bad 89]. Hier liegt auch die wahre Rechtfertigung für die Integration der Eingabe von fließend gesprochenen Sätzen in die Bedienoberfläche. Die typischen Befehle sind derart, daß sie den Sätzen der zwischenmenschlichen Kommunikation äußerst nahe kommen.

Die Sprache ist ein Medium mit der Möglichkeit, ein interaktives System zu erstellen, das einen Menschen oder Roboter, der Befehle und Aufgaben durchführt, ziemlich nahe simulieren kann. Der Mensch gibt seine Befehle oder ganze Handlungspläne in natürlicher Sprache ein und verändert oder bewegt Objekte der virtuellen Welt direkt durch taktile Eingabegeräte. Das System analysiert die Aktionspläne und bildet sie auf elemetare Befehle ab. Unsere nächsten Schritte werden untersuchen, wie das System für die Erkennung fließend gesprocher Sprache [Akt89] mit einem Task-Level Animationssystem verknüpft werden kann.

Zusammenfassung

Die Erstellung von Computer-Animationen ist sehr aufwendig sowohl was Rechenzeit als auch insbesondere die menschliche Arbeitszeit betrifft. Die wesentliche Verbesserung der Bedienbarkeit solcher Animationssysteme wird die Techniken einem größeren Nutzerkreis eröffnen.

Die Bereitstellung von Animationssystemen auf sehr hohem Task-Level in Verbindung mit verschiedenen Eingabemedien insbesondere durch fließend gesprochene Sätze, wird ein anschauliches Beispiel liefern, wie der Umgang mit dem Computer sich künftig vereinfachen wird. So werden die dem Menschen zur Verfügung stehenden Kommunikationskanäle besser genutzt und angesprochen.

Literatur

[Akt89]   Aktas A., Höge H.: Real-time recognition of subword units on a hybrid multi-DSP/ ASIC based acoustic front-end; Proc. of the IEEE International Conference on Acoustics, Speech and Signal Processing, pp. 101 - 103, Edinburgh, May 1989

[Bad 89]   Badler N.I.: Communication Tasks and their Performance via Animation and Natural Language; Technical Report University of Pennsylvania, June 1989

[Gom 85]   Gomez J.: TWIXT: A 3D Animation System
Comput. & Graphics Vol.9 No. 3, pp. 291 - 298

[McK89]   M. McKenna, D. Zeltzer: Dynamic Simulation of Autonomous Legged Locomotion, Tch.Report The Media Lab, Massachusetts Institute of Technology, Cambridge, MA, January 1989

[Nie 90]   Niemöller M., Leiner U.: Approximative, Dynamic Simulation of Objects in Computer Animation Systems; Proceedings of Computer Graphics 90 Conference, 6.-8. Nov. 1990, London

[Zue90]   Zünkler K.: Speech-understanding systems: The communication technology of tomorrow; in: Schwärzel and Mizin (Eds.): Advanced Information Processing, pp. 227 - 251, Springer 1990

EIN HYPERTEXT-EDITOR ZUR SOFTWARE-WARTUNG

Johannes Sametinger, Alois Stritzinger

Johannes-Kepler-Universität Linz
Institut für Wirtschaftsinformatik
A-4040 Linz

ZUSAMMENFASSUNG

Dieser Artikel beschreibt einen Hypertext-Editor, der es erleichtert, Softwaresysteme zu warten. Mit Hilfe dieses Editors ist es möglich, die Beziehungen zwischen Klassen und Methoden, bzw. Moduln und Prozeduren, sowie die Beziehungen zwischen Dateien und sogar den Bezeichnern eines Softwaresystems auf einfache Art und Weise zu identifizieren und zum Navigieren durch das System zu verwenden.

Die Anwendung dieses Hypertext-Werkzeuges beschränkt sich nicht auf die Wartung von Softwaresystemen, sondern kann selbstverständlich auch bei der Entwicklung gewinnbringend eingesetzt werden. Bei der Konzeption des Editors wurde aber besonderes Augenmerk auf die Tätigkeiten der Wartung gelegt.

EINLEITUNG

Die Wartung nimmt den größten Teil des Software-Lebenszyklus ein. Nicht selten wird mehr als die Hälfte der Zeit für diese Tätigkgeit aufgewendet [6], [10]. Es ist daher naheliegend, daß einer Verminderung des Wartungsaufwandes große Bedeutung zukommt.

Das Schwierigste beim Ändern eines Softwaresystems ist das Nachvollziehen der Gedanken der ursprünglichen Entwickler (siehe [8], [9]). Diese Analysetätigkeit wiederum nimmt mehr als die Hälfte der Wartungstätigkeit ein. Gute Dokumentation kann hier eine entscheidende Verbesserung bringen. Meistens ist die Dokumentation jedoch weder vollständig noch am aktuellen Stand. In diesem Fall sind Werkzeuge von großem Vorteil, die das Verstehen von Programmen auf Quellcode-Ebene unterstützen (z.B. [2], [3], [11]) und den Dokumentationsprozeß automatisieren oder zumindest die Konsistenzhaltung von Dokumenten unterstützen ([5], [7]).

Wir beschreiben einen Hypertext-Editor, der das Verstehen von Programmen erleichtert, indem er dem Benutzer hilft, die Übersicht in einem großen System zu bewahren, Beziehungen zwischen Systemkomponenten zu identifizieren und bequem an für das Verstehen des Systems benötigte Informationen heranzukommen.

DIE NETZWERK-STRUKTUR VON SOFTWARE-SYSTEMEN

Hypertext ist eine Art von Informations-Management, mit dem in einem Netzwerk von Knoten (Informationsblöcke) navigiert werden kann ([1], [4]). Die Knoten sind aufgrund bestimmter Beziehungen miteinander verbunden. Um Hypertext für das Navigieren in einem Softwaresystem zu verwenden, müssen solche Informationsblöcke, sowie deren Verbindungen untereinander definiert werden.

Im folgenden beschreiben wir kurz einige typische Charakteristika für den Aufbau von Softwaresystemen. Wir unterscheiden dabei objekt-orientierte Systeme, die in C++, und modul-orientierte Systeme, die in Modula-2 implementiert sind. Die Implementierungssprache beeinflußt einerseits den Aufbau (die Struktur) eines Softwaresystems und andererseits (durch ihre syntaktische und semantische Eigenschaften) die Art und Weise, wie Beziehungen zwischen den einzelnen Systemkomponenten beschrieben werden.

Objekt-orientierte Softwaresysteme

Ein objekt-orientiertes in C++ geschriebenes Programm besteht aus einer Reihe von Dateien, die Klassen-Definitionen, Methoden-Beschreibungen und globale Deklarationen enthalten ([14]). Globale Deklarationen können in mehreren Klassen und Definitionen verwendet werden. Was den Inhalt einer Datei betrifft, so gibt es keinerlei Einschränkungen. Eine Datei kann mehrere Klassen-Definitionen, Methoden-Beschreibungen und auch globale Deklarationen enthalten (z.B. verschiedene Dialogkomponenten für eine graphische Benutzerschnittstelle). Die Beschreibung einer Klasse kann auch auf mehrere Dateien verteilt sein (beispielsweise um die Methoden für die Ein-/Ausgabe mehrerer Klassen zusammenzufassen). Um in einer Datei den Inhalt einer anderen Datei verwenden zu können wird diese *inkludiert* (dies geschieht mit einer speziellen Preprozessor-Anweisung).

Es bestehen somit eine Reihe von Beziehungen zwischen den Dateien, Klassen und Methoden in einem in C++ geschriebenen Softwaresystem:

- Eine Klasse wird in einer Datei beschrieben.

- Eine Klasse erbt von einer anderen Klasse.

- Eine Methode wird ebenfalls in einer bestimmten Datei beschrieben.

- Eine Methode gehört zu einer bestimmten Klasse.

- Eine Methode wird in einer Unterklasse überschrieben.

- Eine Datei wird von anderen Dateien *inkludiert*.

Es existieren noch weitere Beziehungen auf der Ebene der Bezeichner:

- Ein Bezeichner wird in einer Klasse oder Methode definiert, oder er steht in einer Datei und ist global verfügbar.

- Die Verwendung eines Bezeichners steht in Verbindung mit der Definition dieses Bezeichners und mit allen anderen Verwendungen desselben Bezeichners.

- Ein Kommentar kann Erläuterungen zu einem Bezeichner enthalten, z.B. die Beschreibung einer Klasse, einer Methode, oder einer Instanzvariablen (das sind Variablen einer Klasse).

Modul-orientierte Softwaresysteme

Ähnlich ist der Aufbau von modulorientierten Systemen. Für Modula-2 können beispielsweise folgende Beziehungen zwischen Moduln, Prozeduren (bzw. Funktionen) und Dateien definiert werden ([17]):

- Ein Modul besteht aus einem Definitions- und einem Implementierungsteil.

- Ein Modul importiert andere Modul(definitione)n.

- Eine Prozedur gehört zu einem bestimmten Modul.

- Sowohl Definition als auch Implementierung eines Moduls stehen in einer eigenen Datei.

- Eine Modulimplementierung gehört zu einer bestimmten Moduldefinition.

Für Bezeichner gilt gleiches wie für objekt-orientierte Systeme, d.h. auch sie stehen untereinander in Verbindung und können in Kommentaren erläutert werden.

Wir verwenden diese Beziehungen, um mit dem Hypertext-Editor durch ein Software-System zu navigieren und nützliche Informationen für das Verstehen und Warten eines Systems bereitzustellen.

DER HYPERTEXT-EDITOR

Der Hypertext-Editor zerlegt den Quellcode automatisch beim Einlesen eines Software-systems (das sind einfach eine Reihe von C++- oder Modula-2-Dateien) in oben beschriebene Komponenten (Klassen und Methoden, bzw. Moduln und Prozeduren). Außerdem werden — durch syntaktische Analyse — die Beziehungen zwischen diesen

Komponenten und den Bezeichnern in diesem System hergestellt. Mit Hilfe dieser Informationen wird dem Benutzer sowohl ein sehr einfaches Navigieren durch das System ermöglicht, als auch eine Reihe von sehr nützlichen Informationen zum Verstehen des Systems bereitgestellt (siehe auch [12]).

Benutzerschnittstelle

Die Benutzerschnittstelle basiert auf den Konzepten moderner graphischer Dialogschnittstellen (siehe [13], [15], [16]).

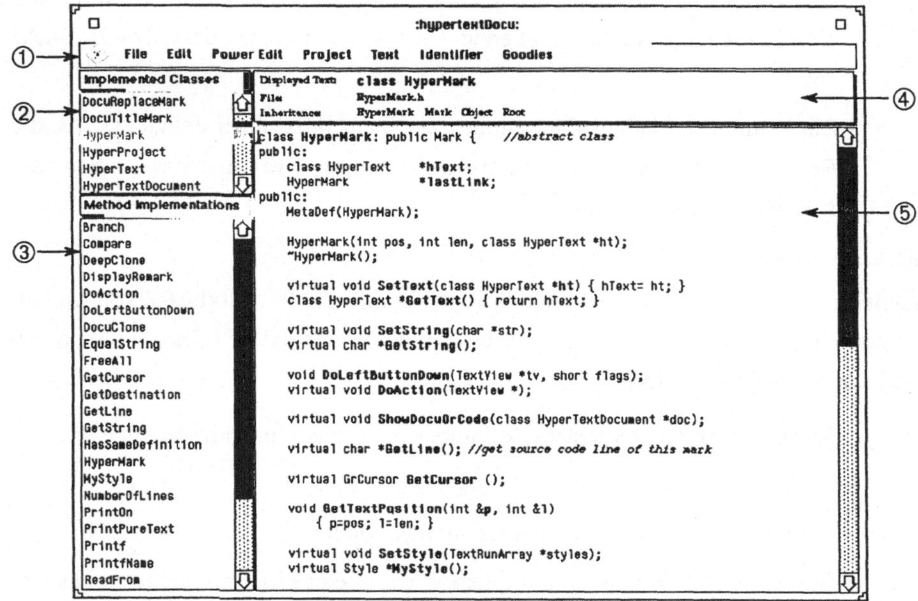

Abb. 1: Benutzerschnittstelle

Sie besteht aus einer Menüzeile (siehe ① in Abb. 1), zwei Listen (② und ③), einer Informationsbox (④), sowie einem Texteditor (⑤). Mit Hilfe der Menüs können verschiedenste Kommandos ausgeführt werden, die obere Liste zeigt Dateien, Klassen oder Moduln des Systems an, und die zweite Liste zeigt jeweils die Methoden, Prozeduren, Unterklassen oder *inkludierte*, bzw. importierte Dateien des in der oberen Liste ausgewählten Elementes. In der Informationsbox wird angezeigt, welcher Text soeben im Texteditor bearbeitet werden kann, aus welcher Datei dieser Text stammt, und (bei Klassen und Methoden) welche Oberklassen (Vererbungshierarchie) es zu einer Klasse gibt.

Selbstverständlich ist es möglich, mehrere solche in Abbildung 1 gezeigte Fenster zu öffnen. Somit können unterschiedliche Teile eines Softwaresystems gleichzeitig analysiert und bearbeitet werden.

Browsing-Möglichkeiten

Es gibt verschieden Möglichkeiten, durch ein System zu *browsen*. Die einfachste Art und Weise ist, einfach ein Element aus den beiden linken Listen auszuwählen. In diesem Fall erscheint dann im Editor die entsprechende Klasse, Methode, Prozedur oder Datei.

Von großem Vorteil ist die Möglichkeit, einer der vorhin beschriebenen Beziehungen zu folgen und somit sehr einfach wie folgt zu verzweigen:

- von einer Klasse zu deren Oberklasse oder einer der Unterklassen,

- von einer Methode zu derselben Methode in einer der Oberklassen

- von einer Klasse oder Methode zu jener Datei, in der die Klasse oder Methode enthalten ist,

- von einer Datei zu einer der *inkludierten* Dateien,

- von einer Prozedur zu jenem Modul, in dem diese Prozedur enthalten ist,

- ...

Es ist überdies möglich einen Bezeichner im Text auszuwählen und beispielsweise

- zur Definition dieses Bezeichners (unabhängig davon wo man sich gerade befindet)

- zur vorhergehenden oder nächsten Verwendung desselben Bezeichners

zu verzweigen.

Informationen über Bezeichner

Über Bezeichner können jederzeit wichtige Informationen angezeigt werden. Dazu gehören:

- die Stelle, an der dieser Bezeichner deklariert wurde
  (welche(r) Klasse, Methode, Modul, Prozedur, Datei),

- die Zeile, in der die Deklaration enthalten ist,

- eine kurze Beschreibung des Bezeichners (falls vorhanden).

Darüberhinaus ist es möglich, auf einfache Art und Weise festzustellen, wo überall im Softwaresystem ein beliebiger Bezeichner vorkommt. Dazu wird vom Hypertext-Editor in den zwei Listen für jeden Text (Klasse, Methode, etc.) angezeigt, wie oft dieser Bezeichner darin vorkommt. Außerdem wird der Bezeichner in den Texten mit einer anderen Schrift hervorgehoben und kann somit leicht erkannt werden.

Beispiel eines Wartungs-Szenarios

Anhand dieses Beispiels wollen wir zeigen, wie mit Hilfe des vorgestellten Hypertext-Editors das Verstehen von fremden Code erleichtert wird. Nehmen wir an, wir wollen wissen, wie eine bestimmte (in C++ geschriebene) Methode genau funktioniert.

Zu diesem Zweck wählen wir zunächst die Klasse der betreffenden Methode in der oberen Liste aus (siehe ② in Abb. 1). In der zweiten, unteren Liste werden dann sämtliche Methoden dieser Klasse angezeigt, und wir können unsere Auswahl treffen. Im Editor erscheint der Quellcode und in der Informationsbox sehen wir die Bezeichnung der Methode, die Datei, die sie enthält, sowie die Vererbungshierarchie ihrer Klasse. Wenn man die verwendete Klassenbibliothek kennt, dann kann diese Information alleine schon einiges über die Eigenschaften einer Klasse aussagen.

Wir können nun beispielsweise alle lokalen Bezeichner einer Methode (mit einer besonderen Schrift) hervorheben, das sind jene Bezeichner, die in dieser Methode definiert werden (Parameter eingeschlossen). Weiters interessiert uns vielleicht, welche Instanzvariablen der dazugehörigen Klasse in dieser Methode verwendet werden. Zu diesem Zweck verzweigen wir kurz zur Klasse (durch einfaches Anklicken in der oberen Liste) und bewirken dort ebenfalls ein Hervorheben aller lokalen Größen der Klasse, wozu unter anderem auch die Instanzvariablen gehören. Zur besseren Unterscheidung verwenden wir diesmal eine andere Schrift und kehren anschließend wieder zu unserer Methode zurück. Wir können nun auf einen Blick sowohl lokale Größen (in Abb. 2 fett dargestellt, Bezeichnerdefinitionen zusätzlich unterstrichen) als auch Instanzvariablen der Klasse (in Abb. 2 *outlined* dargestellt) erkennen.

```
HyperMark *IdentUseMark::GoDefinition()
{
    if (identDef) {
        int defPos, defLen;  //position and length of the definition
        identDef->GetTextPosition(defPos,defLen);
        identDef->SetLastLink(this);
        if (identDef->hText != hText)
            // make sure text of identDef is visible
            ((TextView*)(hText->GetView()))->SetText(identDef->hText);
        ((TextView*)(hText->GetView()))->
            SetSelection (defPos,defPos+defLen);
        ((TextView*)(hText->GetView()))->RevealSelection();
        identDef->lastLink= this;
        return identDef;
    } else
        NoteAlert.Show("Definition not found!");
}
```

Abb. 2: Informationen über eine Methode

Alle Namen, die in der Methode noch in Normalschrift angezeigt werden sind entweder Schlüsselwörter (auch die könnten wir in einer beliebigen Schrift anzeigen lassen), oder sind in einer der anderen Oberklassen oder sonstwo global in einer Datei definiert.

Es kann nun wichtig sein, einfach und schnell Informationen über diese Bezeichner zu kriegen. Wir können dazu entweder direkt zu den Definitionen der Bezeichner verzweigen, oder wichtige Informationen einblenden. Dies ist beim Verstehen von Code von besonderer Wichtigkeit. Wir erhalten so sehr einfach Name, Deklaration, Datei und Vererbung eines beliebigen Bezeichners. Außerdem wird — sofern vorhanden — eine kurze Beschreibung dieses Bezeichners eingeblendet.

ZUSAMMENFASSUNG

Die Implementierung des Hypertext-Editors erfolgte auf SUN Workstations in C++ [14] unter Verwendung des *Application Frameworks* ET++ ([15], [16]). Der Editor wird seit Mitte dieses Jahres sowohl an unserem Institiut bei Forschungsprojekten und für die Lehre als auch bei Partnern aus der Industrie eingesetzt.

Die Verwendung umfangreicher Klassen- oder Modulbibliotheken (z.B. Application Frameworks) gewinnt für die Entwicklung anspruchsvoller Softwaresysteme mehr und mehr an Bedeutung. Dem Verständnis solcher wiederverwendbarer Bausteine (sowohl deren Schnittstelle als auch manchmal deren Implementierung) kommt daher besondere Bedeutung zu. Daraus folgt, daß nicht nur bei der Wartung sondern auch schon bei der Entwicklung komplexer Software das Analysieren und Verstehen von existierendem Code zunehmend wichtiger wird. Das vorgestellte Werkzeug unterstützt durch sein Hypertext-Konzept das Auffinden relevanter Informationen sehr effektiv. Unsere Erfahrungen haben gezeigt, daß durch derartige Werkzeuge die Produktivität sowohl bei der Software-Wartung als auch bei der Entwicklung wesentlich verbessert werden kann. Es bleibt zu hoffen, daß eine ähnliche Unterstützung künftig in moderenen Programmierumgebungen integriert sein wird.

LITERATUR

[1] Bigelow J.: Hypertext and CASE, IEEE Software, pp. 23-27, March 1988.

[2] Cleveland L.: An Environment for Understanding Programs, Proc. of the 21st Annual Hawaii Int. Conf. on System Sciences, Vol. 2, 1988.

[3] Cleveland L.: A User Interface for an Environment to Support Program Understanding, Proceedings of the Conference on Software Maintenance, pp. 86-91, 1988.

[4] Conklin J.: Hypertext: An Introduction and Survey, Computer Vol. 20, No. 9, pp 17-41, Sept.87.

[5] Fletton N. T., Munro M.: Redocumenting Software Systems Using Hypertext Technology, Proceedings of the Conference on Software Maintenance, pp. 54-59, 1988.

[6] Gibson V. R., Senn J. A.: System Structure and Software Maintenance Performance, CACM, Vol. 32, No. 3, pp. 347-358, 1989.

[7] Landis L. D., et al.: Documentation in a Software Maintenance Environment, Proceedings of the Conference on Software Maintenance, pp. 66-73, 1988.

[8] Letovsky S., Soloway E.: Delocalized Plans and Program Comprehension, IEEE Software, pp. 41-49, May 1986.

[9] Parikh G., Zvegintzov N.: Tutorial on Software Maintenance, IEEE Computer Society, pp. 61-62, 1983.

[10] Parikh G.: Techniques of Program and System Maintenance, Second Edition, QED Information Sciences, Inc. 1988.

[11] Rajlich V., et al.: VIFOR: A Tool for Software Maintenance, Software—Practice and Experience, Vol. 20, No. 1, pp. 67-77, January 1990.

[12] Sametinger J.: A Tool for the Maintenance of C++ Programs, Proceedings of the Conference on Software Maintenance, San Diego, 1990.

[13] Shneiderman B., et al.: Display Strategies for Program Browsing: Concepts and Experiment, IEEE Software, pp. 7-15, May 1986.

[14] Stroustrup B.: The C++ Programming Language, Addison-Wesley, 1886.

[15] Weinand A., Gamma E., Marty R.: ET++ — An Object Oriented Application Framework in C++, OOPSLA '88, SIGPLAN Notices, Vol. 23, No. 11, pp. 46-57, 1988.

[16] Weinand A., Gamma E., Marty R.: Design and Implementation of ET++, a Seamless Object-Oriented Application Framework, Structured Programming, Vol. 10, No.2, Springer International 1989.

[17] Wirth N.: Programming in Modula-2, 3rd corrected edition, Springer-Verlag, New York, NY, 1985.

LinkWorks

- Connecting Application Information Together -

Joachim Schaper
Digital Equipment Corporation, CEC Karlsruhe
Vincenz-Prießnitz-Str.1, D-7500 Karlsruhe 1

Abstract

Most of today's on-line information is organized differently foreach application. Worse yet, most existing applications have only limited ways of incorporating information from outside into their own world. This isolates tools
from each other and makes cross-referencing difficult. It leads to 'islands'
of information and prevents the user from linking related information.

HyperInformation services (LinkWorks) is a framework which uses the
hypertext paradigm. The basic idea is to provide hypertext support for the
end user, so that he is able to build his own networks of information using
such daily applications as mail, calendar, cardfiler, and any other DECwindows applications which have been 'hyperized'. The following sections describe the architecture and its basic components. An example shows the
main operations used to build networks. A subsequent section gives a overview of how an existing application can easily be changed into a 'hyperized'
tool.

Introduction

The introduction of computers as a daily resource for creating, retrieving and manipulating information increases the problem of information overload foreseen by Bush more
than 40 years ago [Bush 45].

People have built huge databases and document repositories which they are unable to integrate with most current hypertext tools (e.g. Intermedia [IRIS 88] has his own set of
editors and an import facility to incorporate external data). With LinkWorks a user can,
with very little programming, create information networks which include existing data.

The LinkWorks approach is to separate the node and link information from the original
content and to work on surrogates that describe the content. This information is collected
into repositories that can be distributed in an enterprise-wide network.

The following sections introduce the terminology of the LinkWorks and give a short overview of the system architecture. A walk-through example demonstrates the current user interface to 'hyperized' applications.

Basic LinkWorks Objects

LinkWorks services are object-oriented, that is, data types are defined as objects that have internal state, and a set of manipulation functions which operate on the state. The following section will briefly describe each LinkWorks object type. The related object hierarchy provided by LinkWorks services is shown in Figure 1.

Surrogate

While the LinkWorks architecture uses the object-oriented model, many applications are built using a different model. To overcome this problem and to allow the incorporation of all existing information LinkWorks defines an object type called a surrogate. It is a description of some information in the application domain.

Connection

A connection is an object which represents a relationship between two surrogate objects. It has a set of properties including a relationship type and a Source and Target surrogate. A connection has a direction (Source --> Target), but can be navigated in either direction.

Network and composite network

A network is a collection of surrogates and the connections between them. It can be regarded as a graph consisting of nodes and links. A composite network is a collection of networks that are logically related but do not necessarily form a connected graph.

Step

LinkWorks also defines another object called a step, which records a navigational event during a navigation session. It includes properties such as a target surrogate, a connection and an operation that was performed on the information object associated with the target surrogate.

Path and composite path

A path is a sequence of steps. The path that belongs to an actual navigational session is called a trail and is automatically recorded by the system. Paths may be edited and used to document how e.g. a certain procedure in an administration is performed. A composite path is an ordered collection of paths that form a logical sequence of steps.

User Interface Elements

LinkWorks services also has a set of user interface elements which provide a standardized way of integrating LinkWorks functionality into any DECwindows application.

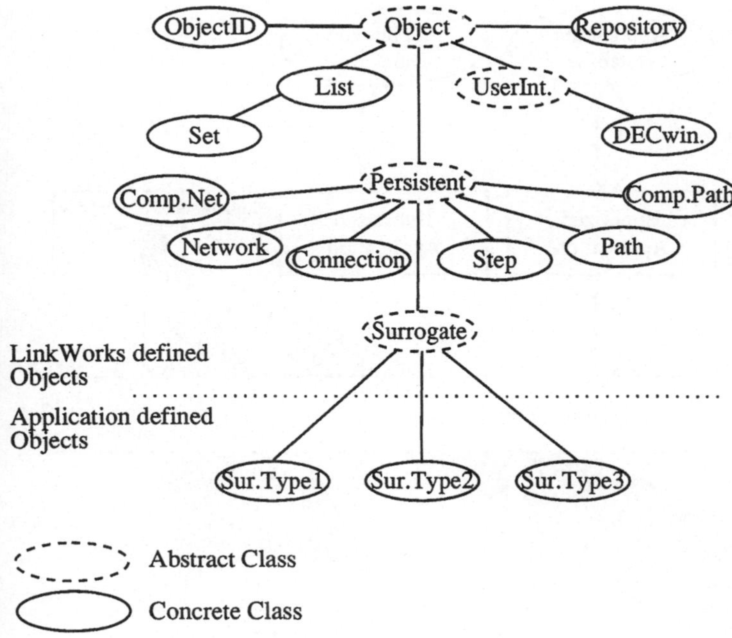

Figure 1: Object Hierarchy

All LinkWorks objects are stored in a LinkWorks repository which can be partitioned to any granularity. The same information objects can be referenced by multiple networks to give multiple views of the domain information.

Architecture

The LinkWorks architecture consists of three basic elements, LinkWorks services, hyperized applications, and the LinkWorks session manager [DEC 90a]. As shown in Figure 2 the LinkWorks service layer controls access to the LinkWorks repositories which keep the LinkWorks objects, like e.g. surrogates, networks, and paths, as persistent objects. Hyperized applications use these services to provide HyperInformation functionality to the user.

The application that organizes the set of repositories used to build networks and paths is called the LinkWorks session manager. It allows the user to create, maintain and select repositories as needed. The figure shows a set of 3 repositories, two of which are currently selected for use.

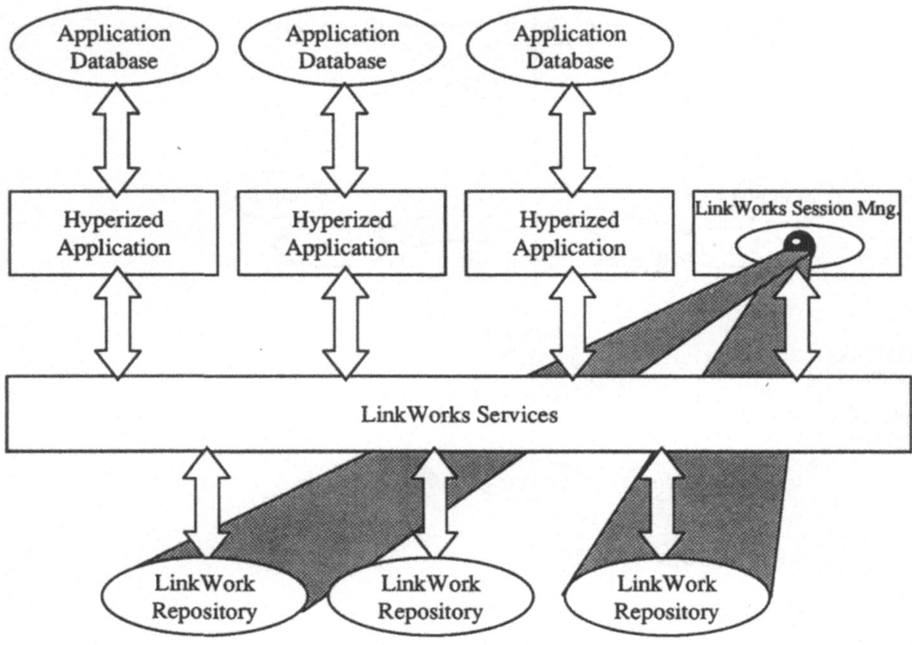

Figure 2: Architecture

User's view

This chapter describes an example usage of the LinkWorks system by a university researcher. The example does not cover the overall LinkWorks functionality, but gives an overview of the user interface and the working style in a 'hyperized' application world.

The applications used are CardFiler, which handles electronic index cards, Calendar, and Electronic-Mail. The following scenario shows how an author of a scientific article would use LinkWorks to interconnect his application data.

A researcher reads his daily mail and receives an announcement called "Call for Papers: Hypertext/Hypermedia 1991 in Graz". He decides to participate in the conference and makes a few entries in his electronic calendar recording the dates of the abstract and paper submissions. Then he connects the entry in mail with the calendar entry "send HT abstract to Graz".

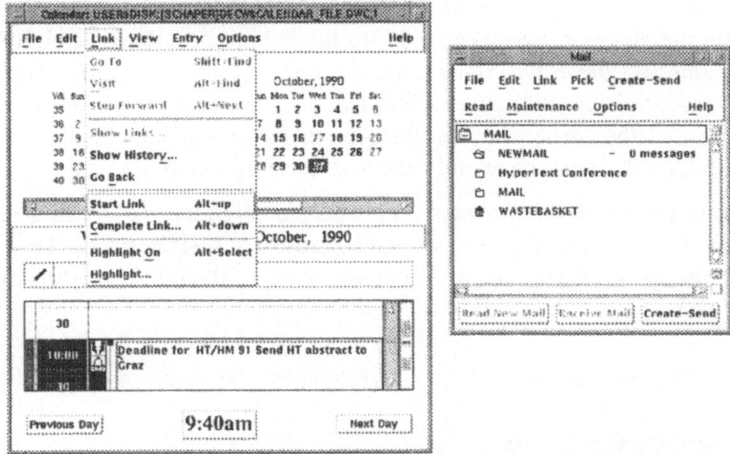

Figure 3: Set a start point of a link

To do this he selects the calendar entry and chooses <Start Link> from the link menu (see figure 3). Then he selects the associated mail entry and chooses <Complete Link> from the link menu in mail. Next, he fills in some link information such as the kind of link and a link description. Clicking the <OK> button creates the link and its surrogates (see figure 4).

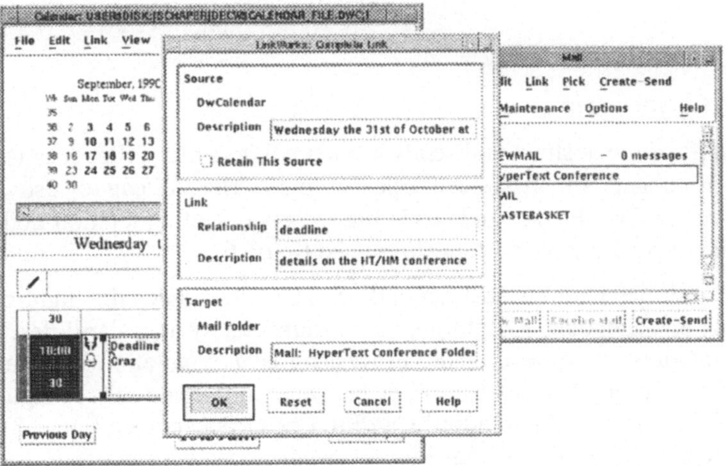

Figure 4: Complete the connection by defining the link attributes

The researcher also decides to reserve a couple of days (calendar entry: "write HT abstract") to write the abstract, two weeks before the submission date "send HT abstract to Graz". So he connects these two dates together choosing the same link type as before. Then he calls up CardFiler and makes a link from the calendar entry "write HT abstract" to the card title just the same way he did before. He stores this small network (linear chain) in his LinkWorks repository and continues reading his mails.

When the date to complete the abstract nears and his calendar gives him a reminder, the researcher selects the calendar entry and chooses <Visit> from the Link menu. LinkWorks starts up the CardFiler and focuses on the 'abstract' entry in the index list (see also figure 5).

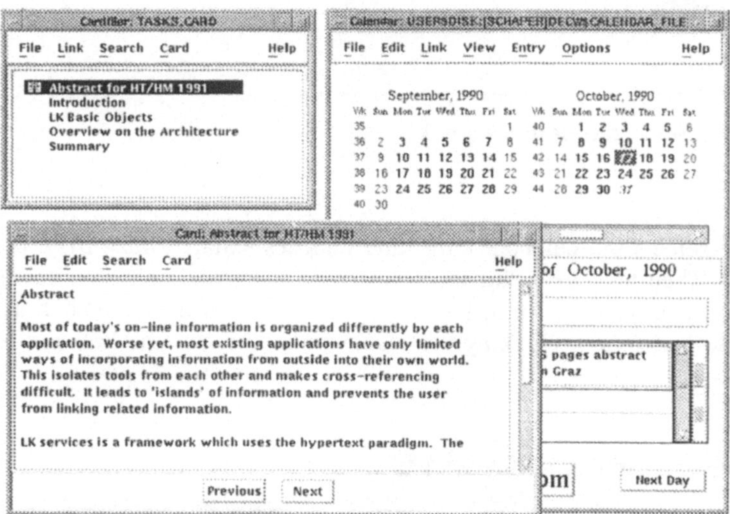

Figure 5: Navigiation step

He finishes the draft of the abstract and sends it, via mail, to some colleagues for review. A few days later he gets the first feedback per mail. His colleague also has used LinkWorks to annotate his abstract and sends him a network of annotation nodes which the researcher adds to his LinkWorks repository (see figure 6).

He starts up the CardFiler with his abstract outline. Then he enables the highlight option of the Link menu by choosing <Highlight on>. Immediately the CardFiler views all places where annotations have been made. Processing each annotation is a simple task. He just selects a source point in his CardFiler list (e.g. 'Introduction' see figure 7) and then chooses <Visit> and the 'Annotation' CardFiler box appears (see figure 8) containing the review information of his colleague.

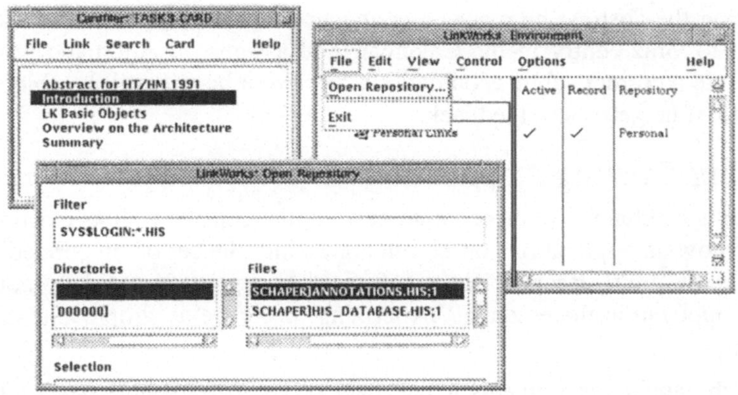

Figure 6: Open Repository "Annotations"

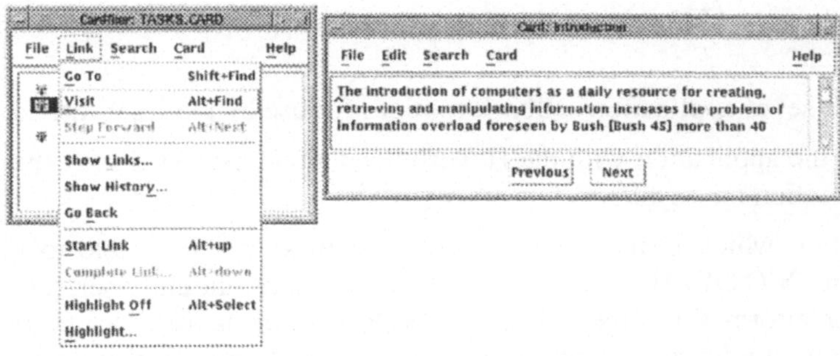

Figure 7: Follow the links ...

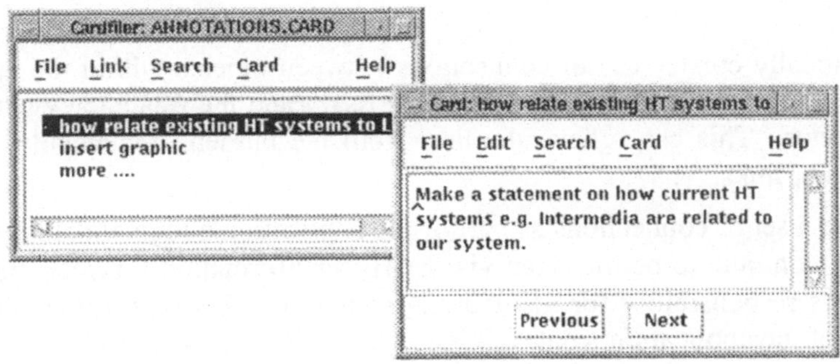

Figure 8: ... read the annotation

After updating the abstract he makes a connection between the document and the "send HT abstract to Graz" entry in the Calendar, and assigns an automatic print/send command to ensure a correct submission date. In any event he will still be able to change the abstract again if he gets more feedback.

Integrating Existing Applications

As LinkWorks is intended to incorporate new applications as well as existing ones, a description of how an application can be integrated into the set of 'hyperized' applications is outlined [DEC 90b]. Because HyperInformation support is typically not the primary focus of an application the essential 'hyperizing' tasks are as simple and straightforward as possible:

- Identify the application objects which may serve as the source or target of HyperInformation connections.

- Define HyperInformation-compatible descriptions for these objects

- Include the HyperInformation User Interface Elements (Connection Menu, etc.) in the application.

- Provide a set of application callback routines for use by the User Interface Elements.

- Register the application with the HyperInformation Services during the installation of the application on a system.

An application which is modified according to these rules, is able to participate in a DECwindow (MOTIF) HyperEnvironment. This means, an end user can establish links to any other information object in his HyperEnvironment. In order to achieve an even better integration with the HyperInformation technology an application programmer may add the following features:

- Augment the Connection Menu with application-specific linking or navigation features.

- Automatically create useful connections between objects within the application domain (e.g. automatic linkage between a glossary and the related keywords in a document editor). This can relieve the user from the burden of manually creating large numbers of links.

- Maintain a set of connections as part of the application's logical database. These connections continue to be managed via the HyperInformation services, but the application takes responsibility for maintaining consistency between these connections and the rest of the application's data.

- In cooperation with the HyperInformation User Interface, allow the navigation of connections represented within the application's private data. These application-private connections are logically merged with explicit HyperInformation connections.

The system components that will enable the application programmer to 'hyperize' new applications will consist of a HyperApplication Developer's toolkit. This toolkit will consist of an API (Application Programmer Interface in various programming languages), a special version of the HyperInformation Services, a HyperInformation Repository Manager for testing and debugging of the LinkWorks repositories and various other development and debugging aids.

Future possibilities

Natural extensions to the current set of HyperInformation facilities would be a graphical representation of paths and networks together with retrieval functionality, which allows the user to retrieve link information of his repositories (e.g. "Select all links which have link-type 'annotation'" or "Find all my links from Calendar to Mail").

Summary

The presented paper gave a brief overview of the work done within Digital to develop a set of services to provide HyperInformation technology for the user-community. The described services will allow the user to build and maintain his own HyperInformation networks by associating relevant information. The standard hypertext structures like networks of nodes and links are supplemented by the introduction of paths, trails and composite networks. The User interface is simple and comprehensive. Multiple, overlapping networks can provide different 'views' of information. The "Hyper Session Manager" allows the user to create, maintain and select networks. LinkWorks will be available in the same way an operating system or a window system is available to the user. It is thought to be a base service for daily work.

Acknowledge

I would like to express my special thanks to Doug Raynor and Ward Clark and all the other people from the LinkWorks project, who have done a great job in coming a step closer to Bush's vision, and who helped me to understand what the problems in HyperInformation are and how the solutions could be built.

Bibliography

[Bush 45]   As We May Think, Vannevar Bush, Atlantic Monthly, July 1945

[IRIS 88]   IRIS Intermedia - User's Guide Release 3.0, Brown University 1988

[DEC 90a]   DECwindows Hyperapplication User's Guide, DEC, April 1990

[DEC 90b]   DECwindows Hypperapplication Developer's Guide, DEC, April 1990

SmallCard - ein Hypertext-System zur Erstellung
rechnergestützter Lerneinheiten

L.Schmitz, K.Meusel

Fakultät für Informatik, UniBw München,
Werner-Heisenberg-Weg 39, 8014 Neubiberg

Abstract: Das Hypertext-System SmallCard ist in Smalltalk/V286 implementiert. Bei den für Hypertext -Systeme gebräuchlichen Werkzeugen wurde besonderer Wert auf drei graphische Browser gelegt: Durch das Anbieten mehrerer Sichten soll eine übersichtliche graphische Darstellung der Datenbasis entstehen. Hier wird SmallCard als Autorensystem verwendet. Sowohl beim Erstellen als auch beim Bearbeiten von Lerntexten können die Möglichkeiten und Werkzeuge von SmallCard nutzbringend eingesetzt werden.

Einleitung

Von den vielfältigen Einsatzmöglichkeiten von Hypertext und Hypermedia im Zusammenhang mit rechnerunterstütztem Unterricht handelt der Tagungsband [JoM 90]. [DeH 90] berichten über positive Erfahrungen bei Entwicklung und Einsatz eines Informatik- Einführungskurses in Form von HyperCard-Stapeln. Die verschiedenen Formen rechnergestützten Unterrichts und ihr lerntheoretischer Hintergrund werden ausführlich in [Sta 83] und [Jon 88] diskutiert. Das hier vorzustellende System *SmallCard* wurde u.a. mit dem Ziel entwickelt, zu bestehenden Lernprogrammen vom Typ 'Simulation und Modellierung' Begleitmaterialien in adäquater Form bereitzustellen.

Die Simulationsprogramme (eine AVL-Baum-Demo, ein interaktiver Compiler-Compiler [KrS 91] und Visualisierungen verschiedener Konstruktionen aus dem Bereich 'Formale Sprachen') sind in Smalltalk/V implementiert worden. Nach unseren Erfahrungen (vgl. [Sch 90]) bieten der objektorientierte Ansatz wegen der günstigen Wiederverwendungs- und Anpassungsmöglichkeiten und insbesondere die reich mit Datenstrukturen und Oberflächenelementen ausgestattete Klassenbibliothek von Smalltalk günstige Voraussetzungen für die Entwicklung interaktiver 'Lernwerkzeuge'. Da andererseits die Simulationsprogramme nur innerhalb der Smalltalk-Umgebung ausführbar sind, ergab sich der Wunsch, Smalltalk mit Hypertextkomponenten zu ergänzen anstatt ein eigenständiges Hypertext- oder Autorensystem zu verwenden.

Das Hypertext-System SmallCard

SmallCard wurde als Prototyp eines Hypertext-Systems im Rahmen einer Diplomarbeit entwickelt. SmallCard ist in Smalltalk/V286 [Dig 88] implementiert und auf IBM PC's lauffähig.

In Anlehnung an Apple's HyperCard™ wird mit Karten und Karten-Stapeln gearbeitet. Den Schwerpunkt des Systems bildet ein umfangreiches (mit der Maus zu bedienendes) Instrumentarium zur Navigationshilfe und Lösung des 'getting lost'-Problems: Graphische Browser für unterschiedliche Sichten (lokal, global), ein detailliertes Protokoll der Sitzung (das ebenso wie ein 'Notizzettel für Leser' abgespeichert und später wieder neu geladen werden kann) und ein Werkzeug zum Arbeiten mit Lesezeichen zu unterschiedlichen Thematiken unterstützen das Navigieren ebenso wie Mechanismen zum Ausnutzen impliziter Links. In einer Autorensystem-Komponente wird eine leicht verständliche Sprache angeboten, mit deren Hilfe Knöpfe 'programmiert' werden können. Dadurch sind auch rudimentäre Erweiterungen der Funktionalität des Hypertext-Systems möglich.

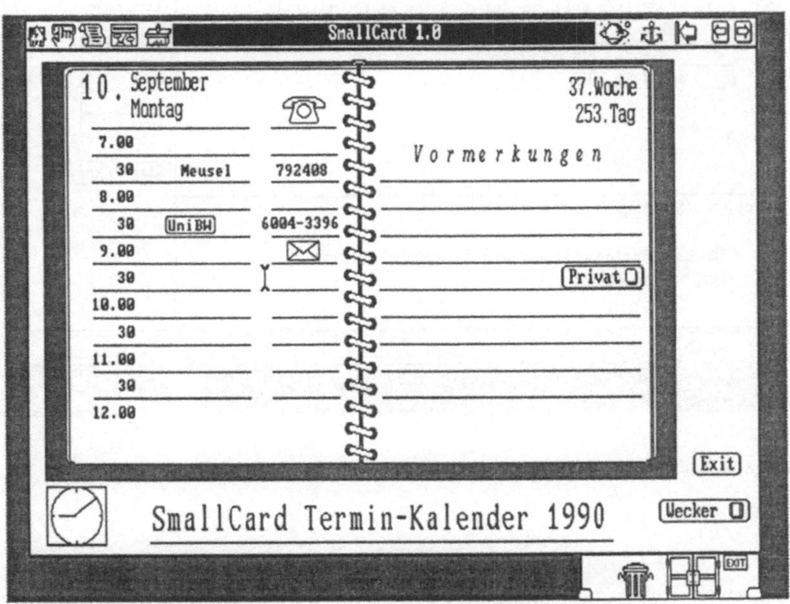

Abb. 1 Das Front-End von SmallCard. Graphik (Kalender) und Text (Termine ...) sind ineinander verschmolzen und bilden zusammen mit den Icons am oberen und am unteren Rand des Fensters die Benutzeroberfläche.

Im Unterschied zu HyperCard sind bei SmallCard die Link-Quellen in den fließenden Text einbettet. Um die Quellen beim Bearbeiten des Textes korrekt mitzuversetzen, wurde der Smalltalk Text-Editor entsprechend abgeändert. Ebenso wurden die Operationen zum Selektieren, Kopieren und Löschen von Text geändert.

Der Einsatz von SmallCard als Autorensystem und ein damit erstellter Lerntext

Grundgedanke von Autorensystemen: Ein Autor erstellt Lerntexte und vermittelt seinen 'Schülern' (den Lernenden) über den Rechner Lerninhalte. Durch diesen Übergang zum 'Unterricht am Rechner' (CUU, 'computerunterstützter Unterricht') entstehen eine Reihe von Vorteilen (vgl. [NiV 83]): Flexible Arbeitszeit, individuelles Arbeitstempo, vielfältige Lerninhalte, individuelle Lernstrategien, Präsentationsmöglichkeiten (Graphik, Geräusche, Animation),

Schulungssoftware über billiges Medium (wenn die Lerntexte auf Diskette ausgetauscht werden; [MaT 90] diskutiert die Kosten bei einer Verbreitung über Rechnernetze).

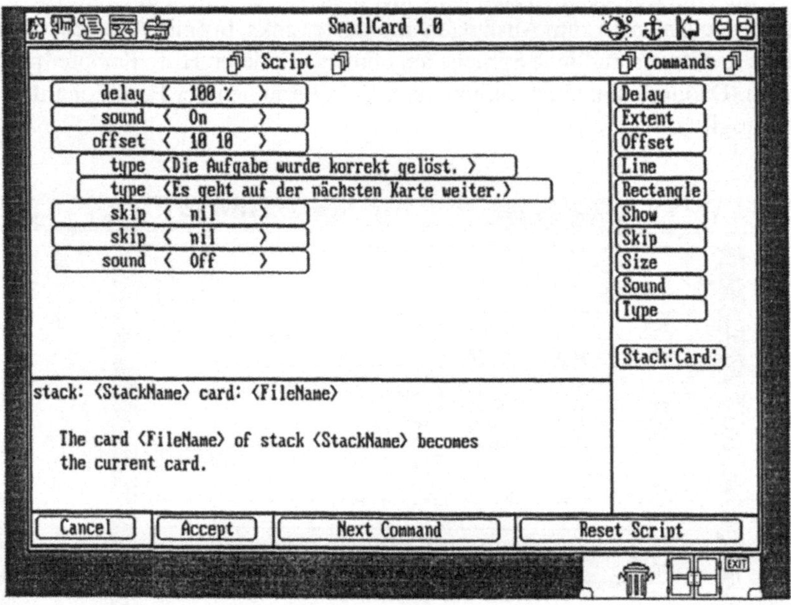

Abb. 2 Die Autoren-Komponente von SmallCard

Es kommen zwei Kreise von Benutzern mit dem System in Berührung: Der Autor und die Lernenden. Der Autor ist Spezialist auf seinem Fachgebiet. Ein Verständnis der Implementierungssprache des Hypertext-Systems kann aber nur selten vorausgesetzt werden. Damit der Autor die Lerninhalte trotzdem zweckmäßig vorbereiten kann, ist es sinnvoll, eine einfache Sprache zum Erweitern der Funktionalität anzubieten, die direkt in das Hypertext-System integriert ist. Abb. 2 zeigt einige von SmallCard angebotene, leicht verständliche Sprachkonstrukte. Durch Mausklick kann der Autor ein einfaches 'Script' zusammenstellen.

Abb. 3 zeigt einen Lerntext, der durch den Einsatz von SmallCard als Autorensystem erstellt wurde. Der Computer wird hierbei in dreierlei Weise als ' *simuliertes Labor, als Vorführ- und individuelles Lerngerät*' genutzt [NiV 83], da ein programmiertes, benutzergesteuertes Modell des behandelten Gegenstandes in den Lerntext eingebunden ist. Das Paket ist dann für Präsentation und Selbststudium gleichermaßen geeignet.

Im Lerntext wird sowohl die Theorie der AVL-Bäume (eine besonders eingängige Darstellung findet man in [NiH 86]) als auch die Realisierung der Datenstruktur 'AVL-Baum' in Smalltalk besprochen. Die Theorie wurde in Kapitel unterteilt (modularisiert; siehe [Con 87]: *'Das Modularisieren von Ideen'*) wie 'Einfügen in einen AVL-Baum' oder 'Löschen in einem AVL-Baum'. Für jedes Kapitel wurde vom Autor ein eigener Kartenstapel eingerichtet. Zu jedem Kapitel existiert eine Folie (Graphik) mit der Darstellung mehrerer Phasen eines Baumes, die dieser während eines Einfüge- oder Löschvorganges durchläuft. Diese Folien wurden vom Autor gezeichnet (FreeDrawing-Tool von Smalltalk/V268) und den einzelnen Kapiteln im Lerntext (Kartenstapeln) zugeordnet. Anschließend wurden diese Folien (ebenfalls vom Autor) auf den einzelnen Karten eines Stapels so beschriftet, daß die Theorie der AVL-Bäume anhand dieser Illustrationen Schritt für Schritt gelernt werden kann.

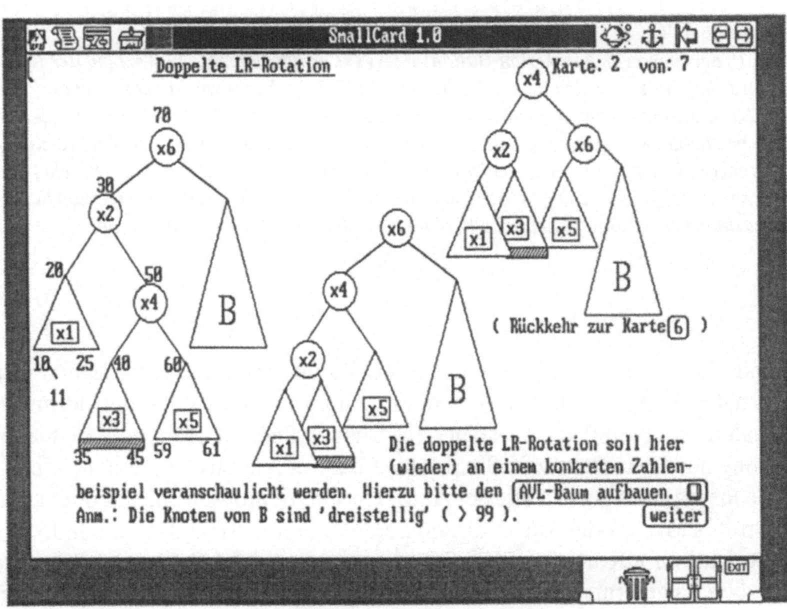

Abb. 3 Ein Lerntext,der durch den Einsatz von SmallCard als Autorensystem erstellt wurde. Lerninhalt: Die Theorie der AVL-Bäume und die Realisierung von AVL-Bäumen in Smalltalk/V.

An einigen Stellen wurden vom Autor Querverweise (Links) in andere Kapitel angebracht. Er regt den Lernenden hierdurch dazu an, Sachverhalte aus unterschiedlichen Blickwinkeln zu sehen und miteinander zu vergleichen. Ebenso wurden Links zu Karten mit vertiefenden Beispielen und zum Wiederholen von Teilen einer Lektion eingerichtet (ebenfalls Anregungen des Autors, die vom Lernenden aber nicht unbedingt eingehalten werden müssen).

Um den Unterricht lebendig zu gestalten, wurden vom Autor noch Beispiele vorbereitet, die Operationen auf konkreten AVL-Bäumen als Abfolge von Bildern aufzeigen. Der Lernende kann per Tastendruck jeweils das nächste Bild auf den Bildschirm holen (vergleichbar einem Dia-Vortrag).

Das hierfür nötige Programm (Implementierung der Datenstruktur 'AVL-Baum', graphische Darstellung eines Baumes etc.) konnte der Autor fertig übernehmen (in Smalltalk/V realisiert). Durch das Programmieren von Knöpfen (Action-Buttons, siehe Abb. 4) mußte der Autor nur noch dafür sorgen, daß der Lernende die Beispiele nach eigenem Geschmack (d.h. beispielsweise auch mehrmals hintereinander) ablaufen lassen kann.

<table>
<tr>
<td>

Baum := AvlTree new.

Baum add: 2.
Baum add: 1.
Baum add: 7.

Baum showAdd: 10.

</td>
<td>

Baum showAdd: 10.

</td>
<td>

Baum := AvlTree new.

</td>
</tr>
</table>

Abb. 4 Das Programmieren von Action-Buttons im AVL-Lerntext. Der Quell-Text auf der linken Seite: Zunächst wird der Urzustand des Beispieles hergestellt (2-1-7). Dann wird genau einmal das Einfügen des Wertes 10 veranschaulicht (showAdd: 10). Die gleiche Abfolge von Bildern kann also mehrmals hintereinander betrachtet werden. Der Quell-Text in der Mitte: In den Baum wird der Wert 10 eingefügt, ohne den Zustand des Baumes vorher zu verändern. Ein mehrmaliges Ausführen dieses Befehls führt zu unterschiedlichen Abfolgen von Bildern (der Baum wächst). Der Quell-Text auf der rechten Seite: Es wird der Grundzustand (leerer Baum) hergestellt, ohne eine Abfolge von Bildern anzustoßen.

Der Lernende kann nun die Theorie der AVL-Bäume am Rechner erlernen (Karten lesen, Links verfolgen, per Knopfdruck 'Dia-Vorträge' steuern). Er kann wichtige Definitionen und Ergebnisse festhalten (im NotePad) und später ausdrucken.Durch Bearbeiten des Kapitels über die Implementierung der AVL-Bäume in Smalltalk/V kann er jedoch auch lernen, wie er eigene Beispiele ablaufen lassen kann (genau wie der Autor Knöpfe zu programmieren oder aber kleine Programmstücke mit 'show it' oder 'do it' zu evaluieren). Aus der Sicht des Lernenden sind folgende Hypertext-Aspekte beim Bearbeiten eines Lerntextes interessant: Orientierung im Lerntext (wo), wieviel wurde bereits gelernt, was kann nachhause getragen werden (Notizen, Historie, Lernpfade), etc. Diese Punkte werden durch die Werkzeuge von SmallCard abgedeckt (siehe Abb. 5).

Beim Lernstoff 'AVL-Bäume' ist ein Verständnis der Vorgänge beim Einfügen/Löschen wichtiger als auswendig gelernte Definitionen etc. (vgl. [NiV 83]). Durch das Programmieren von SmallCard-Knöpfen besteht die Möglichkeit, Aufgaben anzubieten, die bei jedem Besuch der Lernkarte neu generiert werden und somit nicht auswendig gelernt werden können.

Die graphischen Browser von SmallCard

In vielen Hypertext-Systemen werden graphische Browser als Navigations- und Orientierungs-Werkzeuge angeboten. [Nie 90] diskutiert die Nützlichkeit von graphischen Browsern. Ein häufiges Gegenargument ist die mögliche Verwirrung des Lesers durch unübersichtliche, überfrachtete graphische Darstellungen, die vom System erstellt wurden. Die Erfahrungen mit von Hand gezeichneten Übersichten in [Nie 90] zeigen jedoch auch, daß graphische Darstellungen eines geeigneten Ausschnitts der Hypertext-Datenbasis sehr hilfreich für den Leser sind. Dies wurde allerdings durch eine nicht akzeptable Belastung des Autors erkauft. Hier wird nun ein möglicher Ausweg geschildert.

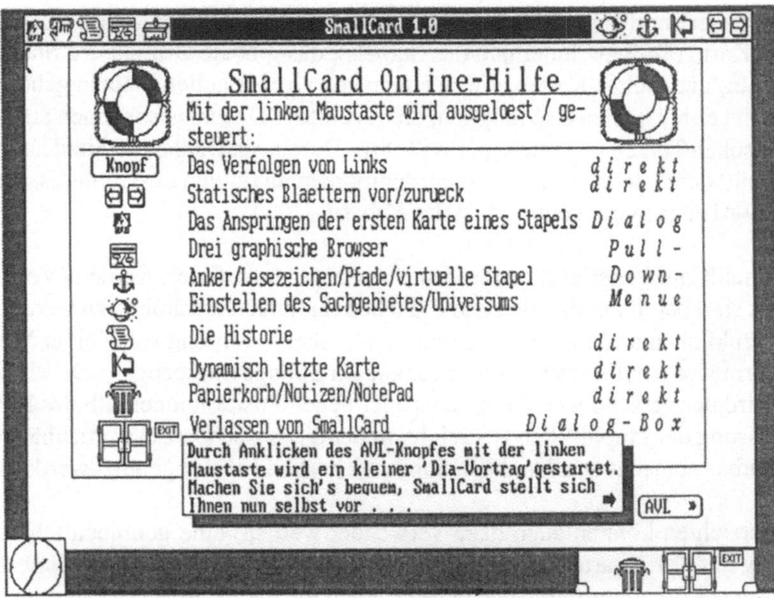

Abb. 5 *Die Werkzeuge von SmallCard.*

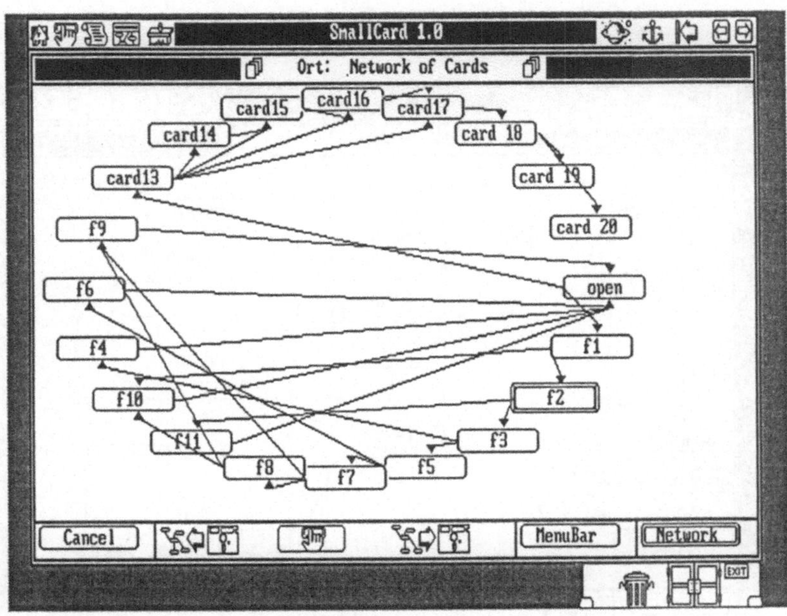

Abb. 6 *Der graphische Browser von SmallCard für die lokale Sicht (Karten und Links innerhalb eines Stapels). Das Layout wurde von SmallCard generiert.*

SmallCard bietet graphische Browser für drei unterschiedliche Sichten an: Das lokale Umfeld der aktuellen Karte (Teilnetz innerhalb des Stapels), das globale Umfeld des Stapels (Links zu anderen Stapeln) und Anker-Karten, die zu einem von vier virtuellen Stapeln gehören (durch virtuelle Stapel ist es beispielsweise möglich, die Hypertext-Datenbasis in einen statischen und in einen dynamischen Teil zu trennen; vgl. [MaT 90]). Durch Auswahl einer Sicht kann das System einen Ausschnitt der Datenbasis bestimmen, der momentan für den Leser interessant ist. Für dieses Teilnetz wird ein Layout generiert (siehe Abb. 6).

Das von SmallCard generierte Layout kann von Hand modifiziert werden (Vorteil: Die Knoten und Links sind bereits vorhanden und brauchen nur noch verschoben zu werden). Hierzu ist ein Knopf anzuklicken und mit der Maus zu verschieben. Während solch einer Wanderung auf dem Bildschirm werden die am Knopf eingehängten Stränge mitgezogen . Durch einen zweiten Mausklick wird der verschobene Knopf an seiner neuen Position innerhalb des Rahmens abgelegt. Eine Fassung der graphischen Übersicht, in der die logischen Zusammenhänge durch Verschieben sichtbar gemacht wurden, kann abgespeichert und später genutzt werden.

Diese Übersichten können auch dazu verwendet werden, eine gebräuchliche Lernstrategie beim Umgang mit Karteikarten zu verwirklichen [Sch 89]. Man wird dort oft die Karten mit dem bereits gelernten Stoff aussortieren und beiseite legen. In SmallCard werden hierzu bei Übersichten die in der Historie enthaltenen Karten besonders gekennzeichnet. Schließlich hat der Leser auch die Möglichkeit, diese Kennung zu löschen, um dadurch Karten in den Lernprozeß neu einzubringen.

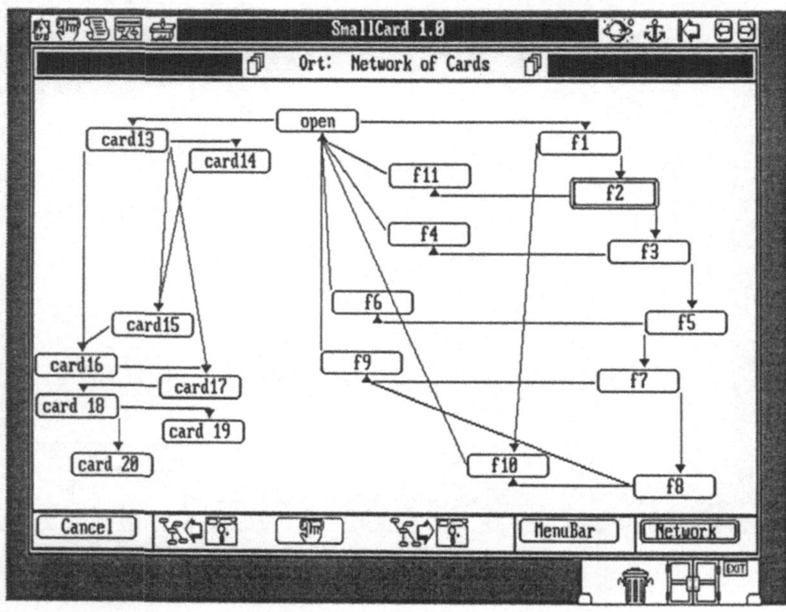

Abb.7 Der graphische Browser von SmallCard für die lokale Sicht (Karten und Links innerhalb eines Stapels). Das Layout wurde von Hand modifiziert.

Literatur:

[Con 87]   Conklin, Jeff: *'Hypertext: An Introduction and Survey'*, IEEE Computer, September 1987, S.17-41.

[Dig 88]   Digitalk Inc.: Smalltalk/V286 - Tutorial and ProgrammingHandbook. Digitalk Inc., Los Angeles 1988.

[DeH 90]   Decker, R.; Hirshfield, S.: *'A Survey Course in Computer Science Using HyperCard'*, ACM SIG-CSE Bulletin, 1990, S. 229 - 239.

[JoM 90]   Jonassen, David H.; Mandl, Heinz: *'Designing Hypermedia for Learning'*, Nato ASI Series, Springer Verlag, 1990.

[Jon 88]   Jonassen, David H. (ed): *'Instructional Designs for Microcomputer Courseware'*, Lawrence Erlbaum Ass., Hillsdale N.J., 1988.

[KrS 91]   Kröger, Jörg; Schmitz, Lothar: *'IPG-An Interactive Parser Generator'*, Kurzvortrag und Systemvorführung auf der STACS'91.

[KüS 89]   Küffner, H.; Seidel, C.(ed): *'Computerlernen und Autorensysteme'*, Verlag für Angewandte Psychologie, Stuttgart, 1989.

[MaT 90]   Maurer, Hermann; Tomek, Ivan: *'Hypermedia in Teleteaching'*, Computers in Education, IFIP 1990.

[Nie 90]   Nielsen, Jakob: *'Hypertext and Hypermedia'*,
Academic Press, 1990.

[NiH 86]   Nievergelt, Jörg; Hinrichs, Klaus: *'Programmierung und Datenstrukturen'*, Springer, 1986.

[NiV 83]   Nievergelt, Jörg; Ventura, Andrea: *'Die Gestaltung interaktiver Programme'*, Teubner, Stuttgart 1983.

[Sch 89]   Schulmeister, Rolf: *'Autorensysteme und Alternativen (Teil lll) - Die Philosophie des Blätterns'*, Computer Anwendungen Universität Karlsruhe, Oktober 1989, S.35-43.

[Sch 90]   Schmitz, Lothar: *'Zur Gestaltung und Implementierung einiger rechnergestützter Lernwerkzeuge'*, Bericht Nr. 9008 der Fakultät für Informatik, UniBw München, 1990.

[Sta 83]   State of the Art Report 11:4 on Computer-based learning, Pergamon Infotech Ltd., Maidenhead, Berksh., England, 1983.

Konzepte zur Versionenverwaltung
für die Hyperdokumenterstellung
in einer hypertextbasierten Publikationsumgebung

Anja Weber

GMD / Institut für Integrierte Publikations– und Informationssysteme (IPSI)
Postfach 104326, D – 6100 Darmstadt, e–mail: weber@darmstadt.gmd.dbp.de

Volker Schoepf
TU Berlin, Institut für Angewandte Informatik, FG AEDV
Franklinstr. 28/29, D – 1000 Berlin 10

1   Einleitung

Die Verwaltung von Versionen ist ein Kernproblem beim Erstellen von Hyperdokumenten [8]. Versionenunterstützung soll Autoren von Hyperdokumenten ermöglichen, einerseits die Geschichte der Änderungen an ihren Hyperdokumenten festzuhalten und andererseits gleichzeitig mehrere Alternativen von Dokumentkonfigurationen zu verwalten.

Erste Hypertextsysteme mit Versionenverwaltung haben als Anwendungsgebiet überwiegend den Software Engineering Bereich. So wurden zum Beispiel die Basismechanismen zur Versionenverwaltung der HAM [2] erfolgreich für zwei Hypertextsysteme genutzt: Neptune [4] für generelle Designaufgaben und Dynamic-Design [1] für die Verwaltung von C–Programmen. DIF (Document Integration Facility) [5] verwaltet Konfigurationen von Software und zugehöriger Dokumentation.

Die Analyse der Benutzeranforderungen an die Versionenverwaltung von Dokumenten beim elektronischen Publizieren zeigt, daß sich der Umgang mit Versionen besonders während der kreativen Aufgaben des Publizierens (Planen, Schreiben, Redigieren und Erstellen von Layouts) vom Umgang mit Versionen in anderen Disziplinen unterscheidet. So kommt beispielsweise der Mehrfach– und Wiedernutzung von Materialien nicht nur zwischen den Versionen eines Dokumentes, sondern auch zwischen den Versionen verschiedener Dokumente eine besondere Bedeutung zu. Die genauen Anforderungen an eine Versionenverwaltung variieren außerdem für spezifische Publikationsaufgaben. Ziel bei der Entwicklung von Versionenunterstützung im Publikationsprozeß muß es daher sein, Modellierungskonzepte allgemeinerer Art zu definieren, auf deren Basis konkrete Publikationswerkzeuge aufgabenspezifische Modellierungen bereitstellen können.

Diese Arbeit definiert zunächst den Begriff der Publikationsumgebung und erläutert das Publizieren von Hyperdokumenten in einer hypertextbasierten Publikationsumgebung (Abschnitt 2). Ausgehend vom typischen Publikationsprozeß stellen wir die Anforderungen an eine Versionenunterstützung beim elektronischen Publizieren von Hyperdokumenten vor (Abschnitt 3). Im Hauptteil dieser Arbeit (Abschnitt 4) entwickeln wir Konzepte zur Versionenverwaltung, die den gestellten Anforderungen Rechnung tragen. Am Beispiel der Erstellung eines konkreten Hyperdokuments demonstrieren wir die Versionenverwaltung mittels der vorgestellten Konzepte (Abschnitt 5). Abschließend ziehen wir Vergleiche mit anderen Ansätzen zur Versionenverwaltung von Hypertexten (Abschnitt 6).

2   *Erstellen von Hyperdokumenten in einer Publikationsumgebung*

Eine Publikationsumgebung besteht aus mehreren Werkzeugen, die die aufgabenspezifische Manipulation der in einem Datenpool gehaltenen Publikationsdaten ermöglichen. Der Datenpool umfaßt Planungs– und Durchführungsunterlagen, Material– und Inhaltssammlungen, die in Form von Text, Graphik oder Video vorliegen können und bei der Erstellung des Dokumentes herangezogen werden, und natürlich das zu erstellende Dokument selbst. Auf diesen Daten operieren Publikationswerkzeuge, wie zum Beispiel Autorenumgebungen, Redaktionssysteme und Systeme zur Gestaltung von Layouts. Ein Beispiel für eine hypertextbasierte Autorenumgebung ist das Autorensystem SEPIA [15], [7], das Autoren durch das Activity Space Konzept einen adäquaten Umgang mit diesen Daten ermöglicht.

Dabei gehen wir von einer Zwei–Schichten–Architektur aus: Ein anwendungsunabhängiges Hypertextbasissystem übernimmt die zentrale Datenhaltung und bietet grundlegende Modellierungs– und Manipulationskonzepte für die Publikationsdaten an (erstmals vorgeschlagen in der HAM [2] und aufgegriffen in HyperBase [13]). Auf diesem Hypertextbasissystem werden über eine Anwendungsschnittstelle konkrete Hypertextanwendungen realisiert. Alle Arten multimedialer Hyperdokumente, die mit der Erstellung des eigentlichen Produktes in Verbindung stehen und den Publikationsprozeß begleiten, können vernetzt in einem System abgelegt und verwaltet und durch aufgabenspezifische Publikationswerkzeuge manipuliert werden.

Für die Diskussion der Versionenkontrollmechanismen setzen wir auf das allgemeine Hypertextmodell von HyperBase [13] auf. HyperBase unterstützt das Anlegen, Manipulieren und Speichern von Hypertextobjekten: Knoten, Links und zusammengesetzte Objekte (Composites). Jedes Hypertextobjekt ist durch einen Objektidentifikator (Surrogat), der nicht vom Benutzer modifiziert werden kann, eindeutig identifiziert. Jedes Objekt trägt die systemverwalteten Attribute 'Autor' und 'Erzeugungsdatum'. Darüberhinaus kann eine beliebig große Menge applikationsdefinierter Attribute zu einem Objekt definiert werden.

Ein Knoten hat insbesondere einen Inhalt. Er kann als reserviertes Attribut aufgefaßt werden, zu dem zu jeder Zeit eine Wertangabe vorliegen muß.

Ein Link enthält genau zwei Referenzen zu beliebigen anderen Objekten, seinem Start– und Zielobjekt. Folglich sind auch Links auf Links modellierbar. Ein Objekt mit einem solchen Identifikator muß existieren, d.h. die referentielle Integrität wird von HyperBase garantiert.

Ein zusammengesetztes Objekt läßt sich als Multimenge über andere Objekte auffassen und besteht neben Attributen aus Referenzen zu den enthaltenen Komponenten. Über einen lokal eindeutigen Zusatzidentifikator werden mehrfache Vorkommen von Referenzen eindeutig identifiziert. Durch die optionale Angabe des lokalen Identifikators eines Vaterobjekts und eines linken Bruderobjekts können Ordnungen bis hin zu Wäldern (Menge von Bäumen) auf der Objektmenge induziert werden. Die referenzierte Objektmenge ist in sich abgeschlossen in dem Sinne, daß ein zusammengesetztes Objekt zu jeder Referenz auf einen Link ebenfalls eine Referenz auf das Start– und Zielobjekt des Links enthält. Objekte können von verschiedenen zusammengesetzten Objekten referenziert werden (gemeinsam genutzte Objekte).

Auf dieses allgemeine Hypertextmodell setzen konkrete Applikationen ihr anwendungsbezogenes Hyperdokumentmodell und Anwendungssystem auf. Für die Modellierung von Publikationsanwendungen auf HyperBase ist hervorzuheben, daß zusammengesetzte Objekte sowohl für die Modellierung von Arbeitsbereichen oder Kontexten (z.B. Datenraum eines Activity Spaces), als auch für die Modellierung hierarchisch strukturierter Dokumente geeignet sind: Die Inhalte eines Dokumentes werden in Knoten, nicht–lineare Beziehungen durch Links und hierarchische Beziehungen zwischen den Inhalten durch zusammengesetzte Objekte repräsentiert. Da zusammengesetzte Objekte zum Modellieren hierarchischer Strukturen von Dokumenten eingesetzt werden, bezeichnen wir Knoten auch als atomare Knoten und zusammengesetzte Objekte als zusammengesetzte Knoten. Der Begriff Knoten wird – wo ohne Mißverständnisse möglich – auch als Sammelbegriff für beide Arten von Hypertextobjekten benutzt.

3   Anforderungen an die Versionenverwaltung beim Publizieren

Publizieren kann als kooperatives, inkrementelles Erstellen von Dokumenten charakterisiert werden. Die Versionenverwaltung sieht sich dabei Anforderungen gegenüber, die nach Art der Publikation variieren können. Die erste Anforderung richtet sich deshalb daran, die Versionenverwaltung eines Hypertextbasissystems in gewissem Maße flexibel zu halten, um unterschiedliche Versionierungsstrategien für Anwendungen realisieren zu können (Anforderung 1). Ähnlich wie in anderen Anwendungsbereichen läßt sich jedoch eine Menge allgemeiner und konkreter Anforderungen identifizieren, die für die breite Menge von Publikationswerkzeugen gleichermaßen anwendbar und adaptierbar ist. Diese Anforderungen (Anforderungen 2 –7) müssen durch entsprechende Versionenkonzepte besonders unterstützt werden.

1. Selektive Versionierung: Die Identifikation derjenigen Zustände eines Hyperdokument(enteil)s, die im Rahmen der Versionenverwaltung verfügbar sein müssen, soll bedarfsgerecht von der Applikation und nicht von Automatismen geregelt werden. Die Unterstützung muß nicht im Sinne des Festhaltens aller Zustände des Pools verlaufsorientiert sein (cf. "versioning of the overall database" [14]), vielmehr müssen die Zustände einzelner Hyperdokumente (Zwischenergebnisse) und wichtige Aspekte ihrer Entstehung (z.B. Zeitpunkt, Weiterentwicklung und Wiedernutzung von (Zwischen)ergebnissen) benutzer– und aufgabengerecht festgehalten werden (cf. "versioning at the node/link level" [14]).

2. Integration versionierter und nicht–versionierter Objekte: Unter Zuhilfenahme von Materialsammlungen, z.B. hypertextbasierter Zettelkästen und (Teile) früherer Hyperdokumente, entstehen schritt– bzw. phasenweise (vgl. [9]) unterschiedlichste Konfigurationen eines Hyperdokumentes: Teile eines Dokumentes können schon endgültig vorliegen, während andere sich noch in der Entwicklung befinden oder noch gar nicht bearbeitet sind. Versionierte und nicht–versionierte Dokumente und Dokumententeile müssen deshalb in einem System verwaltet werden können.

3. Dokumentation des Entwicklungsverlaufs: Fassungen von Hyperdokument(teil)en werden nicht nur weiterentwickelt, sondern dienen oft als Ausgangspunkt für neue Dokument(teil)e. Die kreativen Aufgaben des Schreibens, Gestaltens, und Redigierens erfordern das vergleichende Zurückgreifen auf frühere Entwürfe und Fassungen – auch anderer Publikationen, die als Ausgangspunkt für die gerade bearbeitete Publikation dienen – um Entscheidungen über das weitere Vorgehen zu fällen (open–ended design task, vgl. [11]). Darum muß die Wiedernutzung und Weiterentwicklung von Dokumentbestandteilen – auch über Dokumentgrenzen hinweg – aufgezeichnet werden.

4. Dokumentation der Entwicklung zusammengesetzter Knoten: Das Erstellen eines Hyperdokumentes kann in einem atomaren (Text–)Knoten beginnen, der sich im Laufe der Arbeiten zu einem komplexen Hyperdokument entwickelt. Dieses Hyperdokument ist durch einen zusammengesetzten Knoten präsentiert. Ein zusammengesetzter Knoten kann durch Verschmelzen seiner Komponenten (z.B. Konkatenation zweier

Abschnitte) auch zu einem Knoten zurückgebildet werden. Die Entwicklung von atomaren Knoten zu zusammengesetzten Knoten und umgekehrt muß deshalb festgehalten werden können.

5. Konfiguration von Versionen zusammengesetzter Knoten: Eine häufige Operation bei der Erstellung eines komplex strukturierten Hyperdokumentes besteht darin, eine Reihe von alten Versionen von Dokumententeilen durch neue Versionen zu ersetzen. Das korrekte Erzeugen aller Referenzen von zusammengesetzten Objekten oder Links auf die neuen Versionen und die rekursiv anfallende Erzeugung von Referenzen auf die neu erzeugten Objekte ist eine mühsame, unübersichtliche Aufgabe. Darum muß die Konfiguration von Hyperdokumenten aus Versionen von Teildokumenten unterstützt werden.

6. Änder– und Konservierbarkeit von Zuständen: Einerseits treten oftmals nur kleine Änderungen an Dokumenten auf, zum Beispiel die Korrektur von Rechtschreibfehlern, die nicht zu neuen Versionen, sondern nur zu Änderung des Dokuments führen sollen. Andererseits müssen schützenswerte Zustände von Dokumenten vor unbeabsichtigtem Verändern bewahrt werden können.

7. Hinweise auf Zustandsänderungen: Wenn sich Veränderungen referenzierter Objekte ergeben, stellt sich die Frage, inwieweit referenzierende Objekte betroffen sind. Wird zum Beispiel eine neue Version eines Knotens angelegt, muß entschieden werden, ob referenzierende Links auf die neue oder alte Version zeigen. Die automatische Generierung von Versionen referenzierender Objekte ist im allgemeinen nicht sinnvoll, da auf diese Weise eine Unzahl von Zuständen entstehen, die von der Applikation nicht intendiert sind. (vgl. auch Diskussion in [10] und Anforderung 1). Da die Referenzstruktur in einem Hyperdokument aber sehr unübersichtlich werden kann, müssen Hinweise auf Zustandsänderungen die Korrektheitsüberprüfung von Referenzen unterstützen.

Neben diesen Anforderungen existieren weitere Kernanforderungen etwa bezüglich der Dokumentation von Varianten, der Unterstützung für die aufgabenorientierte Versionenverwaltung, oder der Behandlung von Kommentaren als Auslöser für neue Versionen von Dokumenten, die wir im Rahmen dieses Beitrags nicht behandeln können.

4   *Konzepte zur Versionenverwaltung*

Dieser Abschnitt stellt Modellierungskonzepte für Versionen vor, die die obigen Anforderungen erfüllen. Wir führen die Konzepte als eine Erweiterung des Hypertextbasismodells durch neue Objekttypen und Operatio-

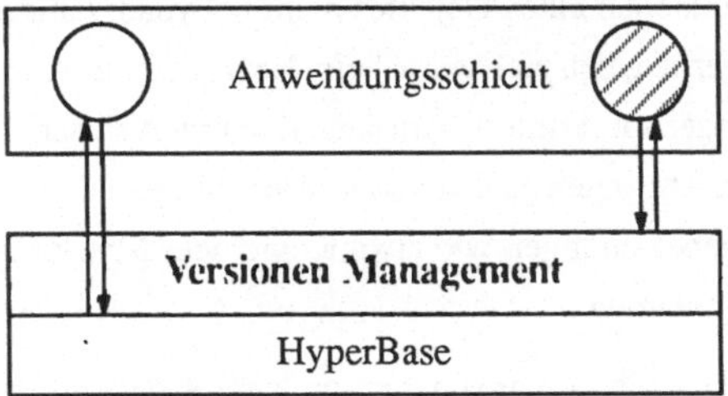

Abbildung 1: Schichtenarchitektur von Anwendungen mit und ohne Versionenunterstützung

nen ein. Diese Konzepte können auf dem Hypertextbasismodell implementiert und den Anwendungsprogrammen als Programmierschnittstelle zur Verfügung gestellt werden (s. Abbildung 1).

Das Konzept der *Single State Objects* (Snobs) modelliert Hypertextobjekte, die nur in einem Zustand vorkommen (nicht versionierte Hypertextobjekte), *Multi State Objects* (Mobs) repräsentieren Hypertextobjekte, die in mehreren Zuständen vorkommen (versionierte Hypertextobjekte) (Anforderung 2). Die in einen Mob enthaltenen Zustände eines versionierten Hypertextobjekts bezeichnen wir als Versionen. Alle drei Konzepte sind als Spezialisierung von Hypertextobjekten aufzufassen, d.h. sie tragen die Attribute Autor und Erzeugungsdatum. Transformationen von einem Snob in einen Mob und umgekehrt von einer Version eines Mobs in einen Snob erlauben den nahtlosen Übergang zwischen Versionieren und Nicht–Versionieren eines Dokument(bestandteil)s.

Snobs tragen die Zustandsinformation eines nicht versionierten Hypertextobjekts (Snob–Knoten, Snob–Link, Snob–Composite), *Versionen* repräsentieren die Zustände eines versionierten Hyperdokumentes (Versionen–Knoten, Versionen–Link, Versionen–Composite). Der Zustand eines Knotens definiert sich durch seinen Inhalt und seine Attribute, der Zustand eines Links durch seine Attribute und die Zustände von Start- und Zielobjekt, der Zustand eines zusammengesetzten Objekts durch seine Attribute, Ordnungsinformation und die Zustände der referenzierten Objekte.

Ein *Mob* aggregiert die Versionen eines versionierten Hyperdokumentes zu einer identifizierbaren Einheit. Für einen Mob können Attribute definiert werden, die zur Beschreibung der zustandsunabhängigen Aspekte des Hypertextobjekts dienen. Um einerseits die Entwicklung von Links, Knoten und zusammengesetzten Objekten, sowie andererseits die Entwicklung von atomaren Knoten zu zusammengesetzten Knoten und umgekehrt dokumentieren zu können (Anforderung 4), unterscheiden wir zwei Sorten von Mobs: Ein Mob enthält entweder Knoten und/oder zusammengesetzte Objekte (*Knoten–Mob*), oder nur Links (*Link–Mob*).

Ein Snob– oder Versionen–Link, ein zusammengesetzter Snob oder eine zusammengesetzte Version kann Referenzen auf beliebige andere Versionen und Snobs enthalten. Insbesondere können zusammengesetzte Snobs und Versionen gleichzeitig verschiedene Versionen ein und desselben Mobs referenzieren, so daß mehrere Versionen eines Hyperdokument(enteil)s zu Vergleichszwecken oder als Alternativvorschläge in ein Hyperdokument eingebunden werden können.

Die *Deszendenz* ist eine gerichtete, azyklische, nicht versionierbare Beziehung, die Nachfolge– und Wiedernutzungsaspekte über Dokument(teil)grenzen hinweg ausdrückt. (Anforderung 3). Der Nachfolger referenziert den Vorgänger, aus dem er hervorgegangen ist. Die Deszendenz ist auf Versionen und Snobs definiert. Man beachte, daß die Versionen eines Mobs nicht notwendig in einem zusammenhängenden Deszendenzgraphen angeordnet sein müssen, da Versionen eines Objektes nicht notwendig aus anderen, vorhergehenden Zuständen des Objektes abgeleitet werden, beispielsweise beim Entwurf einer Alternative einer veranschaulichenden Graphik. Die Beziehung trägt vordefinierte Attribute (Datum, Autoreninformation, log_message) und kann mit applikationsdefinierten Attributen qualifiziert werden. Insbesondere können durch Benennung verschiedene semantische Nachfolgebeziehungen wie etwa Kopie oder Mischung modelliert werden. Die Deszendenz kann als Link aufgefaßt werden.

Da Links sich als Links und Knoten sich als atomare oder zusamengesetzte Knoten weiterentwickeln, unterscheiden wir zwei Typen der Deszendenz: Die *Link–Deszendenz* dokumentiert die Weiterentwicklung von Links, die *Knoten–Deszendenz* die Weiterentwicklung von atomaren und/oder zusammengesetzten Knoten. Bei der Erzeugung von Versionen oder Snobs als Kopien von Versionen oder Snobs wird systemgesteuert ein Deszendenz–Link etabliert. Deszendenz–Links können aber auch von der Applikation angelegt und gelöscht werden. Wird ein Snob oder eine Version gelöscht, so werden seine Deszendenz–Links gelöscht, und die Vorgänger mit den Nachfolgern durch neue Deszendenz–Links verbunden.

Um Hypertextobjekte in ihrem aktuellen Zustand irreversibel zu konservieren, können Snobs oder Versionen durch eine Operation 'freeze' *explizit eingefroren* werden. Damit der eingefrorene Zustand eines Links oder eines zusammengesetzten Objekts durch Verändern der referenzierten Objekte nicht zerstört werden kann, werden die referenzierten Objekte *implizit* durch das explizit eingefrorene Objekt mit *eingefroren*. Explizit oder implizit eingefrorene Hypertextobjekte können gelesen, aber nicht verändert werden. Sie können nur dann gelöscht werden, wenn sie nicht implizit durch andere Objekte eingefroren sind, da sonst konservierte Zustände zerstört würden.

Wird ein eingefrorener Link oder ein eingefrorenes zusammengesetztes Objekt gelöscht, so bleiben die von ihnen referenzierten Objekte nur dann weiterhin eingefroren, wenn sie durch andere Objekte implizt, oder ohnehin explizit eingefroren sind. Das 'Auftauen' von implizit eingefrorenen Hypertextobjekten erfolgt, da durch das Löschen des referenzierenden Objekts, das zu einem impliziten Einfrieren des Hypertextobjekts geführt hat, das Interesse am Konservieren des Hypertextobjekts erlischt.

Nicht jede Änderung eines Hyperdokumentes soll zu einen neuen Zustand der manipulierten Objekte führen. Deshalb geschieht die Erzeugung von Snobs, Mobs und Versionen applikationsinitiiert (Anforderung 1). Versionen werden explizit durch die Applikation angelegt und lassen sich modifizieren, bis sie eventuell eingefroren werden (Anforderung 6). Zu jeder Zeit können neue Versionen oder Snobs von ihnen abgeleitet werden.

Ein *Konfigurationsoperator* unterstützt das Generieren neuer Versionen zusammengesetzter Objekte aus einer Menge neuer Versionen von Teilobjekten (Anforderung 5). Für jedes Unterobjekt, das eine zu ersetzende Version referenziert, wird rekursiv eine neue Version angelegt, die die Ersetzung referenziert.

Notizen unterstützen das gezielte Propagieren von Änderungen (Anforderung 7). Eine *Notiz* ist ein systemerzeugter Knoten, der von der Applikation weder gelöscht noch modifiziert werden kann. Sie enthält Hinweise auf die Art der Änderung (z.B. Update, Hinzufügen eines Links auf einen Knoten oder Anlegen einer neuen Version eines Hypertextobjekts) und wenn nötig die Information, die zur Herstellung der ursprünglichen Situation erforderlich ist (z.B. Deltainformation bei dem Update eines Textknotens, oder Referenzen auf ursprüngliche Knoten bei dem Update eines Links). *Notifikationen,* dies sind spezielle, systemerzeugte Links, verbinden die Objekte, die informiert werden wollen, mit den Notizen. Die Applikation löscht Notifikationen, wenn die Notiz für ein Objekt nicht mehr benötigt wird. Notizen werden automatisch vom System gelöscht, wenn die letzte auf sie verweisende Notifikation gelöscht wird.

Die Erzeugung von Notizen kann von der Applikation kontrolliert werden, indem Referenzen von Links oder zusammengesetzten Objekten als *sensitiv* für bestimmte Änderungen der referenzierten Objekte definiert werden. Die Sensitivitätsbeschreibung gibt an, über welche Änderungen des referenzierten Objekts das referenzierende Objekt informiert werden soll. Bei einer entsprechenden Änderung wird vom System die geeignete Notiz erzeugt und über eine Notifikation das referenzierende Objekt mit der Notiz verbunden.

Die Konzepte lassen sich als eine objekt–orientierte Erweiterung des Klassenschemas von HyperBase um zusätzliche Unterklassen und Operationen auffassen (s. Abbildung 2). Zentrale Erweiterungen sind die Einfrierbarkeit von Knoten, Links und zusammengesetzten Objekten, sowie die Sensitivität von Referenzen in Links und zusammengesetzten Objekten. Diese Funktionalität kann durch direkte Spezialisierungen

Ext_Knoten, Ext_Link, und Ext_Composite modelliert werden, die die Basistypen um Operationen wie etwa 'freeze' oder 'make_sensitive' erweitern.

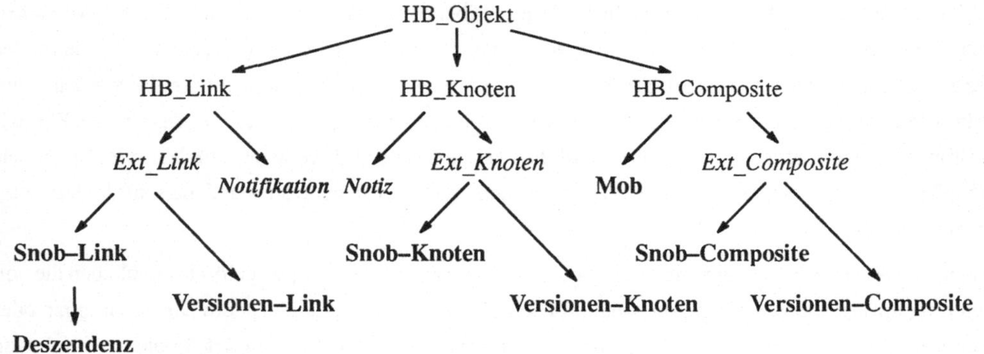

Abbildung 2: Versionenorientierte Erweiterung der HyperBase Objekttypen

5 Ein Anwendungsbeispiel: ipsiLex

Ein Beispiel für das Erstellen eines Hyperdokuments in einer Publikationsumgebung ist das Hypermedia–Fachlexikon ipsiLex. Ziel dieser Publikation ist es, die Kommunikation beim interdisziplinären Arbeiten zu verbessern. Durch die Dokumentation von Fachbegriffen soll das Verständnis zwischen den Disziplinen erhöht und oft vorkommenden Mißverständnissen durch unterschiedlichen Gebrauch gleichlautender Wörter (Homographen) oder gleichen Gebrauch unterschiedlicher Wörter (Synonyme) vorgebeugt werden.

Das Anwendungsszenario stellt sich wie folgt dar: Mitarbeiter verschiedener wissenschaftlicher Disziplinen aus verschiedenen Abteilungen dokumentieren ihre Terminologie in Lexika. Jeder Mitarbeiter arbeitet in einem privaten Lexikon, in dem er seine persönliche Begriffsbildung festhalten, aber auch Begriffe mit Kollegen gemeinsam nutzen, entwickeln und diskutieren kann. Zu gegebenen Zeitpunkten wird aus den aktuellen Arbeitslexika von einem Team von Redakteuren eine abteilungsübergreifende Fassung des Lexikons (genannt ipsiLex) hergestellt.

Ein Lexikon kann (aus lexikalischer Sicht stark vereinfacht) wie folgt beschrieben werden: Es besteht aus einer Menge von lexikalischen Einträgen oder sogenannten Lexikonartikeln, die je einen Begriff definieren. Jeder Lexikonartikel kann den Erfordernissen der Erläuterung entsprechend strukturiert und gestaltet werden. Lexikalische Informationen, wie Verweise auf Synonyme, auf Ober– und Unterbegriffe, und aus Lexikonartikeln zu anderen Einträgen, oder Kommentare sind wesentliche Bestandteile des Lexikons.

Ein Lexikon läßt sich durch das im vorherigen Abschnitt vorgestellte Hypertextmodell wie folgt realisieren: Das Lexikon, Lexikonartikel und ihre Strukturierungseinheiten (z.B. Abschnitte und Absätze) werden als zusammengesetzte Objekte (zusammengesetzte Knoten) bzw. als Knoten (atomare Knoten) repräsentiert. Links modellieren die angesprochenen lexikalischen Informationen und Verweise, z.B. einen symmetrischen Verweis zwischen Einträgen ('siehe ebenfalls'–Verweis), oder den gerichteten Verweis aus einem Lexikonartikel auf einen anderen Lexikonartikel.

Zur Erläuterung der Versionenkonzepte betrachten wir eine typische Arbeitssituation bei der Lexikonerstellung. Ein Autor möchte einen Begriff in einem Lexikonartikel beschreiben. Er beginnt mit einer Ideensammlung, die einmal überarbeitet wird, bevor er sich dazu entschließt, den Artikel in eine Definition und ein erläuterndes Beispiel zu gliedern. Die Definition enthält neben Materialien aus der Ideensammlung eine Kopie eines Absatzes aus einem anderen Lexikonartikel.

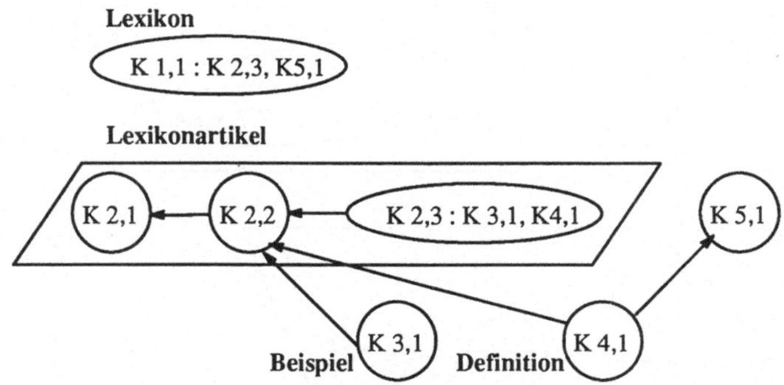

Abbildung 3: Deszendenz zwischen Dokumentteilen

Abbildung 3 zeigt die Modellierung des Lexikons als zusammengesetzten Knoten (K 1,1), der die letzte Version des Lexikonartikels enthält. Atomare Knoten sind als Kreise, zusammengesetzte Knoten und Links durch Ellipsen, Mobs durch Parallelogramme, und Deszendenz–Links durch Pfeile dargestellt. Knoten werden mit K, Links mit L, gefolgt von zwei Nummern, angegeben. Die erste Nummer identifiziert das Objekt, die zweite Nummer den Zustand des Objekts. Referenzen in zusammengesetzten Knoten und Links sind direkt hinter der Objektidentifikation angegeben.

Objekte, die nur in einem Zustand existieren, sind als Snobs repräsentiert, d.h. sie gehören zu keinem Mob. Die Versionen des Lexikonartikels sind in einem Mob zusammengefaßt. Ein Deszendenz–Link zeigt die Entwicklung des Lexikonartikels von einer Ideensammlung (K 2,1) zu einem strukturierten Dokument (K 2,3). Sowohl das Beispiel (K 3,1) als auch die Definition (K 4,1) übernehmen Inhalte aus der Ideensammlung (K 2,2). Der Text stützt sich auf Informationen eines anderen Eintrages (K 5,1). Deszendenz–Links dokumentieren diese Wiedernutzungs– und Weiterentwicklungsaspekte über Dokumentgrenzen hinweg.

Die Ausarbeitung des Beispiels (K 3,1) führt in mehreren Schritten und über mehrere Versuche zum Ziel. Nur zufriedenstellende Fassungen des Beispiels führen zu neuen Versionen des Artikels (s. Abbildung 4a). Der Mob faßt die Versionen der Definition in eine identifizierbare Einheit zusammen. Deszendenz–Links kennzeichnen die Entwicklung der Versionen der Definition (Entwicklungsgeschichte). Projektionen auf Versionen mit bestimmmten Eigenschaften zeigen weitere Aspekte der Geschichte der Versionen, zum Beispiel die zeitliche Reihenfolge über den Zeitstempel (Entstehungsgeschichte), oder die Benutzung in zusammengesetzten Objekten (Nutzungsgeschichte) bezüglich Weiterentwicklung, oder zeitlicher Nachfolge (s. Abbildung 4b).

Ein Arbeitsschritt besteht in der Einbindung des neuen Lexikonartikels in andere Artikel. Aus der Definition setzt der Autor einen gerichteten Querverweis (L 1,1) auf einen anderen Eintrag (K 6,1) und von einem weiteren Eintrag (K 7,1) einen bidirektionalen Verweis (L 2,1) ('siehe ebenfalls'–Verweis) auf den neuen Artikel. In einem weiteren Arbeitsschritt kommt es zu einer Überarbeitung und einer neuen Version der Definition, die in das Lexikon aufgenommen werden muß. Über den Konfigurationsoperator wird die alte Version der

Definition (K 4,1) durch die neue Version der Definition (K 4,2) ersetzt, indem rekursiv neue Versionen aller betroffenen referenzierenden Objekte erzeugt werden (s. Abbildung 5).

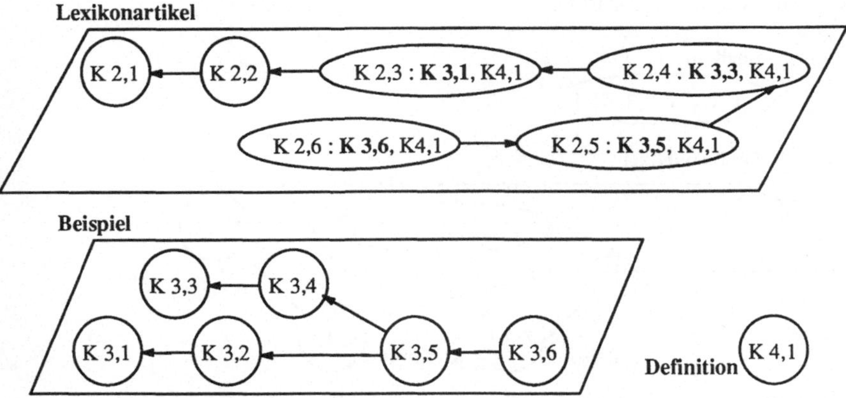

Abbildung 4a: Entwicklung des Beispiel–Knotens und des Lexikonartikels

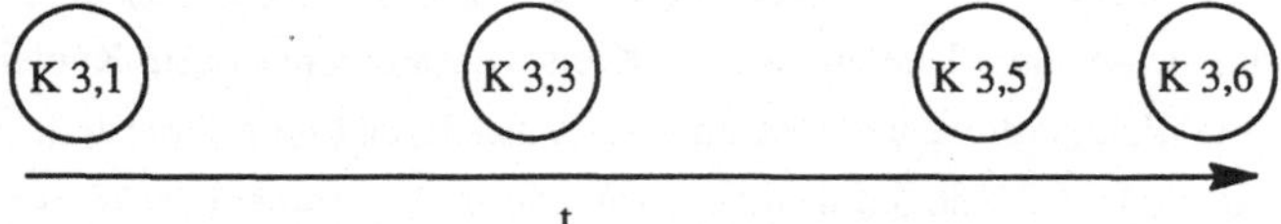

Abbildung 4b: Zeitliche Entstehung des Beispiel–Knotens, eingeschränkt durch die Nutzung im Lexikonartikel

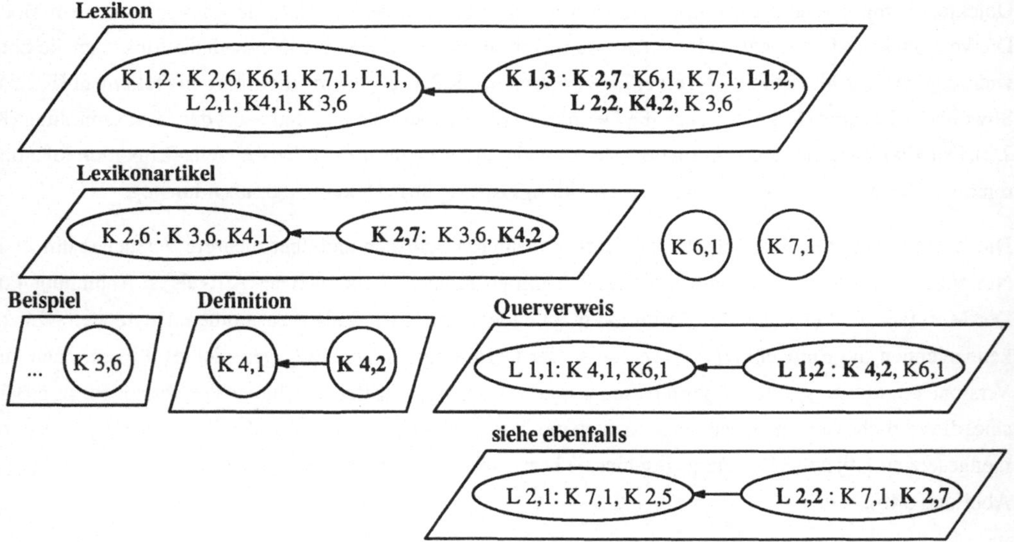

Abbildung 5: Konfiguration einer neuen Version des Lexikons durch Ersetzung von K 4,1 durch **K 4,2**

Lexikonartikel können von mehreren Autoren weiterentwickelt werden. Möchte ein Redakteur aus den verschiedenen Fassungen unterschiedlicher Autoren eine neue Version des abteilungsübergreifenden Lexikons erstellen, kann er beliebige Versionen ein und desselben Objekts in einem neuen zusammengesetzten Objekt als Arbeitslexikon zusammenstellen. Durch Einfrieren dieses Arbeitslexikons wird verhindert, daß die referenzierten Versionen durch nachfolgende Arbeiten anderer Personen zerstört werden. Jede Weiterentwicklung muß nun in einer neuen Versionen festgehalten werden.

Erachtet der Lektor die Version eines Begriffs als noch nicht ausreichend, kann er einen versionensensitiven Link auf die Version setzen. Wann immer eine neue Version des Begriffs erzeugt wird, etwa durch einen Autor, der unabhängig vom Lekor an seinem Artikel weiterarbeitet, wird der Arbeitslexikonknoten durch eine Notiz informiert. Diese kann vom Lekor genutzt werden, um gezielt neue Zustände von Knoten zu untersuchen und sie eventuell in sein Arbeitslexikon aufzunehmen.

6 Vergleich mit anderen Ansätzen

Die Versionenverwaltung der HAM [2], [4] beruht auf Zeitstempeln und sogenannten Kontexten. Es findet keine Verwaltung der Versionen eines Knotens oder Links in einer identifizierbaren Einheit statt. Insbesondere werden unabhängige oder alternative Entwicklungen eines Hypertextobjekts nicht in einem expliziten, unzusammenhängendem Deszendenzgraphen aufgezeichnet. Vielmehr wird die Versionengeschichte indirekt durch die Verwendung von Versionen in Kontexten festgehalten und ist somit über Kontexte verstreut. Alternative Entwicklungszustände eines Knotens müssen über Kontexte modelliert werden, so daß bei vielen alternativen Ansätzen auch entsprechend viele Kontexte angelegt werden müssen.

Ein Kontext hält die zeitliche Abfolge von Versionen in einem Versionenfaden fest. Versionen, die nicht voneinander abstammen, erscheinen als Nachfolger im Versionengraphen. Die Abstammung von Versionen muß indirekt über 'back pointer' erschlossen werden, die zu den Ursprungsversionen zeigen. Die Abstammung von Versionen anderer Objekte oder die Entwicklung von Knoten zu komplex strukturierten Hyperdokumenten, etwa durch Aufzeichnung der Entwicklung von Knoten zu Kontexten, kann nicht festgehalten werden.

Die HAM erzeugt neue Versionen von Objekten bei jedem Update eines Objekts. Für Knoten kann unterschieden werden, ob Änderungen des Inhalts zu neuen Versionen führen sollen (archived–node), oder nie in Versionen festgehalten werden (non–archived node). Nicht gewünschte Versionen können durch die Applikation gelöscht werden. Unser Ansatz erlaubt dagegen die flexible Realisierung verschiedenster Strategien zur Versionierung. Durch den Update von Versionen kann in unserem Modell das Aufzeichnen unerwünschter Versionen von vornherein vermieden werden. Notizen unterstützen die Information über Updates von Versionen.

Prevelakis [12] hat die Anregung von Halasz [8] aufgegriffen, die Konzepte von PIE [6] zur Versionenverwaltung für die Smalltalkprogrammierung auf Hypertext zu übertragen. Bei diesem Ansatz steht die Modellierung zusammenhängender Änderungen von Knoten und Links im Vordergrund. Ein Overlay (in PIE ein Layer) faßt die Änderungen an einer Menge von Knoten und Links als Delta (–Operationen) in eine identifizierbare Einheit zusammen. Ein Zustand des Netzwerkes wird durch eine Folge nacheinander angewendeter Overlays in einer Perspective (in PIE Context) beschrieben. Overlays und Perspectives werden explizit vom Benutzer angelegt und bewirken somit die Erzeugung von Versionen der Einzelobjekte. Die Dokumentation alternativer Entwicklungen von Knoten erfordert das Anlegen neuer Overlays, so daß es auch bei diesem Ansatz zu einer Explosion von Overlays kommt.

Unser hier vorgestelltes Modell enthält keine Konzepte zur Erfassung zusammenhängender Änderungen. Solche Mechanismen können jedoch durch das Anwendungsprogramm unter Verwendung zusammengesetzter Objekte realisiert werden.

7 Zusammenfassung und Ausblick

Ein wesentliches Merkmal unseres Ansatzes ist die zentrale Verwaltung der Versionengeschichte für jedes Hypertextobjekt, inklusive Links, in einem Mob. Dabei trennen wir die Abstammung der Versionen (Deszendenz) klar von ihrer zeitlichen Entstehungsfolge (Zeitstempel). Die Geschichte der Verwendung dieser Versionen in zusammengesetzten Objekten wird über die Versionen der zusammengesetzten Objekte getrennt verwaltet. Das Anlegen von Versionen geschieht applikationsinitiiert. Notizen unterstützen die gezielte Information über Änderungen in Hyperdokumenten. Ein Konfigurationsoperator unterstützt das Erzeugen von Versionen zusammengesetzter Objekte aus neuen Versionen von Komponenten.

Die Deszendenz kann nicht nur innerhalb eines Mobs, sondern auch über Objektgrenzen hinweg dokumentiert werden. Ein neuer, publikationsspezifischer Aspekt ist dabei die Erzeugung unzusammenhängender Versionengraphen für ein Hypertextobjekt. Dieses ist von besonderer Bedeutung, da das Entwerfen von alternativen Dokumentenversionen auch ad hoc, ohne Wiedernutzung anderer Materialien, oder durch parallele Weiterentwicklung beim kooperativen Arbeiten geschieht.

Die vorgestellten Konzepte wurden in laufende Arbeiten des europäischen Projektes Telepublishing (RACE–Programm, Projekt 1075) eingebracht [16] und werden am IPSI und der TU Berlin fortentwickelt. Insbesondere werden die Konzepte auf HyperBase [13] implementiert und in einer Programmierschnittstelle Hypertextapplikationen zur Verfügung gestellt. Als erste Anwendung wird ein Hypertexteditor realisiert, der das benutzerinitiierte Anlegen von Hypertextknoten und –links ermöglicht. Nachfolgend sollen konkrete Hypertextanwendungen mit vordefinierter Versionenunterstützung realisiert werden, bei denen zum Beispiel am Ende jeder Sitzung alle manipulierten Objekte in eingefrorenen Versionen festgehalten werden.

Der geplante Hypertexteditor erlaubt den interaktiven, explorativen Zugriff auf frühere Versionen von Textknoten, Verweisstrukturen, oder zusammengesetzte Knoten. Er unterstützt die Navigation auf Versionen von Objekten bezüglich der Entstehungs–, Entwicklungs– und Nutzungsgeschichte (vgl. Abbildung 4). Neben dem navigatorischen Zugriff auf Versionen sollte aber auch der Zugriff auf Versionen über deklarative Beschreibungen von Zuständen möglich sein. Hierbei spielt die Beschreibung von Versionen durch Beziehungen zu anderen Objekten eine bedeutende Rolle. Es soll eine Anfragesprache für versionierten Hypertext entwickelt werden.

Die hier vorgestellten Konzepte umfassen keine direkte Unterstützung für zusammenhängende Änderungen. In Ergänzung der hier vorgestellten Konzepte entwickeln wir deshalb ein Konzept zur aufgabenorientierten Verwaltung von Versionen. Die Übertragung von Konzepten zur Job-Control auf hypertextbasierte Publikationsumgebungen, wie sie von Clemm für eine Software-Engineering Umgebung definiert wurden [3], scheint für die Unterstützung zusammenhängender Änderungen bei der Hyperdokumenterstellung ein vielversprechender Ansatz zu sein.

Danksagung

Wir danken unseren Kollegen Jörg Haake, Christoph Hüser, Kurt Sandkuhl, Kai Schwidder, Jörg Littmann-Stöwer, Helge Schütt und Manfred Thüring für ihre anregenden Kommentare.

Literatur

[1]   James Bigelow & Victor Riley. Manipulating Source Code in DynamicDesign. In *Hypertext '87 papers*, pages 397–408, Chapel Hill, N.C., November 1987.

[2]   Brad Campbell & Joseph M. Goodman. HAM: A General Purpose Hypertext Abstract Machine. *Communications of the ACM*, 31(7):856–861, July 1988.

[3]   Geoffrey M. Clemm. Replacing Version-Control with Job-Control. In Jürgen F. H. Winkler, editor, *Proceedings of the 2nd International Workshop on Software Configuration Management*, pages 162–169, Princeton, New Jersey, October 24 1989.

[4]   Norman M. Delisle & Mayer D. Schwartz. Contexts - A Partitioning Concept for Hypertext. *ACM Transactions on Office Information Systems*, 5(2):168–186, April 1987.

[5]   Pankaj K. Garg & Walt Scacchi. On Designing Intelligent Hypertext Systems for Information Management in Software Engineering. In *Hypertext '87 Papers*, pages 409–432, Chapel Hill, N.C., November 1987.

[6]   I. Goldstein & D. Bobrow. A Layered Approach to Software Design. In D. Barstow, H. Shrobe, and E. Sandewall, editors, *Interactive Programming Environments*, pages 387–413. Mc Graw Hill, 1984.

[7]   Jörg Haake & Helge Schütt. Eine Systemarchitektur für ein wissensbasiertes Hypertext-Autorensystem. In Peter Gloor and Norbert Streitz, editors, *Hypertext und Hypermedia: Von theoretischen Konzepten zu praktischen Anwendungen, Informatik-Fachberichte, Heidelberg*, Darmstadt, April 1990.

[8]   Frank G. Halasz. Reflections on NoteCards: Seven Issues for the Next Generation of Hypermedia Systems. *Communications of the ACM*, 31(7):836–852, July 1988.

[9]   John R. Hayes, Linda S. Flower, Karen S. Schriver, James F. Stratman, & Linda Carey. Cognitive processes in revision. In S. Rozenberg, editor, *Advances in applied psycholinguistics*, pages 176–240. Cambridge University Press, 1980.

[10]   R.H. Katz & E. Chang. Managing Change in a Computer-Aided Design Database. In *Proceedings of the 13-th International Conference VLDB*, pages 400–407, 1987.

[11]   Christine M. Neuwirth & David S. Kaufer. The Role of External Representations in the Writing Process: Implications for the Design of Hypertext-Based Writing Tools. In Frank Halasz and Rob Akscyn, editors, *Hypertext 89 Proceedings, Special Isuue of SIGCHI Bulletin*, pages 319–341, Pittsburgh, Pensylvania, November 5-8 1989.

[12]   Vassilis Prevelakis. Versioning Issues for Hypertext Systems. In Dennis Tsichritzis, editor, *Object Management*, pages 89–105. Atélier d' Impression de l' Université de Genève, July 1990.

[13]   Helge Schütt & Norbert A. Streitz. HyperBase: A Hypermedia Engine Based on a Relational Database Management System. In A. Rizk, N.Streitz, and J. André, editors, *Proceedings of the European Conference on Hypertext (ECHT-90): Hypertext: Concepts, Systems, and Applications*, pages 95–108, Versailles, France, Cambridge Series on Electronic Publishing, November 27-30 1990.

[14]   Ben Shneiderman & Greg Kearsley. *Hypertext - Hands-On! An Introduction to a New Way of Organizing and Accessing Information.* Addison-Wesley, 1989.

[15]   Norbert A. Streitz, Jörg Hannemann, & Manfred Thüring. From Ideas and Arguments to Hyperdocuments: Travelling Through Activity Spaces. In Frank Halasz and Rob Akscyn, editors, *Hypertext' 89 Proceedings, Special Issue of SIGCHI Bulletin*, pages 343–364, Pittsburgh, Pennsylvania, November 1989.

[16]   Anja Weber & Volker Schoepf. Formal Model of a User–Oriented Versioning Concept. *Deliverable D/WP 4.1.2, RACE–Programme, Telepublishing–Project (1075)*, September 1990.

EINE HYPERTEXT-KOMPONENTE ZU EINEM EXPERTENSYSTEM: BENUTZERFRAGEN FÜR ERKLÄRUNGSDIALOGE

Fahri Yetim

Informationswissenschaft, Universität Konstanz
Postfach 5560, D-7750 Konstanz

Abstract

In diesem Beitrag wird eine Erklärungskomponente vorgestellt, die auf dem Hypertext-Konzept beruht. Die Arbeit beschäftigt sich schwerpunktmäßig mit den Fragen, die vom Benutzer in erklärungsbedürftigen Situationen gestellt werden können. Durch die Analyse der möglichen Erklärungssituationen und deren Zuordnung zu Frageklassen wird der Versuch unternommen, dem Benutzer situationsädaquate Ausdrucksmöglichkeiten im Erklärungsdialog anzubieten. Desweiteren wird auf Aspekte der Repräsentation von Benutzerfragen mittels Frames sowie auf Regeln zur Bestimmung relevanter Fragen eingegangen.

1. Einleitung

1.1. Das Erklärungsproblem in Expertensystemen

Erklärungen in wissensbasierten Systemen dienen im allgemeinen dazu, die Vorgehensweise des Systems transparent zu machen. Erklärungskomponenten übernehmen diese Aufgabe und dienen als Dialogwerkzeug für den Benutzer, um das Systemverhalten kritisch auswerten bzw. überprüfen zu können. In der Fachliteratur der Künstlichen Intelligenz über Erklärung wird häufig argumentiert, daß eine solche Komponente unterschiedliche Aspekte berücksichtigen muß, wie Benutzerfragen, den Wissensstand des Benutzers, die Dialoghistorie sowie den Kontext (vgl. Kobsa/Wahlster 1989, Moore/Swartout 1989, Klee 1989, Joung 1989). Bisherige Systeme unterstützen jedoch nur die Beantwortung bestimmter Standardfragetypen wie 'Warum'-Fragen, 'Wie'-Fragen etc., die durch Angabe der durchgeführten Deduktionsschritte erfolgt. Die Anzeige der Sequenz von Regeln, die zu dem Ergebnis geführt hat, ist sinnvoll für die Fehlersuche in einem System und für die Darstellung bestimmter Aspekte seines Funktionierens. Jedoch liefert eine solche Darstellung kaum akzeptable Erklärungen für den Benutzer. Denn die Erklärungssequenz ist vorab festgelegt und bietet somit keine Möglichkeit zur Variation der Reihenfolge und ebenfalls keine Möglichkeit auf Benutzerbedürfnisse einzugehen.

Die in der Wissenschaftstheorie geführte Diskussion über Erklären und Verstehen (vgl. Schurz 1988) und die Erkenntnis, daß Erklären Verstehen bewirken soll, sowie die Diskussion der Frage, ob Computer dieser Anforderung gerecht werden können (vgl. Winograd/Flores 1986, Herrmann 1989), legt einen Erklärungsansatz nahe, bei dem der Benutzer aktiv Erklärungseinheiten entsprechend seinen Bedürfnissen aufsuchen und rezipieren kann. Genau diese Möglichkeit des flexiblen Umgangs mit einem System ist charakteristisch für Hypertexte (vgl. Conklin 1987, Kuhlen 1991). Deshalb sind Hypertexte ein geeignetes Werkzeug zur flexiblen Gestaltung von Erklärungen (vgl. Yetim 1990/91). Denn "making oneself understood often requires the ability to present the same information in multiple ways or to provide different information to illustrate the same point" (Moore/Swartout 1989, 1505).

1.2 Hypertext als Erklärungskomponente für Expertensysteme

In jüngster Zeit werden zunehmend Versuche unternommen, Hypertext und KI-Systeme zu koppeln bzw. Hypertext in KI-Systeme zu integrieren. Auch im Konstanzer Projekt WISKREDAS haben wir bei der Gestaltung der Mensch-Maschine-Schnittstelle auf Hypertextkonzepte zurückgegriffen (vgl. Dambon/Yetim 1990) und einen integrierten Ansatz verfolgt, der den benutzerorientierten und technologieorientierten Ansatz vereinigt (vgl. Eberts/Eberts 1989, Shneiderman 1987). Die Möglichkeit der Anwendung der Hypertextidee auf die Entwicklung einer Erklärungskomponente wurde an anderer Stelle bereits allgemein diskutiert (vgl. Yetim 1990/91) und soll hier deshalb nur kurz wiederholt werden.

Die dem Hypertext-Konzept inhärente Flexibilität sowohl bei der Repräsentation als auch bei der Präsentation von Wissen kommt den Anforderungen an eine 'gute' Erklärung entgegen. Eine angemessene Repräsentation ermöglicht verschiedenartige, situationsspezifische Präsentationen, deren Form wegen der Beeinflussung der Wahrnehmung von Erklärungsinhalten eine große Bedeutung zukommt. Eine auf Hypertext-Konzept beruhende Erklärungskomponente setzt prinzipiell die Integration formalisierten Wissens mit nicht-formalisiertem Wissen voraus, das für die Erklärung relevant ist. Für die Präsentation ergeben sich in Abhängigkeit vom Erklärungsgegenstand unterschiedliche Gestaltungsmöglichkeiten, die z.B. bei verbalen Darstellungsformen im Spektrum von der Ausgabe des Programmcodes bis hin zu natürlichsprachigen Erklärungstexten liegen.

Die Eigenschaften von Hypertexten machen es möglich, die Spuren von vorausgegangenen Informationsverarbeitungsprozessen flexibel zu verfolgen. Durch die Navigationsmöglichkeit, die das Hypertext-Konzept bietet, ist der Benutzer im Erklärungsdialog nicht mehr an einen einzigen vorgegebenen Weg gebunden (wie in herkömmlichen Trace-Funktionen, wo man eine vorgegebene Kette von Gründen bzw. Argumenten zu verfolgen hat), sondern er kann sich selbst Erklärungen erarbeiten. Den für Erklärungen generierten Hypertext kann er auf beliebigen Pfaden durchlaufen und dabei die für ihn 'richtigen' Informationen in der ihm angemessenen Reihenfolge in sein Vorwissen einbetten. Erklärung im Hypertextkontext erfordert demnach beim Benutzer ein aktives Vorgehen, welches als entscheidendes Mittel zum Kennenlernen des Systems erachtet wird (vgl. Caroll 1982). Die Wege, die ihn zu seinen Informationen führen, bilden die Erklärung. Der Inhalt der Erklärung wird vom Benutzer in Abhängigkeit von seinem Vorwissen und subjektiven Informationsbedarf bestimmt.

Für die Entwicklung einer hypertext-basierten Erklärungskomponente sind folgende Punkte zu spezifizieren: (a) wie wird der Erklärungsbedarf vom Benutzer geäußert; (b) wie werden Erklärungsinhalte bestimmt, strukturiert und präsentiert. Gegenstand dieser Arbeit ist im allgemeinen die Interaktion der Benutzer mit einem wissensbasierten System über eine Hypertext-Erklärungskomponente und im speziellen die systemseitige Bereitstellung von situationsadäquaten Ausdrucksmöglichkeiten bzw. Fragen, durch die der Erklärungsbedarf vom Benutzer geäußert werden kann.

1.3 Die Rolle der Fragen in Hypertextumgebungen

Im Hypertextkontext kann man Fragen als getypte Hypertext-Kanten (-Links)[1] auffassen,

---

1 Einige Konstanzer Arbeiten zu diesem Aspekt, jedoch im Kontext des intelligenten Information Retrieval, sind in Yetim 1989 bzw. Kuhlen/Yetim 1989 sowie Hammwöhner 1990 beschrieben.

deren semantische und pragmatische Aspekte durch die Typisierung erfaßt werden. In einer hypertext-basierten Erklärungsumgebung führen Benutzerfragen dazu, daß nach semantischen sowie pragmatischen Gesichtspunkten aus den strukturell möglichen Antworten eine Teilmenge ausgesondert und dadurch der Bereich, der Kontext, bestimmt wird, in dem der Benutzer selbst für ihn sinnvolle Antworten auf eine Frage erarbeiten kann. Die Form der Erklärung (bzw. die Strukturierung des erklärungsrelevanten Wissens) ist somit vom Fragetyp abhängig. Während z.B. 'Was'-Fragen eher deskriptive Antworten verlangen (z.B. Definitionen, vorformulierte, explizite Erklärungen auf Fragen in der Form 'Was bedeutet x?'), können sich 'Wie'-Fragen beispielsweise darauf beziehen, auf welche Art und Weise das System zu seinem Schluß kam. Die Form der Erklärung auf 'Warum'-Fragen (bzw. 'Warum-nicht'-Fragen) kann dagegen argumentativ sein, wobei auch Mischformen möglich sind. In Abhängigkeit vom Fragetyp können unterschiedliche Kontexte gebildet werden (vgl. Yetim 1991). Im Dialog kann sowohl in einem Kontext als auch zwischen unterschiedlichen Kontexten navigiert werden, wodurch das Rezipieren und Aufsuchen der die eigentliche Erklärung konstituierenden Einheiten durch den Erklärungssuchenden nach seinen Bedürfnissen entsprechend erfolgt.

Fragen zu stellen, bedeutet im Hypertextkontext, mittels einer Maus Kanten (Fragen) zu selektieren. Diese Eigenschaft der auf die Interaktion bezogenen hypertext-basierten Benutzeroberfläche ermöglicht eine vereinfachte Handhabung des Systems: Der Benutzer hat dadurch nicht die bekannten Probleme, denen er bei einer natürlichsprachlichen Eingabe begegnet (wie z.B. eintippen langer Zeichenketten und dabei auftretende Rechtschreibfehler)[2]. Die Aufgabe, dem Benutzer im Dialog die situationsadäquaten Ausdrucksmöglichkeiten, nämlich Fragen als Menü anzubieten, erfordert die Bestimmung der für eine gegebene Situation relevanten Fragen aus einer Menge von möglichen Fragen. Diese kann sich auf Kriterien stützen, die eine Auswertung der aktuellen Erklärungssituation der Dialoghistorie und einer Modellierung der Benutzerklasse erlauben. Für den Fall, daß der Inhalt des Menüs den Erwartungen des Benutzers nicht entspricht, bietet sich die Möglichkeit des Zugriffes auf die Gesamtmenge der erlaubten Fragen (z.B. über einen Struktur-Browser).

Im folgenden wird zunächst geklärt, welche Arten von Fragen gestellt werden können und wie diese Fragen klassifiziert werden müssen, damit sie flexible und situationsspezifische Erklärungsdialoge erlauben.

2. Erklärungssituationen und Benutzerfragen

Es gibt eine ganze Reihe von Fragetypen, die in wissensbasierten Systemen zur Abwicklung der Interaktion und insbesondere bei der Erklärungskomponente nötig sind, und deren Inhalte primär vom Anwendungsgebiet abhängen. Bislang liegen einige Arbeiten im Bereich der Künstlichen Intelligenz vor, die Fragen mit Bezug auf unterschiedliche Anwendungen klassifizieren. Lehnert's Klassifikation von Fragen wurde dazu verwendet, eine Geschichte (in Verbindung mit dem SAM-System) zu verstehen (Lehnert 1978). Hughes (Hughes 1986) überprüfte und kritisierte diese Klassifikation im Hinblick auf die Anwendbarkeit auf regelbasierte Systeme und schlug eine neue Klassifikation der Fragen vor, die (im Gegensatz zu Lehnert's Klassifikation)

---

2 Für diese Art der Interaktion sprechen ebenso einige experimentelle Studien, die zeigen, daß unerfahrene Benutzer Schwierigkeiten dabei haben, ihren spezifischen Informationsbedarf zu erkennen und ihre Fragen klar auszudrücken ('anomalous state of knowledge', vgl. Belkin et al. 1982).

hierarchisch geordnet ist. Die Arbeit von Hartley/Smith 1988 im Rahmen des EUROHELP-Projektes ordnete allgemeine Klassen von Fragen zu Benutzeraktivitäten in einer UNIX-Umgebung zu, um bei der Benutzung von UNIX-Mail 'intelligente' Hilfe zu leisten.

Wie eingangs angedeutet, kann der Benutzer im Rahmen einer hypertext-basierten Erklärungskomponente über eine feste Anzahl von Fragetypen, die in einzelnen Gruppen unterteilt und strukturiert werden können, auf das Wissen zugreifen. Denn "a fairly natural way of arriving at a typology of explanation is to consider the various ways in which we might couch a question to which an explanation or justification will be the answer" (Ellis 1989, 111). Es besteht also ein Zusammenhang zwischen den Fragen und der Erklärung. Die Analyse der möglichen Erklärungssituationen und deren sinnvolle Zuordnung zu den relevanten Fragekategorien ermöglicht dem System, im Dialog dem Benutzer die für die Situation relevanten Fragen anzubieten, wie auch die intendierte Bedeutung einer Frage zu erkennen[3]. Zur weiteren Einschränkung des möglichen Frageraumes mit vielfältigen Fragen kann, wie später gezeigt wird, ebenso die Dialoghistorie und die Benutzerklasse herangezogen werden. Im folgenden Unterkapitel wird zunächst auf die Erklärungssituationen eingegangen, die für die Dialoggestaltung relevant sind.

2.1 Erklärungssituationen

Allgemein können folgende Situationen im Umgang mit Dialogsystemen als Erklärungsbedarf auslösend bezeichnet werden (vgl. Wahlster 1981, Abelson/Lalljee 1988, Stoyan 1989):

S1: Präsentation eines Ergebnisses bzw. Zwischenergebnisses

> Die Reaktionen des Benutzers[4] könnten sein: er möchte prüfen, ob das von ihm als relevant betrachtete Wissen bei der Berechnung des Ergebnisses vom System berücksichtigt wurde; ob die Problemlösungsstrategien des Systems zufriedenstellend sind; ob alle vom System berücksichtigten Daten für den Problemstand relevant sind; oder er möchte zum besseren Verständnis des Ergebnisses von alternativen Präsentationsmöglichkeiten des Systems Gebrauch machen.

S2: Stellen einer Frage durch das System

> Der Benutzer fordert Erklärungen zum System: er möchte wissen, warum die Eingabe benötigt wird (Zweck der Beantwortung der vom System gestellten Frage) oder prüfen, was die Eingabe bewirkt (zum Testen des Systemverhalten), sowie sich darüber informieren, welche Alternativen für die Eingabe bestehen.

Die häufig in der Literatur erwähnten Typen von Erklärungen in o.g. Situationen (S1-S2) beziehen sich auf Erklärungen über dynamisches Wissen, worunter das in einer konkreten Problemsituation aktuelle Schlußfolgerungswissen subsummiert wird. Der Erklärungsbedarf wird in diesen Fällen durch das System ausgelöst[5]. Darüberhinaus kann beim Benutzer jedoch ebenso Erklärungsbedarf in folgenden Situationen entstehen:

S3: Fehlen des domänenspezifischen Wissens

> Die Reaktion des Benutzers beruht auf seinem Wissensmangel, der Erklärungen über statisches Wissen erfordert, worunter Wissenselemente unabhängig von einer konkreten Problemlösungssituation zu verstehen sind (Wissen über Begriffe, über die Beziehungen

---

3 z.B. eine 'Warum'-Frage, die mehrere Bedeutungen haben kann (s. Kapitel 3).
4 An dieser Stelle wird zunächst auf eine Unterscheidung zwischen den Benutzerklassen verzichtet.
5 Das Vorkommen dieser beiden Situationen kann daher im Gegensatz zu den Situationen S3 und S4 seitens des System ohne weiteres erkannt werden.

zwischen Begriffen, Regeln, etc.). Diese Situation tritt auch dann auf, falls das System zu Ausbildungszwecken eingesetzt wird, und der Lernende Zusammenhänge in der Wissensbasis gezielt verfolgen und durch eigene Initiative sein Wissen erweitern möchte.

S4: Mangel an Ausdrucksmöglichkeiten des Systems

Diese Situation kann auftreten, wenn die vom System angebotenen Frage-Menüs den Bedürfnissen des Benutzers nicht entsprechen. Der Benutzer kann dann selber aktiv werden und in der Wissensbasis 'browsen'.

Aus den unterschiedlichen Erklärungssituationen und den darin möglicherweise entstehenden Benutzerreaktionen wird ersichtlich, daß nicht alle Fragen für jede Situation notwendig sind. Es bedarf einer Strukturierung der Fragen vor allem unter Berücksichtigung dieser Erklärungssituationen, um eine für die Anwendung adäquate Ordnung zu erhalten.

2.2 Klassifikation von Benutzerfragen

Die Klassifikation von Fragen in hierarchischer Form, wie sie Hughes 1986 im Gegensatz von Lehnert's 'single level hierarchie' vorgeschlagen hat, erscheint nicht nur für regelbasierte Systeme, sondern auch für andere wissensbasierte Problemlösungssysteme sinnvoll. Durch die Hierarchisierung wird mehr Struktur in der Klassifikation erkennbar, welche eine flexible Handhabung seitens des Systems (situationsspezifische Operationen bzw. Vererbungsmöglichkeiten) und des Benutzers (z.B. 'browsen' in Frage-Hierarchie) ermöglicht. Abb. 1 zeigt die Hierarchie von Hughes, wobei sie bzgl. der hier betrachteten konkreten Anwendung, nämlich Erklärung, leicht abgeändert ist[6].

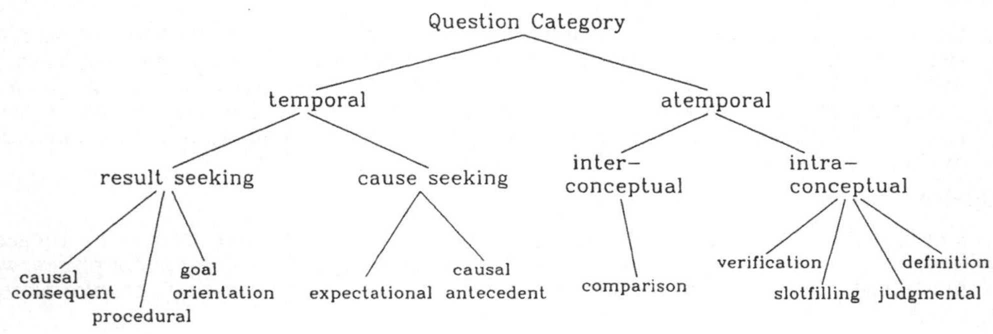

Abb. 1.: Frage-Kategorien

Durch die Bildung zweier Kategorien *'temporal'* und *'atemporal'* erfolgt die globale Unterscheidung zwischen Fragen zu dynamischem und statischem Wissen, wobei ersteres das Laufen eines Prozesses voraussetzt. *'Result-seeking'*-Kategorien werden dadurch charakterisiert, daß die Aufmerksamkeit auf der kausalen Kette vom aktuellen Stand auf den noch in der Zukunft liegenden Ergebniszustand gelenkt wird. In dieser Unter-Klasse wird (z.B. in einem regelbasierten System) die kausale Kette (Links) vorwärts traversiert, ausgehend vom aktuellen Zustand zu einem Ergebniszustand. Zu dieser Unter-Kategorie gehörende Frage-Kategorien sind *'causal consequent'* und *'goal orientation'*. Fragen der Kategorie *'causal-consequent'* erwarten Antworten, die die Konsequenzen bestimmter Aktionen erklären (z.B. Fragen der Art 'Was geschieht, wenn

---

6 siehe folgende Fußnote!

die die Konsequenzen bestimmter Aktionen erklären (z.B. Fragen der Art 'Was geschieht, wenn X?'). Fragen der *'goal-orientation'*-Kategorie beziehen sich auf die Ziele und Zwecke einer Aktion (wie die Frage eines Benutzers als Reaktion auf eine vom System gestellte Frage: 'Warum stellst Du die Frage?'). Die *'procedural'*-Kategorie der Fragen beziehen sich auf abstrakte, domänen-unabhängige Beschreibungen (z.B. 'Wie beweist Du, daß X wahr ist?'), d.h. auf das, was das System tut, und setzen voraus, daß ein solches Wissen im System für Erklärungszwecke vorhanden ist.

'Cause-seeking'-Kategorien lösen ebenso das Traversieren kausaler Ketten aus, um eine Antwort auf die Frage zu finden. In dieser Unter-Klasse wird die kausale Kette rückwärts traversiert, ausgehend vom aktuellen Zustand zum verursachenden Zustand. Diese Kategorie unterscheidet sich von der *'result-seeking'*-Kategorie darin, daß hier die Aktionen (Ergebnisse) schon ausgeführt sind. Zu dieser Unter-Kategorie gehörende Frage-Kategorien sind 'causal antecedent' und 'expectational'. Fragen der 'causal antecedent'-Kategorie beziehen sich auf Zustände bzw. Ereignisse, die den aktuellen Zustand bzw. das Ereignis verursacht haben (z.B. die Frage 'Warum ist die Entscheidung negativ bewertet?'). Fragen der *'expectational'*-Kategorie drücken die Verletzung der Erwartungen eines Benutzers aus und können als negativer Ausdruck von 'causal-Antecedent'-Fragen angesehen werden (z.B. 'Warum nicht X?').

'Atemporal'-Kategorien sind im Gegensatz zu *'temporal'*-Kategorien unabhängig von bestimmten dynamischen Prozessen. Sie beziehen sich auf statisches Wissen in der Wissensbasis, wie z.B. Wissen über einzelne Konzepte sowie Meinungen, Stellungnahmen von Experten zu Konzepten (*intraconceptual*) und Wissen über ihre Beziehungen zu- bzw. Vergleiche miteinander (*interconceptual*)[7, 8].

2.3. Beziehungen zwischen den Erklärungssituationen und Benutzerfragen

Die Absicht, in der gegebenen Erklärungssituation die relevanten Fragen aus einer Menge von möglichen Fragen zu qualifizieren, erfordert die Überprüfung der Zusammenhänge zwischen den oben vorgestellten prototypischen Erklärungssituationen und den Klassen von Fragen, sowie die Herstellung einer sinnvollen Zuordnung:

S1 <=> cause-seeking
S2 <=> result-seeking
S3 < = > atemporal
S4 < = > weitere System-Möglichkeiten zum Browsen

Die Beziehung der einzelnen konkreten Fragen zu Erklärungssituationen lassen sich aus der Beziehung ihrer zugehörigen Klassen ableiten, wie es im folgenden anhand der Bedeutungen einiger ausgewählter Fragetypen erörtert wird, die in wissensbasierten Systemen im

---

7 Nach Hughes gehören die Fragen der 'Judgmental'-Kategorie unverständlicher Weise zu 'interconceptual'-Kategorie. Da diese Fragen Aussagen über einzelne Konzepte verlangen, wie z.B. mit Hughes's Beispiel-Frage 'What do you think of bitumen Coatings?', werden sie zur 'intraconceptual'-Kategorie angehörig betrachtet.

8 Weitere in Hypertextumgebungen relevante Fragen, wie z.B. die Orientierungsfragen der Art "Wo bin ich? Wie komme ich hierher? Wo kann ich hin?" (vgl. Nievergelt 1983, 33), die sich nicht auf den Inhalt der Erklärung, sondern auf den Umgang mit dem System beziehen, bleiben hier unberücksichtigt.

Zusammenhang mit Erklärungskomponenten gestellt werden:[9, 10]

'Warum'-Fragen (vgl. Wahlster 1981) zielen entweder auf die Erklärung einer Tatsache bzw. Behauptung (Klasse: *causal antecedent*) oder auf die Begründung einer Frage bzw. Aufforderung des Systems ab (*goal orientation*).

'Warum-nicht'-Fragen (Richter 1989) werden als negative 'Warum'-Fragen bezeichnet und verlangen die Erklärung, warum eine Lösung nicht ausgewählt wurde und können auch gestellt werden, um zu testen, ob z.B. bestimmte Ursachen nicht vorliegen (*expectational*).

'Wie'-Fragen können sich darauf beziehen, auf welche Art und Weise das System zu einem Ergebnis kam, z.B. die Frage " Wie wurde eine Struktur abgeleitet?" (*procedural*).

'Was-Wenn'-Fragen sind hypothetisch (vgl. Ellis 1989). Das System verhält sich so, als wäre das gegebene Faktum wahr und prüft die Konsequenzen, was z.B. eine Eingabe bewirkt (*causal consequent*).

'Was'-Fragen können sich auf die Definitionen, wie die Frage 'Was bedeutet X?' (*intraconceptual*) oder Vergleiche von Begriffen (*comparison*) beziehen, wie z.B. 'Was ist der Unterschied zwischen X und Y?'.

Darüberhinaus lassen sich ebenso Fragen, die sich auf die Systemperformanz und Statistik beziehen und somit für die Wartung des Systems relevant sind, den Frageklassen zuordnen.

3. Repräsentation von Fragen als Frames

Jeder mögliche Fragetyp läßt sich als ein eigenes Objekt repräsentieren. Aufgrund der im experimentellen System WISKREDAS (Dambon et al. 1989) zur Wissensrepräsentation eingesetzten Framestrukturen und der Ähnlichkeit zwischen dem 'Objekt' und dem 'Frame'-Begriff (vgl. Stefik/Bobrow 1986) liegt es nahe, zur Modellierung dieser als Objekt aufgefaßten Fragen Frames zu wählen. Denn Frames können die intendierte flexible Handhabung der Fragen ermöglichen, da sie zum einen mit prozeduralen Anhängseln (*Attached Procedures*) versehen werden können, die die Berücksichtigung impliziter Beziehungen unter den Eigenschaften bei der Gewinnung von Eigenschaftsausprägungen auf natürliche Weise nachvollziehen, zum anderen die Darstellung von Objekten verschiedenen Abstraktionsgrades durch die Möglichkeit der Vererbung von Eigenschaften erlauben.

In Abb. 2. wird das allgemeine Frame-Konzept zur Modellierung der Fragen dargestellt, welches aus dem Frame-Namen, einer Menge von möglichen Eigenschaften (*Slots*) und erlaubten Slot-Einträgen besteht. Dieses allgemeine Frame-Konzept mit den Slot-Eintrag-Spezifikationen[11] dient u.a. zur interaktiven Erzeugung von Frage-Repräsentationen.

---

9 Das Ergebnis des von Rogers 1988 durchgeführten Experimentes, in dem Fragetypen ausgewertet werden, die Benutzer stellen, wenn sie in einem benutzerinitiierten Dialog Information und Vorschläge vom Expertensystem bekommen, zeigt, daß meistens die (im englischen) sog. 'wh-questions' (why, who, what, where und when) gestellt werden.

10 Wobei hier literarische Bedeutungen von Fragen sowie Sprechhandlungen, welche Einladungen, Vorschläge etc. äußern, nicht berücksichtigt werden.

11 Dabei bezeichnen die erlaubten Einträge mit den kleinen Buchstaben Konstanten und mit den großen Anfangsbuchstaben Mengen.

Name
Is-a: *question*
May-be-a: *{Question-category}*
Description: *{String}*
Obj-specification: *{Objects}*
Expl-situation: *{s1,s2,s3,s4}*
User-class: *{expert, end-user, programmer}*
Dialog-history: *{yes, no}*
Explanation-pattern: *{Predicates}*
Actions: *{link(explanation), add(dialog_history)}*

Abb. 2.: Das allgemeine Frame-Konzept zur Repräsentation der Fragen

Da eine Frage in Abhängigkeit von der Erklärungssituation verschiedene Rollen einnehmen kann, die durch Frageklassen (vgl. Abb. 1) beschrieben sind, läßt sich diese Beziehung durch den Slot 'may-be-a' realisieren[12]. Im obigen Frame-Konzept enthalten die beiden Slots 'is-a' (Spezialisierungsbeziehung) und 'may-be-a' (Rollen-Beziehung) als Einträge die Bezeichner entsprechender Klassen und ermöglichen Vererbungen der Eigenschaften. Zu jeder Frage gehört eine textuelle Beschreibung 'Description' und eine Menge von Restriktionen bzw. Rahmenbedingungen, die die pragmatische Relevanz der Frage bestimmen: i.e. Angaben darüber, für welche Menge von Objekten (*Obj-specification*) die betreffende Frage eingesetzt werden kann, in welchen Situationen (*expl-situation*) und für welche Benutzerklassen (*user-class*)[13] die entsprechende Frage sinnvoll ist, sowie Angaben darüber, ob eine Frage in die Dialog-Historie aufgenommen werden darf[14]. Die Information im Slot 'Obj-specification' kann den Benutzer, falls er eine Frage ohne eine vorausgehende Angabe von Objekten aktiviert hat, bei der Auswahl eines Objektes gezielt unterstützen. Einer Frage können Erklärungsmuster (*Explanation-pattern*[15]) zugeordnet werden, deren Gesamtheit die prozedurale Semantik der Frage und somit die Aktionen, die diese Frage in der Wissensbasis ausführt, beschreiben. Der Benutzer hat dadurch die Möglichkeit, auch einzelne Erklärungsmuster nach seinem Interesse zu aktivieren oder (in der Rolle des Systementwicklers) ihre Verhalten zu prüfen. Der Slot 'Actions' enthält Prozeduren, die die eigentliche Erklärung realisieren (d.h. u.a. die entsprechenden Erklärungsmuster aktivieren, sowie die Aktion einer hypertext-artigen Aufbereitung der Erklärung anstoßen). Diese Prozeduren werden erst dann aktiviert, wenn die bisher erwähnten Bedingungen erfüllt sind.

---

12 vgl. hierzu Reimer 1991.

13 Es werden hier Stereotypen von Benutzern unterschieden, die für unsere Anwendung relevant sind.

14 z.B. Fragen wie 'Was-Wenn' (engl: What-if), deren Ausgangsbedingungen (z.B. Eingaben, deren Konsequenzen getestet werden sollen) nicht von der aktuellen Wissensbasis abhängen und somit beliebig sein können, brauchen nicht in die Dialog-Historie (hier ist vielmehr die Frage-Historie gemeint) aufgenommen zu werden.

15 vgl. Schank 1986.

In Abb. 3. wird eine Beispiel-Repräsentation gezeigt, wobei wegen der übersichtlichen Darstellung die graphische Form gewählt wurde und die dargestellten Beziehungskanten als Slot vorzustellen sind. Bei den Fragen wird unterschieden, ob sie prinzipiell zur Auswahl als Menü-Option stehen können. Während die Frageklassen in Abb. 1, zwischen denen nur die Spezialisierungsbeziehung 'is-a' besteht, keine Menü-Option sein können und die Rollen einer Frage beschreiben, besitzen die Framekonstrukte der als Menü-Option erlaubten Fragen neben dem Slot 'is-a' auch den Slot 'may-be-a'. Der oberste Frame 'cause-seeking' in Abb. 3 ist nur für die Erklärungssituation 'result-presented' (d.h. wenn das System End- oder Zwischenergebnis präsentiert hat) relevant, wohingegen der Frame 'result-seeking' in der Erklärungssituation 'sys-request' (d.h. wenn das System Fragen gestellt hat) zum Tragen kommt. Zur Anfragezeit vererbt sich die Erklärungssituation auf alle Unterklassen. Aufgrund der bestehenden 'May-be-a'-Beziehung sowohl zwischen der Frage 'Why-goal' und der Klasse 'goal-orientation' als auch zwischen der Frage 'Why-causal' und der Klasse 'causal-antecedent' wird es möglich, in der aktuellen Situation zur Anfragezeit durch die Vererbung der Erklärungssituation zu bestimmen, welche Variante der 'Warum'-Frage relevant ist. Die Darstellung der Fragen auf unterschiedliche Abstraktionsebenen erlaubt, die Fragen entsprechend der Benutzerklasse zu qualifizieren: z.B. unter Berücksichtigung der aktuellen Benutzerklasse kann sich anstatt der gültigen Variante (z.B. 'Why-goal') deren Abstraktion ('Why') als Menu-Option qualifizieren.

Nach dem der Benutzer im Frage-Menü eine Frage selektiert hat, wird ein Instanz-Frame generiert, der beschreibt, auf welches konkrete Objekt sich die Frage in gegebener Situation bezieht. In unserem Beispiel handelt es sich um das Konzept 'Umsatz' (*turnover*). Der Instanz-Frame wird in die Dialog-Historie - hier ist die Frage-Historie gemeint - aufgenommen, soweit dies von der Restriktion im Slot *'Dialog-History'* des entsprechenden Frame zugelassen ist.

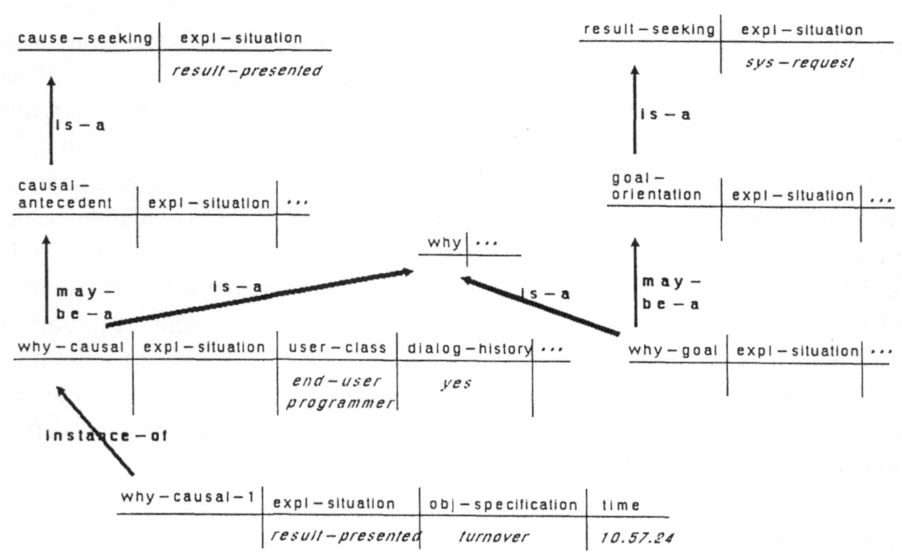

Abb. 3.: Eine Beispiel-Repräsentation

4. Bestimmung der relevanten Fragen

Die Abhängigkeit der relevanten Fragen von den o.g. pragmatischen Rahmenbedingungen läßt sich formal als eine Funktion aus dem Kreuzprodukt der Mengen ES (Menge aller Erklärungssituationen), DH (die Potenzmenge Dialoghistorien), UC (Menge aller Benutzerklassen) und OB (die Potenzmenge Objekte) in die Menge Q darstellen:

$$relevant\text{-}questions(ES*UC*\underline{DH}*\underline{OB}) \implies Q$$

In einer algorithmischen Sicht kann die Funktion 'relevant-questions' als Relation folgendermaßen definiert werden:

$$relevant\text{-}questions(KB, es, uc, DH, OB, Q) \iff$$

(1) $\quad \exists Q_1 : \;\; (\forall f : \;\; (is\text{-}frame(KB, f) \;\wedge$

(2) $\qquad\qquad\qquad is\text{-}slot\text{-}entry(KB, f, \text{'}expl\text{-}situation\text{'}, es) \;\wedge$

(3) $\qquad\qquad\qquad is\text{-}slot\text{-}entry(KB, f, \text{'}user\text{-}class\text{'}, uc) \;\wedge$

(4) $\qquad\qquad\qquad \exists o_1 \in OB \; \neg \exists f_1 : \;\; (is\text{-}slot\text{-}entry(KB, f, \text{'}obj\text{-}specification\text{'}, o_1) \;\wedge$

(5) $\qquad\qquad\qquad\qquad\qquad instance\text{-}of(KB, f_1, f) \;\wedge$

(6) $\qquad\qquad\qquad\qquad\qquad is\text{-}slot\text{-}entry(KB, f_1, \text{'}obj\text{-}specification\text{'}, o_1) \;\wedge$

(7) $\qquad\qquad\qquad\qquad\qquad is\text{-}slot\text{-}entry(KB, f_1, \text{'}expl\text{-}situation\text{'}, es) \;) \implies$

(8) $\qquad\qquad\qquad f \in Q_1 \;) \;\wedge$

(9) $\qquad\qquad \forall f_2 \in Q : \;\; f_2 \in Q_1 \;\wedge\; best\text{-}chain\text{-}member(KB, f_2, Q_1) \;)$

(1) Zunächst wird eine Menge (Q1) der potentiell relevanten Fragen bestimmt, so daß jedes Element der Menge Q1 ein Frame f in der Wissensbasis KB ist, der noch folgende Bedingungen erfüllen muß:

(2) dieser Frame muß sowohl für die aktuelle Erklärungssituation als auch

(3) für die spezifizierte Benutzerklasse und

(4-7) mindestens für ein Objekt aus der spezifizierten Objektmenge relevant sein: d.h. es muß mindestens ein Objekt aus der spezifizierten Objektmenge geben, das als Slot-Eintrag im Frame f vorhanden ist, wobei es keine Instanz dieses Frame geben darf, deren Sloteinträge die aktuelle Erklärungssituation und das Objekt sind. Dadurch wird eine Frage eliminiert, die auf alle spezifizierten Objekte in derselben Situation bereits angewendet worden ist (es wird angenommen, daß der Benutzer darüber informiert ist).

(8) Erfüllt ein Frame diese Bedingungen, so gehört er zu der Menge Q1.

(9) Die so gebildete Menge Q1 enthält möglicherweise auch Frames, zwischen denen Spezialisierungsbeziehungen bestehen, wie z.B. die Frames 'Why' und 'Why-goal', die als Frame-Ketten betrachtet werden können. Alle Frames derselben Kette dürfen nicht gleichzeitig als Menü-Option zur Auswahl stehen. Aus der Menge Q1 wird daher eine Teilmenge Q ausgesondert, die das Frage-Menü bildet, und deren Elemente (Frames) eindeutig sind. Die Bestimmung der relevanten Frames aus Frame-Ketten der Menge Q1 erfolgt durch das Prädikat 'best-chain-member', das dann wahr ist, wenn der Frame entweder den allgemeinen Frame in der entsprechenden Frame-Kette darstellt (falls die Kette linear ist) oder denjenigen Frame in der Frame-Kette (falls die Kette baumartige Form aufweist), der mit mindestens einem weiteren Frame die Spezialisierung ein und desselben Frame ist, wobei im letzten Fall (als zusätzliche Bedingung) die darunterliegende Teilkette linear sein muß. Dadurch wird zur Vermeidung der Mehrdeutigkeit sichergestellt, daß mehrere qualifizierte Bedeutungsvarianten einer Frage nicht durch ihre gemeinsame Oberklasse vertreten werden.

Die Menge der Fragen, die vom Benutzer während des bisherigen Dialogverlaufs gestellt wurden, können sich sowohl auf statisches als auch auf dynamisches Wissen beziehen. Wenn für den Fall des dynamischen Wissens beispielsweise die während des bisherigen Dialoges durchlaufene Sequenz von Fragen keine Änderung der aktuellen Wissensgrundlage zur Folge hat, dann stehen bereits gestellte Fragen, wie die Frage "Wie wurde die Struktur abgeleitet?", dem Benutzer solange nicht zur Verfügung, bis vom System neue Verarbeitungsschritte unternommen werden, die eine Änderung der bisherigen Wissensgrundlage bewirken. Dies erfordert jedoch die Überwachung und Repräsentation des Systemstatus, auf den die Frage-Komponente zurückgreifen kann. Ebenso setzt die Bestimmung der Fragen die Repräsentation der aktuell präsentierten und bereits selektierten Objekte im System[16] voraus, die als Parameter in die obige Funktion eingehen. Die folgende Regel soll zur Illustration einer Meta-Regel dienen, die die obige Funktion aufruft:

$$run(KB) \iff$$

$$(1) \quad \exists es: \; is\text{-}expl\text{-}situation(KB, es) \; \wedge$$

$$(2) \quad \exists uc: \; is\text{-}user\text{-}class(KB, uc) \; \wedge$$

$$(3) \quad \exists DH: \; is\text{-}dialog\text{-}history(KB, DH) \; \wedge$$

$$(4) \quad \exists OB, OB_1, OB_2: \; (\; (selected\text{-}obj(OB_1) \; \wedge \; OB_1 \neq \emptyset \; \implies \; OB = OB_1 \;) \; \vee$$

$$(5) \quad\quad\quad\quad\quad\quad\quad (presented\text{-}obj(OB_2) \; \implies \; OB = OB_2 \;) \;) \; \wedge$$

$$(6) \quad \exists Q: \; relevant\text{-}questions(KB, es, uc, DH, OB, Q) \; \wedge$$

$$(7) \quad present(Q) \; \wedge \; ...$$

(1) Die aktuell gültige Erklärungssituation,
(2) Benutzerklasse und
(3) Dialog-Historie;
(4-5) die Festlegung, welche Objekte zur weiteren Operation selektiert sind; im Falle, daß kein Objekt selektiert ist, werden alle auf dem Bildschirm präsentierten Objekte betrachtet;
(6-7) die Bestimmung und Präsentation der relevanten Fragen.

Als Basis zur Realisierung dieser konzeptuellen Arbeiten dient das wissensbasierte System WISKREDAS, auf das im folgenden Kapitel kurz eingegangen wird.

5. Das System WISKREDAS

Der im Rahmen des Sonderforschungsbereichs 221 an der Universität Konstanz entwickelte Prototyp WISKREDAS[17] hat zum Ziel, einen komplexen Entscheidungsvorgang in einer Kreditabsicherungsbank informationell zu unterstützen (Dambon et al. 1989). Die Unterstützung besteht im wesentlichen darin, daß das System alle Informationen, die zur Bearbeitung eines Kreditantrags eines Existenzgründers benötigt werden, verwaltet, zum Teil automatisch einholt, diese nach Regeln, die auf dem Fachwissen des Sachbearbeiters beruhen, verarbeitet und schließlich, wenn die informationelle Basis als ausreichend eingeschätzt wird, einen Entscheidungsvorschlag macht, der im Ergebnis eindeutig sein muß: Empfehlung auf Ablehnung oder Übernahme der beantragten Bürgschaft.

Die grundlegende Repräsentationseinheit von WISKREDAS ist der sogenannte Makroframe, in dem das gesamte statische Fallwissen in einer Framestruktur modelliert ist. Den Makroframe kann man sich als Netz vorstellen, dessen Knoten Konzepte (Frames) und dessen Kanten Beziehungen (Relationen) zwischen den Konzepten repräsentieren (vgl. Dambon/Yetim 1990). Die Erklärungskomponente im WISKREDAS bezieht sich u.a. auf die Erklärung der bereits getroffenen Entscheidung. Als Grundlage dazu dienen einerseits die statische

---

16 vgl. hierzu Thiel 1990.
17 Der Prototyp wurde auf einer Micro-Vax unter Verwendung von PROLOG realisiert.

Wissensbasis, die den Makroframe und die Entscheidungsregeln enthält, und andererseits ein vom System jeweils nach einer Fallbearbeitung generierter 'Entscheidungsbaum' sowie fallspezifische entscheidungsrelevante Daten, welche zum dynamischen Wissen zählen. Beim gegenwärtigen Stand der Entwicklung bilden die expliziten Beziehungen zwischen den Objekten die Hypertextpfade. Erweiterung der Navigationsmöglichkeiten in der Wissensbasis werden durch die Realisierung der in dieser Arbeit vorgestellten Fragen intendiert.

6. Zusammenfassung und Ausblick

Diese Arbeit beschäftigt sich im allgemeinen mit der Interaktion der Benutzer mit einem wissensbasierten System über eine Hypertext-Erklärungskomponente und im speziellen mit den Fragen, die vom Erklärungssuchenden in unterschiedlichen erklärungsbedürftigen Situationen gestellt werden. Die hierarchische Organisation der Fragen mit mehrfachen Klassenbeziehungen und somit unterschiedlichen Gesichtspunkten, sowie die Zuordnung zu Erklärungssituationen ermöglichen, Erklärungsdialoge flexibel, benutzerspezifisch und situationsadäquat zu gestalten. Die hier beschriebenen Verfahren zur Bestimmung der relevanten Teilmenge der Fragen unter Berücksichtigung pragmatischer Rahmenbedingungen erlauben, u.a. Frage-Intentionen zu erkennen. Die Form der Organisation von Fragen stellt ebenso einen Beitrag zur automatischen Kontrolle der in großen Hypertexten schwierig zu beherschenden Hypertext-Funktionen (-Links) dar. Gegenwärtige Arbeiten beschäftigen sich mit der Thematik der Beantwortung der diskutierten Fragen, insbesondere mit der Strukturierung und hypertextartigen Aufbereitung der Antworten.

Literatur

Abelson, R. P.; Lalljee, M. (1988): Knowledge Structures and Causal Explanation. In: Hilton, D. (ed.): Contemporary Science and Natural Explanation. The Harvester Press.

Belkin, N.J.; Oddy, R.N.; Brooks, H.M. (1982): ASK for Information Retrieval: Part I. Background and Theory. In: J. Dokumentation, Vol. 38, No. 2, Juni 1982, 61-71.

Carroll, J (1982): The Adventure of Getting to Know a Computer. In: IEEE Computer 1982, 14-20.

Conklin, J. (1987): Hypertext - An introduction and a survey. IEEE Computer, Sept., 18-41.

Dambon, P.; Glasen, F.; Kuhlen, R.; Thost, M. (1989): WISKREDAS: Ein Wissensbasiertes Kreditabsicherungssystem. Bericht SFB 221 B3-3/89, Konstanz, August 1989.

Dambon, P. / Yetim, F. (1990): Integration of Hypertext into a Decision Support System. In: Herget, J.; Kuhlen, R. (eds.): Pragmatische Aspekte beim Entwurf und Betrieb von Informationssystemen. Konstanz: Universitätsverlag, 64-77.

Eberts, R.E.; Eberts, C.G. (1989): Four Aproaches to Human Computer Interaction. In: Hancock, P. A.; Chignell, M. H. (eds.): Intelligent Interface: Theory, Research and Design. Amsterdam et al: North Holland, 69-128.

Ellis, C. (1989): Explanation in intelligent systems. In: Ellis, C. (ed.): Expert Knowledge and Explanation. The Knowledge-Language Interface. New York et al:Halsted Press, 108-126.

Hammwöhner, R. (1990): Automatischer Aufbau von Hypertext-Basen aus deskriptiv expositorischen Texten - Ein Hypertext-Modell für das Information-Retrieval. Universität Konstanz (Dissertation).

Hartley, J.R.; Smith, M.J. (1988): Question answering and explanation giving in on-line help systems. In: Artificial Intelligence and Human Learning. London: Chapman & Hall Computing, 338-360.

Herrmann, T. (1989): Verständigungsprobleme und ihre Bedeutung für die computergestützte Vermittlung von Erklärungen. In: Stoyan, H. (ed.): Erklärung als Gespräch - Erklärung als Mensch-Maschine-Kommunikation, Symposium in Darmstadt, Juli 1989.

Hughes, S. (1986): HOW and WHY: HOW far will they take us, WHY should we need any more?. In: Proceedings of a Workshop on Explanation. London: Alvey, 69-82.

Joung, R.M. (1989): Human interface aspects of expert systems. In: Murray, L.A., Richardson, J.T.E. (eds.), Intelligent Systems in a Human Context. Development, Implications, and Applications. Oxford et al.:Oxford University, 20-34.

Klee, H. W. (1989): Zur Akzeptanz von Expertensystemen. Eine empirische Analyse der Relevanz und Angemessenheit der Erklärungskomponente, Köln: Verlag Josef Eul (Dissertation).

Kobsa, A. / Wahlster, W. (1989) (eds.): User Models in Dialog Systems. Berlin et al: Springer

Kuhlen, R. (1991): Hypertext - ein nicht-lineares Medium zur Darstellung von Wissen und Erarbeitung von Information. Berlin et al.: Springer.

Kuhlen, R.; Yetim, F. (1989): HYPER-TOPIC: - a System for the Automatic Construction of a Hypertext-Base with Intertextual Relations; in: Online'89 - 13th Int. Online Meeting, London, December 1989, Learned Information, 257-264.

Lehnert, W. G. (1978): The Process of Question Answering. A Computer Simulation of Cognition. Hillsdale, New Jersey: Lawrence Erlbaum Associates.

Moore, J. D. ; Swartout, W. R. (1989): A Reactive Approach to Explanation. In: Proceedings of IJCAI'89, 1504-1510.

Nievergelt, J. (1983): Die Gestaltung der Mensch-Maschine-Schnittstelle. In: GI-13. Jahrestagung, Berlin et al:Springer, 41-50.

Reimer, U. (1991): Einführung in die Wissensrepräsentation, Stuttgart: Teubner.

Richter, M. (1989): Prinzipien der Künstlichen Intelligenz. Stuttgart: Teubner.

Rogers, Y. (1988): User Requirements for Expert System Explanation: What, Why and When?. In: Jones, D.M./ Winder, R. (ed): People and Computers IV. Proceedings of the Forth Conference of the British Computer Soviety. Cambridge: University Press, 547-564.

Schank, R. C. (1986): Explanation Patterns. Understanding mechanically and creatively. Hillsdale, New Jersey.

Schneiderman, B. (1987): Designing the user interface. Strategies for effective human-computer interaction. Reading MA: Addison-Weseley.

Schurz, G. (1988) (ed.): Erklären und Verstehen in der Wissenschaft, München: Oldenburg.

Stefik, M.; Bobrow, D. G. (1986): Object Oriented Programming: Themes and Variations. In: The AI Magazine, Vol. 6, No. 4, 1986, 40-62.

Stoyan, H. (1989): Erklärungen und Beweise. In: Stoyan, H. (ed.): Erklärung als Gespräch - Erkärung als Mensch-Maschine-Kommunikation, Symposium in Darmstadt, Juli 1989.

Thiel, U. (1990): Konversationale graphische Interaktion mit Informationssystemen: Ein sprechakttheoretischer Ansatz, Universität Konstanz (Dissertation).

Wahlster, W. (1981): Natürlichsprachliche Argumentation in Dialogsystemen. KI-Verfahren zur Rekonstruktion und Erklärung approximaler Inferenzprozesse. Berlin et al.: Springer.

Winograd, T; Flores, F. (1986): Understanding computers and Cognition: A new Foundation for Design. Norwood, New Jersey: Ablex Publishing.

Yetim, F. (1989): Ein intertextuelles Hypertextmodell als Weiterentwicklung eines Volltextanalysesystems. In: Informationsmethoden: Neue Ansätze und Techniken. Proc. Deutscher Dokumentartag 89, DGD, Bremen, Oktober 1989, 197-212.

Yetim, F. (1990): Hypertext und Erklärung: Überlegungen zu einem pragmatischen Ansatz. Beitrag zum 2. Workshop "Hypertext und KI", Bayerisches Forschungszentrum, Erlangen, 2. Oktober 1990

Yetim, F. (1991): A Hypertext Approach to Explanation. (Eingereicht zur Veröffentlichung).

Autorenindex